Oxford A Level
Religious Studies
for OCR

Christianity, Philosophy and Ethics

Year 2

Libby Ahluwalia • Robert Bowie

OXFORD
UNIVERSITY PRESS

OXFORD
UNIVERSITY PRESS

Great Clarendon Street, Oxford, OX2 6DP, United Kingdom

Oxford University Press is a department of the University of Oxford. It furthers the University's objective of excellence in research, scholarship, and education by publishing worldwide. Oxford is a registered trade mark of Oxford University Press in the UK and in certain other countries

British Library Cataloguing in Publication Data
Data available

978-0-19-837533-3

Kindle edition: 978-0-19-841269-4

3 5 7 9 10 8 6 4 2

Paper used in the production of this book is a natural, recyclable product made from wood grown in sustainable forests.

The manufacturing process conforms to the environmental regulations of the country of origin.

Printed in Great Britain by Bell and Bain Ltd. Glasgow

Links to third party websites are provided by Oxford in good faith and for information only. Oxford disclaims any responsibility for the materials contained in any third party website referenced in this work.

Thank You

The publishers would like to thank Revd Dr Mark Griffiths, Philip Robinson, RE Adviser to the CES, and Julie Haigh for their guidance.

MIX
Paper from
responsible sources
FSC® C007785
www.fsc.org

Contents

Exam support

Introduction

By this second year of your A level course, if you have been doing your homework regularly, you will already have had plenty of practice writing essays and you will have received feedback from your teacher to help you build your skills. If you have not been doing your homework regularly, it is not too late to change your habits. Essay skills develop over time, with constant practice, and they will not magically appear on the day of the exam. You need to do some work in advance.

Developing your skills

You should, by now, understand that you will be assessed in two different skills in your exams:

AO1 (Assessment Objective 1)

This assesses your knowledge and understanding. For high marks in AO1, you need to learn and understand the material. You need to have a firm grip on the different issues under discussion. You need to be able to explain different people's views with accuracy and confidence, for example showing that you know it was Aquinas who thought X and Kant who thought Y. Although you do not need to learn long quotations by heart, it can be very useful to memorise short quotes when they are good summaries of a scholar's key points.

Some people seem to think that because this subject relies heavily on written arguments and persuasion, it is possible to gain good marks without learning very much, as long as you can think on your feet and argue well when it comes to the exam. However, this is not really true. You will not be able to get a grade that does you justice unless you learn the material well, however much skill you have in arguing. Without sufficient knowledge of the course content, you will have nothing of substance to argue about. Inadequate revision will leave you resembling a painter who over-relies on his artistic skill but has not equipped himself with enough paint.

Your knowledge and understanding will develop if you take time over your homework essays, making careful notes and paying attention to the details as you write. You can help yourself to remember key thinkers and key facts by using memory aids such as flashcards, and by reading over your class notes on a regular basis. There are a lot of good resources online, such as podcasts, revision websites and YouTube videos. Of course not everything on the Internet is accurate or reliable, so use your judgement and ask your teacher for advice about good sites to help you consolidate your knowledge.

AO2 (Assessment Objective 2)

This assesses your skills in critical thinking and persuasive argument. For high marks in AO2, you need to think about the different topics under discussion and formulate an opinion of your own. When you read or hear the views of others, you need to decide whether you find them convincing, and be clear in your own mind about your reasons for agreeing or disagreeing with them. In your essays, your opinion and your reasoning should be evident throughout your writing, not just at the end.

Learning all of the material in your textbook and class notes will not be enough to get you high marks for AO2. You need to engage with it and have the confidence to think for yourself and assert your own point of view.

One way of developing your skills in AO2 is to involve yourself fully in class discussions, and perhaps also in a debating society or philosophy club. Taking part in discussion helps you to articulate your views and to find the right words with which to defend them against the criticism of others. It might also persuade you to change your mind if someone points out a problem in your way of thinking. Listening is also an important skill in discussion. Try to take in what other people are saying and think about the extent to which you agree with them, rather than just waiting for your turn to speak. Hearing views that are different from your own will help you to present a balanced argument. It will also give you the opportunity to develop your critical skills when you are working out what you think is wrong with the other person's argument and challenging them about it.

Sometimes people mistakenly think that in order to offer a balanced argument you have to give 'a middle of the road' opinion. This is not true; if you agree or disagree strongly with something, you are entitled to say so. A balanced argument is one that treats different views fairly before giving a judgement of them. In order to present a balanced argument, you should make sure that the different viewpoints you explore are presented accurately. You should try to give each different point of view roughly the same number of words in your essay. Some people rapidly dismiss anything with which they disagree and concentrate on their own perspective, but this is one-sided and not balanced. Explain the different points of view carefully, showing that you understand why some people might think this way, before offering your critique of them.

When you are writing about the strengths and weaknesses of an argument, remember that this often involves the skill of critical evaluation as well as memorising knowledge. Some people write things like, 'A weakness of Kant's ethical theory is that he does not allow for individual circumstances', as if it is a firmly established fact that this is a weakness. However, some people might argue that it is a strength; they might think that the same rules should apply to everyone regardless of circumstances. If you are writing about the strengths and weaknesses of a point of view, try to explain why you think they are strengths and weaknesses, rather than simply asserting that they are. This will help you to gain higher marks for AO2.

Keeping on top of things

The second year of an A level course can be a very busy time, especially if you are applying for university during the year. Try to plan ahead so that you can avoid too many times when you feel overwhelmed by work. Be realistic about your work goals. For example, if you are going to a friend's party on a Saturday evening, you may not succeed in completing the big piece of work that you planned to tackle on the Sunday. Work out in advance when you have university open days, school productions, parties or sporting fixtures, and try to make a sensible schedule for your work so that you can keep on top of it while still having time to enjoy yourself.

Taking Religious Studies beyond A level

If you have been enjoying this course and feel that you are doing well, you might be considering taking the subject further by studying it for a degree.

Choosing your course

There are many different routes that you could take in furthering your education in this subject. For example, there are degree courses available in Religious Studies, Biblical Studies, Theology and Philosophy. It is important to do some research to make sure that you choose a course which is appropriate for your interests, as there can be big differences between courses. If you go through the UCAS 'clearing' system to find a university place, be wary of accepting the first place you are offered. Read about the course before you decide whether to accept the offer.

You could start by looking at courses that have entry requirements that roughly match your predicted grades. There is nothing wrong with being aspirational and applying to universities that ask for top grades, but it is a good idea to also have alternatives, which will be open to you if you do not quite achieve the highest marks in the exam.

Some courses, for example those at Bible colleges, might be aimed specifically at those who are hoping to go into Christian work in a leadership role. The courses might concentrate on studying the text of the Bible and on Christian theology. Other courses might offer options to study a range of world religions or to specialise in one in particular, such as Islam, or in one 'family' of religions, such as Eastern religion. Some courses require that you study a language such as New Testament Greek, Arabic or Sanskrit as one of your modules, while for other courses this is optional or it may not be possible. A course in Philosophy is not the same as a course in Religious Studies. Philosophy courses need not include any reference to religion at all (although philosophy of religion might be an optional module), but they might concentrate instead on logic, philosophy of science or philosophy of art. Many university courses have a range of different modules and allow you to choose your own route through your degree. Many also have some modules that are compulsory, particularly in the first year. In some degree courses the majority of your marks will come from extended pieces of writing that you submit throughout the course, but others rely more heavily on timed exams. This is something you might want to take into consideration when making your choices. Some universities offer the possibility of studying 'joint honours', where you choose two subjects rather than just one, for example studying both Theology and Education, or Religious Studies and Sociology. Some offer the opportunity to spend a year studying abroad, which might be an exciting option.

Be wary of applying to a university because a friend is going there or because it is close to home without first checking that it offers a course you want to follow. Some universities do not offer courses in Religious Studies or related subjects.

If a university offers a course that appeals to you, try to visit on one of its Open Days. You will be able to see the buildings and accommodation, hear people speak in lecture halls, ask questions and pick up informational literature, and get a sense of what it might be like to spend three or four years there. Some people like universities that are in big, vibrant cities where there is plenty going on, such as London, Manchester or Birmingham. Other people prefer quieter and more intimate places, such as Durham or St Andrews. You might enjoy a university that is in a city, or you might prefer one that is on a campus (where the university is like a little town of its own, outside the main city). The architecture of the university can influence some people's decisions too. Older accommodation with high ceilings and wide staircases can be lovely, but you are less likely to have a private bathroom and the rooms might not be as warm, so think about your personal priorities. The distance of the university from your home can also be a consideration. Think about whether you want to visit your home often and have your family visit you, or whether you would prefer some distance, and think about how much fares might cost.

There are numerous factors to consider when choosing to apply for a course at a particular university and it can seem overwhelming. However, your priority should be the content of the course itself. You will enjoy your university time much more if you are genuinely interested in the things you are studying. Do your research before committing yourself to an application.

Preparing a good application for Religious Studies and related subjects

The most important aspect of your application for a degree course will be your grades. If you are applying post A level you will already know your grades; otherwise, your predicted grades will be important. Your school will predict your grades based on your performance throughout the course as well as in any practice exams. No one in the university admissions department will look at your extra-curricular activities unless you seem to be of sufficient academic calibre for the degree course, so do not imagine that you can compensate for a lax work ethic and poor grades by excelling on the sports field.

Alongside your grades, you will also need to provide a personal statement in support of your application to most universities. This personal statement has a strict word count. It gives you the opportunity to tell the university admissions office something about yourself and your academic interests and achievements.

Some people make the mistake of using the personal statement to write all about the subject they hope to study and to say how great it is. The reader is likely to know already that this is a fascinating subject and that religion is important in the world today. What they

are curious about is whether you are a good applicant, so your personal statement should concentrate on marketing yourself, not your chosen subject.

In your personal statement, try to give the reader little snapshots that illustrate what kind of a person you are, rather than just making assertions about yourself. For example, someone might say: 'I am a hard-working person and I find other people's beliefs about the afterlife fascinating.' However, someone else might say, much more effectively: 'When I was volunteering at a care home for the elderly, I realised the extent to which faith in an afterlife can affect people's attitudes.' This second example shows that you are hard-working and interested in other people, without you having to pay yourself a compliment. It shows that you can relate academic ideas to real life and that you recognise their importance. You might not have done anything particularly remarkable with your life yet, but you can still use illustrations to show that you are a thinking person, such as referring to conversations in class that made you think, or world events, or ideas in books. Show that you are the kind of person who actively engages with ideas, who is thoughtful and who loves to learn.

Your personal statement should concentrate on demonstrating that you would be an enthusiastic, able, independent and committed student of the subject you are applying to study.

Enthusiasm

Try to demonstrate your enthusiasm for the subject with examples. Saying 'I am passionate about…' is not as effective as an example that illustrates your passion. If, perhaps, you are interested in situation ethics, rather than simply saying, 'I am interested in situation ethics', you could say, 'When I was reading Fletcher's book *Situation Ethics*, I was struck by…/it made me think about…' or, 'When I saw X event on the news recently, it made me consider how situation ethics might be applied…' or, 'When I went to a lecture about ethics recently, I realised…'.

Simply saying that different topics in the course are fascinating does not tell the reader anything about you. Illustrate your claim that you are enthusiastic by showing what you have done. It is difficult to convince someone that you are fascinated by something if you have done nothing to follow up on that enthusiasm. Most importantly, read about your academic interests, not only on the Internet but also in high-quality books and in the news. You will find some suggestions for further reading at the end of each of the chapters in this book. When you write about your reading, explain why you chose the books and what they made you think about. If you have read nothing more than the textbooks and the pieces you have been given for homework, and you have not made any effort to extend your knowledge beyond this, it does not suggest that you are really keen on the subject.

If you are interested in world religions, try to visit a place of worship, talk to people from the faith community and develop your knowledge through reading. In some towns and cities there are lectures you can attend. All of these can be used as examples in your personal statement to show that your enthusiasm is genuine and you are keen to learn.

Ability

Your grades and school reference will demonstrate your academic abilities, but you can also show them in your personal statement. Entering essay competitions and writing articles on philosophical, ethical and religious topics for your school magazine can give you an opportunity to showcase your skills in Religious Studies. It is worth mentioning these things in your personal statement, as well as involvement in debating societies and philosophy clubs for example, especially if you take part in competitions.

Make sure that your personal statement is written in good English and that you have not made any factual mistakes in it.

Independence and commitment

Universities like to know that you are able to work independently, will not need constant guidance and reassurance every step of the way, and will not give up easily. You could include things on your personal statement to show that you can work independently. For example, you might have done an extended essay or some other kind of academic project. Your examples do not have to focus on Religious Studies as

a subject area – perhaps you have organised a charity event or given an assembly. You might have been helping in a care home or at Guides in a committed way for a substantial length of time. See if you can think of something that shows that you can initiate a task and then see it through to the end.

Extra-curricular activities and work experience

It can be good in a personal statement to show that you have a wide range of interests as this gives the admissions tutors some idea of what you are like as a person, but this should not dominate the personal statement. You might belong to clubs and societies, you might play sport or a musical instrument or have other interests and talents. These can be mentioned, but you do not need to go into great detail about them. If you have done something outstanding, such as run a marathon or won a national award, that is something that can enhance your application.

Some degree courses, such as veterinary medicine, require you to have undertaken relevant work experience before applying. Work experience can be useful in helping you to mature and giving you a taste of possible careers so that you can form a judgement about what you enjoy. However, no one will expect you to have relevant work experience before undertaking a degree in Religious Studies. Take opportunities if they arise, but do not feel that this is something you have to do, as your application does not depend on it.

Interviews

Some universities like to interview applicants before deciding whether to offer them a place. Oxford and Cambridge have rigorous interviews, and some other universities also include an interview as part of the selection process. The point of the interview is to see how well you respond to questions and ideas that you have not rehearsed. In many respects it is impossible to prepare for an interview, because you cannot know what you will be asked about. However, you can practise by talking about your ideas with others, and your school might be able to offer you a practice interview with a visitor.

Make sure that you re-read your personal statement before an interview, as the interviewer might want to use it as a starting point for questions. If, on your personal statement, you say you have read something, then make sure you actually have read it and have another look at it before the interview to refresh your memory.

Wear something reasonably respectable and comfortable to the interview. It does not have to be a suit, but if you feel more confident in a suit then wear one.

If you are nervous in the interview that will not count against you. Take your time with the questions, if necessary ask the interviewer to repeat them, and feel free to change your mind during the conversation if you want to.

What can I do with a degree in Religious Studies or a degree in a related subject?

People who study for degrees in Religious Studies and related subjects go into a wide variety of careers. As with other humanities subjects, the degree course will help to develop your skills in research, in writing reports and in paying attention to detail. Religious Studies will enhance your critical abilities, help you learn to form incisive arguments, give you empathy for people whose beliefs are different from your own and help you to understand what it means to live in a culturally diverse world.

A degree in this subject could lead to a career in the civil service, the armed forces, politics or the police service. It could lead you into a caring profession such as nursing, diversity training or social work, or it could lead to a career in law, education, writing or the performing arts. All kinds of career opportunities will be open to you as employers increasingly understand the need to engage with a changing world and diversity of beliefs and values.

Studying philosophy of religion

What do people mean by the term 'God'?

Do the different attributes traditionally ascribed to God, such as omnipotence and omniscience, make coherent sense?

How can people use normal everyday language to communicate ideas about God?

Are all attempts to discuss supernatural ideas ultimately meaningless?

In the second year of this A level course, study in philosophy of religion is focused on two areas: beliefs about the nature of God and issues in religious language. These two areas are closely related. Beliefs about the nature of God are expressed through language, but difficulties arise when people try to describe a being whose nature is so very different from anything in the physical world that none of the words we use seem adequate. Although questions about these two areas have been discussed for centuries, they have a great deal of significance today, as Christianity re-evaluates how it understands God's action in the world and where Christianity stands in relation to other world religions.

Discussion of the nature of God includes issues such as what it means to call God 'omnipotent'. Does this mean that God can do absolutely anything, even the impossible and the nonsensical? Is omnipotence, in itself, a coherent concept, or is it perhaps self-contradictory? For example, God is omnipotent so there is nothing he cannot do, including fail; but if he cannot fail then he cannot do everything. Omniscience is another characteristic that is ascribed to God, but this also raises issues.

For example, there is the issue of whether our freedom to make real choices is compromised if God already knows with certainty what we are going to do. God's relationship with time is also discussed, with a consideration of whether God exists outside time or whether God travels along the same timeline that we do. Did God know in advance about events such as terrorist attacks or natural disasters? Could he have used his powers to prevent it from happening?

These issues continue to have relevance in the modern world. The two World Wars of the twentieth century, in particular, made people think again about their ideas of a God of power, foreknowledge and love. Scholars have tried to find new ways of understanding how God interacts with the world and have asked whether God deliberately limits his own powers in order to allow humanity the freedom to make its own choices.

Developments in discussions of religious language have also led people to question whether religious believers have been too literal in trying to understand God in terms of human characteristics. Perhaps the terms people use when they are trying to explain the nature of God are best understood as analogy or as symbol, rather than as literally true. Or perhaps it would be better to use only negative terms for God, saying what God is not rather than trying and failing to describe God in terms that are always going to be too small to encapsulate God's nature.

Religious language is an issue that has dominated the philosophy of religion in the last century. Some thinkers, such as A.J. Ayer and Antony Flew, have posed challenges to religious believers by suggesting that statements made about God are meaningless. They cannot be tested using the senses; they cannot be falsified. So perhaps they are not really asserting anything at all, but are empty statements. This debate about the meaningfulness of religious language has at least in part been inspired by the thinking of Wittgenstein, one of the most exciting philosophers of the last century. It relates closely to meta-ethics, where very similar questions of meaning are discussed.

The two areas of study in this second year of the course are important because of the influence they have had on shaping modern Christianity. If religious language is to be understood as symbolic, for example, does this mean that other world religions, with their different ways of symbolising God, could be just as true (or false) as Christianity? Debates in philosophy of religion, therefore, link closely to debates in ethics and in Christianity, and have encouraged people to look at the Christian faith in new ways and find fresh approaches, for example by suggesting that God's power is not actually total, or interpreting all religious language as symbolic rather than literal.

Chapter 1.1

The nature or attributes of God

Does the omnipotence of God mean that there is nothing God cannot do?

If God can do anything, can this be compatible with God being perfectly good?

If God knows the future with certainty, does this restrict human free will?

If God exists at all, does God exist outside time or does he move along the same timeline that we do?

Key Terms

Omnipotent: all-powerful

Omniscient: all-knowing

Omnibenevolent: all-good and all-loving

Eternal: timeless, atemporal, being outside the constraints of time

Everlasting: sempiternal, lasting forever on the same timeline as humanity

Free will: the ability to make independent choices between real options

Existentialism: a way of thinking that emphasises personal freedom of choice

Immutable: incapable of changing or being affected

Specification requirements

Developments in the understanding of:

- omnipotence
- omniscience
- (omni)benevolence
- eternity
- free will

Introduction

One of the most fundamental questions in the philosophy of religion is, what do people mean when they talk about 'God' or 'gods'? Theists are people who believe that God exists, but what exactly is it that they are saying exists, and what are they asking other people to believe in? Are they talking about an object, one amongst all the other objects in the universe? Are they, perhaps, talking about 'Existence-Itself', encompassing the entire universe? What do they understand the nature of God to be?

Different religions have different understandings of the nature and attributes of God, although there are also many ideas in common. In the Hindu tradition, for example, one God can be understood and experienced in many different forms through different deities such as Krishna, Ganesha and Lakshmi. The Hindu deities illustrate the many facets of God. They can be male or female, both creative and destructive, and both gently benevolent and fiercely aggressive. In the Muslim tradition, the oneness of Allah is emphasised alongside the complete dependence of humanity on Allah.

The Christian tradition also has a distinctive way of understanding the nature and attributes of God. Because Christianity began and grew within the context of the Greco-Roman world, Christian understandings of the nature of God developed from the interweaving of biblical ideas and concepts from the ancient Greek philosophers.

Christians inherited the language, symbolism and poetry of the Old Testament, in which God is anthropomorphised (made to seem like a human person), involved with the world and unpredictable. The God of the Old Testament seems to have thoughts and feelings: he is satisfied when people obey his Commandments, and angry and disappointed when they fail. He sometimes seems to have to wait and see what people will do next, and gives them warnings and promises, as if the future is as unknown to God as it is to his people. God is concerned about moral behaviour, taking an interest in what people do and passing judgement on the decisions they make, suggesting that whatever they do is their own choice and that, when they do wrong, it is their own fault.

However, the writers of the New Testament and the Christians who were responsible for shaping early Christian thought also came from a culture in which classical ideas of a timeless, spaceless, unchanging First Cause were very attractive. In particular, ideas from Plato and Aristotle were adopted and woven into Christian interpretations of the nature of God – sometimes successfully, and sometimes in a way that produces apparent contradictions. If God has perfect power, does this mean that he is in total control of everything that ever happens (in which case, can we ever be free to make independent decisions)? Can God be entirely loving in nature, and yet also powerful to the extent that he can do anything at all (including unloving things)? Can God be infinite and outside time, and yet be concerned with a finite creation that exists within time?

Think question

Do you think different religions believe in different gods, or do they just express their ideas about the same God differently?

Think question

If someone told you that they believed in God, what would you understand them to be saying?

The idea of God as omnipotent raises questions about whether there is anything God cannot do

Can God know the future with perfect knowledge, and yet still allow us to be free to choose our own futures and be responsible for our own actions?

Many theists, including Christians, assert that God is **omnipotent, omniscient, omnibenevolent,** and **eternal** or **everlasting**, and they sometimes have differing views about what these attributes mean. Philosophers of religion work to explore whether traditional beliefs about the nature or attributes of God make coherent sense, and whether these beliefs can be held simultaneously without creating contradictions.

The idea of divine power

The idea that God is omnipotent, or all-powerful, is a familiar one in Christian thought. However, it has caused a considerable amount of controversy.

One question that immediately arises is whether omnipotence is a coherent concept, whether applied to God or to anything else. For example, people have for years debated the questions of whether God can create a stone too heavy for himself to lift, or a knot that he cannot himself untie. Can there be such a thing as omnipotence, or does it necessarily involve logical contradictions? On the one hand, omnipotence involves (allegedly) being able to do absolutely anything. On the other hand, there are some actions that seem impossible for an omnipotent being to do, such as 'fail at a task' or 'be defeated by another being'. If omnipotence itself is impossible, then there cannot be any omnipotent beings. These problems are often referred to as 'the omnipotence paradox', where the whole notion of total power seems to be self-contradictory.

Another question that arises is whether omnipotence can be compatible with other characteristics traditionally ascribed to the Christian God. People discuss whether God's omnipotence is compatible with his being all-loving, since it would be illogical for God to be both able to do evil (because he is able to do absolutely everything) and unable to do evil (because he is perfectly loving) at the same time. Perhaps God's omnipotence is incompatible with his omniscience, since it would be illogical for God to be both able to add to his knowledge (because he is able to do everything) and at the same time unable to add to his knowledge (because he already knows everything).

Such questions then lead on to the further question of what the concept of 'an omnipotent being' might actually mean. Does it mean 'a being that is able to do absolutely anything, including the impossible'? Does it mean 'a being that is able to do everything possible'? Perhaps it means 'a being that has maximal power (more power than any other being in existence)' without this necessarily implying total power and all the difficulties that entails.

There are many passages in the Bible that support the view that God is omnipotent in some sense. The creation stories at the beginning of the book of Genesis, the references to creation in the Psalms, the words of the prophets, the ending of the book of Job, the miracle stories and the resurrection of Jesus are all examples that point to a God who has such power that he just has to want something to happen for it to come about:

> 66 And God said 'Let there be light' and there was light. 99
>
> Genesis 1:3, New International Version

The prophet Amos speaks of a God who has total power over nature:

> 66 He who made the Pleiades and Orion,
>   who turns midnight into dawn
>   and darkens day into night,
> who calls for the waters of the sea
>   and pours them out over the face of the land—
>   the Lord is his name. 99
>
> Amos 5:8, New International Version

God's omnipotence is also shown in his dealings with individuals, where he makes things happen for them that would never have occurred without the help of God. For example, in the book of Genesis, there is the story of Abraham and his wife Sarah, who showed kindness and hospitality to three strangers, bringing them water and preparing a meal for them to refresh them before they went on their way. As a reward, God told Abraham that he and Sarah would have the son they had always longed for, even though Sarah was well past child-bearing age. The idea was so ridiculous to her that she could not help laughing and God immediately knew her secret thoughts. But, the story emphasises, she should have realised there is nothing that is too hard for God:

> 66 Then one of them said, 'I will surely return to you about this time next year, and Sarah your wife will have a son.'
>
> Now Sarah was listening at the entrance to the tent, which was behind him. Abraham and Sarah were already very old, and Sarah was past the age of childbearing. So Sarah laughed to herself as she thought, 'After I am worn out and my master is old, will I now have this pleasure?'
>
> Then the Lord said to Abraham, 'Why did Sarah laugh and say, "Will I really have a child, now that I am old?" Is anything too hard for the Lord? I will return to you at the appointed time next year, and Sarah will have a son.'
>
> Sarah was afraid, so she lied and said, 'I did not laugh.'
> But he said, 'Yes, you did laugh.' 99
>
> Genesis 18:10–15, New International Version

The Bible emphasises the power of God to create and perform miracles

There is a similar story in Luke's gospel, where Mary the mother of Jesus hears from the angel that her cousin Elizabeth is pregnant with John the Baptist, despite the fact that Elizabeth, like Sarah, has passed the menopause and has never been able to have children:

> 66 Even Elizabeth your relative is going to have a child in her old age, and she who was said to be unable to conceive is in her sixth month. For no word from God will ever fail. 99
>
> Luke 1:36–37, New International Version

Even performing miracles that go against the laws of nature are within the power of God. Stories of Jesus in the gospels present Jesus as a miracle worker to show his divine nature. Jesus is shown to be someone who could walk on water, turn water into wine, raise the dead and calm storms just by giving a command.

In the New Testament, God's omnipotence is declared by Jesus in the context of the story of the rich young ruler. He asked Jesus what he needed to do in order to be saved and was told that he needed to sell all he had and give the money to the poor:

> 66 Then Jesus said to his disciples, 'Truly I tell you, it is hard for someone who is rich to enter the kingdom of heaven. Again I tell you, it is easier for a camel to go through the eye of a needle than for someone who is rich to enter the kingdom of God.'
>
> When the disciples heard this, they were greatly astonished and asked, 'Who then can be saved?'
>
> Jesus looked at them and said, 'With man this is impossible, but with God all things are possible.' 99
>
> Matthew 19:23–26

Christian theologians have taken the view that if God did not have supreme power, he would not be able to do the things that are necessary for human salvation. Unless God had omnipotence, he would not be able to create and carry out his plans for the universe; he would not be able to save people from their sins; he would not be able to resurrect people from death; he would not be able to give them eternal life in heaven. Both Anselm and Descartes depended on this understanding of God when they formed their ontological arguments, claiming that God is 'that than which nothing greater can be conceived' (Anselm), and that God has all the perfections (including perfect power). If God were anything less than omnipotent, then we would be able to conceive of a greater, more perfect and more powerful being; so God, by definition, must be omnipotent.

Apply your knowledge

1. In the passage from Matthew's gospel, what do you think Jesus meant when he said 'with God all things are possible'? Do you think he meant that God can do absolutely anything? Give reasons for your answer.

2. Look up the story of Jesus' temptation in the wilderness before he began his ministry (Matthew 4:1–11). In the story, Jesus is tempted to use his supernatural powers, but he resists the temptation. What do you think the story is trying to show about Jesus' power? Why does Jesus refuse to use it?

Think question

How convincing do you find the view that God, by definition, must be omnipotent?

Different understandings of omnipotence

Different thinkers have considered the problems raised by the notion that God is omnipotent, and have developed a variety of ways of understanding what the omnipotence of God might mean.

Perhaps omnipotence means that God can do absolutely anything, including the impossible and the self-contradictory

When Descartes explored what it meant for God to be perfectly powerful, he came to the conclusion that God can do absolutely anything, even that which is logically impossible. According to Descartes, God could make a square circle, or make $2 + 2 = 5$, because God is the supreme perfection and, therefore, he can have no limitations at all. God is the source of logic and has the power to suspend logic or replace it whenever he wants to. Descartes argued that the laws of mathematics only exist in the way that they do because God created them that way, and God can change them or override them whenever he likes. Descartes rejected any other understandings of omnipotence because he thought that they put limits on the greatness of God and dishonoured God's greatness. Saying God had to conform to the laws of logic made it sound as though the God of Christianity was no more powerful than Zeus, who was at the mercy of the Fates.

For Descartes, God could be capable of doing evil (because of his omnipotence), and incapable (because of his love) at the same time, even though this involves a logical contradiction. Although we cannot see how such a God could exist, this (for Descartes) is because we are limited by logic and by the smallness of human understanding. God can see how to be self-contradictory because he is omnipotent God.

However, most Christian scholars have argued that this kind of understanding of omnipotence is mistaken. God can do anything; but logical contradictions are not 'things'. It is not a lack of power that prevents God from making a square circle, or a lack of knowledge that would prevent God from scoring more than 100 per cent on a test. It is the fact that square circles and test scores of more than 100 per cent are nonsense.

Descartes' view also turns God into an unpredictable and arbitrary tyrant, who might do anything (and therefore cannot be relied upon). If God is really all-powerful in the sense that he can do anything at all, then God has to be capable of doing evil, of being unforgiving, of turning against us, and of failing. He has to be capable of being self-contradictory by, for example, making unbreakable promises and then breaking them. It presents God as a being that humans cannot hope to understand or rely upon. It means that God's moral rules might change at any minute, or be both true and false at the same time. It makes it impossible for people to have a relationship with God or trust in him for their salvation.

Descartes thought that an omnipotent God should be able to do anything at all, even the logically impossible

Descartes' view creates difficulties for theodicy (attempts to justify God in the face of the existence of evil). The theodicies that have been put forward by most Christian thinkers, such as Irenaeus, Augustine and John Hick, suggest that God could not act in any other way than the way he does without depriving us of our **free will**. Suffering is a price that has to be paid in order for us to make free choices and be autonomous moral agents. However, if Descartes is correct and God is capable of absolutely anything, such as suspending the laws of logic to allow us to have free will without the consequent evil, then the existence of evil in the world becomes something that God could change if he wanted to, but which he chooses to inflict on us even though there is no justification for it. This then becomes difficult to reconcile with the idea that God is perfectly loving.

It could also be argued that Descartes' understanding of absolute omnipotence is not wholly supported by the Bible. For example, Numbers 23:19 claims that because God is God and not human, he cannot fail in some of the ways that humans fail:

> 66 God is not human, that he should lie,
> not a human being, that he should change his mind.
> Does he speak and then not act?
> Does he promise and not fulfill? 99
>
> Numbers 23:19, New International Version

Hebrews 6:18 states that 'it is impossible for God to lie' (Hebrews 6:18, New International Version).

The Bible certainly emphasises that the greatness and power of God is on a scale way beyond anything that humans can do or imagine, but it does not necessarily support Descartes' idea that literally nothing is impossible for God.

Perhaps omnipotence means that God can do everything that is within his own nature, and which is logically possible

In the Abraham story from Genesis, where Sarah is promised a child, God asks a rhetorical question, 'Is anything too hard for God?', implying that God can do anything and everything that he wants to. It is this idea of 'everything that he wants to' that has given many Christian thinkers an opportunity to try to resolve the difficulties of God's omnipotence. If God is capable of doing anything that he wants to do, then he is omnipotent – but there are things that God would never want to do because they are against his nature, such as breaking the laws of logic, failing or doing something unjust.

Thomas Aquinas argued that God is completely omnipotent in the sense of being in charge of the whole world, creating it and keeping it in existence. Aquinas said that God is omnipotent because: 'he can do everything that is absolutely possible', qualified by saying that 'everything that does not imply

Think question

Do you think that Matthew 19:26 and Hebrews 6:18 contradict each other? How might someone defend the view that both verses are true, if at all?

Aquinas argued that God could do anything that is non-contradictory and that is within the nature of God

a contradiction is among those possibilities in respect of which God is called omnipotent' (Aquinas, *Summa Theologica*, 1265–74, Part I, Q25.4).

So Aquinas is saying that God can do anything logically possible, but if it is not logically possible then it cannot be done, even by God. If something is logically contradictory, such as a square circle, then it is not a thing that can be made at all.

From this, then, it follows that God cannot do anything that is inconsistent with his nature because that would imply a contradiction. God is incorporeal (he has no body) for example, and therefore cannot swim, or die, or become tired. God is perfectly good, and therefore cannot deceive or do any other form of evil.

The modern theologian and philosopher of religion, Richard Swinburne (b. 1934), also takes this view. In his book *The Coherence of Theism* (1977), he argues that God's omnipotence means that God can do everything – but 'everything' has to be understood properly. God can do and create all 'things', but self-contradictory definitions do not refer to 'things'. A square circle is not a 'thing', so God cannot make one. A 'stone too heavy for God to lift' could not be a thing, and a 'knot that God could not untie' could not be a thing, so God could not make them. This, for Swinburne, is not a challenge to God's omnipotence, because God remains capable of doing and creating everything.

Swinburne argues that God can do anything, but not the logically impossible, because impossible things are not things

Perhaps God deliberately limits his own power for our benefit

In *The Puzzle of Evil* (1992), Peter Vardy (b. 1945) suggests that God's omnipotence is much more limited than many Christians have previously suggested. God is not in control of the whole of history, able to move anything around like pieces on a chessboard, Vardy argues, and it is wrong to suggest that everything that happens is because of the will of God.

Vardy suggests that God created the universe in such a way that his ability to act is necessarily limited. The whole of the universe is finely tuned in such a way that if God acted in any different way, everything would not be able to exist in the way that it does. He argues that the universe is perfectly suited for the existence of free, rational human beings, and that in order for it to remain this way, God's omnipotence has to be very much limited. However, this limitation is self-imposed. God chose to create the universe in this way, knowing what it would mean, and therefore it is still right to call God omnipotent because nothing limits his power except when he chooses.

66 To call God Almighty, therefore, is to recognise the ultimate dependence of the universe and all things within it on God. It is to recognise God's creative and sustaining power. However, it specifically does not mean that God has total power to do anything he wishes. God is limited by the universe he has chosen to create […] his limitation does not, however, lessen God in any significant way. It

> is rather a recognition of God's wish to create a universe in which human beings can be brought into a loving relationship with him. 99

Peter Vardy, *The Puzzle of Evil*, 1992, p. 124

Many leading Christian thinkers point out that limits on God's omnipotence are self-imposed. God chooses to limit his own power for our benefit

John Macquarrie makes a similar point in *Principles of Christian Theology* (1966). Like Aquinas in the thirteenth century and Peter Vardy today, Macquarrie emphasises that any limitations on God's omnipotence are self-imposed. God is not constrained by logic, nor by the physical world, nor by the actions of human beings, but is constrained in his omnipotence merely because he chooses to limit his own power out of love for humanity.

This idea of God being self-limited is one that has been explored by Christian theologians, particularly in the context of Christology (a branch of theology involved with understanding the nature of Christ). In answer to the puzzle of how Jesus could have been the Son of God, given that Jesus did not always display God's attributes of omnipotence or timelessness or being without a body, theologians have developed a doctrine known as kenosis. This means 'self-emptying'; in other words, God deliberately emptied himself of some of his divine attributes before coming to earth, in order to make Jesus' encounter with humanity possible. Jesus had to have human limitations in order to be human at all, and this was because of God's own choice and freely given love. The doctrine is based on a passage from the letter to the Philippians in the New Testament, where the writer encourages his readers to imitate Christ's humility:

66 In your relationships with one another, have the same mindset as Christ Jesus:

Who, being in very nature God,
  did not consider equality with God something to be used to his own advantage;
rather he made himself nothing
  by taking the very nature of a servant,
  being made in human likeness.
And being found in appearance as a man,
  he humbled himself
  and became obedient to death—
  even death on a cross! 99

Philippians 2:5–8, New International Version

This idea has gained in popularity in the twentieth and twenty-first centuries, perhaps because of the need for Christians to re-evaluate the idea of God's omnipotence after the horrors of the twentieth century wars, and perhaps also because of rising interest in **existentialist** ways of thinking, where free will and finding personal meaning is emphasised.

Perhaps problems with the idea of God's omnipotence are an issue of religious language

Macquarrie and other thinkers emphasise the need for believers to remember that when they speak of the power of God, they are using analogy, and should understand that God's power is very different from our own. They need to remember that the word 'power' refers to power within this world, so when it is applied to God, it cannot be applied literally because God is infinitely greater than we are. Following Aquinas, he argues that there will always be aspects of God's nature that remain unknowable to us. Even if we can understand them partially, and express them partially with the use of analogy, we should nevertheless bear in mind that if God's omnipotence is something we have difficulty comprehending, that is only to be expected given that we have small fallible human minds whereas God is God. When we think of 'perfect power', we think of the kinds of power that we know and understand from our limited human world. We try and magnify them in our minds and imagine what power might be like on an infinite, divine scale. However, the kinds of power we know are fallible, and our imaginations are limited, and therefore if we struggle to understand God's power we should not be surprised.

Perhaps total omnipotence is not a great quality, and God should be understood as 'unsurpassably great' rather than totally powerful

Another interesting position in the debate about God's omnipotence comes from thinkers such as A.N. Whitehead (1861–1947) and Charles Hartshorne (1897–2000). They argued that absolute omnipotence in the sense of total power would not in reality be a perfect quality, and that it would be better to think of God as a being whose power cannot be surpassed by any other being, rather than as a being with total power. Hartshorne argues that total power, when we examine the idea, is not actually all that impressive.

Hartshorne considers that total power means that nothing else is able to put up any resistance at all to that power. If something else can offer resistance, then the power is not total. Omnipotence for Hartshorne means having total influence and effect. A totally omnipotent God would have total control over everything, and nothing would be able to do anything unless God allowed it and controlled it.

If I want to tidy the garden and cut a small overhanging branch off the roses, the rose will offer some resistance. I have to squeeze the clippers quite hard to get through the branch. I am stronger than the rose branch and so I can do the clipping. But if I were omnipotent, the branch would offer no resistance at all; clipping it would be like slicing through melted butter or I could just will the rose to be the shape I wanted and it would happen. Hartshorne asks us what would be so impressive about a being who can conquer things that can put up no resistance? It would be like praising someone who came first in a race with no other competitors.

> *See the discussion of religious language in Chapters 1.2 and 1.3. Aquinas argues that when we speak of God's attributes we need to remember that we are using analogy and not speaking literally.*

Thinkers such as Aquinas and Macquarrie point to issues with religious language as a key to understanding the attributes of God

Apply your knowledge

3. **a.** Which of the different understandings of God's omnipotence, if any, do you find the most coherent? What do you think are its strengths?

   b. Which of the views do you find the least convincing and why?

4. Some scholars have argued that difficulties arise for us because we cannot conceive of the power of God, and the problems stem from our own limitations of understanding rather than because ideas about God are nonsense. Do you think this is a fair point? Give reasons for your answer.

Hartshorne argued that God's omnipotence is only impressive if it is not total

For Hartshorne, it is important for an understanding of God's power that we recognise that other beings, through their free will, are capable of putting up resistance to God. Therefore, God's power over them is not total, although his power is always greater than that of any other being. This, for Hartshorne, is more impressive than a being that nothing can challenge. In his view, God's omnipotence means that God can overcome all resistance, not that God will meet no resistance.

Divine omniscience and God's relationship with time

What does it mean to say that God is omniscient?

Most people understand the omniscience of God to mean that God knows everything; there is nothing that he cannot know. However, it also means that God has no false beliefs and cannot be mistaken. If God knows something, then that thing is true.

If God is omniscient, God's knowledge includes things that are unavailable to the human mind. For example, God knows details of history that humanity has long forgotten; he knows whether there is life on other planets, in other galaxies; he knows whether there are other universes besides this one. He knows people's secret thoughts even when they are never expressed.

Omniscience, when attributed to God, is also closely linked with the idea of wisdom. God always knows the right thing to do, the best choices to make, which moral rules to give and when to intervene in the world. If God does something, then that action is the best action and it is done at exactly the right time.

However, attributing omniscience to God raises questions. If God knows everything, does this include events in the future as well as those in the past? Particularly significant for theology is the question of whether God knows in advance all the moral decisions that people will make in their lives. If he does know these decisions (and if his knowledge is always certain and never mistaken) then it raises the issue of whether people have any real freedom of choice.

For example, if God knows for all time that someone will steal an item this Friday, and God's knowledge is certain, then perhaps when Friday comes that person has no choice but to steal it. God's certain knowledge that it will happen might 'fix' the event and make it unchangeable. The person might feel that they are making a choice to steal the item, but in actual fact there was no possibility that they could have decided at the last minute not to steal it after all. And if there was no possibility that they could have acted otherwise, then it becomes difficult to blame them for following the only course of action open to them.

In Christianity, Judaism and Islam, alongside the belief that God is omniscient is the belief that humans are morally responsible for at least some of the actions they perform. It is believed that people have genuinely free choices about what they do. God does not compel them to choose one way rather than another, but leaves it to each individual to decide, independently, what to do in different situations as they arise. This means that they can then be held responsible for their choices. Islam, in particular, stresses that this earthly life is a testing place, where people make choices between right and wrong. Their responses to these choices are judged by Allah, and their place in heaven depends on whether they make the right decisions. Similarly, in Christianity, people are held to have a free choice about their moral decisions and about where they place their faith, and they are judged by God accordingly.

There is, then, a firm belief that it is possible both for people to have genuinely free will and for there to be an omniscient God. Within Christianity, different thinkers have offered different possible solutions to the problems this raises.

Friedrich Schleiermacher (1768–1834) argued that there is a possible solution to the problem of whether God's omniscience restricts our freedom. He drew the analogy of the knowledge that close friends have of each other's future behaviour to conclude that God could be omniscient while still allowing people to act freely:

Think question

What do you think are the differences between knowledge, belief and wisdom? If God is omniscient, could he have 'beliefs'?

23

> 66 In the same way, we estimate the intimacy between two persons by the foreknowledge one has of the actions of the other, without supposing that in either case, the one or the other's freedom is thereby endangered. So even the divine foreknowledge cannot endanger freedom. 99
>
> Friedrich Schleiermacher, *The Christian Faith*, 1831, trans. W.E. Matthew, p. 228

Perhaps Schleiermacher is right. If I go to an Indian restaurant with my husband and Amritsar fish is on the menu, I can be fairly certain that he will choose it as it is his favourite meal. He can be very certain that I will avoid meat dishes, as I am vegetarian. Does our knowledge of each other's future choices mean that in some way we are restricting each other's freedom of choice? Most would say that the answer is no; because although I *know* what my husband will choose, I am only making a *reliable guess*. There is a possibility that I could be wrong; he might prefer something else this time. There is nothing in my knowledge of what he likes to eat that compels him to choose the dish I think he will choose. His knowledge that I am vegetarian, too, does not force me to make a vegetarian choice. I would make the same choice regardless of what my companion knew. I am not going to choose anything that is not vegetarian, but this is not *because* my husband knows this. There is nothing in his knowledge or lack of knowledge that forces my choice. For Schleiermacher, this is comparable with God's knowledge of our actions. His knowledge does not force or affect what we choose to do, and therefore we can still be held morally responsible and still make genuinely free choices.

Schleiermacher thought that the knowledge God has of us is like the knowledge close friends have of each other

See Chapter 2.3 of the AS and Year 1 book for more about Kant's understanding of ethics.

The problems with Schleiermacher's idea are that, unlike the knowledge partners or friends have of each other, God's knowledge is said to be infallible. I could be wrong in guessing what my husband will eat, but God cannot be wrong; he never makes mistakes. There is nothing that God knows that could turn out to be untrue. God is also said to *know* the future, rather than making a reliable prediction of it. It is the certainty of omniscient knowledge that makes it difficult to reconcile with human freedom of choice.

If our freedom to act morally were only apparent, then there would be serious implications. We would not be able to be held morally responsible for our actions because we would not have been able to behave in any other way. A genuine freedom of choice is considered by ethicists to be essential as a basis for morality. Kant, for example, argued that without freedom, there can be no moral choices. We have to have genuine options available to us to choose between, not just an illusion that we are making a free choice.

If God's omniscience determines our choices, then God cannot justifiably punish us when we do wrong or reward us when we do good.

The problem for our moral freedom becomes even more acute when belief in God's omniscience is coupled with the belief that God intends and creates every individual life, fashioning each person in accordance with his plans. God could have chosen to make us differently, or he could have chosen not to make us at all. If God not only knows the future with certainty, but knew when he made us and from the beginning of time exactly what we would choose at every point of our lives, perhaps God can be held responsible for all kinds of evil, including so-called moral evil.

There is the added difficulty that God might know, for all time, each person's religious choices. Perhaps God knows from the beginning of time which of us will have faith and which will doubt or disbelieve. Perhaps God knows, even before we are born, whether we will end up in heaven or hell, so that there is nothing we can do about it.

If, however, God does not have a clue what we will do, and wondered when he made each individual how they would turn out, and was sometimes taken aback by the choices they made, then this seems to imply a less than all-powerful God. It suggests that God can be surprised, or can make choices that turn out to have been unwise. God's capabilities seem to be limited.

Different Christian thinkers have formed different responses to the issues raised by the idea that God is omniscient. The ideas of Boethius and Anselm have been particularly influential. The modern philosopher Richard Swinburne has also contributed to the debate.

Discussion of what it means for God to be omniscient, and whether this restricts our free will, is closely linked to different understandings of God's relationship with time. Is the future already known to God, or does God have to wait and see what happens, just as we do?

God's relationship with time

Christianity claims that God is eternal, but what does this mean? There are two main views.

1. The view most commonly adopted by classical theologians, is that God is timeless. In other words, God is outside time, and is not bound by time; God is the creator of time. God is described as 'eternal' or 'atemporal'.

2. The other view is that God is everlasting. In other words, it is the belief that God moves along the same timeline that we do but never begins or ends. The past is past for God as well as for us, and past events are fixed for God just as they are for us. The future is unknown to us and is also, to some extent at least, unknown to God because it has not happened yet. In this view of God, he is described as 'sempiternal'.

Our understanding of what it means for God to be eternal is important because it affects many other ideas about the attributes of God. It affects ideas such as:

- Omniscience: Can God know with certainty the details of events that have not yet happened?

Apply your knowledge

5. Look up Romans 11:33–34 and Hebrews 4:13.

   a. What do these verses say about the knowledge of God?

   b. Do you think these verses support the view that God is omniscient?

6. Do you think that if God is omniscient, this must mean that he knows all our future choices? Give reasons for your answer.

7. It could be argued that to call God omniscient does not have to mean that God knows everything. It could mean that God's knowledge is unsurpassed by the knowledge of any other being. What do you think of this argument?

- The problem of evil: Can God see the whole picture from the beginning, in which case can he be at least partly blamed for things being the way that they are, because he knew in advance what would happen?

- Omnipotence: Can God change the past, and make events that have already happened un-happen, or is that beyond his power?

- Justice: Can God justifiably blame us for actions he knew we would perform even before he made us?

- Prayer: Is there any point in praying for something if God already knows what he will do and the future is fixed?

The view that God is timeless (atemporal)

This is the view that has been the more popular among Christian thinkers, and has been held by, for example, Augustine, Boethius, Anselm, Aquinas and Schleiermacher. It is the idea that God exists outside time, and can see the past, the present and the future, all with perfect knowledge. Time, it is argued, is an aspect of the created world, like space, and God is in control of it. God is not bound by space, in the Christian view; he can be and is everywhere at once. In the same kind of way, he is not bound by time but exists in every part of history and in every part of the future while being present in the world today.

This view is popular because it shows that God is not limited. As an aspect of the created world, time is something introduced by God rather than something to which God is subject. God's omnipotence is not threatened if God is not bound by the constraints of time – perhaps a God who could not know the future would be less powerful than one who could. It is a view that also allows for the belief that God is **immutable** (unchangeable), which is argued by some thinkers to be necessary if God is perfect.

People who support the idea that God is eternal argue that if God were bound by time, then he would be much more limited. He would not know what the outcomes of actions might be; he would have to wait and see how events turn out before deciding what to do next. There might be times when God's plans were thwarted because of unforeseen difficulties – and then God would have to resort to a different plan. His omnipotence and omniscience would be reduced to a point where God could hardly be called *all*-powerful and *all*-knowing. A God who was sempiternal rather than atemporal would not meet Anselm's definition of 'a being than which nothing greater can be conceived', because we would be able to conceive of a greater being than one who was constrained by having to exist within time.

Those who defend the view that God is outside time argue that other concepts of God's relationship with time do not recognise the uniqueness of God. God can bring things about in time, and cause changes in people without being changed himself, because God is not a person in the same way that we are. There are things that are possible for God, because of the unique nature of his existence, even if we cannot see how they are possible with our limited understanding.

The classical view of God's relationship with time is that he exists eternally, outside time and is unconstrained by time

Think question

Do you think that a God who exists outside time would be greater than a God who moves along the same time line that we do?

The view that God is everlasting (sempiternal)

Other people have raised objections to the view that God is timeless, saying that it creates more problems than it resolves.

One problem is that it seems to limit our free will: when God already knows what we are going to choose and how things will work out for us, in a fixed and certain way, there is nothing we can influence or change, and nothing for which we can be held responsible.

Another difficulty is connected with the problem of evil: it is difficult to reconcile the idea of a loving God with the idea of a God who knows that terrible natural disasters, acts of terrorism and diseases will happen and yet does not step in. This is linked to the issue of how God can act in the world at all if there is no 'before' and 'after' for God. Some scholars have therefore taken the view that God acts within time, responding to events and to people as they happen and as they act. This is the view of theologians such as Charles Hartshorne, as well as other thinkers such as Richard Swinburne.

Some Christian thinkers, such as Swinburne, offer the view that God is everlasting rather than existing outside time

God as timeless in the thinking of Augustine and Aquinas

In the fourth century, Augustine considered the question of whether the Bible supports the idea of a God who is atemporal, or a God who is sempiternal, and Augustine reached the opposite conclusion from Swinburne. For Augustine, the problem was that God had made the world at a particular point in time, which raised the issue of what God had been doing all the while beforehand if God moves along the same time line as we do. Augustine wondered why, if God is everlasting, he picked that particular moment to create the universe, and how God might have been spending his time (because God would have had time, just as we understand it) in the eternity before the universe existed. For Augustine, the biblical account of creation points towards a timeless God, who chooses to create day and night, and chooses to create the seasons, as described in Genesis, but who transcends notions of 'before' and 'after'. For Augustine, there cannot have been a 'before' for God.

Augustine and Aquinas both wrote extensively about the idea of an unchanging, eternal God, and have influenced much of Christian thought. According to Augustine, in his book *The City of God*, God is absolutely immutable, completely unchangeable, and cannot be other than he is. This is firmly bound to the idea that God is timeless. Aquinas followed Augustine's view, adding the important point that when we speak of God, we need to recognise that the language we use is analogical and not univocal. This means that any words that we use to describe God cannot be applied directly, because God is not like us. We have to use words from our own experience of the world when we speak, because those are the only words that human language has. But God is not like anything else in the world, and so when we use language, according to Aquinas, we have to use analogy, mentally putting the characteristics that we ascribe to God into inverted commas. We might say that God 'moves' in mysterious ways – and

See Chapters 1.2 and 1.3. Aquinas pointed out that when we talk of God we have to remember that God's existence is very different from our own.

when we do, we are using the word 'moves' analogically. We are not saying that God goes from one place to another so that he is not in the former place any more. We might say that God is a 'loving father' – and when we do, we are not saying that God's love is limited to the kind of love a human is capable of feeling and expressing, nor that God can only do as much for us as a human father can do. Aquinas, then, wanted to point out that some of the philosophical difficulties people have when trying to understand the attributes of God, arise because we are taking our own language too literally, and failing to take account of the unknowability of God.

One of the questions that arises with the view that God is outside time is the question of whether an unchanging being that exists outside time can be capable of love. Some modern scholars argue that love involves emotional response, feeling happy when the loved one is happy and worried when the loved one is unhappy. An unchanging God outside time would feel exactly the same way, all the time, whether people were contentedly worshipping him or suffering terrible pain.

Aquinas did not, of course, criticise later thinkers directly, but he did hold that God could be both loving and unchanging, just because he is God. People cannot be loving and at the same time unchanging; but God is different from us, and things that are not possible for us are possible for God. Aquinas drew a distinction between God's nature combined with God's will, which are immutable (unchangeable), and God making a change in other things: God's activity. Aquinas argued that God's nature, because it is perfect, is unchanging, always love, always perfect goodness. God's will, then, is always the same because God does not change his mind; he knows perfectly what the good is because he is goodness itself, and he does not change his will because of circumstances that he did not expect. However, in Aquinas' view, God's unchanging nature does not prevent God from having relationships. God does not change, but his creation changes. People learn and mature, they can move towards God or away from God, and so there is a dynamic relationship that allows for the existence of love even though God stays the same.

The idea of an eternally timeless God raises issues about whether God can have loving relationships with humanity

Richard Creel, in his book *Divine Impassibility* (1986) also argues that God can be loving as well as immutable. God can know what his own will is, in response to any of an infinite number of possibilities. He does not have to wait until people exercise their free will, then see how they act, and then decide how he will respond to them. Although people have genuine free will, according to Creel, God can still know what all of the possibilities are, and can know in advance what his will is in response to each of those possibilities.

The omniscience and justice of God in relation to human free will

Boethius and *The Consolation of Philosophy*

In the sixth century, the Christian philosopher Boethius took up the problem of God's omniscience and the effect it might have on our moral freedom. He was particularly concerned about the judgement of God, and whether it would be fair of God to praise or blame people if they did not have any real moral freedom and were constrained by what God already knew about their future.

When he wrote his book *The Consolation of Philosophy*, he was a prisoner awaiting execution. He had led a life of great ups and downs. He was born in Greece into a renowned family with excellent connections and received a very good education. In his middle years, he held positions of great power in the government, and he had many academic interests. However, it all went wrong when political rivalries led to an accusation of treason, and Boethius was sentenced to death. He was executed in AD524.

Boethius was worried about the problem of God's omniscience, because it seemed on the surface that if God knows the future, then he is wrong to reward us or punish us for our behaviour. Yet the Bible does teach about divine reward and punishment very clearly. Believing that he was likely to be facing God's judgement in the near future, Boethius wanted to find a solution to this philosophical difficulty.

Thinking aloud in Book V of *The Consolation of Philosophy*, Boethius considers the different possibilities. He asks himself: 'How can God foreknow that these things will happen, if they are uncertain?' (Boethius, *The Consolation of Philosophy*, Book V, Section 3). If God knows that something will happen, when in fact it is uncertain, then God's knowledge is mistaken, and that cannot possibly be. However, if God knows that something might happen, and then again it might not, then it can hardly be called 'knowledge' at all, and it puts God in the position of being no wiser than we are. But if God firmly knows things, then they become inevitable. Things that at the moment seem fair (the reward of the good, and the punishment of the bad) become unfair:

> 66 That which is now judged most equitable, the punishment of the wicked and the reward of the good, will be seen to be the most unjust of all; for men are driven to good or evil not by their own will but by the fixed necessity of what is to be. 99
>
> Boethius, *The Consolation of Philosophy*, Book V, Section 3

After much contemplation, Boethius reaches the conclusion that he has made a mistake. He has forgotten that God can see things in a different way from the way in which we see them. Humans exist within time. They have pasts that are fixed once they have happened, they have a present that is gone in an instant, and futures that are uncertain. And because the future is uncertain, humans have genuine free will.

However, when God is knowing, he does not have the same constraints in time that we have. God, therefore, does not have a past, present and future, and so 'his knowledge, too, transcends all

Boethius argued that God can see us in our past, our present and our future, all simultaneously

temporal change and abides in the immediacy of his presence.' God can look down on us, moving along our timelines, 'as though from a lofty peak above them' (Boethius, *The Consolation of Philosophy*, Book V, Section 6). God can see us in the present; he can also see us in our pasts and in our futures, so that he has perfect knowledge of what we will freely choose to do. He does not know what moral choices we will make in advance of our making them because there is no such thing as 'in advance' for God. All events occur simultaneously for God, in his eternal presence.

Boethius suggested that God can see us simultaneously at different moments in our lives, 'as though from a lofty peak'

As God does not know things in advance of them happening, Boethius thought, it makes no sense to talk of what God should have known in the past or what God will come to know in the future. God cannot be accused of a lack of wisdom in not realising that Adam and Eve would disobey him, nor of a lack of morality in allowing evil dictators to be born. God does not know what we will do in the future because there is no future for God. All time happens in 'simultaneity' for God. Boethius concludes that we, therefore, have a genuine free choice and can be rewarded or punished with justice.

Think question

Do you think that Boethius has successfully solved the problem of God's foreknowledge and human free will?

Anselm's four-dimensionalist approach to the timelessness of God

In the eleventh century, Anselm took up Boethius' ideas of a God who can 'see' all moments of time at once. Anselm developed it further in what has become known as his 'four-dimensionalist' approach to questions of God's relationship with time.

Anselm's view contrasts with a view known as 'presentism'. According to presentism, only the present moment exists. The past is gone, and the future has not happened yet. The only reality is that which exists in this moment. We cannot go back and change what happened yesterday because it is gone. We cannot know what will happen next week because it does not exist yet.

Anselm's understanding of time is different. We humans, he thought, live in a presentist way, but this is not how things are for God. God is timeless, just as he is spaceless, whereas we humans are constrained by time just as we are constrained by space.

A four-dimensionalist view of time, in contrast with a presentist view, is that the past and the future exist in the same way that the present exists. Terms such as 'yesterday', 'the past', 'next week' and 'the future' are relative terms, relative to the person doing the perceiving at any given moment in time, just as 'right next to me' and 'a mile away' and 'the other side of the world' are relative to the person in any given place in space. Time, then, is understood as 'the fourth dimension' alongside height, width and depth which all relate to space.

It can be difficult to imagine the past and the future 'existing' in the way that the present exists. However, works of fiction often make use of the idea, inviting us to imagine that we can 'go back in time' or go forward into the future to see what might happen. Anselm, in any case, did not think that the limits of the human imagination provided any kind of evidence against the eternity of God.

Human beings exist in a particular place in space. There are some places that are near to us and other places which are further away. Different people live in different places, and can only be in one place at a time. In the same way, different people live in different times. The First World War is further away from me than it was from my parents, and my grandparents lived right through it. We are limited by space as well as by time. But because God is eternal, in Anselm's thinking, God is unlimited by either space or time, and therefore God can be in the past, present and future all at once, just as he can be in the whole universe at once. In Anselm's view, God is not just 'in' every time and every space, but every time and space is 'in' God, created and sustained by God. God is not constrained by them but is in control of them.

For Anselm, the four-dimensionalist understanding of the eternity of God means that we do have free will. God can see the free choices that we

A four-dimensionalist view of time holds that the past and the future exist, as the present also exists

Think question

a. Would you like to be able to visit the past or the future? Why, or why not?

b. What are some of the difficulties that might be involved in visiting the past or the future?

make, and have made in the past, and will make in the future. However, Anselm goes a step further than Boethius. Boethius wrote about God being able to see our free actions 'as though' from a lofty peak, whereas Anselm thought there was no 'as though' about it. God literally can see us in our pasts, our presents and our futures, because of his eternal timelessness.

For both Boethius and Anselm, therefore, God can justifiably judge us, and we can be held morally responsible for our actions, which we choose freely and which God can see at all times.

Swinburne's view of a God in time

It has been argued that if God is timeless, and therefore immutable, then God cannot be a person, or be said to have a 'life'. This view has been expressed by, for example, Richard Swinburne. A person with a life has to be changeable, he argues, in order to have relationships and respond to people according to what they do. A timeless God would not be able to love, because a timeless God is immutable and is therefore not affected by anything.

Their argument is that love (even unconditional love which is not because of our deserving but because of the nature of God) cannot be compatible with immutability (unchanging quality). A loving being responds to the object of his or her love, as a process and a sequence of events. Therefore, God has to exist within time for God to be able to respond to us with love. If there is a living God, who has relationships with people as individuals, then God cannot also be timeless.

Richard Swinburne writes that the view of a timeless God contradicts the Bible:

> 66 If God had thus fixed his intentions 'from all eternity' he would be a very lifeless thing; not a person who reacts to men with sympathy or anger, pardon or chastening because he chooses to there and then. Yet [...] the God of the Old Testament, in which Judaism, Islam and Christianity have their roots, is a God in continual interaction with men, moved by men as they speak to him, his action being more often in no way decided in advance. We should note, further, that if God did not change at all, he would not think now of this, now of that. His thoughts would be one thought which lasted for ever. 99
>
> Richard Swinburne, *The Coherence of Theism*, 1977, p. 221

Swinburne argued that the God of the Bible exists within time, responding to his creation and allowing people to have free will

Swinburne argues that the view of a God outside time is not biblical, but has permeated Christian thought through the influence of the ancient Greeks, and was then promoted by Thomas Aquinas. Swinburne does not see why a perfect being should have to be changeless. It was Plato who planted the idea in Western minds that a world of unchanging and unchangeable concepts was inevitably more perfect than the changing world, but we do not have to accept Plato's ideas.

In the Bible, Swinburne argues, God does not have fixed purposes for all eternity. He does not intend for all time that something should happen on a particular day and then remain unchanged in that intention. In contrast, God interacts with people, and God's decisions about what will happen may change because of his ongoing relationships with individuals.

A biblical example, which might support Swinburne's view, is the story in Isaiah of King Hezekiah's illness:

> 66 In those days Hezekiah became ill and was at the point of death. The prophet Isaiah son of Amoz went to him and said, 'This is what the Lord says: Put your house in order, because you are going to die; you will not recover.'
>
> Hezekiah turned his face to the wall and prayed to the Lord, 'Remember, Lord, how I have walked before you faithfully and with wholehearted devotion and have done what is good in your eyes.' And Hezekiah wept bitterly.
>
> Then the word of the Lord came to Isaiah: 'Go and tell Hezekiah, "This is what the Lord, the God of your father David, says: I have heard your prayer and seen your tears; I will add fifteen years to your life."' 99
>
> Isaiah 38:1–5, New International Version

Perhaps, then, Swinburne is right: God had been planning to end Hezekiah's life, but was persuaded to change his mind in response to Hezekiah's prayer. However, there are also passages where the changelessness of God is emphasised:

> 66 God is not human, that he should lie,
> not a human being, that he should change his mind.
> Does he speak and then not act?
> Does he promise and not fulfill? 99
>
> Numbers 23:19, New International Version

In this passage, at least, God does seem to have fixed intentions which do not change. Unlike humanity, God knows with perfect knowledge what he will do, and has no need to alter his views or intentions.

See Chapter 1.1 of the AS and Year 1 book. Plato thought that things that are unchanging, such as concepts, are more perfect than the changeable world of physical objects.

The omnibenevolence and justice of God

The Christian understanding of God holds unequivocally that God's nature is love. This idea is not just a New Testament concept, but can be seen in the Old Testament too. The Old Testament speaks mainly of God's love for Israel rather than for particular individuals. The Hebrew word used is *hesed*. God's love is not caused by any special worth in its object. God did not choose to love Israel because Israel had especially loveable qualities; Israel has special worth because of God's love:

> 66 The Lord did not set his affection on you and choose you because you were more numerous than other peoples, for you were the fewest of all peoples. 99
>
> Deuteronomy 7:7, New International Version

God's love, like God's existence, has no cause. It is not brought into being by something else but is part of the nature of God from the start.

Love as an attribute of God is closely connected to ideas about God's goodness and righteousness. Unlike Plato's static 'Form of the Good', which exists as a concept in the realm of ideas unaffected by anything, the goodness of God described in the Bible is demonstrated as love for the people. Plato's Form of the Good does not have feelings, and does not care whether people measure up to it or not. But the love of the biblical God is a love which is interactive, which requires a response and cares about what that response will be. Aristotle's Prime Mover, too, although seen to be perfect, does not have the characteristics of the Christian God of love. The Prime Mover cannot be affected or changed and so it thinks only of itself and its own perfect nature, whereas the God of the Bible is moved by the way people act, especially by the way they treat those who are weak or in poverty.

In the Bible, God's love is compared with the love of a human parent, full of tenderness for the child and profoundly hurt when the child rejects the love shown:

> 66 To them I was like one who lifts infants to the cheek, and I bent down to feed them. […] Ephraim has surrounded me with lies, Israel with deceit. And Judah is unruly against God, even against the faithful Holy One. 99
>
> Hosea 11:4, 12, New International Version

The loving God of the Bible contrasts with the ideas of Plato and Aristotle. See Chapter 1.1 of the AS and Year 1 book.

The prophet Hosea lived in the eighth century BC and was given the unenviable task of forming a marriage that was to work as a symbol of God's love for Israel. Hosea was told to marry Gomer, a woman known to be adulterous, and this marriage became a kind of visual aid for Hosea as he taught people about their behaviour and its consequences. Gomer was repeatedly unfaithful to Hosea, just as Israel was repeatedly unfaithful to God, but Hosea loved her, and took her back even though he knew she would probably repeat her behaviour. In the same way, Israel is tempted away from God by the attractions of other religions and by a secular lifestyle, and God, because of his love for Israel, is hurt and angry. He is determined to punish the people even though he wants to be able to restore their loving relationship:

> **❝** Woe to them,
>   because they have strayed from me!
> Destruction to them,
>   because they have rebelled against me!
> I long to redeem them
>   but they speak about me falsely. **❞**
>
> Hosea 7:13, New International Version

This understanding of the love of God has created some philosophical problems for Christians. Does God's love come and go, or does it stay the same? Can God be affected, and be hurt, and suffer, and if so, does this imply a limitation to his omnipotence? Does God remain unchanging, and, if so, does this suggest limits to his relationships with us? If God loves his people unconditionally, and is also omnipotent, then why does he not stop them from doing the things that hurt him?

Although the love of God illustrated by Hosea appears to be part of a stormy relationship, in the Psalms the emphasis is on the reliability of the love of God:

> **❝** … and with you, Lord, is unfailing love **❞**
>
> Psalm 62:12, New International Version

> **❝** Because your love is better than life,
>   my lips will praise you. **❞**
>
> Psalm 63:3, New International Version

The love of God is a central theme in Christian scripture and teaching

> **"** Give thanks to the Lord, for he is good;
>   his love endures forever. **"**

Psalm 118:1, New International Version

In the Old Testament there is a strong theme of the love that the people should have for God and for each other as a result of loving God. It is taken for granted that God should be obeyed and that his laws are right. Showing loving concern for each other's welfare is the proper response to the love that God has shown for them. When the Hebrew people have been rescued from slavery in Egypt, have been led to Mount Sinai, and are about to be given the Ten Commandments, they are reminded that they have this special role because of the love that God has shown for them:

> **"** You yourselves have seen what I did to Egypt, and how I carried you on eagles' wings and brought you to myself. Now if you obey me fully and keep my covenant, then out of all nations you will be my treasured possession. Although the whole earth is mine, you will be for me a kingdom of priests and a holy nation. **"**

Exodus 19:4–6, New International Version

Think question

Do you think that the moral commands given by God in the Bible, coupled with warnings of punishment, are compatible with the idea of an all-loving God?

The love shown to the Hebrew people by God results in heavy responsibilities. They are to become a kingdom of priests, setting an example for the rest of the world: a holy nation, set apart because of their relationship with God. God's love seeks moral fellowship with Israel. The love of God cannot be separated from righteousness. It is not sentimental love, and it goes with a demand that the people should keep the Commandments. The idea of an omnibenevolent God is closely linked with a God of justice and of judgement.

God's love is expressed through judgement and forgiveness; his punishment of sin is precisely because of his love. One well-known example comes from the book of the prophet Amos, who, although he was a humble sheep farmer, had great skill in public speaking and addressed the people of his hometown with the messages he believed God had given him. The people were expecting to hear that, although God would punish their neighbours, they would be left alone and protected because they were God's holy nation. However, they were wrong. God's special love for Israel meant that they were to be singled out for punishment:

> **"** You only have I chosen
>   of all the families of the earth;
>   therefore I will punish you
>   for all your sins. **"**

Amos 3:2, New International Version

Some Jewish post-Holocaust theologians have built on this idea, claiming that the Jews were singled out for God's punishment during the twentieth century precisely because they are his chosen people. However, this view is not attractive to everyone, as it implies that the atrocities of the Holocaust were God's own doing, that the Jews deserved them and that God wanted them to happen.

In the New Testament, the word used for Christian love is 'agape'. Agape has the connotations of showing love through action rather than love as simply a feeling or emotion. In the first letter of John, the writer summarises Christian understanding of the love of God. He equates love with God: God is not just the prime example of a loving being, God is the source of love, and demonstrated his love by becoming incarnate in Jesus, giving people the opportunity to see God by seeing his love for the world. The source of all human love is God, and the love of God requires that people reciprocate by showing love for each other:

> 66 Dear friends, let us love one another, for love comes from God. Everyone who loves has been born of God and knows God. Whoever does not love does not know God, because God is love. This is how God showed his love among us: He sent his one and only Son into the world that we might live through him. 99
>
> 1 John 4:7–9, New International Version

In the Christian view, then, God is equated with love; any love shown by humans for each other is a reflection of God. God is not only love in the Platonic sense of being the 'Ideal' love. The theme of God's love is strongly linked with concepts of salvation, reconciliation and redemption. God's love involves activity, shown supremely in the sacrifice and death of Christ. This is taken as evidence of the love of God.

Christian teaching is that all love comes from God and that the essence of God is love

In Christianity, the sacrificial death of Christ is understood to be conclusive evidence of the love of God

The Christian understanding of the love of God is that it is perfect love. It is unconditional (agape). It is personal to each individual, as well as to humanity as a whole: 'even the very hairs of your head are all numbered. So don't be afraid; you are worth more than many sparrows.' (Matthew 10:30–31, New International Version). And it is everlasting. Paul, in his letter to the Corinthians, counts love as the greatest of the three things that last forever. He explains the importance of love underpinning everything else that Christians do, and he explains how the love of God will be revealed in the way that people treat each other:

> **❝** If I speak in the tongues of men or of angels, but do not have love, I am only a resounding gong or a clanging cymbal. If I have the gift of prophecy and can fathom all mysteries and all knowledge, and if I have a faith that can move mountains, but do not have love, I am nothing. If I give all I possess to the poor and give over my body to hardship that I may boast, but do not have love, I gain nothing.
>
> Love is patient, love is kind. It does not envy, it does not boast, it is not proud. It does not dishonour others, it is not self-seeking, it is not easily angered, it keeps no record of wrongs. Love does not delight in evil but rejoices with the truth. It always protects, always trusts, always hopes, always perseveres.
>
> Love never fails. **❞**
>
> 1 Corinthians 13:1–8, New International Version

The existence of evil and suffering in the world appear to some people (such as David Hume and J.S. Mill) to contradict the idea that there is an all-loving, all-powerful God. We might assume that, if a loving God really did exist, then there would be no suffering in the world. Disasters such as tsunamis and earthquakes, epidemics and hurricanes would not happen. No one would die young and everyone would reach a peaceful old age, having lived a happy and contented life of bliss. Perhaps there would be no death at all. However, it is all too obvious that the world is not like this, and nearly all of us encounter hardship and suffering of some kind, at some point in our lives.

Aquinas argued that we need to remember that when we speak of the love of God, we are using analogy. We are talking of a love that is like ours in some respects, but we have to bear in mind that God is infinitely greater than us and that we can only understand a tiny proportion of divine love.

The usual Christian view is that we cannot expect to understand the love of God. We experience it whenever we experience love, because all love comes from God, but we do not know why God acts in the ways he does. However, for many Christians, the key is that God does not leave

Aquinas thought it was important that people should remember that everything we say of God is not literally true but is using analogy. See Chapters 1.2 and 1.3 on religious language.

us to suffer on our own. Christians believe that in Christ, God came to earth in human form and suffered with us. They believe that God is with us in our pain, even if we do not understand the reasons for it. This is the theme of Jürgen Moltmann's book *The Crucified God* (1973). Moltmann argues (along with other process theologians) that Christianity shows that God does not just sit outside time being perfect and immutable. He gets involved with us and shares the pains of human existence to the extent of suffering death by torture. Moltmann explored Christian theology as a result of his own experiences in the Second World War and concluded that God exists within time rather than in the timeless, eternal way suggested by Anselm.

In the Christian understanding, we may not understand the love of God or the reasons why people suffer, but we can still be confident of God's love and confident of a life after death when all will be made plain. We cannot understand God's power, God's knowledge and its relation to our freedom of will, or God's relationship with time, because we are limited, but one day we will come to an understanding:

> **66** For now we see only a reflection as in a mirror; then we shall see face to face. Now I know in part; then I shall know fully, even as I am fully known. And now these three remain: faith, hope and love. But the greatest of these is love.'. **99**
>
> 1 Corinthians 13:12–13, New International Version

Apply your knowledge

8. The Greeks had other words for love in addition to the word 'agape' (unconditional love). They also used the words *storge*, *phileo* and *eros*. Find out and make a note of what these different words mean.

9. Do you think the concept of an all-loving God is compatible with the concept of an all-powerful God, or should an all-powerful God be able to do unloving things? Give reasons for your answer.

10. Using your knowledge from Year 1, how do you think the loving God of the Bible compares with Plato's Form of the Good and with Aristotle's Prime Mover?

Discussing the nature or attributes of God

Is it possible, or necessary, to resolve the apparent conflicts between the traditional attributes of God?

One possible way of addressing the apparent conflict between traditional attributes of God is to adopt the view that God cannot be understood by the finite human mind. A God who is infinite in power, in knowledge and in goodness is not going to be readily comprehended by limited people who exist in time and space. Aquinas, in particular, was keen to emphasise this. God is essentially unknowable: we can learn about God, and explore what we understand of God and strive to do the things God seems to want of us, but in the end we will not understand him completely.

Perhaps the idea of God having a range of attributes, such as eternity, love and power, is an effort to break God down into manageable pieces so that

See Chapters 1.2 and 1.3 for a discussion about religious language, especially the via negativa, and the view that human language and concepts are inadequate to encompass the nature of God.

we can comprehend him more easily. If we were trying to understand a magnificent building, we might look at it from the south and then from the north; we might look at a floor plan, go inside and look first at the entrance hall and then at different rooms. We would not be able to take it all in at once because we are so much smaller than the building. This might give rise to apparent contradictions. Some people might argue that windows are for looking in from the outside, while others might argue that they are for looking outward. This demonstrates only the different limited perspectives of the viewers, not that the building could not exist at all.

However, other thinkers are not satisfied with the view that any apparent contradictions are due to our own limitations and that we should not expect to understand. Richard Dawkins (b. 1941), a modern biologist, argues that this 'it's a mystery' kind of thinking is lazy and damaging. He argues that we should not be satisfied to set aside difficult questions and accept that we cannot understand. If the idea of God is unintelligible to us then this, for him, is reason to stop claiming that such a being exists. J.L. Mackie (1917–81) also writes of the 'miracle of theism', claiming ironically that it is a 'miracle' that reasonable people should continue to support Christian beliefs given their incoherence.

Which understanding of the relationship between God and time (that of Boethius and Anselm or Swinburne) is the most useful?

Boethius and Anselm have very similar ideas about the relationship between God and time, each claiming that God exists outside time and is able in some way to know the past, the present and the future.

Swinburne, however, argues that God exists within time and that this understanding fits better with the biblical idea of a God of love who is capable of action and of having dynamic relationships with his people.

Both of these positions have their difficulties. If the view of Boethius and Anselm is adopted, then perhaps there are problems connected with the possibility of people having a relationship with God. It might not be possible to please or anger God if God was outside time and able to be in the future as well as in the past and present. God would always be the same, and so he could not 'become' pleased or angry, no matter what we did. There is the problem of whether a God outside time could really be totally omniscient, as perhaps God could not know what day or what time it is. There is a problem of whether a God outside time can act in the world. In works of fiction, such as novels and films, when time travel is imagined as a possibility it creates all kinds of difficult issues. People who 'go back in time' and meet their life partners at a time before their relationship are trapped, unable to do anything that might jeopardise the relationship and change the future, even though they know what the future holds. Perhaps the same is true for God, where he is unable to act because of his own omniscience. There is also the issue of whether a God outside time is really compatible with our having free will, and the question of whether Boethius and Anselm have successfully resolved this. On the other hand, a timeless God seems to be more perfect than a God who exists in time, capable of offering eternal life to people and able to make promises with certainty.

The idea of a God who is in the same time as us, who has a past and a present and a future, also creates difficulties. Before he came to the conclusion that God is timeless, Augustine wondered what God was doing all the time before he created the universe, and this could be a problem for those who believe that God exists in time in a sempiternal way. It could be argued that a God who exists in time is much less powerful than a timeless God, because he is constrained by time. A God who existed in time would have to wait and see what happens rather than knowing. Perhaps a God who exists in time cannot be all-knowing if he does not know what the future holds and has to deal with unforeseen events. On the other hand, a God who exists in time seems to be more personal and capable of having relationships with us, and this view of a God in time perhaps allows more scope for human free will.

Have Boethius, Anselm or Swinburne successfully resolved problems connected with God's attributes and human free will?

For some people, the thinking of Boethius and Anselm on God's omniscience and timelessness has successfully dealt with problems of human free will. They argue that God can see us at all times in our lives, freely making choices. The fact that God can see us making those choices, and knows what our future choices and their consequences will be, does not restrict our freedom to act freely. Ideas of past, present and future work differently for God. We can still be praised or blamed for our moral choices that we make in time, because God's knowledge of our choices is not foreknowledge (knowledge in advance) as there is no 'in advance' for God. Therefore, our future choices are not fixed before they have even happened.

Others might argue that Boethius and Anselm have not really solved the problem at all. God does still know our choices with certainty, and while this might not be 'beforehand' for God, it is still 'beforehand' for us, as we do exist in time. A related issue is the question of God having free will himself. The timeless, four-dimensionalist God described by Boethius and Anselm does not seem able to make free choices himself. He cannot have options available to him and subsequently choose between them as there is no 'subsequently' for God. God's choices are already made, for all time. Everything God thinks and does is restricted by his timelessness and his perfect nature.

Apply your knowledge

12. Which idea of God's relationship with time seems the most plausible to you? Give reasons for your answer.

13. If all of the suggestions for God's relationship with time create philosophical difficulties, does this demonstrate that God does not exist at all?

Think question

Do you think that the existence of a God who knows all our thoughts and choices would restrict our ability to act freely?

14. Some people argue that we only think we have freedom to act, but actually our actions are completely beyond our control. Known as 'hard determinists', they argue that our sense of ourselves making free choices is just an illusion. How far would you agree with this point of view?

Swinburne's view of a God who exists in time might seem to resolve problems of human free will because the future is not fixed in this model. People can make genuine free choices about what to do next, and no one knows what they will choose, not even God, until it happens, perhaps. However, a God who exists in time may still be omniscient in the sense of knowing everything that can be known. God might know everything about our personalities and the influences on us, our secret wishes as well as the ones we admit to, and know with perfect knowledge how we are likely to respond in any situation. If God cannot be mistaken, then even if God is predicting rather than knowing our choices, he will always predict correctly, which might not be very different from knowing with certainty.

It could be the case that we have no free will, whether God exists or not, outside or within time. We could be so determined by genetics and by external factors that none of our actions are free even if we feel ourselves to be acting freely.

Should the attributes of God be understood as subject to the limits of logical possibility or divine self-limitation?

The idea that God should be subject to the limits of logical possibility is one that has given rise to debate. Descartes' view was that logic is created by God, and that God is not subject to anything. God can, therefore, make some kind of nonsensical object if he so wishes or can act in a way that is contrary to his own nature.

However, most Christian thinkers reject Descartes' view on the grounds that logically impossible 'things' are not 'things' at all and, therefore, cannot be done or created. This does not make God subject to the laws of logic, because the reason God cannot do the logically impossible is not a failure on God's part.

Christian scholars such as Aquinas have argued that God can do everything possible. The question remains as to whether God can change his mind and break the laws of logic, and some of the miracle stories of the Bible suggest that he can. There are several different positions that could be held on the issue, for example:

- a Cartesian view, in which God can do absolutely anything

- a Thomist view (following Thomas Aquinas), in which God can do everything that can be done without contradiction and which is within his nature

- a view that holds that the idea of an omnipotent God makes no sense and is a reason for rejecting theist beliefs.

Many thinkers have struggled with the idea that God is totally powerful, or all-knowing.

These ideas, when explored, seem to present a God whose control over creation and over human life is such that people can put up no resistance to God's will and have no freedom to act. Some have, therefore, concluded that God intentionally limits his own powers in order to allow humanity to live purposefully and responsibly. God creates a world with 'epistemic distance' (a distance in knowledge) between himself and humanity so that it is not so obvious that people have no choice but to believe in him and worship him, it is argued. He also limits his own omnipotence so that we can choose to resist him, and limits his own omniscience so that we can take moral responsibility for our actions.

Others might argue, however, that this is simply making excuses for ideas that do not work. In his discussion of religious language, Antony Flew (1923–2010) argues that theistic beliefs die a 'death of a thousand qualifications' when they are challenged. When sceptical people raise objections to the claims of religious believers, the believers qualify their claims by saying, 'Ah, but God works in mysterious ways', and keep finding ways around problems until there is nothing left of their original statements.

It could also be argued that a God who limits his own omnipotence and omniscience (and who deliberately makes himself obscure from human view) is then not omniscient and omnipotent after all. He may have chosen these limitations for himself, but, even so, they are then limitations and so God's power and knowledge is not absolute.

Think question

a. Do you think it would be better if God made himself more obvious to us, so that religious faith became easier?

Think question

b. Do you think that a God who has chosen to limit his own powers can still be called 'omnipotent'?

Learning support

Points to remember

» When you are offering evaluative comment in response to an essay title, remember that you need to go further than just describing different possible points of view. You need to say which option you find the most convincing, and give your reasons for it. You need to offer criticisms of the opinions you find weaker, and say why you find them unconvincing. You should aim to persuade your reader and not simply display the various options.

» It can be difficult to write evaluative essays about beliefs if you do not hold those beliefs yourself. Discussion of the attributes of God might seem pointless if you do not believe God exists at all. However, in your essays, you are entitled to criticise all of the Christian beliefs if you want to. You could draw the conclusion that none of the suggestions work and that this points to scepticism as a reasonable position. If you do have religious belief, the fact that you believe something is not enough to count as evidence. You need to persuade your reader that your beliefs can stand up.

Enhance your learning

» Novels and films that explore ideas about time travel can be an interesting way of developing your thinking about four-dimensionalism. *The Time Machine* by H.G. Wells (1895, with later film adaptations), *The Time Traveler's Wife* by Audrey Niffenegger (2003, adapted for film in 2009); and *About Time* (a 2013 Richard Curtis film) are good places to start.

» Boethius (*Consolation of Philosophy*, Book V), Anselm (*De Concordia*), Aquinas (*Summa Theologica*, 1265–74), Descartes (*Meditations*, 1641) and Swinburne (*The Coherence of Theism*, 1977, Part II) are all readily available to read in the original, although they can be quite difficult to understand.

» *God, Foreknowledge and Freedom* (1989), edited by John Martin Fischer, is an excellent anthology of articles by different authors on the subject of God's omniscience, which would be interesting further reading for developing your knowledge beyond the demands of the course.

» Matthew 19:23–26 is the passage where Jesus says that with God, all things are possible.

» Sections 2 and 4 of *The Puzzle of God* (1999) by Peter Vardy are very accessible and provide a good supplement to enhance your knowledge.

» Chapter 11 of John Macquarrie's *Principles of Christian Theology* (1966) is a very sound and academic text but also readable.

Practice for exams

At A level, essay questions invite you to demonstrate your knowledge and understanding of factual material (AO1) and also your critical ability in putting forward a coherent, balanced argument (AO2). You should aim to write essays that are persuasive responses to the question throughout, rather than writing a lot of description and then tacking an opinion on at the end of each paragraph.

How convincing is Boethius' view of God's relationship with time?

In this question, you are asked to consider one view of God's relationship with time, and assess the extent to which you find it convincing, so you need to start by deciding whether or not you think Boethius' position is strong or weak.

Your knowledge and understanding can be demonstrated in your explanation of Boethius' views, showing that you understand the problems he faced explaining the relationship between God's omniscience and human free will. Try to make your own argument the key feature of the essay rather than giving a lot of uncritical description. It would be useful to compare the views of Boethius with the views of other thinkers so that you can say whether you find his views more or less persuasive than the alternatives. Give reasons why you find Boethius' position convincing or unconvincing, so that you have a structured argument rather than just an assertion.

Discuss critically the view that God deliberately limits his own powers for the good of humanity.

This question invites a consideration of the popular view that any limits to God's power come about because God chooses to limit himself. For example, the view that God chose to come to earth as a man in Jesus, limiting himself to a physical body. In your answer, you need to explain this view, making reference to thinkers and writers who support it (such as, for example, Peter Vardy), and discuss whether or not you find their arguments convincing. You should also consider different points of view, such as the view that God has the power to do absolutely anything in an unlimited way.

Show clearly what you think about each of the positions you present so that your conclusion naturally follows from the arguments you have been making.

Chapter 1.2

Religious language: negative, analogical or symbolic

If God exists in such a different way from humanity, is it possible to use human language to speak intelligibly about God?

Does human language inevitably make God seem too small?

Can we communicate a more accurate understanding of God by talking about what God is not?

If statements about God cannot be tested using sense experience, does this mean they are nonsense?

Is religious language best understood in terms of analogy or symbol?

Key Terms

Agnosticism: the view that there is insufficient evidence for God, or the view that God cannot be known

Truth-claim: a statement that asserts that something is factually true

Apophatic way (*via negativa*): a way of speaking about God and theological ideas using only terms that say what God is not

Cataphatic way (*via positiva*): a range of ways of speaking about God and theological ideas using only terms that say what God is

Univocal language: words that mean the same thing when used in different contexts

Equivocal language: words that mean different things when used in different contexts

Analogy: a comparison made between one thing and another in an effort to aid understanding

Symbol: a word or other kind of representation used to stand for something else and to shed light on its meaning

Introduction

Many **agnostic** thinkers argue that God is something we can neither know nor speak about. Their view is that God is not available to reason, not accessible to experiment and testing, and that none of the words in the human vocabulary can communicate anything about God. Therefore, they argue, there is no point in discussing God or in making statements claiming that God is like this or like that, as we cannot possibly know if what we are saying is true and we do not have the language to communicate effectively. Some atheist thinkers go further and claim that talk of God or of anything supernatural is just plain nonsense.

Theists, however, have always tried to communicate their understanding of God through language. They give God different titles in order to try and communicate something about his nature. In Islam, for example, there are 99 names for Allah, which include 'The Gracious', 'The Merciful', 'The Compassionate', 'The Light' and 'The Giver of Life'. In the Bhagavad Gita, the Hindu god Krishna is described as 'the goal of all knowledge', 'the cause of all causes' and 'the Supreme Lord of all beings'. Jews describe God as 'the creator', 'the king of the universe' and 'the father of all'. As well as trying to express an understanding of the nature of God, theists also try to communicate other aspects of belief that are outside everyday experience, for example beliefs about the afterlife, about the state of enlightenment and about the nature of the soul. Every religion uses language in an attempt to convey supernatural ideas, and the normal language of ordinary life can often seem inadequate.

One of the issues for philosophers of religion is whether religious language can communicate ideas effectively, even when these are ideas that go way beyond our normal experiences in everyday life. Perhaps the language of our human, finite, limited world is totally inadequate for conveying ideas about a divine, perfect and infinite being, or perhaps there are ways in which at least some understanding of God can be communicated.

> **Think question**
>
> How effective are art forms such as poetry, painting and music at conveying ideas and feelings that are difficult to put into words?

What is religious language?

'Religious language' does not refer only to specialist vocabulary used in the context of religion. There are, of course, many specialist terms that religious people use. They might talk of 'taking part in the Eucharist', or of 'the Messiah', or of 'the sin of shirk' or of 'following one's dharma', using words that a non-religious person might have to look up. Some people think of 'religious language' in terms of old-fashioned words from traditional acts of worship, such as 'thou art' and 'go forth'. However, religious language is a much broader concept than this. It refers to any kind of language used in the context of religious discussion, behaviour and worship – this could be specialist vocabulary or archaic liturgy, but it could also include ordinary everyday words used in a religious context.

Sometimes religious language is used in the context of **truth-claims**. In other words, religious people use language to make statements about what is, or is not, the case. When they say, 'There is no God but Allah, and Muhammad is his prophet', or, 'Jesus is alive today', they are asserting that their religious beliefs are true (and, by implication, that the opposite is false). Much of the debate about religious language in the philosophy of religion is concerned with this kind of use of language. However, there are also other ways in which religious language can be used. When religious believers meet for worship, for rites of passage and for festivals, they do not spend all of their time making truth-claims. They might also use religious language to evoke feelings of worship, to express their personal feelings, to praise God, and to solemnise occasions by saying, 'I baptize you in the name of the Father, the Son and the Holy Spirit', or to pray, for example.

A lot of discussion about religious language revolves around the status of religious 'truth-claims'

Think question

Do you agree that all of the positive language people use when talking about God makes God seem too small? Can you think of any examples of words or phrases applied to God in a positive way that adequately communicate ideas about the infinity of God?

The apophatic way, or *via negativa*, as a way of speaking about God

One of the problems of religious language is that if people are using their normal vocabulary, they have words that apply only to finite, imperfect things that belong in this world. If people speak of God as a 'judge' or a 'father', for example, these are words that make us think of human judges and human fathers. They put pictures in our minds of physical beings with limitations, even if by human standards they are exceptionally good judges or fathers.

Some writers have therefore argued that whatever normal language we use when we try to describe God, we are always going to make God too small, and misrepresent him in a damaging and disrespectful way. They have argued that, instead, it is only possible to speak about God properly if we use negative terms, and talk about what God is not. This is sometimes called the **apophatic way**, or *via negativa* (negative way).

The apophatic way involves speaking of God using only negatives, to emphasise the difference between God and humanity. God is described as 'immortal', 'invisible', 'inaccessible', 'timeless', 'incorporeal', etc. Those in favour of the *via negativa* argue that these descriptions of God are plain statements of fact. They state that those descriptions that try to give God positive attributes are misleading and should be avoided. If we say God is a king, or a shepherd, then we might give people completely the wrong idea, conveying the impression that God has a body, or is male, or has to follow a job description, or has faults. Even if we say something like, 'God is love', then we start making people think of human love with all of its flaws and jealousies, fluctuations and limits. If we say, 'God is good', then we start thinking about our own goodness and our own ideas of what goodness is, because it is the only goodness we know. We imagine that God must possess a goodness like ours. But our own goodness is so flawed and temporary that it is wrong to use the same concept and try to apply it to God. As soon as we try to speak of God in positive terms and suggest that God has attributes that we recognise from the physical world, we start making statements that are so inaccurate that they damage understanding. People who support the *via negativa* believe that it is better to accept the mysteries of God than to try to pin God down using flawed concepts. If we use these, we end up belittling God and imagining that our reason is capable of understanding divine mysteries.

One well-known modern lateral-thinking puzzle uses a similar idea. The puzzle is that you are given a 10m length of fencing and asked to enclose the largest space you can. Most people would use the fencing to enclose a circle of land. However, the best answer to the puzzle is to use the fencing to create a very small area, and stand in it and declare yourself to be on the outside of the fence. The whole of the rest of the universe is thereby 'enclosed'. This is the kind of idea that the apophatic way is suggesting: by pointing at what God is not, people can still manage to communicate the infinity and the mystery of God.

One significant Christian thinker from the sixth century was Pseudo-Dionysius the Areopagite. No one knows what he was really called. His writings were for a long time attributed to someone called Dionysius who lived at the Areopagus (an open-air court), but then it was realised that the writings did not fit the dates of Dionysius, and so the anonymous thinker and writer ended up with this strange name. He was a mystic, a Christian who spent a lot of time in deep contemplation, reflecting on his experiences of God in a way that was influential in shaping the writings of many medieval Christians.

Pseudo-Dionysius argued that the *via negativa* is the only way in which we can speak truthfully about God, because God is beyond all human understanding and imagination. Pseudo-Dionysius wrote about religious experience as well as the religious language used to express it. He wrote about the need for the soul to become unified with God by going beyond the realms of sense perception and rationality, entering obscurity, a 'cloud of unknowing' from which God can be approached. He was a follower of Plato, believing in the division between the physical body and the spiritual soul, and believing that the soul's search for God can be held back by the demands of the body and the mind's desire for complete understanding. His ideas about God being beyond knowledge and beyond the realms of rational thought greatly influenced the author of the anonymous medieval

Pseudo-Dionysius was an influential figure in the development of the apophatic way

book *The Cloud of Unknowing* as well as many other thinkers and writers, including Thomas Aquinas.

Pseudo-Dionysius stated that it is counter-productive to speak of God as though God can be perceived by the senses or as though we can reach God through reason. It is only through recognition of the limits of humanity that spiritual progress can be made. People who are genuinely seeking God should put away their need to have the answers to everything; they should stop trying to use logic and arguments. Instead, they should allow God to speak to them in stillness, accepting that God will remain a mystery, and realising that until they are ready to accept this, they will miss the point and end up with an idea of God that is too small.

The great Jewish thinker Moses Maimonides (1135–1204) was also a supporter of the *via negativa*. Maimonides thought that the best way to convey an accurate understanding of the nature of God was to explain what God is not. In this way, he hoped, people could move closer to an understanding of what God is, without limiting God in their thoughts. In his writing, Maimonides used the example of a ship to demonstrate what he meant:

> **66** There is no necessity at all for you to use positive attributes of God with the view of magnifying Him in your thought […] I will give you […] some illustrations, in order that you may better understand the propriety of forming as many negative attributes as possible, and the impropriety of ascribing to God any positive attributes. A person may know for certain that a 'ship' is in existence, but he may not know to what object that name is applied, whether to a substance or to an accident; a second person then learns that a ship is not an accident; a third, that it is not a mineral; a fourth, that it is not a plant growing in the earth; a fifth, that it is not a body whose parts are joined together by nature; a sixth, that it is not a flat object like boards or doors; a seventh, that it is not a sphere; an eight, that it is not pointed; a ninth, that it is not round shaped; nor equilateral; a tenth, that it is not solid. It is clear that this tenth person has almost arrived at the correct notion of a 'ship' by the foregoing negative attributes […] In the same manner you will come nearer to the knowledge and comprehension of God by the negative attributes […] I do not merely declare that he who affirms attributes of God has not sufficient knowledge concerning the Creator […] but I say that he unconsciously loses his belief in God. **99**
>
> Moses Maimonides, *The Guide for the Perplexed*, trans. Michael Friedlander, 1904

The via negativa *uses only negative terms to speak of God, as a way of avoiding belittling God by attributing human qualities to him*

In Buddhist texts, the *via negativa* is used in an attempt to convey central beliefs; the nature of nirvana, and the nature of the Buddha, are concepts that are notoriously difficult to describe. Although Buddhists do not believe in God, they still use the *via negativa* to try to convey the essence of ultimate reality, which cannot be described except as the negation of things we know from the physical world.

The cataphatic way, or *via positiva*, as a way of speaking about God

The '**cataphatic way**' is the term used to describe approaches to religious language that use positive terms in order to convey meaning. It is sometimes called the *via positiva*.

Some thinkers (most notably Aquinas) have argued that we cannot say anything positive that is literally true of God, because the use of ordinary human language automatically limits God, placing his attributes only within our experience and understanding. Aquinas used the term *via eminentiae* (the way of eminence) to show that what we say of God, and indeed what we know of God, is only partial. We should realise that the love of God, for example, is 'eminent'. Our own love and the love that we receive is partial and flawed, but God's love is the prime example of love.

However, Aquinas did not completely follow the *via negativa* in claiming that we should never use positive terms for God. He suggested in *Summa Theologica* (1265–74) that there could be a way of making positive claims about God and conveying positive ideas, as long as we understand that the words we use have an analogical, rather than a literal, application. Aquinas was not suggesting that analogy could be a good way of communicating about God, but was saying that we should remember that this is what we are already doing whenever we make positive claims about God. If people speak about God 'listening' to them, for example, they should remember that this is not literally true, as according to Christian belief God does not have physical ears and does not need people to make a sound when they speak to him. It is an analogy – God 'hearing' us is in many ways analogous to people listening to sounds. One of the most famous analogies in the Christian philosophy of religion is Paley's analogy of the watchmaker, where he claims that God's design of the world is analogous to a watchmaker's design of a watch.

It is important to understand the distinction between analogical language and **univocal** and **equivocal language**.

Sometimes, we use words for two different things in a way that is univocal – which means the same words are used in exactly the same way, for example when we talk about a bath mat and a doormat.

Sometimes, we use words for two different things in a way that is equivocal – which means the same word is used in two completely different ways, such as when we talk about a fruit bat and a cricket bat, or a dining table and

Apply your knowledge

The modern philosopher Mark Vernon wrote an article for *The Guardian's* series 'Face to Faith' in November 2006. In it he explained how, at the end of his life, Aquinas stopped writing about God completely. Use a search engine to find the article online.

1. What reasons does Mark Vernon give in support of the *via negativa*? What does he think are the problems of speaking of God in positive, everyday terms?

2. Do you agree with Mark Vernon's view in this article? Write a paragraph in response, explaining why you either agree or disagree with his perspective.

See Chapter 1.3 of the AS and Year 1 book for a discussion of the analogy Paley used when he offered his design argument for the existence of God.

Aquinas wrote about the need to remember that when we use positive terms about God, we are always using analogy and not saying something that is literally true a periodic table. In different contexts, the word has an entirely different meaning, so that knowing what a dining table is would be of no help at all in gaining an understanding of a periodic table.

In addition, we use words in a way that is **analogical**. This means that the same term is used, in not exactly the same sense, but in a similar or related sense. We use this kind of language in all sorts of contexts, as well as in religious language. For example, we might talk about a smooth floor and a smooth wine. The wine is not smooth in the same way that the floor is smooth, but the word is used in a related way – it is the same kind of idea that is being expressed, of a gliding finish and a lack of roughness. Another example of analogical use of language is when we speak of a woollen blanket and a blanket of snow. Poetry often uses this kind of language in the form of metaphors and similes. As well as the words having their obvious, denotative (literal) meanings, they also carry connotations that help our minds associate them with other related concepts, and in this way we gain greater insights.

Aquinas rejected using univocal language to speak of God because it makes God too small and does not sufficiently convey the greatness and the mystery of God. He also rejected the use of equivocal language (for example where someone might say that God is good but that his goodness is completely different from any goodness we know), because it is not helpful at all in communicating about God. He developed his doctrine of analogical language as a kind of middle path between the two.

Aquinas divided analogies into two main types:

1. **Analogy of attribution**, where there is a causal relationship between the two things being described. For example, a seaside town might be called 'healthy' because it causes the people who live there to be healthy, while a sticky cake might be called 'sickly' because of the effect it has on the person eating it. Aquinas used the earthy example of bull's urine: we call the bull's urine 'healthy' because it is caused by, and can be attributed to, the health of the bull.

   Aquinas thought that it was important when we speak of God to remember that we are using analogy of attribution. When we speak of God as loving, for example, we should think about the causal relationship here and realise that God does not only display love but is the cause of all love. When we speak of God as living, we should remember that God creates and sustains all life. When we speak of God as wise, we should remember that all knowledge and wisdom comes from God. Aquinas made the distinction between God being good, wise and loving in his essence, whereas everything else is good or wise or loving because it participates in the essence of God.

2. **Analogy of proportionality (analogy of proper proportion)**, where the words relate to objects that are different in proportion. For example, we might speak of a clever toddler and a clever scientist, and the words are used in proportion. The toddler is clever in comparison

with other toddlers, and the scientist is clever in comparison with other people. In religious terms, then, Aquinas thought that we can use terms such as 'loving' and 'faithful' when we speak of God, but we have to recognise that God's love, faithfulness and so on are on an infinitely vaster scale than our own.

John Hick, in his book *Philosophy of Religion* ([1963] 1973), gives a useful example to illustrate the idea of analogy of proportionality:

> 66 We sometimes say of a pet dog that it is faithful, and we may also describe a man as faithful. We use the same word in each case because of a similarity of a certain quality exhibited in the behaviour of the dog and the steadfast voluntary adherence to a person of a cause that we call faithfulness in a human being. Because of this similarity we are not using the word 'faithful' equivocally (with totally different senses). But, on the other hand, there is an immense difference in quality between a dog's attitudes and a man's. The one is indefinitely superior to the other in respect of responsible, self-conscious deliberation and the relating of attitudes to moral purposes and ends. Because of this difference we are not using 'faithful' univocally (in exactly the same sense). We are using it analogically, to indicate that at the level of the dog's consciousness there is a quality that corresponds to what at the human level we call faithfulness. 99
>
> John Hick, *Philosophy of Religion*, 1973 p. 70

Ramsey, models and qualifiers

A twentieth-century version of the idea of speaking of God analogically comes from the philosopher Ian Ramsey, who explained his ideas in his 1957 book *Religious Language*. He tried to explain the way in which religious language could usefully describe God by using the terms 'models' and 'qualifiers'. According to Ramsey, we can use 'models' when we speak of God, using words such as 'righteous' or 'loving' – these are words that we understand because we have a reference point in our own human experience. However, to ensure that we do not limit God and that we recognise that his attributes are unlike our own, we also need to use 'qualifiers'. These are adjectives and adverbs such as 'everlasting' or 'perfectly'. In this way, we can anchor our ideas about God within our own experience, so that we at least know what we are talking about; and then we can show that God is different from us proportionally by using the qualifier to point us in the right direction. We might not understand and comprehend exactly the nature of God, because qualifiers such as 'infinitely' or 'perfectly' are in many ways beyond our imagination, but it is intended to be a method of speaking about God positively that aims to avoid either limiting God or speaking incomprehensibly.

Apply your knowledge

4. List some examples of your own that show words being used in univocal ways (the same meaning in different contexts) and equivocal ways (different meanings when used in different contexts).

5. Take the example of a relationship described analogically as 'blossoming'. In what ways could a relationship be similar to a plant coming into flower? In what ways could it be different?

6. If someone described an animal as 'brave', what kind of characteristics would you expect it to display? If you did not know anything about what kind of an animal it was, would the description 'brave' help your understanding?

The cataphatic way, or via positiva, *uses a range of ways of making positive claims about what God is*

Using symbols to talk about God

Analogy is one way of understanding how religious language might be used to say positive things about God. Another way is through the use of **symbols**.

All language, of course, is symbolic, in the sense that we use words to stand for other things. Much language, both religious and non-religious, is symbolic in the sense of being figurative. It is used in a metaphorical way rather than literally. People recognise without needing to be told that when we say, 'I'm dying for a cup of tea', or, 'his face fell', or, 'she was battling her way through the crowd', we are using words figuratively rather than literally. Using religious language symbolically might be a way in which positive claims can be made about God while avoiding the problems of making God seem too small.

Religious people often use language symbolically when they are talking about their relationship with God. They might say that God 'listened' to their prayers, although they believe that God has no body and, therefore, no ears. They might say that God 'walks with them', even though they believe that God is always everywhere and is beyond space. The figurative, symbolic use of language helps to create short cuts, but it can also cause problems if it is not clear whether a phrase is meant as a symbolic metaphor or whether it is meant literally.

People use symbols to describe God and their relationship to God, saying things like, 'The Lord is my shepherd', or, 'God is my rock'. They also use symbols instead of language, to convey meanings that cannot readily be put into words, or to evoke particular feelings, or to identify themselves as members of a particular group of believers so that they can be easily recognised by others.

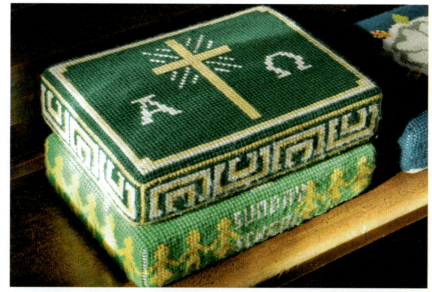

Symbols are often used in religion to communicate ideas that cannot readily be put into words. The Alpha Omega symbol uses the first and last letters of the Greek alphabet to convey the idea that Jesus is at the beginning and at the end of everything

Apply your knowledge

7. Find some examples of company logos, school badges and other symbols that belong to organisations. What kinds of messages are they trying to convey? Do you think the symbol is more effective than simply using literal words?

8. Make a list of ways in which religious people use symbols in ways other than through spoken or written language. You could consider symbolic foods, symbolic dress, symbolic architecture, symbolic objects and artefacts, and symbolic activities.

9. Why do you think light is used as a symbol in all kinds of symbolic contexts? What sorts of meanings and emotions might it convey?

10. In the Bible, look up some examples of symbolic language that you could use as examples in your own writing. Make notes to describe the imagery used, and say what you think the author is trying to convey by using the symbol. You could look at Isaiah 64:8, Psalm 23:1, Psalm 93:1, John 6:35 and 1 Corinthians 12:14–26.

11. Do you think the examples of symbolic language from the Bible that you identified for question 10 have stood the test of time? Do they convey the same kinds of ideas that they might have conveyed when they were first written? Give reasons for your answer.

Tillich's view of religious language as entirely symbolic

Paul Tillich (1886–1965) was a German-American theologian and philosopher, most noted for his books *The Courage to Be* (1952) and *Systematic Theology* (1951–63). He was a Christian existentialist, responding to the human search for meaning in the context of the post-war years. These years were a time of rebuilding and looking forward, deciding which parts of the past should be preserved and which should be discarded. The leading theologians of the time thought that Christian faith should be a part of this process and could not just carry on after the war as if nothing of significance had happened. Tillich had lived in Germany all his life until 1933, when he came into conflict with Nazism and was dismissed from his position as Professor of Theology at the University of Frankfurt. Soon afterwards he was offered a position in the USA and so he settled there.

Within theology, Tillich is probably best known for his 'theology of correlation' ('correlation' meaning a mutual relationship between two or more things). He wanted to show that there was a correlation between the questions raised by philosophy, the arts, the range of world religions, psychology and history, and the answers provided by theology. His aim was to correlate (show the relationship between) faith and culture, in particular a culture in which humanity is searching to find or create meaning. In Tillich's view, all of the 'big questions' raised by people essentially come down to the same question – the question of how to make sense of human existence. What does it mean to live a finite human life in the context of the universe? This fundamental question, he thought, is not only the question that all thoughtful people address whether religious or not, but is the same question that theology addresses and answers. Therefore, for Tillich, theology not only has a place in, but should be central to, modern life and culture.

Tillich was a German-American theologian who was part of a movement working to show Christianity as relevant for people living in post-war society

Think question

Do you think Tillich is right in saying that everyone tries to make sense of human existence? Is this the most important question for people to try to answer?

One of the main ways in which Tillich thought that faith could correlate with culture was by means of symbol. Tillich believed that all religious language is symbolic rather than literal, and therefore it cannot be subjected to tests in order to assess its meaningfulness.

Tillich argued that metaphors and symbols help us to a better understanding of God and of religious experience; they 'open up levels of reality which were otherwise closed to us'. He argued that symbols can take us beyond the world available to our senses into the 'internal reality' of the symbol; a symbol 'unlocks dimensions and elements of our soul'. The language used is intelligible and accessible to us, but it points beyond itself towards an ultimate reality, which is God. He defined symbols very broadly, including visual images, rituals, saints, stories and even ideas. For Tillich, religious language should be seen more like poetry than like prose, more like art than like diagram. A symbol 'participates in' that to which it points, and a religious symbol points towards God, a person's 'ultimate concern' (*Dynamics of Faith*, 1957, pp. 48–60). He made a distinction between signs and symbols, arguing that signs are chosen arbitrarily to stand for something else, and as long as we agree on the meaning of the sign, it does not really matter what form the sign takes. A symbol, on the other hand, according to Tillich, 'participates in' the object represented. He uses the example of a national flag, which evokes feelings of loyalty and patriotism at the same time as it symbolises the country. It is because of this that the act of burning the American flag amounts to an act of defiance against America and everything it stands for; it is not just setting fire to a piece of patterned cloth.

Tillich used the example of a flag to illustrate his thinking about how a symbol 'participates in' the idea it is representing

According to Tillich's thinking, we use religious symbolic language as a means of coming to terms with the meaning of human existence. For example, we use the symbol of God the creator to help us come to terms with our place in the universe, our ambivalent relationship with the natural world and our understanding of our purpose in being here.

Apply your knowledge

12. Make a list of six signs in common usage that are chosen arbitrarily to stand for something, for example a '?' sign indicates a question.

13. **a.** Make a list of six symbols in common usage that Tillich might say 'participate in' the idea or object they represent, for example water being used as a religious symbol for spiritual cleansing.

    b. How easy is it to understand what Tillich means by 'participates in'?

We use the symbol of Jesus the Christ to unlock some of the mystery of the relation between the physical and the spiritual, our tendency to sin, and our desire for freedom in a deterministic world.

Tillich argued that people rarely use language that is not symbolic, except when they are talking about trivial things. All of our most important ideas, concerns, feelings and experiences are expressed through symbol. He also pointed out that symbols only work within particular times and places and cultures, and can lose their power or significance when society changes.

He followed Aquinas in asserting that ordinary human language is inadequate to convey ultimate truth and, like those who support the *via negativa*, Tillich claimed that to use literal language of God is unhelpful and conveys a false impression of the nature of God.

Tillich was critical of the traditional ways of understanding and describing God as a being with characteristics such as omnipotence, omnibenevolence and omniscience. For Tillich, these descriptions of God suggest that God is 'a being', something at the top of the list of all the beings in the universe. But, Tillich argued, this still places God in the same kind of category as created things. If God is 'a being', then it begs the question of who created God and brought him into being. God cannot be the ultimate source of all being if he is a being too. Tillich understood God to be Being-Itself, sometimes expressed as 'the ground of all being'. God does not just exist; he is existence itself, the ground of all existence, the reason why anything and everything else exists. Tillich had no place for arguments for the existence of God because they are arguments that try to settle the question of whether God does or does not exist, whereas in Tillich's view (rather like Anselm's) God is Being-itself, not some 'thing' that might or might not have existence. God is that very existence.

He argued that if we think of God as an existent being instead of realising that such thinking is symbolic, then God does not give us an adequate answer to existential doubt (wondering whether we have any purpose in the universe). We end up, as is symbolised by Christ on the cross, with human anxiety and fear of our own mortality, feeling that God has forsaken us and gone away. It is only when we understand that God is the ground of all being, and that to speak of the 'existence' of God is symbolic, that we have a solid response to the ultimate existential question.

Discussing religious language

Does the apophatic way (*via negativa*) provide an effective method for theological discussion?

For some people, the apophatic way is the best way of attempting to communicate ideas about God, because it is a way of recognising that we have to go beyond our normal everyday experiences and language in order to encounter God. It does not place a limit on God by giving a point of reference that is within the physical world. It is a way of conveying the essential otherness and mystery of God, and underlining the belief that God is not like us.

It can also be seen as a means by which we can say something about God, or about reality, which is literally true and does not need interpretation. Unlike symbolism or analogy, the *via negativa* applies equally well in different cultures and in different periods of history. If we do not use figurative language, which necessarily demands interpretation, we can say things that are understandable and mean the same things across cultures and generations.

The apophatic way could be useful for people who already believe, as a reminder not to belittle God in their speech and their imaginations.

However, the *via negativa* also has disadvantages. If we speak of God only negatively, then it is still not very easy for the person who has no experience of God to know what we mean. To say that white is 'the opposite of black' does not give much help to the person who has never seen, and has no concept of, 'white'. God cannot be reached by a process of elimination if he is outside our experience.

The writer Brian Davies, for example, criticises Maimonides. Davies writes:

> **66** Only saying what something is not gives no indication of what it actually is, and if one can only say what God is not, one cannot understand him at all. Suppose I say that there is something in my room, and suppose I reject every suggestion you make as to what is actually there. In that case, you will get no idea at all about what is in my room. Going back to the quotation from Maimonides […] it is simply unreasonable to say that someone who has all the negations mentioned in it 'has almost arrived at the correct notion of a "ship"'. He could equally well be thinking of a wardrobe or a coffin. **99**
>
> Brian Davies, *An Introduction to the Philosophy of Religion*, 1986, pp. 27–8

Davies, then, points out that Maimonides' method of arriving at the 'right answer' is unlikely to lead people in the right direction at all.

Another objection that could be made to Maimonides' point of view is that when we try to arrive at something by a process of elimination, we need to know before we start what the different possibilities are so that we can know what we have left when the alternatives have been crossed off. Therefore the *via negativa* might not work for someone who begins by knowing nothing of God.

Think question

Do you agree with Davies' criticism of Maimonides' view? Why, or why not?

Antony Flew, in his paper 'Theology and Falsification' (Flew and MacIntyre [eds], *New Essays in Philosophical Theology*, 1955), argued that if we try to explain God by saying that he is invisible, soundless, incorporeal, etc. there is very little difference between our definition of God and our definition of nothingness. We argue God out of existence by 'a thousand qualifications', as will be discussed in Chapter 1.3.

Many of the holy scriptures of the world's religions do make positive statements about God. For example, the Bible makes positive claims that God is a king, a judge, a father, a shepherd, a rock. If it is believed that holy scripture comes from God, then this would suggest that in the right context it can be appropriate to make positive claims about God.

Anselm, in the ontological argument, described God in both negative and positive terms as, 'that than which nothing greater can be conceived'. Anselm is careful here to tread a line between making a positive claim about God while still being mindful of the need not to make God too small. He does not say that God is limited to being the greatest thing we can imagine, but points to a God beyond our imaginations.

> *See Chapter 1.3. Some thinkers argue that to speak of God only in negative terms shows that there is no genuine content to religious language.*

> *See Chapter 1.4 of the AS and Year 1 book for a discussion of Anselm's ontological argument.*

Apply your knowledge

14. How effective do you think that the *via negativa* could be in explaining ideas about God to someone who has no religious belief?

15. Might the *via negativa* work better in some contexts than in others? For example, might it work better for talking to other believers than for talking to non-believers? Give reasons for your answer.

Do Aquinas' analogical approaches support effective expression of language about God?

Some people argue that speaking of God using analogy is unhelpful because we have to translate the analogies into univocal language before they mean anything. We have to know how God's love relates to human love before we understand anything. This method of speaking about God still leaves us with an unclear picture, where we know something about the nature of God, but not a great deal. If we are speaking of the faithfulness of a dog in comparison with the faithfulness of a man, then we can understand that the dog's faithfulness is a partial, smaller shadow of human faithfulness, and this makes understanding a dog's faithfulness fairly easy. However, if the analogy is looking 'upwards' (as Hicks puts it) into infinity, and we start with the partial shadow that is human qualities such as human love and wisdom, and we have to use this partial shadow as our only tool for understanding the love and wisdom of God, then perhaps the analogy is not as useful.

> *See Chapter 1.5 of the AS and Year 1 book. People who believe that they have had religious experiences of God often use analogies to communicate their encounter with God.*

Aquinas and other writers answer this objection by saying that there is nothing wrong with accepting that God is mysterious and that our knowledge of him is limited, as long as the believer understands enough to be able to worship. The 'otherness' of God, described by Rudolf Otto

Apply your knowledge

16. Revisit some of the examples of people you have studied who claimed to have had experiences of God.

   a. How did they try to communicate what they believed they had experienced?

   b. Can you find examples of the apophatic way and the cataphatic way in their writings?

as '*mysterium tremendum et fascinans*' (a fearful and fascinating mystery) (*The Idea of the Holy*, 1917), is something that our language ought to convey, not disguise.

When Jesus was teaching, he often used analogy in order to communicate a message. God's influence on earth is described by Jesus as a 'kingdom', which is sometimes compared with a mustard seed in order to communicate ideas about its ability to grow. Jesus describes people who have fallen away from God's teaching as being analogous to lost sheep and lost coins. Jesus teaches about neighbourliness by giving a story about a good Samaritan.

Can religious discourse be comprehensible if religious language is understood as symbolic?

It has been argued, by, for example John Hick in his book *Philosophy of Religion* (1973, pp. 71–4), that Tillich over-emphasises the aesthetic, artistic nature of the religious symbol, making it appear very subjective and open to every kind of interpretation. Tillich's view almost seems to suggest that there is no factual content in religious language and that it is an appeal to an emotional response rather than a means of conveying knowledge.

It could be argued that symbols leave us with no way of knowing what is a valid insight into ultimate reality and what is not. Without help, we might not know if we are interpreting a symbol correctly, or, if we take a symbol to be pointing beyond itself, whether we are pointing it in the right direction. For example, when looking at a highly symbolic piece of artwork in a gallery, if there is no commentary available and no guide to explain the work, we might miss many of the important aspects that the artist is trying to convey.

Symbols can also be very dependent on cultural context in order to carry meaning. For example, in visual art, the butterfly can have symbolic meaning, but this is not the same across all cultures. In different cultures the butterfly in art represents love, fickleness, long life, the shortness of life and, in Christianity, resurrection. It would be easy for someone from one time and culture to misunderstand a painting showing a butterfly painted in a different time and culture. A striking example of a symbol being used in different ways can be seen in the swastika, used as a decoration and symbol of good luck in Hindu cultures but as a symbol of fascism in modern Europe.

Symbolism in religious language might face similar problems. It could be misinterpreted by someone from a different culture, with the result that the symbol could be unhelpful. If God is symbolised as a father, for example, this will carry very different connotations for people from different backgrounds, perhaps where a father is authoritarian or lenient, closely involved with the upbringing of children or absent.

The swastika has very different symbolic meanings in Eastern and Western cultures

However, there are aspects of symbolism that make it very powerful in conveying meaning, not only in words but also on deeper levels. Many religions use symbolic washing as a way of feeling cleansed from sin and closer to God. Jews use the Mikveh (ritual bath) as a purification symbol, Christians use baptism, Muslims perform wudu (ritual washing) before prayer, Hindus bathe in the Ganges, and Sikhs immerse themselves in the Pool of Nectar at Amritsar. For people who are bereaved, a symbol such as lighted candle can offer comfort in a way that is difficult to express in literal language. Symbols such as badges can evoke a sense of belonging and loyalty. Wedding rings can prompt married people to remember the promises they have made to each other.

The ways in which symbols are open to interpretation by different individuals could be seen as an advantage as well as a disadvantage. The symbol does not simply carry an intrinsic meaning which the individual has to guess correctly, but it can mean different things to different people at different times in their lives, allowing them to have a relationship with the symbol and opening the possibility for it to provide them with new levels of meaning when they look at it or hear it again.

> **Think question**
>
> Can you see any symbols from where you sitting at the moment? What do they symbolise and what kinds of feelings do they evoke?

How do the apophatic way (*via negativa*) and the cataphatic way (*via positiva*) compare as approaches to religious language?

The apophatic way and the cataphatic way are very different approaches to religious language, with supporters of the apophatic way claiming that it is wrong to try and speak positively of God. Neither approach is without its difficulties.

The apophatic way aims to provide opportunities for saying things that are literally true of God. It tries to avoid the need for people to guess what an analogy or a symbol might mean. Saying that God is 'invisible' does not require interpretation and it means the same thing today as it meant for the writers of the Bible. It is not trying to hint at something else and does not need us to try and work out what that might be. However, it is often accused of not being as helpful as it could be. It might be successful in conveying the mystery of God but less successful in helping someone who has no idea of God towards an understanding of what religious believers mean when they are talking about God. Also, it is not consistent with the ways in which the Bible communicates ideas about God, where there is analogy, symbol, poetry, truth-claims and all kinds of other positive statements of God alongside passages that convey God's otherness.

Analogy and symbol, as examples of the cataphatic way, also have advantages, in that they help people to gain a picture of what the believer is trying to get them to understand. They leave open the possibility for different people to have their own individual understanding, without necessarily judging one interpretation as right and the others as wrong. This openness can be an advantage in allowing freedom for people to believe in their own way, but can also be problematic if there is too much diversity of understanding that could lead to conflict.

The fact that we use analogies and symbols so often in non-religious contexts is testament to their usefulness. Someone trying to explain the sensation of a migraine to a person who has never suffered from migraines will probably need to use analogy; for example, saying that it is like a vice gripping the head or like a blinding light or the worst hangover. However, they may mislead the listener, who will probably not understand quite what it is like to have a migraine unless they experience it for themselves.

In practice, rather than sticking to one method of communication, religious believers tend to use a range of methods depending on the context in which the communication is happening. Analogies, especially in the form of stories and parables, are often used to teach children, whereas the apophatic way might be used in the context of worship by people who already have a strong faith.

Apply your knowledge

17. Find or invent some examples of the apophatic way (the *via negativa*) and the cataphatic way (symbol and analogy) being used in contexts other than religious language. (For example, 'the film is nothing like the book.') Explain the different connotations of using negative and positive language to convey meaning.

Learning support

Points to remember

» In order to clarify your writing and show that you have developed your own thinking, try to use examples from religious language and literature of the *via negativa* or of analogy or symbol.

» For your essays, you need to develop your own line of thinking, deciding which opinions seem to you to be more convincing and giving your reasons for your point of view.

Enhance your learning

» The fourteenth-century book *The Cloud of Unknowing* is available online and worth dipping into to gain a sense of the religious language used by medieval Christians to express their understanding of God.

» Look at some examples of religious art and listen to some examples of religious music to explore ways that people have tried to convey religious ideas other than through the use of literal written and spoken language.

» Look at an example of a religious ceremony online and see if you can find examples of the apophatic way and the cataphatic way being used in the words spoken. Look at examples of religious symbolism used in art or in other non-verbal ways.

» Aquinas' views on religious language can be found in *Summa Theologica*, Part I, Q13, which is worth looking at but might be more easily understood with a commentary.

» Paul Tillich's views of language as symbolic are in Part 3 of *Dynamics of Faith* (1957). However, Tillich is not very easy to read.

» Find out more about the 'I am' sayings of Jesus in John's gospel, to see how Jesus used analogy and symbol in his own teaching.

» A.J. Ayer's *Language, Truth and Logic* (1936) is a classic text in the debate about religious language, although Ayer rejected most of the views expressed in it in his later life.

» Richard Swinburne's 'God-talk is Not Evidently Nonsense' in B. Davies, *Philosophy of Religion: A Guide and Anthology*, 2000, is a useful excerpt from Swinburne's writings.

» The 'Religious language' entry in the *Internet Encyclopedia of Philosophy* (www.iep.utm.edu/rel-lang) is an excellent resource for extending your knowledge of this topic.

Practice for exams

At A level, essay questions invite you to demonstrate your knowledge and understanding of factual material (AO1) and also your critical ability in putting forward a coherent, balanced argument (AO2). You should aim to write essays that are persuasive responses to the question throughout, rather than writing a lot of description and then tacking an opinion on at the end of each paragraph.

'The only way in which meaningful statements can be made about God is the *via negativa*.' Discuss.

This question suggests that only the apophatic way is appropriate as a means of talking about God. You need to decide at the start whether you think this is true.

Your essay should demonstrate knowledge and understanding of the *via negativa*. Examples will help to clarify your meaning and show your understanding. You will need to compare the *via negativa* with other ways of speaking about God, such as analogy and symbol. You might decide that all of them are meaningful, that none of them are, or that one method is better than others.

Aim to present an argument rather than simply a list of the different possibilities.

To what extent is symbol an effective way of communicating religious ideas?

This question focuses specifically on symbol, so it is not essential to compare symbol with other ways of communicating religious ideas. You should refer to scholarly views, such as those of Tillich, and you should give examples of symbol being used in religious contexts, in written and spoken form and also in non-verbal ways.

You are asked to discuss whether symbol is effective, so you will need to think about what 'effective' means here.

Try to present a balanced argument, where you consider more than one point of view.

Chapter 1.3

Religious language: twentieth-century perspectives and philosophical comparisons

What criteria should we use to determine whether language is meaningful?

Is religious language about facts, or does it perform some other function?

Does religious language make claims that can be tested?

Can religious language be defended against claims that it is meaningless?

How do cognitive and non-cognitive approaches to religious language compare?

Key Terms

Logical positivism: a movement that claimed that assertions have to be capable of being tested empirically if they are to be meaningful

Cognitive: having a factual quality that is available to knowledge, where words are labels for things in the world

Non-cognitive: not having a factual quality that is available to knowledge; words are tools used to achieve something rather than labels for things

Empirical: available to be experienced by the five senses

Verification: providing evidence to determine that something is true

Symposium: a group of people who meet to discuss a particular question or theme

Falsification: providing evidence to determine that something is false

Demythologising: removing the mythical elements from a narrative to expose the central message

Specification requirements

- Logical positivism
- Wittgenstein's views on language games and forms of life
- Discussion about the factual quality of religious language in the falsification symposium

Introduction

Some philosophers have argued that religious truth-claims, such as 'God exists', 'God is love' and so on, are neither true nor false but meaningless. We can only usefully discuss statements that mean something, and according to some thinkers, religious statements lack any kind of meaning at all. They say there is no point in even raising questions about whether God exists within or outside time or what heaven might be like, how God might save people from sin or what attributes God might have, because there is nothing to talk about. The **logical positivists** of the twentieth century posed a challenge to religious believers by suggesting that, if language is to be meaningful, its claims have to be capable of being tested using the five senses. A long-lasting debate was sparked by A.J. Ayer's book *Language, Truth and Logic* (1936), in which Ayer suggested tests that might be used to judge the meaningfulness of language. Many philosophers contributed to the debate, offering various different understandings of how the claims made by religious believers might be understood, discussing whether they were talking about facts or whether the claims should be understood in different ways, and drawing conclusions about whether religious language meant anything at all or was just made up of empty words.

Philosophical discussion about meaning often identifies two different ways in which a word or phrase might mean something:

- *Denotation:* this is when the word stands for something, as a label for it, such as the word 'window' standing for the part of the wall that has glass in it. The word has a clear literal meaning, which can be taken at face value.

- *Connotation:* this is when the word carries other associations with it. So 'window' might carry associations of opportunity, or of finding a space in a busy period. Connotation can carry meaning beyond the literal sense of the words, and sometimes words can mean different things to different people or in different contexts. Sometimes they can also convey meaning that was unintended by the speaker.

These two different ways in which a word or phrase might mean something are closely linked to a division that is made between **cognitive** and **non-cognitive** uses of language. When we make truth-claims, asserting that we are stating a fact, then we are speaking

Cognitive language is about facts that can be known. Non-cognitive language is different and cannot be determined 'true' or 'false' but has a different kind of function

Apply your knowledge

1. Look at the following phrases and decide whether they are examples of cognitive or non-cognitive uses of language.
   a. Good morning.
   b. It is much colder than it was yesterday.
   c. Ouch!
   d. You are standing on his foot.
   e. Sorry about that.
   f. Does this train stop at Doncaster?
   g. There is a timetable on the wall over there.

2. Think about the statement 'People should not scribble on public property.' Do you think ethical statements such as this are cognitive or non-cognitive? Do they refer to facts so that they can be true or false, or are they perhaps a way of expressing feelings? Different philosophers hold different views about this. What is your own view and how would you defend it?

cognitively. We are talking about something that we think can be known, and that can be either true or false. A statement spoken cognitively might be something like 'It is foggy today', or 'My essay is due on Friday', or 'The Uffizi gallery is in Florence'.

There are also other kinds of statement and other uses of language that are different and do not, and are not meant to, describe facts. These kinds of language are non-cognitive, and they cannot be determined to be either true or false. Statements such as 'Happy birthday!' and 'What a pity' express wishes and feelings rather than asserting facts, and are therefore non-cognitive. Questions, such as 'What temperature is it in the greenhouse?' and 'What colour were velociraptors?' are non-cognitive. Instructions and commands, such as 'Gently whisk four egg whites' and 'Remember to set your alarm clock' are also examples of non-cognitive uses of language. None of these statements could be said to be true or false; they have non-cognitive meanings.

The distinctions between denotative and connotative language, and between cognitive and non-cognitive language, raises issues for religious language. There is the question of whether people, when they make religious truth-claims, intend them to be understood as denotative, cognitive statements. For example, if someone says, 'God created the heavens and the earth', do they mean literally that the word 'God' applies as a label for some kind of being, and that this being literally made supernatural worlds and the natural world? Perhaps they mean the words both cognitively and symbolically, where 'God' is a word for something unimaginable, beyond the powers of human thought, and 'heaven and earth' is a poetic way of describing all that exists. Perhaps they mean it in a connotative and non-cognitive way, in which case they might be trying to encourage others towards showing great respect for the earth or they might be trying to convey their own emotional feelings of awe as a response to the existence of the world. There is also the question of whether, logically, the truth-claims of religious language can be considered to be either true or false, regardless of what the speaker or writer might have intended.

The challenge to religious language from logical positivism

Ludwig Wittgenstein (1889–1951), one of the most remarkable philosophers of the twentieth century, raised the whole question of the meaning of language, and inspired debates around the world. People talked about 'the meaning of meaning', how meaning is conveyed from one person to another, and what might be the necessary conditions for something to have any meaning at all. Wittgenstein, as a philosopher, was keen to establish the limits of human knowledge and imagination, and to work out where the line should be drawn between what people could know and understand and what was beyond the grasp of human knowledge.

His writings were a strong influence on the Vienna Circle, a group of philosophers who met after the First World War at the University of Vienna and carried on getting together in the 1920s and 1930s. The Vienna Circle did not always agree with Wittgenstein's conclusions, but it was interested in the questions he raised, and it developed its own approaches to them. Wittgenstein was not a member of this group, but he followed its debates closely.

The Vienna Circle was led by a writer called Moritz Schlick (who, incidentally, was murdered by one of his former students). The group met regularly and discussed issues arising in logic, in mathematics, in the newly developing social sciences and in philosophy. Following the thinking of the nineteenth-century writer Auguste Comte (1798–1857), the Vienna Circle members generally believed that theological interpretations of events and experiences belonged in the past, to an unenlightened age when 'God' was used as an explanation for anything that science had not yet completely mastered. They thought that it was time to move away from seeing things as being designed or guided by God, and time, instead, to develop more scientific ways of understanding the questions raised by twentieth-century life.

The Vienna Circle met at the University of Vienna for discussions, including discussions about religious language

Before the Vienna Circle was established, Comte had claimed that people's thinking had passed through various stages over time. He thought that the growing understanding of science led people to abandon what he saw as old-fashioned ways of explaining things in favour of more accurate and sophisticated ideas. Comte said that there had been a 'theological' era, when people attributed all the things they did not understand to God. He thought this was replaced by the 'metaphysical' era, when concepts from philosophy were used as a replacement for the gods, to fill in the gaps left by science. Finally, Comte said there was the 'positivist' age, when the only useful form of evidence for investigation

Comte influenced the Vienna Circle by claiming that theological explanations were outdated in a scientific age

See Chapter 1.4 of the AS and Year 1 book for a discussion of ontological arguments making use of the distinction between analytic and synthetic statements.

was that which was available to the senses (**empirical** evidence) and which could be tested in a scientific way.

Comte, then, held the view that a theological way of looking at reality was outdated and unnecessary in a scientific age, and the Vienna Circle took up this idea. It concluded that empirical evidence was the key to understanding what was meaningful and what was not. A claim was meaningful if it could be tested using sense experience, and it was meaningless if it could not. This position became known as logical positivism, and the members of the Vienna Circle were, therefore, known as logical positivists.

A.J. Ayer (1910–89) was a British philosopher who spent some time at the University of Vienna after he graduated from the University of Oxford. He became known for his support of logical positivism. In 1936, when he was only 26, he wrote a very influential book called *Language, Truth and Logic*. Taking up the ideas of Wittgenstein and of the Vienna Circle, he attempted to set down rules by which language can be judged to see whether it really means anything.

The main argument of logical positivism, as articulated by Ayer, was that statements are only meaningful if they fall into one of two categories. They should be either 1) analytic or 2) verifiable using the senses.

Philosophers often divide statements into two kinds, analytic and synthetic:

1. *Analytic statements*: These are propositions that are true by definition. We do not have to go and check whether they are true. Analytic statements just give us information about what words mean. A dictionary is full of analytic statements. These statements are true or false depending on whether the words in the statement actually mean what is suggested. An example of an analytic statement is: 'A rug is a floor covering'. The logical positivists also included some other kinds of statement in this group, for example tautologies (statements that say the same thing twice, such as 'ice is icy'), and mathematical statements such as '$3 \times 4 = 12$'. Analytic statements merely define how a word is being used and do not give us any extra information.

   The logical positivists decided that analytic statements were meaningful.

2. *Synthetic statements*: These give information that goes beyond just defining our use of language. 'Rebecca is allergic to nuts' and 'The village church is made of grey stone' are examples of synthetic statements. 'Allergic to nuts' is not part of the definition of 'Rebecca', and 'is made of grey stone' is not part of what 'the village church' means. They are additional pieces of information.

   The logical positivists decided that in order for synthetic statements to qualify as meaningful, they had to be verifiable using empirical evidence – in other words, it had to be possible to test the truth of the statement using the experience available to the five senses.

Think question

Think of some more examples of analytic and synthetic statements.

We can test whether Rebecca is allergic to nuts, and we can see what the village church looks like and is made from, so both qualify as meaningful statements.

The verifiability theory, then, says that if a statement is neither analytic nor empirically verifiable, it says nothing about reality and is therefore meaningless. This way of thinking followed that of David Hume, who argued that if a statement does not contain any abstract reasoning (such as that found in mathematics) or any experimental reasoning, then it says nothing at all. Statements, if they go beyond giving mere definitions, have to be verifiable in order to mean anything. They have to be capable of being tested, to find out whether or not they are true. We have to know under what conditions we would call their claims 'true' or 'false'. This way of judging the meaningfulness of language is known as the '**verification** principle'.

In *Language, Truth and Logic*, A.J. Ayer agreed that in order for any statement to be meaningful, in principle it has to be verifiable using empirical methods. For example, before we can judge whether our claim is meaningful, we do not necessarily have to go as far as testing to find out whether Rebecca really does have a nut allergy. But we have to know what kind of test could be applied to find out whether our statement is true or false.

In principle, our claim that 'Rebecca is allergic to nuts' is verifiable. We know under what circumstances we would call it true: if Rebecca had some kind of allergic reaction after being in contact with nuts. We know under what circumstances we would call it false: if Rebecca came into contact with nuts and they had no effect on her health. Therefore, 'Rebecca is allergic to nuts' as a claim, passes the test set by the verification principle and can be considered meaningful.

The verification principle says that if a synthetic statement is to be meaningful, it has to be capable of being tested empirically

Think question

How would you test the claim that it is Wednesday today? Is 'It is Wednesday today' a meaningful statement?

A.J. Ayer's book *Language, Truth and Logic* (1936) was profoundly influential in sparking discussion of the meaningfulness of religious language

Apply your knowledge

3. Can you think of a way of testing the claim 'God created the world' that uses any of the five senses? For example, is there anything that people could see or hear that could demonstrate that the claim is true or false?

4. Can you think of circumstances under which the claim 'the Lord is my Shepherd' could be shown to be true or false?

5. Do you agree with the logical positivists that statements are only meaningful if they can be verified using the senses? Give reasons for your answer.

If synthetic statements are only meaningful if they can be tested empirically, then religious claims could be considered meaningless. According to the logical positivists, claims such as 'God created the world', 'God has a plan for each of us', or 'the Lord is my Shepherd' cannot be shown to be either true or false using the senses. Religious believers cannot state under what circumstances they would call these claims true or false, and they cannot suggest what kind of test would settle the matter.

Wittgenstein's views on language games and forms of life

Ludwig Wittgenstein was a fascinating character whom many believe to be the greatest philosopher of the twentieth century. He was the youngest of eight children in a very wealthy and influential Viennese Jewish family. His father had become rich in the steel business and Ludwig Wittgenstein inherited a fortune, which allowed him to pursue his own interests. Ludwig Wittgenstein went to school with Adolf Hitler and, according to some sources, Hitler's hatred of the Jews was sparked in his childhood by an intense dislike and jealousy of Wittgenstein because Wittgenstein was so rich and clever.

Ludwig Wittgenstein was at school with Adolf Hitler in Vienna. Hitler can be seen in the top right of this photograph. Wittgenstein is in the second row from the top, third from the right

Although Wittgenstein was Viennese, he could not stay in Vienna during the war because he was of Jewish descent, and he spent most of his working life as a philosopher in Cambridge. As a student he followed an engineering course and became intrigued by philosophical questions raised by mathematics. One of the conclusions that he drew, and continued to believe throughout his life, was that reality is not all completely intelligible to us. Wittgenstein thought that it was important to recognise this. There are many aspects of reality that we can experience with our senses, and that we can talk about using commonly understood terms. However, there are other aspects that we cannot experience, that we have difficulty understanding and which we find it hard to conceptualise, for example the nature of infinity or the concept of timelessness. In Wittgenstein's view, people should confine themselves to talking only about those parts of reality that can be conceptualised. The other areas may have reality and truth, or they may not, but we will never know, and we will always be unable to talk about them meaningfully. Wittgenstein's best-known saying relates to these ideas: 'Whereof one cannot speak, thereof one must remain silent.'

In his early work *Tractatus Logico-Philosophicus* (1921), Wittgenstein attempted to set out principles to demonstrate what could and could not be expressed in language. In doing this, he hoped also to show the scope and the limitations of philosophy and of human reason. This was the book that had such a profound effect on the Vienna Circle and the logical positivist school of thought. However, although he was quite convinced at the time that he had found answers to many philosophical problems with this work, in later life Wittgenstein began to think that he might have been wrong about the limitations of the meaningfulness of language, and that his criteria for determining meaningfulness might have been too narrow.

Wittgenstein's later work explored the ways in which language can have meaning in different ways and on different levels. He looked at how words can indicate more than one idea at the same time, and how language is a process, developing and changing as it is used by different people at different times in history. He also explored the idea of language usage in different contexts, showing how groups of people, when they are all engaged in the same activity, can use words with a meaning that they might not have in a different context.

For example, a sports commentator might use the word 'result' to indicate the outcome of a match, whereas someone working in a laboratory might use it to indicate a piece of data collected during an experiment. A university admissions tutor might use the word 'result' in a similar but not identical way, when looking at the scores achieved in exams by applicants. The meaning of the term is best understood in its context, when it is being used. Wittgenstein used the term '*Lebensform*' or 'form of life' to denote the context in which language might be used. Sports commentating is a 'form of life', as is laboratory work and also working in an admissions office.

Wittgenstein thought it would be useful to think of language in terms of a game, which we know how to play once we understand the rules. He was not implying that language is trivial, or that words are used as a way of playing tricks, but he thought that the analogy of a game would be useful as a way of highlighting and explaining the scope and limitations of language.

We can say that we know what a word means once we can use it in context, he argued. Learning a language is like learning a game, where we understand how and when to use particular words by seeing how they are used. We accept that words are used in certain ways because we recognise the role they have in the whole game. Wittgenstein uses the example of a chess piece. We might learn that a certain piece is called a 'king', but we will not really understand this until we have played chess and understand the significance of the king within the game. There is no point in arguing about how language is used. It might seem unreasonable that we use certain words in certain ways, but if you want to play the language game you just accept the rules that have been agreed by everyone else. The '*Lebensform*' or 'form of life' of a chess player has its own rules.

In another of Wittgenstein's illustrations he asks us to imagine being in the driver's cabin of a steam train. We would be able to see all sorts of different buttons, pedals and levers, but we would not really understand them properly unless we had a go at driving the train. Then we would understand which were the really important controls and which were only used in some circumstances, which ones only worked if you used them in conjunction with others and which ones had to be handled with special care.

For Wittgenstein, religion is a 'Lebensform' (a form of life), which has its own rules for language usage

Wittgenstein used the example of a steam train to illustrate his ideas about language games

In *On Certainty* (1969), Wittgenstein showed that language makes statements that are groundless. For example, we cannot justify the statement 'this is a piece of paper'; we cannot find reasoning to support why we call it this, it is just how we were educated to conceptualise the world. Definitions are 'groundless beliefs', but they shape the way in which we understand the world to an enormous extent. Wittgenstein argued that religious belief shapes the way the world is seen in a similar sort of way. Our beliefs about whether or not there is a Last Judgement, for example, will be groundless whether we believe them or not, as we cannot produce any evidence for or against them. However, they will shape the way we think and the decisions we make.

The philosopher D.Z. Phillips (1934–2006) took a Wittgensteinian approach and argued that religious language is just a way of defining the rules of the game of religion. He argued that 'God is love' is not a description of an actual existent being, but a way of showing how the word 'God' is to be used. Religious language is meaningful for those who genuinely use it, and it does not need to be justified to those who do not participate in that particular language game. Many of the terms and concepts only make sense within the context of participation in the 'game' of religion. It might not make sense to talk of salvation, sin, prayer, enlightenment or communion outside the context of religious participation, but for those who are involved in religious belief and who see the world through the lens of religion, the words do have meaning.

In his book *Religious Language* (1976), Peter Donovan explains Wittgenstein's thinking about language-games:

66 It is only when we are engaged in the Jewish and Christian religious language-games that the question 'Was Jesus the Messiah?' can be properly understood, and as we know, it is answered differently within each of those two language-games. […] The same is true, equally, of the many actions, gestures and forms of worship which make up religious behaviour. They mean what they do because of their connections with other parts of the religious system and its thought-world. Statements in religious language, like moves in games, are context-dependent. It has thus become quite common amongst philosophers of religion to speak of the way language is used in a certain religious tradition as the 'language-game' of that religion. That way of speaking is a useful reminder that misunderstanding and confusion are likely to result if statements are taken away from their context, and analysed without regard to the usual circumstances in which they are uttered, the moves they are used to make, and the point of the game as a whole. 99

Peter Donovan, *Religious Language*,
1976, p. 89

Apply your knowledge

6. How might the word 'clutch' be understood by a seller of handbags, a driving instructor and a writer of ghost stories?

7. How might the word 'natural' be understood in different contexts?

Think question

How might the word 'defend' be used in the context of a Religious Studies debate? How might the word 'defend' be used on the hockey field?

As with a game, according to Wittgenstein, the more people participate in religious behaviour, the more they will understand the language and the special meanings and nuances of its use. Other aspects of games can also be used in this analogy: with religion, as well as with games, there is the concept of developing skill, of having goals, of achieving success, of training and practice, of emotional commitment and loyalty.

So for Wittgenstein, religious language was not necessarily about facts. His was a more non-cognitive approach. A statement such as 'God loves us' operates, in his view, rather like a rule in a game. In chess, someone might say, 'the bishop can only move diagonally', but this is not a statement of fact. If you wanted to, you could move the bishop straight ahead on the board, or take him off the board completely and move him about on the table, and once the game is over he can be tipped back into the box in any old direction. But within the rules of the game of chess and while a game is in play, the bishop can only move diagonally, and if you want to understand and participate in a game of chess then you have to accept that the bishop can only move diagonally, otherwise the game of chess is meaningless. As you become better at chess, you will see the implications of the bishop moving only diagonally. You will be able to anticipate how this might work to your advantage and how to beware your opponent's bishop. Similarly, if you want to participate in and understand Christianity, then the statement 'God loves us' is something that you have to accept in agreement with the rest of the community of believers. As you become more immersed in the community of Christianity (Christianity as a *Lebensform*) you will develop a deeper understanding of what 'God loves us' means in this context, and you will be able to apply it to your own life and understand its implications.

> *Wittgenstein put forward the view that the meaningfulness of language, including religious language, can be illustrated if we think in terms of 'language games'*

The factual quality of religious language in the falsification symposium debates

Antony Flew and 'Theology and Falsification'

Antony Flew's article 'Theology and Falsification' (Flew and MacIntyre [eds], *New Essays in Philosophical Theology*, 1955) has become one of the best-known pieces of writing on the subject of religious language. After the Second World War, philosophical discussion about language was one of the key interests at the University of Oxford. However, the debate between the logical positivists and those who wanted to defend religious language had reached something of a stalemate. The logical positivists said that religious language was meaningless, and that statements that sounded like assertions were no more than 'utterances' without any genuine content or significance. Defenders of religious belief and religious language disagreed with this conclusion, and the discussion did not appear to be making any progress. Antony Flew wanted to turn the debate in a more fruitful direction by raising some fresh issues and questions. In a **symposium** of Oxford philosophers in 1950, Flew presented 'Theology and Falsification' and invited responses from his colleagues R.M. Hare and Basil Mitchell.

In his article, Flew returned to the debate begun by the logical positivists, but he suggested that instead of insisting that a statement should be verifiable, it should instead be **falsifiable**. What he meant by this was that we do not necessarily have to be in a position of being able to provide supporting evidence for what we are saying, but we should know, when we say something, what we are ruling out when we make our claims.

Flew began his article by referring to a parable from John Wisdom's paper 'Gods' (*Proceedings of the Aristotelian Society,* 1944–5). In this parable, two explorers come across a clearing in the jungle, and in the clearing there are both flowers and weeds. One of the explorers, who is called the Believer, is convinced that there must be a gardener who comes to the clearing and looks after it, but the other, the Sceptic, disagrees.

The two explorers decide to settle their argument by lying in wait for the gardener and watching for his arrival. However, the gardener never appears. The one who believes in the existence of the gardener suggests that perhaps he is an invisible gardener, so they set up all sorts of traps that might detect his presence, but still no gardener is found. The Believer continues to qualify his assertion that there is a gardener, by saying that he is invisible, silent, intangible, etc. until eventually the Sceptic asks:

> 66 But what remains of your original assertion? Just how does what you call an invisible, intangible, eternally elusive gardener differ from an imaginary gardener or even from no gardener at all? 99

> Antony Flew, 'Theology and Falsification'. In *New Essays in Philosophical Theology*, eds Flew and MacIntyre, 1955

One of Flew's points, then, is that if religious believers keep on saying that 'God is different from us', 'the usual characteristics of a being don't apply to God', and so on whenever they are challenged, then they end up with a description of God that has no content.

Flew moves on in his article to draw a parallel between the Believer and a religious person who makes claims such as 'God loves us as a father loves his children' and 'God has a plan'. According to Flew, when these beliefs are challenged, for example when evil and suffering are encountered, religious believers do not accept that they are wrong and that God does not love us after all, or that God has no plan. Instead, they qualify their claim by saying that God's love is not like human love, or that God's

Apply your knowledge

8. Find Flew's article online and read it carefully in order to understand the discussions in this chapter.

Flew used a parable of two people in a jungle to set out his views on religious language

plans are a mystery to us. Every time something happens to challenge their belief, religious people meet it with further modifications, until eventually there is nothing left of the original assertion. Flew concludes that the claims religious believers make about the nature and activity of God die a 'death by a thousand qualifications' – in the end the believers are saying nothing at all, because their statements are empty. They are not meaningful but 'vacuous'.

For Flew, if a statement is to have any meaning, it has to assert something, and at the same time deny the opposite of that assertion. Saying 'x is y,' has at the same time to say 'x is not–y' in order to be meaningful. An assertion has to rule out some states of affairs. If I say, 'Dan came top of the class,' then I am ruling out a state of affairs in which Dan got the lowest score. If I say, 'My car won't start' then I am ruling out the possibility that the engine is running normally.

In *Philosophy of Religion* (1982), C.S. Evans describes Flew's point of view as:

> 66 An assertion which does not rule out anything, but rather is compatible with any conceivable state of affairs, does not appear to assert anything either. 99
>
> C.S. Evans, *Philosophy of Religion*, 1982, p. 145

So, to give another example, if I said I am spending the morning baking a fruit cake, that would rule out some states of affairs. I would not be in a coma, for example, or on a transatlantic flight, or in a swimming pool. If you asked, 'Under what circumstances would your claim to be baking a fruit cake be false?' I could answer with these examples. This is how alibis work in court. If the defendant can show that they were doing something else at the time of the crime, then participation in the crime can be ruled out.

But, Flew argues, when theists talk of God and his attributes, they refuse to rule out any states of affairs. If asked, 'Under what circumstances would your statement that God loves us be false?' they would not be able to think of any. Whatever happened, however cruel or frightening, they would still cling to their original assertion, all the while qualifying it with claims that God's love is mysterious or does not operate in accordance with the normal ways we expect love to work. For Flew, a claim that cannot be falsified is not really saying anything at all. In order for the claim 'God loves us' to have any meaningful content, we need to know what the world would look like if God did not love us.

Flew was writing and speaking only a few years after the end of the Second World War, when the horrors of fighting, the concentration camps and prisoner of war camps, and the effects of the atomic bomb were very much in living memory. Although he does not refer to the events of the war in his article, his listeners and readers must have wondered whether he was right to question whether faith in the loving care of God really meant anything if it did not provide any guarantee against suffering.

R.M. Hare's response to 'Theology and Falsification'

R.M. Hare gave the first and probably the most radical response to Flew's article. He agreed that Flew had succeeded in demonstrating the failure of religious language to make meaningful truth-claims. However, Hare suggested that when people use religious language, they should not be interpreted as truth-claims in a cognitive sense, but as expressions of what he called a 'blik' (Hare made up the word 'blik' because no word existed that encapsulated what he wanted to say). Hare responded to Flew, in the journal *New Essays in Philosophical Theology* (1955), with a parable of his own. He asked us to imagine (using language that is not considered appropriate today) a 'lunatic' who is convinced that all university dons want to murder him. No matter how many kindly dons he meets, he is not shaken from his belief that they are only pretending to be kind as part of their plots to kill him. There is nothing that the dons could ever do to persuade him that he is wrong in his belief.

Hare invented the word 'blik' to describe this man's unfalsifiable conviction. Hare's argument is that we all have our own 'bliks', with which we approach the world and make judgements about it: we all have unfalsifiable ways of framing our understanding of our experiences which help us to find meaning in the world. The belief that everything happens by chance is just as much a 'blik' as the belief that things happen according to the will of God or that everything is 'meant to be'. Religious people have 'bliks', but so do atheists, and each person

Apply your knowledge

A child wants to join the local choir, but the choir teacher has heard rumours that the child is very naughty. The child's mother assures the choir teacher that her child is not naughty at all. The choir teacher asks about the stories that the child has been bullying smaller children, does not pay attention at school, steals from the local shops and is rude to adults. Every time, the mother explains that her child is not naughty. Other children are telltales with no fighting spirit. Her child is not being stretched enough at school. Her child has a wonderfully independent personality, is creative, has an excellent sense of humour, enjoys being daring, and so on.

9. Should the choir teacher be reassured that the child is not naughty?

10. What are the mother's assurances that her child is not naughty actually worth? Do you think the child could do anything that would make the mother decide that, actually, her child is naughty after all?

11. Do you think there is anything that could happen which might persuade religious believers that God does not love them, or does not exist, after all? Is Flew right?

uses their 'blik' as a framework for understanding the world and finding meaning in it.

Hare writes:

> A certain lunatic is convinced that all dons want to murder him. His friends introduce him to all the mildest and most respectable dons that they can find, and after each of them has retired, they say, 'You see, he doesn't really want to murder you; he spoke to you in a most cordial manner; surely you are convinced now?' But the lunatic replies, 'Yes, but that was only his diabolical cunning; he's really plotting against me the whole time, like the rest of them; I know it I tell you'. However many kindly dons are produced, the reaction is still the same.
>
> Now we say that such a person is deluded. But what is he deluded about? About the truth or falsity of an assertion? Let us apply Flew's test to him. There is no behavior of dons that can be enacted which he will accept as counting against his theory; and therefore his theory, on this test, asserts nothing. But it does not follow that there is no difference between what he thinks about dons and what most of us think about them – otherwise we should not call him a lunatic and ourselves sane, and dons would have no reason to feel uneasy about his presence in Oxford.
>
> Let us call that, in which we differ from this lunatic, our respective bliks. He has an insane blik about dons; we have a sane one. It is important to realise that we have a sane one, not no blik at all; for there must be two sides to any argument – if he has a wrong blik, then those who are right about dons must have a right one. Flew has shown that a blik does not consist in an assertion or system of them; but nevertheless it is very important to have the right blik.

R.M. Hare, *New Essays in Philosophical Theology*, eds Flew and MacIntyre, 1955

Hare did not go on to expand his ideas further in writing, but other thinkers did take up the possibility that religious language is unfalsifiable as a way of defending religious language. For example, the philosopher D.Z. Phillips, who was greatly influenced by Wittgenstein, wrote extensively about non-cognitive understandings of religious language and developed Hare's thinking, by claiming that religious statements are not cognitive truth-claims at all but fall into a different category of language usage. For Hare, religious claims are expressions of personal attitudes or commitments to particular ways of life. They are not testable assertions that x or y is the case, but they are a way of saying how the speaker intends to view the world and frame their interpretations of it.

Hare responded to Flew by suggesting that religious language is not cognitive but that religious belief is an unfalsifiable 'blik'

Basil Mitchell and the 'parable of the partisan'

Basil Mitchell also responded to Antony Flew with his own story, known as the 'parable of the partisan'. In his parable, a country is occupied by the enemy during war and the 'partisan' is a resistance fighter. The partisan meets a stranger who makes a strongly favourable impression on him. The stranger asks the partisan to trust him, even though the stranger will sometimes need to behave in ways that make it seem as though he is on the enemy side. The partisan makes a commitment to trust the stranger. Sometimes the stranger is clearly helping the resistance, and the partisan reassures other resistance members that the stranger is on their side and can be trusted. However, sometimes the stranger can be seen working alongside the enemy and helping in the capture of resistance fighters. The partisan has made a commitment to trust the stranger and continues with this commitment even when faced with counter-evidence. He admits that sometimes he doubts his own decision to trust the stranger but he tells himself that there is a reasonable explanation for the stranger's behaviour, even if he does not always know the details of it.

Mitchell's view is different from that of Hare because he is arguing that religious beliefs, statements and commitments do have a factual content (are cognitive). The partisan might find out, eventually and if he survives the war, whether or not he was right to trust the stranger, because there is truth and falsity to be found. While the war is going on, the partisan has to make a decision whether or not to trust the stranger on the basis of incomplete and ambiguous evidence. Mitchell makes a parallel between this and belief in a loving God. While we are in the world, the evidence for a loving God can seem incomplete and can be ambiguous, but, according to Mitchell, there is still a factual content to religious assertions of the existence of a loving God. 'God loves us' is, in the end, either true or false, even if at the moment we cannot offer a definitive test for it and just have to choose whether or not to trust the claim. In this respect, Mitchell also differs from Hare in that Hare claimed that our 'bliks' are groundless whereas, for Mitchell, the partisan's trust in the stranger is not groundless. The partisan makes a deliberate choice to trust the stranger because of the impression made on him when they first met.

Mitchell argues that religious language is cognitive even if people need to make a commitment to religion based on trust rather than facts

Apply your knowledge

12. Do you think that either Hare or Mitchell made a persuasive response to Flew's challenge? Give reasons for your answer.

Discussing religious language: twentieth-century perspectives and philosophical comparisons

Does the verification principle successfully demonstrate that religious language is meaningless?

Not surprisingly, the verification principle of meaning was not universally welcomed.

The most significant criticism was that the statement of the theory itself does not pass the test and is not, consequently, a meaningful statement. The verifiability theory cannot be verified by sense experience (we cannot tell, using the senses, if these are the only types of statement to have any meaning) and so is not a meaningful synthetic statement. And if it is analytic, it is giving a new sense to the word 'meaningful', a new definition that we do not necessarily have to accept. If the theory fails its own test then it cannot be successful.

The idea that all meaningful synthetic statements have to be empirically verifiable also rules out far more than the logical positivists intended. The logical positivists wanted to dismiss as meaningless all claims that were made about God and the supernatural, while keeping scientific statements as meaningful. However, many of the claims made by advances in science, such as the existence and nature of black holes, cannot be verified by sense experience. The human senses are insufficient for many scientific experiments and need to be extended with the use of artificial 'senses', such as X-rays and ultrasonic equipment, but, even with these aids, there are still claims in science that have to be accepted without it being possible to test them using the senses. The science of psychology, for example, often depends on people explaining and describing their feelings and symptoms, but a doctor cannot use their senses to verify a claim such as 'I feel a terrible sense of imminent doom'.

Similarly, historical statements, where claims are made about events that happened in the past, cannot be tested using the senses. We cannot use our eyes and ears to verify whether Henry VIII died in 1547. We can read other people's accounts of his death, but that only verifies that someone wrote an account and does not verify that the account is true. Ethical claims also present problems of meaning. For example, if someone claims that 'torture is wrong' this cannot be verified empirically. We can see the outcomes of torture and that it produces undesirable results, but we cannot tell whether torture itself is right or wrong.

Logical positivists accepted that there was a problem with the verification principle, and that they were disallowing too much as meaningless, so the theory was weakened to allow for 'indirect experience' and 'weak verification'. In later life, Ayer also accepted that much of *Language, Truth and Logic* (1936) was wrong. However, there was still a desire to dismiss as meaningless all talk of the supernatural, of God, of life after death, and of other theological concepts such as sin and salvation.

Some philosophers, most notably John Hick, have argued that even if we do accept that a claim must be verifiable in order to be meaningful, religious truth-claims are verifiable because they are 'eschatologically verifiable'. By this, he meant that although we cannot test and see at the moment, in this life and this world, whether the good will be rewarded,

Think question

a. Can you think of other examples of claims that you consider meaningful and yet are incapable of being tested using the senses?

Think question

b. Do you think claims about the future are verifiable in any way other than 'wait and see'? For example, if someone claims that Arsenal will win the FA cup next year, is that claim empirically verifiable? Is it meaningless?

or whether God really does exist and love us, after death these claims will be verified.

Critics of Hick have argued that 'eschatological verification' is not an acceptable way out of the problem, because even if there is an afterlife and even if we do have physical senses in it with which to perceive things, they will not necessarily be the same senses that we have now and so it is likely they will not count as 'empirical'. And if there is no afterlife, then there will be no one to do the verifying.

Eventually it became clear, and Ayer himself agreed, that the theory could not be adjusted so that scientific and historical statements were seen to be meaningful and yet religious claims were ruled out. However, there were and still are those who consider that there are some assertions that, because of the lack of any possibility of empirical evidence, are meaningless. The falsification principle was developed as a modification of the verification principle, once it had been accepted that the verification principle was unsound.

Did any of the participants in the falsification symposium present a convincing approach to the understanding of religious language?

During the falsification symposium, Flew, Hare and Mitchell each contributed their suggestions and then Flew responded. Flew criticised the position presented by Hare:

....

66 Hare's approach is fresh and bold. He confesses that 'on the ground marked out by Flew, he seems to me to be completely victorious'. He therefore introduces the concept of blik. But while I think that there is room for some such concept in philosophy, and that philosophers should be grateful to Hare for his invention, I nevertheless want to insist that any attempt to analyse Christian religious utterances as expressions or affirmations of a blik rather than as (at least would-be) assertions about the cosmos is fundamentally misguided. First, because thus interpreted they would be entirely unorthodox. If Hare's religion really is a blik, involving no cosmological assertions about the nature and activities of a supposed personal creator, then surely he is not a Christian at, all? Second, because thus interpreted, they could scarcely do the job they do. If they were not even intended as assertions, then many religious activities would become fraudulent, or merely silly. If 'You ought because it is God's will' asserts no more than 'You ought', then the person who prefers the former phraseology is not really giving a reason, but a fraudulent substitute for one, a dialectical dud

Apply your knowledge

13. Do you think that Hick is right to suggest that we will find out after death whether religious claims are right or wrong? Give reasons for your answer.

14. Do some research and find out about reports that Ayer became less convinced about atheism in his later life. What allegedly persuaded him that there might be truth in religious claims after all?

cheque. If 'My soul must be immortal because God loves his children, etc.' asserts no more than 'My soul must be immortal', then the man who reassures himself with theological arguments for immortality is being as silly as the man who tries to clear his overdraft by writing his bank a cheque on the same account. (Of course neither of these utterances would be distinctively Christian: but this discussion never pretended to be so confined.) Religious utterances may indeed express false or even bogus assertions: but I simply do not believe that they are not both intended and interpreted to be or at any rate to presuppose assertions, at least in the context of religious practice; whatever shifts may be demanded, in another context, by the exigencies of theological apologetic. **"**

Antony Flew speaking at the Symposium on Theology and Falsification, 1950

Flew is arguing that Hare's assessment of religious language as non-cognitive has problems. If religious language is just an assertion of 'picture preference', talking about how someone chooses to view the world rather than making claims about facts, then there does not seem to be much difference between a religious claim and a non-religious claim. Also, religious believers intend their claims to be cognitive. When Christians say that Jesus rose from the dead, they mean that Jesus' tomb really was empty and Jesus really had been resurrected. They do not just mean that they prefer to see the world as if Jesus had risen from the dead in some kind of symbolic way.

Hare's approach, however, could be seen as convincing. A non-cognitive approach to religious language might allow new possibilities and make religious faith more vivid and personal. Paul Tillich argued that God is not 'a being' but 'being-itself', and that religious language is not cognitive (talking about things that can be known) but symbolic. Symbols are not the same as facts, and therefore it is wrong to criticise them as if they were. Symbols cannot be verifiable or falsifiable. If someone says, 'My love is like a red red rose', it would not make sense to ask if this was true or false. Symbols need not be meaningless, even if they are unverifiable; they can be effective or ineffective ways of drawing religious believers to 'the power of being'. In the same way a 'blik' could be intensely meaningful to the person who had it.

> *Tillich presents a view of religious language as wholly symbolic; see Chapter 1.2.*

Hare talks about the importance of having the right 'blik' rather than the wrong one. In the context of his parable, the right 'blik' is to understand that the dons really do mean no harm. However, other thinkers have found this aspect of his response unconvincing. For example, in his book *Philosophy of Religion* (1982), C.S. Evans points out that Hare gives us no way of being able to judge whether a 'blik' is right or wrong. If there are no facts to support religious claims and they are just expressions of a preferred world view, the whole idea of 'right' and 'wrong' becomes meaningless.

Perhaps Hare's parable of the 'lunatic' does not serve him very well in making his point, but nevertheless there could be something worthwhile in taking a non-cognitive approach to religious language.

Mitchell's response to Flew seems to be closer to the way in which religious people normally defend their position. He argues that we have to place our trust in things sometimes, and give them our commitment even when we lack sufficient evidence to know that they are true. Mitchell does not think it is possible to say when such faith is reasonable or unreasonable. We do not know the point at which the partisan ought to stop trusting the stranger. Similarly, although there is evil and suffering in the world, as Flew indicates, Mitchell argues that we cannot know at what point this might start to count decisively against belief in a good and loving God. However, although this position might seem convincing, it does have its problems. The parable of the partisan and the stranger does not totally correspond to the believer's trust in God because, in Mitchell's story, the partisan does have grounds for his trust. He meets the stranger face-to-face and is impressed by him, and this meeting is the justification for the trust. Religious believers often claim to have had a direct encounter with God, but perhaps not in the same sense as when two physical people meet.

Flew's own position can be criticised in other ways as well as those offered by Hare and Mitchell. It could be argued that Flew's confidence in empirical evidence as the final test of meaning is, in itself, unfalsifiable. Flew's article finishes with the question: 'What would have to occur or to have occurred to constitute for you a disproof of the love of, or the existence of, God?' The religious believer might want to respond to him with a similar question: 'What would have to occur or to have occurred to constitute for you a disproof of the primacy of empirical evidence?' If Flew could not think of any circumstances under which he would be prepared to say that empirical evidence was not necessary after all, then perhaps his assertion that we need empirical evidence is also empty.

Another possible counter to Flew might be to return to Anselm and his argument that God is necessarily existent. Anselm, in his ontological argument of the eleventh century, argued that 'the fool says in his heart that there is no God' because the fool does not understand that God exists in a way that is necessary rather than contingent. Contingent beings might exist, or they might not. There will be times when they exist and times when they stop existing. However, if God's necessary existence is different from this, then the question of what kind of evidence might be offered against the existence of God becomes a meaningless question. If God's necessary existence means that there is no 'might or might not'

See Chapter 1.4 of the AS and Year 1 book for a more extensive discussion of Anselm's ontological argument.

Apply your knowledge

15. Do you think that the symposium ended up with a clear winner of the debates? Give reasons for your answer.

16. Flew's article has become one of the most influential pieces of writing in the philosophy of religion. Why do you think it has had such a profound effect?

about his existence, then there could be no possible circumstances that are incompatible with his existence, so no wonder religious believers cannot think of any. However, this kind of argument is unlikely to impress Flew's followers, who would respond by saying that God's existence cannot be established simply by asserting that God exists necessarily.

After the symposium many other writers added their views to the debate. In response to Flew, Richard Swinburne argues that we do not have to be able to specify what would count against an assertion in order for that assertion to be meaningful. In *The Coherence of Theism* (1977) he argues that we cannot specify what would count against scientific theories of the beginnings of the universe, for example, because we do not know enough about the scientific theories involved, but this does not make the theories meaningless to us. This is because we accept that there is undoubtedly something that, hypothetically at least, could count against those theories if only we understood what their implications were. For Swinburne's objection to work, we have to allow that something could count against the existence of God, or the nature of God as traditionally understood, even if we cannot specify what that might be.

How do the ideas of Aquinas on religious language compare with those of Wittgenstein?

Aquinas and Wittgenstein were obviously coming from very different contexts when they wrote about religious language. Aquinas was writing in the thirteenth century as a committed Christian priest and leader, whereas Wittgenstein was writing in the twentieth century, from a Jewish background and as an agnostic philosopher. Aquinas addressed his writing mainly to other believing Christians, attempting to explore what the Christian concepts mean in a philosophical way in order to aid understanding and faith. Wittgenstein did not assume that his readers had religious faith and did not assume that Christian beliefs are true.

However, both shared concerns about the extent to which human language is adequate to convey ideas about God, and both investigated how such language might be meaningful. Both Aquinas and Wittgenstein held the belief that God is essentially unknowable. Although Aquinas was a Christian, throughout his life and writings he maintained an element of agnosticism, arguing that God cannot be fully known by the finite human mind and that there are limitations to what we can expect to understand of the nature of God. Wittgenstein was not a traditionally religious man, but he too argued that questions of God are beyond the limitations of what humans can know. Both Aquinas and Wittgenstein argued that religious language has to be understood in a particular way if it is to have meaning.

Aquinas' argument was that religious language has to be understood analogically. When we use religious terms or make religious truth-claims, we have to understand that we are not using words from the finite human world in a univocal way when they are applied to God. The language has to be understood as analogy, giving us an indication of God but not giving us such a clear picture that God can be completely comprehended. Aquinas was using religious language cognitively, making claims that he thought were factually true.

Wittgenstein's argument was that religious language is best understood by those who are within the 'game' or 'form of life' of religion. Those who use religious language regularly, within a community of believers, find meaning in the language, which others outside that language-game might think meaningless. Wittgenstein's approach, along with its developments by his followers such as D.Z. Phillips, is a non-cognitive approach, where the assertions made in religious language are not assertions that can be identified as true or false, relating to facts, but which are more like the rules of a game.

Does a cognitive approach or a non-cognitive approach present the better way of making sense of religious language?

A cognitive approach to religious language, such as Aquinas' thinking on analogy, has been the more popular approach among religious believers. When Christians make assertions about their faith, they usually mean to imply that they are referring to facts. When they speak of the existence and the love of God, they usually intend to refer to a real being who has a love for humanity that is in some ways comparable to, although also much greater than, the love that humans can experience in this world. They are unlikely to mean 'I prefer to look at the world using the imagery of a supernatural being', or 'I like to think that there is something especially powerful about love'.

However, cognitive approaches to religious language do present some issues that need to be resolved. One of the issues is whether assertions made in the form of truth-claims can be regarded as meaningful if the person making the claim cannot produce any evidence to support it and does not know what would count as evidence either for or against it. The challenges made by Ayer and by Flew are significant and need to be met.

Wittgenstein's approach to religious language suggests that there is nothing intrinsically meaningful or meaningless about religious language (or, indeed, any other kind of language). Words and phrases do not simply have meaning, regardless of their context. For Wittgenstein, meaning is something given to words and phrases by those who use them in a context (*Lebensform*). In his view, those who are not participating in the 'game' of religious language are not in a position to determine the meaningfulness of the language.

See Chapter 1.2 for a discussion of Aquinas' understanding of religious language as analogical.

Apply your knowledge

17. Are you more inclined towards the thinking of Aquinas, or the thinking of Wittgenstein? What do you find persuasive about their ideas, and what do you find less convincing?

Think question

Do you think a poem has a meaning if no one is reading it and the writer is dead? Or does it only have a meaning when it is meaningful to a reader? Give reasons for your answer.

Non-cognitive approaches to religious language also raise issues, therefore. If a claim such as 'God loves us' is not asserting a fact, and cannot be subjected to the question 'Is that true or false?', it is difficult to see exactly what such a claim is worth. Wittgenstein's approach, for example, does not help us to resolve the 'big questions' of whether there is a God, whether we are created beings and whether human life is purposeful. It places such questions outside the realm of what can be known. But many religious believers argue that revelation from God does give us facts that can be known, even if they have to be believed with faith rather than because of empirical evidence.

What has been the influence of non-cognitive approaches to religious language on the interpretation of religious texts?

See Chapters 3.1 and 3.2 for further discussion of how Christianity might be understood in a multi-faith context.

Non-cognitive approaches to religious language have had a profound effect on the ways in which some thinkers have interpreted religious texts. Some people have found these approaches challenging and even threatening to the Christian faith, while others have found them liberating and refreshing, offering new opportunities for modern people to relate to Christian ideas and providing possibilities for positive discussions in a multi-faith world.

For most Christians, the Bible contains cognitive assertions. It makes claims that are factual, such as that God created the world, that Jesus was the Son of God, that there is a heaven after death, that there will be a Day of Judgement and that Jesus rose from the dead on the first Easter Sunday. These are claims that Christians say are true, and which they say are open to being judged as either true or false. There is not a body of evidence to draw upon to demonstrate the truth of the claims, and, therefore, faith is required to accept them and commit to them, but, nevertheless, they are offered as cognitive claims.

However, non-cognitive approaches to religious language suggest that perhaps religious texts are not making cognitive assertions that can be judged to be true or false, but are doing something else. Perhaps they are offering a 'picture preference', a way of looking at the world that is figurative rather than literal. Some thinkers have developed different ways of understanding the Bible by taking non-cognitive approaches in different directions.

Sometimes, non-cognitive approaches have been adopted as a way of addressing the challenges to religious belief presented by modern science, where scientific evidence and empirical observation makes it difficult for modern people to believe in some of the claims of the Bible as being factually true. During Charles Darwin's lifetime, and after the publication of his works detailing his theories of evolution through natural selection, people questioned whether the creation accounts in Genesis were best understood as literally, historically accurate descriptions or whether they were best understood in other ways. For many, it made more sense to understand the creation narratives as figurative, mythological ways of presenting a way of understanding the world in relation to God, rather than trying to believe them as literally true. The creation stories began to be understood in different ways by some Christians. Some interpret the stories symbolically, seeing them as poetic ways of presenting cognitively meaningful truths, such as that an almighty being brought the world into existence. Others interpret them non-cognitively, seeing them as serving a function within a community rather than as making reference to historical facts.

In his essay 'New Testament and Mythology' (1941), the German theologian Rudolf Bultmann went further. He argued that the writers of the New Testament were never trying to make a record of accurate historical fact, but that they had expressed their beliefs through the language of myth. Bultmann's work was considered radical because it took a non-cognitive approach to the Gospels as well as to the Old Testament. It suggested that perhaps they were not cognitive assertions about facts and real events, but had a different function and could be interpreted differently.

The real point of the gospel message, for Bultmann, was the need for individuals to reach a personal decision about the direction they wanted their lives to take in relation to God. In Bultmann's view, the modern, intelligent, literate person could not take seriously the supernatural elements of the Gospel stories, such as visitations by angels, the virgin birth and miraculous events, but this did not have to mean that the whole of Christianity should be rejected. Bultmann advocated the '**demythologising**' of the New Testament as well as the Old, to enable Christianity to hold what he saw as its rightful place as an essential, vital option in a fast-changing world.

Other writers have also caused controversy by taking a non-cognitive approach to religious language. Two books written in 1963, *Honest to God* by John Robinson and *The Secular Meaning of the Gospel* by Paul van Buren, also took up the idea that biblical teaching might not necessarily be interpreted as being about facts, but could be more usefully understood in terms of the choices and attitudes it offered to modern people. In 1977, a book called *The Myth of God Incarnate*, which was edited by John Hick, became notorious because of its suggestion that the idea of Jesus being God as a man on earth could be a pictorial, non-cognitive way of expressing meaning rather than an historical fact.

Many Christian thinkers and writers have continued to interpret biblical texts in the same way that they have always done, by assuming their truth and looking for ways in which their teachings can be applied to modern life. Those who have taken a more radical approach have sometimes been regarded as not Christian at all, because they appear to be denying the factual truth of many of the key elements of the Christian faith, such as the Virgin Birth, the miracles and the resurrection of Christ. Perhaps a non-cognitive approach to religious texts reduces them to no more than general advice to be nice to other people and to value relationships more than material possessions. Those who support a non-cognitive interpretation of the Bible point out that trying to force oneself to believe miracle stories is missing the point of Christianity. They argue that belief is not just giving assent to a list of unevidenced truth-claims, but is about personal choices and attitudes, and that a non-cognitive approach can free people to find meaning within the Christian faith in new ways.

To what extent is Aquinas' analogical view of theological language valuable in philosophy of religion?

Aquinas' view of religious language as analogy is still very popular within Christianity, especially within the Catholic tradition. Many Christians find it helpful to think of the truth-claims of Christianity as cognitive, with real factual content, even if in this life our finite minds cannot understand or access those facts. However, modern discussions about the factual quality of religious language have presented serious challenges to this view. Whether or not religious believers think that their assertions are about facts, the challenge remains for them to provide evidence of the truth of what they are saying.

For Aquinas, the revelation of God to individuals through religious experience, through the words of the Bible and the teachings of the church, provided sufficient evidence to support claims such as 'God loves us'. Philosophers today are likely to argue that we need more than just someone's claim that God revealed truths to them, and that we would not accept other truth-claims, such as those of science, on the basis of a reported vision or holy text. But Christians will argue that religious faith demands a trust in the truth of a claim even without evidence.

Learning support

Points to remember

» There is quite a lot of specialist technical vocabulary to remember for this topic. Doing some further reading to supplement your knowledge will help you to remember it and use it with confidence. In particular, be clear about the distinction between cognitive and non-cognitive uses of language.

» It is important to remember which thinkers held which points of view, as you might be asked a question about one of them in the exam.

» As well as developing your understanding of different viewpoints on issues of religious language, remember that you need to develop your own perspective and think about the reasons why you find it the most convincing position.

Enhance your learning

» Ayer's book *Language, Truth and Logic* (1936) is an interesting read which captures the enthusiasm that the young Ayer felt for the ideas of the Vienna Circle. There is a useful extract from it in Brian Davies' anthology *Philosophy of Religion: A Guide and Anthology* (2000, p. 143). Davies has given the extract the title 'God-talk is Evidently Nonsense'. It is followed in the anthology, on p. 147, by an extract from Swinburne's *The Coherence of Theism* (1977), which Davies has called 'God-talk is Not Evidently Nonsense', and which provides a useful contrast.

» Ludwig Wittgenstein's *Philosophical Investigations* (1953) contains much of his writing about language games. It is considered a very difficult text by many.

» *The Coherence of Theism* (1977) by Richard Swinburne is a demanding read, but Part 1 covers the issues for religious language in depth, from a Christian perspective.

» The 'Religious Language' entry in the *Internet Encyclopedia of Philosophy* is aimed at university level but is a very thorough and informative source to add to your knowledge: www.iep.utm.edu/rel-lang.

» To extend your understanding of this topic further, it would be interesting to dip into some of the books that were influenced by non-cognitive discussions of religious language. Some notable examples are:

○ Paul van Buren's *The Secular Meaning of the Gospel* (1963). Van Buren was an American theologian and ordained priest who in this book discusses ways in which the Christian Gospels could be reinterpreted for a secular age.

○ John Robinson's book *Honest to God* (1963) was very controversial when first published as it seemed to interpret Christianity too radically for many.

○ John Hick edited a book called *The Myth of God Incarnate* (1977) in which the contributors argue that the idea of Jesus as God incarnate (God in human form) was not to be taken literally but should be interpreted non-cognitively.

○ Don Cupitt's book *Taking Leave of God* (1988) follows the same kind of radical thinking as *The Myth of God Incarnate* (Hick, 1977) in suggesting that it is time to move on from a literal understanding of religious language about God.

Practice for exams

At A level, essay questions invite you to demonstrate your knowledge and understanding of factual material (AO1) and also your critical ability in putting forward a coherent, balanced argument (AO2). You should aim to write essays that are persuasive responses to the question throughout, rather than writing a lot of description and then tacking an opinion on at the end of each paragraph.

'Antony Flew's falsification principle presents a significant challenge to religious language.' Discuss.

This question requires you to make a critical evaluation of Flew's challenge to religious language. You will need to be familiar with his ideas as expressed in the Symposium on Theology and Falsification in order to demonstrate your knowledge and understanding. You should also be confident in your understanding of the responses given by Hare and Mitchell.

Rather than simply describing what each of them said, you should form and articulate your own view about whether Flew's challenge is significant. You might think that the points Flew made successfully demonstrate that religious language is empty talk. However, you might think that some or all of the responses made to Flew are good counter-arguments. You might have ideas of your own to contribute. Make sure that your essay expresses your point of view throughout, so that your conclusion is well supported.

Discuss critically the issues arising from taking a non-cognitive approach to religious texts.

For this essay you need to have a firm understanding of the difference between cognitive and non-cognitive approaches to religious language in order to score well in AO1. You should show how a non-cognitive approach might be used to interpret biblical texts, and for high marks you will need to demonstrate that you understand that there might be different ways of doing this.

For AO2 marks, you are asked to 'discuss critically the issues arising', so you will need to decide which issues are raised. One way of structuring this essay might be to take several issues one by one and give your view of each in turn, supporting it with reasoning.

Studying religion and ethics

What does the language of ethics really mean?

What is the best way of explaining having a sense of right or wrong and feelings of guilt?

What are the most important moral questions in sexual ethics?

Your study of ethics in your second year of A level brings you up to date, with an exploration of modern discussions around what we mean by the ethical language that we use (meta-ethics), an examination of conscience from a classical philosophical perspective and a modern psychological perspective, and an investigation into an important area of applied ethics in the form of sexual ethics.

First there is an exploration of three meta-ethical theories: naturalism, which holds that moral values can be defined absolutely in terms of the natural world, discernable through empirical ways of knowing; intuitionism, which holds that we use a special knowledge to discern moral values rather than our empirical senses; and emotivism, which rejects the concept that there are any moral values that really exist, and holds that moral utterances are relative to our emotions or preferences. These questions are important because they ask deep questions about whether we can discern moral values and, if we can, how we do it.

Next there is a discussion of conscience, exploring the theory of an important philosopher, Thomas Aquinas, and an important psychologist, Sigmund Freud. Conscience touches on a key part of ethics, namely our ability to be moral and our sense that we might be doing right or wrong. Philosophy and theology are not the only disciplines to respond to questions about our sense of conscience. The secular science of psychology also offers insight into the development of the human mind and how it behaves, often challenging philosophical and theological thinking.

Finally there is a study of sexual ethics, exploring important but contested questions about the morality of premarital, extramarital and homosexual sexual relationships. These questions are significant because in recent times there have been radical changes in the way Western liberal societies have legislated around matters of sexual ethics, and social norms have undergone seismic shifts.

Chapter 2.1 : Meta-ethical theories

Is morality an observable feature of the world?
Is morality discerned by intuition?
Is morality nothing more than emotion?

Key Terms

Absolutism: the view that morals are fixed, unchanging truths that everyone should always follow

Relativism: the view that moral truths are not fixed and are not absolute. What is right changes according to the individual, the situation, the culture, the time and the place

Naturalism: ethical theories that hold that morals are part of the natural world and can be recognised or observed in some way

Intuitionism: ethical theories that hold that moral knowledge is received in a different way from science and logic

Vienna Circle: a group of philosophers known as logical positivists who rejected claims that moral truth can be verified as objectively true

Emotivism: ethical theories that hold that moral statements are not statements of fact but are either beliefs or emotions

Hume's Law: you cannot go from an 'is' (a statement of fact) to an 'ought' (a moral)

Naturalistic fallacy: G.E. Moore's argument that it is a mistake to define moral terms with reference to other properties (a mistake to break Hume's law)

Specification requirements

*   Naturalism
*   Intuitionism
*   Emotivism

Introduction

For relativists, moral statements might be practically useful, cultural practices, personal opinions or even just arbitrary preferences. For absolutists, moral statements say something real about the world, something solid that does not change.

Absolutism and **relativism** are two ethical standpoints that are important to understanding what meta-ethics is all about. Absolutism is the idea that morals are fixed, unchanging truths that everyone should always follow.

Apply your knowledge

1. Consider the following and note true or false against each one:

   a. Morals are absolute facts that can be perceived through our senses like other kinds of facts (naturalism).

   b. Morals are absolute facts that can be perceived through a special kind of knowing that is different from our regular senses (intuitionism).

   c. Morals may not be objectively real but we can still have a moral duty.

   d. Morals are relative to our emotions, they are outbursts that are devoid of any other meaning (emotivism).

   e. Morals are comments made by people who want others to agree with them (prescriptivism).

2. When you have read the remainder of this chapter, revisit this question to see if you still agree with your initial answers.

See Chapter 1.3 for more about the Vienna Circle.

If killing a person is wrong, then for an absolutist it is always wrong for everyone to kill a person. Relativism takes the view that moral truths (moral assertions, rules or beliefs) are not fixed and are not absolute. What is right changes according to the individual, the situation (as situationists claim), the culture, the time and the place. Relativism and absolutism do not disagree about what is moral; they disagree about what it means to make a moral statement of any kind.

'Meta-ethics' relates to the modern philosophical debate surrounding the language of ethics. It is concerned with whether moral utterances refer to fixed truths or facts, as with ethical absolutism, or are relative to something like emotions or beliefs, as with relativism. It is also concerned with how we come to know morals – whether it is through some sort of knowing through our senses and observations (as with other observable things), a special kind of intuitive knowing, or whether there is no knowledge in morality at all. There are three different and contradictory strands to the debate.

Naturalism is an ethical theory that holds that morals are fixed absolutes in the universe and they can, consequently, be recognised or observed. Naturalists, such as F.H. Bradley (1846–1924) and Philippa Foot (1920–2010), believe that morals can be perceived in the world in the same way that other features of the world are identified. Naturalism can be linked to absolutism, the theory that there are fixed moral norms.

Intuitionism can be thought of as beginning with the work of G.E. Moore (1873–1958) in *Principia Ethica* (1903). Moore rejects Naturalism's presumption that you can simply see right and wrong in the social order, instead suggesting that morality is perceived through a different mechanism: intuition. H.A. Prichard (1871–1947) is an intuitionist who defined the way people intuit (detect or perceive) the moral dimension. The intuitionist W.D. Ross (1877–1971) accepted that moral principles cannot be absolute, but advanced a theory to justify moral duties, based around character. Intuitionist philosophers have contributed to deeper insights into what is meant by the term 'good'.

Empiricists hold that morals arise from human sentiment, not things that are observed. British philosopher A.J. Ayer (1910–89) and his book *Language, Truth and Logic* (1936) represents a departure from the claim that moral language has some kind of absolute meaning. Ayer belonged to the **Vienna Circle** of philosophers, a group of philosophers known as logical positivists who rejected claims that objective moral truth can be verified as true. They drew on the thinking of David Hume (1711–76). Ayer was an ethical non-naturalist because he rejected claims that ethics can be seen in the natural world. He was an **emotivist** because he held that moral statements are an emotional outburst in favour of, or against, something. Morals are relative to emotions and therefore have no fixed meaning. The American Philosopher C.L. Stevenson (1908–79) developed Ayer's ideas, suggesting that moral judgements are linked to our beliefs about morals rather than simply emotional outbursts. Emotivism is a striking example of relativism.

Naturalism

Ethical naturalists are absolutists. They hold that moral evil and goodness are absolute facts of the natural world, like other kinds of facts. They are fixed things that do not change according to situation, results or cultural practice. Morals are not about 'your point of view' or 'my opinion' but are objectively true. So when someone says, 'euthanasia is evil' or 'everyone has human rights', ethical naturalists argue that they are expressing a moral truth, part of the reality of the universe, and not an opinion.

Think question

Are morals absolute, like other facts in reality, or are they closer to opinions that can differ?

F.H. Bradley

F.H. Bradley (1846–1924)

Historically, naturalism linked claims about moral truth to the rise of modern science and the idea that truths about the world we live in can be proved. F.H. Bradley was an ethical naturalist and in his book, *Ethical Studies* (1876), he wrote:

> 66 What is it then that I am to realise? We have said it in 'my station and its duties'. To know what a man is (as we have seen) you must not take him in isolation. He is one of a people, he was born in a family, he lives in a certain society, in a certain state. What he has to do depends on what his place is, what his function is, and that all comes from his station in the organism. 99
>
> F.H. Bradley, *Ethical Studies,* 1876, p. 173

Bradley went on, stating that our duty is universal and concrete, it is objective with real identity, and, finally, that it realises the whole person, teaching us to 'identify others and ourselves with the station we fill; to consider that as good, by virtue of that to consider others and ourselves good too' (Bradley, *Ethical Studies*, 1876, p. 181).

See Chapter 2.1 of the AS and Year 1 book for a discussion of Aquinas' natural law.

Think question

When you see video footage of a terrorist attack that has killed innocent children, are there observable features that show wrongness?

Ethics is something that can be explained by the concrete absolute reality we observe; in much the same way we observe other things in the universe. The particular focus is on the place we hold in society, which directs what we should do.

Bradley represented the naturalism of the nineteenth century, but there are conceptual links to the natural moral law of Aquinas and his argument that we can look to the world and perceive morals from the purposes of life that we see in the world.

Theological naturalists, such as Thomas Aquinas, link goodness to divine will and the kind of creatures God has made humans to be. For these creatures, adultery is wrong, as it limits or prevents human flourishing. Hedonic naturalists link goodness to pleasure or happiness: the thing that causes happiness is right; moral statements are justified by some other thing. Bradley claims that morals are observable as part of the concrete world. The social order and your position in that order decides your moral duties. The position you hold in a community is not an incidental thing, it is a structure of reality, but is it correct to interpret the social order as a fixed fact? The twentieth century saw radical changes in many Western countries, where the roles of men and women changed and where hierarchical social roles came under significant pressure. The idea of individual freedom or self-determination and equality for all undermined concepts of class, fixed gender roles and institutions such as marriage. Bradley's fixed moral social order is, therefore, highly questionable. However, social orders fixed to absolute ideas about right and wrong seem to remain a feature of much of the rest of the world and among many migrant communities in Western countries. The breakdown of social order in Western society is linked to family breakdown and to marriage breakdown. In this way, naturalism sustains absolutism in so far as it labels these breakdowns as moral failures.

Empiricist challenges to naturalism

David Hume (1711–76)

There is a long-running British empiricist challenge to the claims of naturalism and the idea that morals are absolute facts. David Hume argued that moral claims are not derived from reason, but rather from sentiment. In *A Treatise of Human Nature* (1738), he rejected the idea that moral good or evil can be distinguished using reason. They are explained by the sentiment of the observer, not his or her reason. He goes on to suggest that morals excite passions and produce or prevent actions, but reason is impotent in matters of morality. The rules of morality are not the result of our applying our reason. Hume disagreed with Aquinas in this respect. Hume challenges us that when we see something we think is wrong, the 'wrongness' comes from our sentiment, not from our observations.

66 Take any action allowed to be vicious: Wilful murder, for instance. Examine it in all lights, and see if you can find that matter of fact, or real existence, which you call vice. In whichever way you take it, you find only certain passions, motives, volitions and thoughts. There is no other matter of fact in the case. The vice entirely escapes you, as long as you consider the object. You never can find it, till you turn your reflexion into your own breast, and find a sentiment of disapprobation, which arises in you, towards this action. Here is a matter of fact; but 'tis the object of feeling, not of reason. It lies in yourself, not in the object. So that when you pronounce any action or character to be vicious, you mean nothing, but that from the constitution of your nature you have a feeling or sentiment of blame from the contemplation of it. Vice and virtue, therefore, may be compared to sounds, colours, heat and cold, which, according to modern philosophy, are not qualities in objects, but perceptions in the mind. 99

David Hume, *A Treatise of Human Nature*, 1738, from www.gutenberg.org/files/4705/4705-h/4705-h.htm

Hume observed that writers on morality often move from 'is' statements (statements of fact) to 'ought/ought not' statements (statements prescribing what should be done). A person tells a lie and the moral philosophers says 'you ought not to lie'. Hume argues that this move creates an entirely unjustified new relationship between the words. This is sometimes called **Hume's Law:** you cannot go from an 'is' to an 'ought'. Charles R. Pigden suggests, 'Naturalists, in short, resort to all sorts of supposed facts – sociological psychological, scientific even metaphysical or supernatural' (Pigden, 'Naturalism'. In *A Companion to Ethics* [Blackwell Companions to Philosophy], ed. Singer, 1991, p. 422).

Philippa Foot

Philippa Foot (1920–2010)

However, Hume can be challenged. The British naturalist philosopher Philippa Foot suggested that moral evil is 'a kind of natural defect'. '[T]he fact that a human action or disposition is good of its kind [...] [is] a fact about a given feature of a certain kind of living thing' (Foot, *Natural Goodness*, 2001, p. 5). She argued that when we call a person a 'just man' or an 'honest woman' we are referring to something, to a person who recognises certain considerations (such as promise keeping, or helping your neighbour) as things that are powerful, compelling reasons to act. The moral person is someone who keeps promises, who defends those whose rights are being violated. A moral person has qualities which, for them, are the reasons they carry out certain actions, and this can be observed. We know if someone cannot be trusted to keep promises. Perhaps, therefore, there are some absolute morals after all.

Foot is arguing that there are virtues, characteristics or behaviours that aim at some good, an idea she takes from Aristotle. However, the key thing to understand is that she thinks these virtues can be recognised or observed by watching how a person acts in consideration of those virtues. The person who acts in consideration of honesty does honest things, and the honest things can be identified though observation. In this way, we can perceive the moral absolutes that empiricists argue we cannot measure.

When we call a person a 'just man' or an 'honest woman' we are referring to something

> 66 [...] a moral judgement says something about the action of any individual to whom it applies: namely something about the reason that there is for *him* to do it or not do it, whether or not he recognizes that, and whether or not, if he does recognize, he also acts on it as he should. 99

Philippa Foot, *Natural Goodness*, 2001, p. 18

Foot draws on Aristotle's observation that the natural world includes a good way of doing things. Life offers patterns of excellence and defect, related to the function and purpose of living things, and these apply to morality as much as anything else:

1. There is a *life cycle* consisting of self-maintenance and reproduction.

2. *Self-maintenance and reproduction* can be achieved differently in each species depending on how they feed themselves, how they develop and how they reproduce.

3. From all of this, certain *norms* can be deduced, such as the swiftness of the deer or the night vision of the owl.

4. By applying these norms to individual members of the species, *members can be judged to be effective or defective.* An owl with poor night vision is a defective owl, for example.

There is no difference between saying a living thing has 'good roots' and saying a human being has 'good dispositions of will'.

Foot gives the example of evaluating an oak tree:

> 66 We are, let us suppose, evaluating the roots of a particular oak tree, saying perhaps that it has good roots because they are as sturdy and deep as an oak's roots should be. Had its roots been spindly and all near the surface they would have been bad roots but as it is they are good. Oak trees need to stay upright because, unlike creeping plants, they have no possibility of life on the ground, and they are tall, heavy trees. Therefore oaks need to have deep sturdy roots: there is something wrong with them if they do not 99

Philippa Foot, *Natural Goodness*, 2001, p. 46

Oak trees need to have deep sturdy roots

Foot then applies her thinking to an example from Peter Kropotkin's *Memoirs of a Revolutionist* (1971), and the tale of Mikluko-Makláy, a geographer and anthropologist sent from Russia to study the peoples of the Malayan archipelago. Kropotkin says:

> ❝ [H]e had with him a native who had entered into his service on the express condition of never being photographed. The natives, as every one knows, consider that something is taken out of them when their likeness is taken by photography. One day when the native was fast asleep, Makláy, who was collecting anthropological materials, confessed that he was awfully tempted to photograph his native, the more so as he was a typical representative of his tribe and would never have known that he had been photographed. But he remembered his agreement and refrained. ❞

Peter Kropotkin, *Memoirs of a Revolutionist*, 1971, p. 229.
Cited in Philippa Foot, *Natural Goodness*, 2001, p. 47

Naturalism implies there is something absolute about morality

Think question

Should the Commandment be written more precisely as, for example, 'You ought not to kill' rather than 'Do not kill'? Does this make any difference?

This shows the wrongness associated with breaking a promise. It could be considered that taking the photograph would do no harm because the servant was asleep. However, trust and respect are things that matter. To take advantage of a person in this way would have been wrong. Trust matters in human communities. Human happiness has something to do with justice. Humans have developed ways to live well together and have developed rules (moral rules) to ensure that everyone can live happily together. These rules are natural and absolute, and whether or not people follow them they can be observed.

J.L. Mackie

J.L. Mackie (1917–81)

J.L. Mackie was a philosopher who found difficulty with claims about absolute or natural approaches to morality. In his book *Ethics: Inventing Right and Wrong* (1977), he noted that it is possible to describe an institution from the outside, such as the institution or social practice of promising or making chess moves in a game. The institution makes demands that promises are kept. However, we can also make observations from the inside; we can speak within the institution. For example, 'Don't break a promise John', or 'Don't move that rook as it will leave your king in check'. Thus Mackie argued, the injunction to not break promises depends on the rules of the institution having already being accepted. The rules themselves are not hard and fast facts; they are accepted to varying degrees by all those inside the institution.

> 66 Do the desires and especially the sufferings of other people, if known to me, constitute a reason for me to do something, if I can, or to try to do something that satisfies those desires or to relieve those sufferings? It would be natural to say that they constitute some reason; how strong a reason, how easily over-ruled by other considerations, may be a matter of dispute. 99
>
> J.L. Mackie, *Ethics: Inventing Right and Wrong*, 1977, p. 78

The degree to which moral rules should be applied can be disputed, depending on our relationship with the people affected. Should we be more inclined to keep the promises we make to our family and friends than those we make to strangers? We use an institution, a moral tradition to resolve these disputes, to guide whether or not we should show concern for the well-being of family and friends more readily than we show concern for the well-being of strangers. Following the rules of an institution is not the same as acting logically in response to agreed upon facts. It is acting in accordance with social expectations; it is responding to an understanding of the demands that will be made, and what will be approved of and what will be disapproved of. Mackie, as a naturalist, believes that moral rules can be observed but believes they are based on tradition rather than being absolute constructs.

Intuitionism

Intuitionists provide deeper insights into what we might mean by the term 'good,' and how we might distinguish 'good' from ideas like 'right'.

The naturalistic fallacy and G.E. Moore

G.E. Moore published *Principia Ethica* in 1903. He thought that intrinsically good things exist for their own sake. They cannot be analysed, or broken down, like other things in the physical world. Nonetheless, they can be recognised. It is not about *proving* these things but rather *seeing* them. He thought that we should do the thing that causes most good to exist. Good, according to Moore, is a simple indefinable thing. Moore was particularly concerned with rejecting utilitarians, who argued that goodness can be defined, measured, quantified and qualified.

Apply your knowledge

3. Identify human actions that you think could constitute natural, observable moral absolutes. Telling lies is one example.

4. The preamble to the *Universal Declaration of Human Rights* says, 'Whereas recognition of the inherent dignity and of the equal and inalienable rights of all members of the human family is the foundation of freedom, justice and peace in the world' (www.un.org/en/universal-declaration-human-rights). Discuss to what extent human rights declarations 'prove' there are moral facts in the world. What might Hume, Foot and Mackie each say?

5. Consider keeping promises:
   a. Are Foot and Kropotkin right about keeping promises?
   b. Is it correct to say that there is never a time when breaking a promise is right?
   c. How might Mackie respond?

6. Can human development be compared to the development of a tree? Are there ways in which human beings develop that trees do not?

G.E. Moore (1873–1958)

See Chapter 2.4 of the AS and Year 1 book for a discussion of utilitarianism

Moore thought that attempts to define good in terms of something else is the **naturalistic fallacy**. So, for instance, if we try to define good by saying it is the thing that gives us most pleasure, we have broken good down into something else. This is not possible as good is a simple thing and cannot be broken down into constituent parts.

> **❝** If I am asked 'What is good?' my answer is that good is good, and that is the end of the matter. Or if I am asked 'How is good to be defined?' my answer is that it cannot be defined, and that is all I have to say about it. **❞**
>
> G.E. Moore, *Principia Ethica*, 1903, p. 6

Good is a simple notion, just as yellow is a simple notion – you know it when you see it. A horse is a complex notion because it can be broken down into different qualities. A horse is a quadruped, an animal, a mammal and so on. We might say that yellow is in fact made up of light waves of some kind and other elements, but what we perceive is yellow, not the waves or the particles. Good is good. Moore wrote, 'everything is what it is and not another thing' (Moore, *Principia Ethica*, 1903, p. 206).

Philosophers who define good as being made up of something else, or based on other things, are making it a complex notion. They define good as the greatest happiness or the pursuit of self-interest. These become some property of good. The essential mistake they are making is to look into the world for some physical thing they can define (or substitute) in place of good. This turns the moral judgement into a judgement about the physical world, and that is wrong. Although Moore did not define himself as an intuitionist in the strict sense, he did place importance on intuition as the thing that perceives moral goodness, rather than our senses. He argued that there is no place for discussion about proof because methods of proving require evidence from the empirical world and intuition cannot be measured empirically.

Moore asserts a number of things that he holds are good and indefinable.

> 66 By far the most valuable thing which we know or can imagine, are certain states of consciousness, which may roughly be described as the pleasures of human intercourse and the enjoyment of beautiful objects 99
>
> Moore, *Principia Ethica*, 1903, p. 188

Beautiful art is good in and of itself, but our awareness or appreciation of beauty cannot be defined because it is intuitive. However, in the absence of any recourse to some kind of proof, which Moore says we cannot rely on in moral matters, we simply have his word for the existence of these intuitions. It is also unclear how we can enter into an argument about the validity of his list or anyone else's list, given the person making the list provides no evidence to support their point of view.

H.A. Prichard

H.A. Prichard (1871–1947)

H.A. Prichard was a leading British moral philosopher in the 1920s and 1930s. In his article 'Does moral philosophy rest on mistake?' (Prichard, *Mind*, vol. 21, 1912, pp. 21–37), he argues that it is a hopeless quest to try to find arguments to determine what our moral obligations are. When we are asked why should we do this or that, answers usually involve recourse to happiness or the justification that it achieves some good. Perhaps both of these can be achieved: 'Do the right thing because it will be best for you and will, in the end, make you happy.' However, Prichard argues there is a gap between the good thing and the idea of what things I have a duty to bring about. The course of action X might be best, but why should I bring such a course of action about? Duty and the good are separate things. Duty is something beyond the good thing to do.

> 66 Suppose we ask ourselves whether our sense that we ought to pay our debts or to tell the truth arises from our recognition that in doing so we should be originating something good, e.g., material comfort in A or true belief in B, i.e., suppose we ask ourselves whether it is this aspect of the action which leads to our recognition that we ought to do it. We, at once, and without hesitation answer 'No.' […]
>
> This apprehension is immediate, in precisely the sense in which a mathematical apprehension is immediate, e.g., the apprehension that this three-sided figure, in virtue of its being three-sided, must have three angles. Both apprehensions are immediate in the sense that in both insights into the nature of the subject directly leads us to recognise its possession of the predicate; and it is only stating this fact from the other side to say that in both cases the fact apprehended is self-evident. 99
>
> H.A. Prichard, 'Does Moral Philosophy Rest on a Mistake?' *Mind*, vol. 21, 1912, pp. 27–8

There are two different kinds of thinking taking place: intuition and reasoning. Reason collects the facts and intuition determines which course to follow. In deciding whether to give to a charity, reason collects all of the data on the charity and the alternative uses of the resource, the people concerned and the various possible outcomes. Intuition determines what we should do. Ethical dilemmas are about making a choice between different actions where there are conflicting moral obligations. In the case of giving to charity, which charity? Should the money be used for other purposes? Intuition identifies which obligation is greater. Moral obligations are not linked to the intrinsic goodness of any action. One simply considers the different obligations in the situation at hand.

Reason collects the facts concerned and intuition determines which course to follow

Prichard does not explain how we discriminate between different options when different people have different intuitions about what is right. How we decide which option is more enlightened is not that clear. Prichard notes that not all people seem to be able to intuit moral truth to the same extent as others. Morals differ because some people have more clarity around moral intuitions; they are more enlightened. We may experience doubt, but this is because we need to think things through more clearly and let our moral capacities of thinking do their work. This might require us to use our imagination to hypothesise what we would think if we were in the same situation, or we may need to put ourselves in the same situation before we can intuit the correct course of action.

Some think Prichard's most important contribution to meta-ethics is to show the importance of many moral words; not just 'good', but also 'right', 'obligation' and 'duty', giving us a more complex range of moral vocabulary.

W.D. Ross

W.D. Ross (1877–1971)

W.D. Ross was Prichard's student and he built on the work of both Moore and Pritchard in his books *The Right and the Good* (1930) and *Foundations of Ethics* (1939). Ross set out to try to understand the sorts of moral principles that people might use when answering a moral question.

Principles can sometimes conflict. For instance, to keep a promise I may have to tell a lie. For example, 'Promise you won't tell him I am hiding in the attic', says the younger sister. 'Tell the truth now, where is she hiding', says the older brother. Another problem is that principles may change from one culture to another. Consider this sentiment, which might seem odd in one culture and normal in another: 'Take the husband your parents have chosen for you. Your personal freedom is not as important as an experienced judgement that the whole family approves of.'

Apply your knowledge

10. Are you convinced by Prichard's claim that our intuition about the right course of action is separate from our perception of the facts of the situation? Consider something that provokes a strong moral response in you, and that you also feel some sense of duty about (for example, some people express a duty to be a vegetarian because of the treatment of animals). Do you think your sense of duty arises from the facts of what you perceive, or is it a separate thing?

11. How might intuition be explained? Consider conscience, God, feeling/ emotions, memory.

12. In 2016, a UK court considered the case of a father who imprisoned his daughter in a cage in an overseas apartment to save her from going off the rails, socialising with her friends in the UK and going out to clubs. The British courts said she should be freed and allowed to return to the UK. The father believed he was doing the right thing. How do we decide which intuition is right, the father's or that of the British courts?

Ross argues, therefore, that principles should not be taken as absolute:

> **❝** The only way to save the authority of such rules is to recognise them not as rules guaranteeing the rightness of any act which falls under them, but as rules guaranteeing that any act which falls under them tends so far as that aspect of its nature goes, to be right, and can be rendered wrong only if in virtue of another aspect of its nature it comes under another rule by reason of which it tends more decidedly to be wrong. **❞**

W.D. Ross, *The Right and the Good*, 1930, p. 312

Ross, like Moore, thought goodness cannot be defined in natural terms. Moral principles cannot be absolute. They argued that moral theories are lists of principles from which we deduce courses of action. Utilitarianism, natural law and Kantian ethics offer different lists of moral principles that operate in this way.

Ross proposed prima facie duties; duties that are 'at first appearance'. When faced with a moral problem, various duties or obligations are apparent. A prima facie duty is a moral obligation that binds us to follow it *unless there's an overriding obligation*. We follow a particular duty unless a higher duty exists that compels us to pursue that instead.

Ross identified seven foundational prima facie duties that are clearly moral (though there might be more). 'There is nothing arbitrary about these prima facie duties. Each rests on a definite circumstance which cannot seriously be held to be without moral significance' (Ross, *The Right and the Good*, 1930, p. 20). They are: promise-keeping, reparation for harm done, gratitude, justice, beneficence, self-improvement and non-maleficence. These are not a list of absolutes, but they emphasise a personal character of duty. It is a matter of judgement when deciding how to balance these duties in a moral dilemma. It is not the case that one over-riding principle (such as the utilitarian idea of the greatest good for the greatest number or the Kantian act you can universalise) always applies. The duties do not tell us what to do and they are not in priority order. They can only be considered in a particular situation: 'it is more important that our theory fit the facts than it be simple' (Ross, *The Right and the Good*, 1930, p. 19). In making a moral decision, our intuition identifies our prima facie duties, although our actual action is not self-evident; it is the outcome of a process of judgement.

Making judgements is difficult and not without error. We may not have absolute certainty about what to do or absolute knowledge of the situation, and whilst we may know what we think the right thing to do is, others may see the situation very differently. It is possible, however, to improve our ability to make judgements through experience of previous moral decision-making.

Ross developed intuitionism into an approach that took account of clashes of apparent absolutes, when a dilemma forces a choice that must lead to the abandonment of one principle or another. Ross helps to provide a solution to the Kantian problem of a son who is required to be honest to a murderer's enquiry about the whereabouts of his father because one must always be truthful. Ross proposes a theory that allows discernment between the requirement to be truthful and the obligation to try and preserve life – he would place life preservation over honesty. Ross' view of morality is that it is a difficult area to navigate, and one in which certainty is hard to find. Ross' thinking may be uncomfortable for those who wish to assert absolutes in life–and–death situations.

Intuitionists provide some clarification about what we might mean by the term 'good', but other philosophers provide a very different explanation for such terms.

Apply your knowledge

13. Ross' approach to ethics acknowledges a degree of uncertainty about decision-making, in contrast to the confidence of the utilitarian or Kantian approaches. Which is the more realistic way of thinking about ethical decision-making in your view? Give reasons.

14. Ross suggests seven foundational prima facie duties (promise-keeping, reparation for harm done, gratitude, justice, beneficence, self-improvement and non-maleficence). He thought these were right, but he did not give reasons for his choice. Explain why these are important duties and which you find hardest to justify including as one of the seven foundational prima facie duties.

15. Ross also thought the list was not complete. Suggest an additional prima facie duty (for example modesty, charity, inclusiveness, the golden rule) and make an argument to support it.

Emotivism

Intuitionists reject the naturalist claim that moral knowledge is absolute and can be seen in the facts of the world as perceived by our senses. They propose alternative kinds of information as the source for our moral responsibilities. Some philosophers agree with the intuitionists that the naturalists are wrong, but conclude that the intuitionists are wrong as well because morality is no kind of fact at all; it is entirely relative. The Vienna Circle was one such group of philosophers. In the 1920s the group developed the idea of logical positivism. They accepted David Hume's idea that you cannot go from an 'is' to an 'ought', from a fact to a moral, and they accepted his conclusion that all morality was sentiment, a feeling for the common person, and nothing more. Intuitionists think it is possible to identify morality even if verifiable science does not reveal it; logical positivists reject the existence of things that cannot be known through verifiable science. Logical positivists are relativists.

A.J. Ayer

A.J. Ayer (1910–89)

Only things that can be verified through scientific and mathematic propositions are facts

An important British example of logical positivism was the emotivist philosopher A.J. Ayer. He thought there were three kinds of judgements: logical (analytical) judgements, factual (synthetic) judgements and moral judgements. Emotivism is ethical non-naturalism because it rejects the view that morals tell you anything about the external world. Only things that can be verified through scientific and mathematic propositions can do that. Morals are relative only to our feelings or emotions. They tell us about the person and their emotions, not the external world. Ayer's thinking is, therefore, part of relativism, which holds that there can be no known, fixed moral truths.

A meaningful statement about the world is one that can be verified. There are two categories of meaningful statement about the world. Factual (*synthetic*) statements can be verified using our senses, particularly through observation. 'It is raining outside' is a factual statement because you can see and feel the rain. Logical statements can be verified *analytically*; they are true by definition: '2 + 2 = 4', 'All widows are women' and 'All bachelors are men' are logical statements.

Moral judgements, and also theological ones, are not observable (e.g. you can see the features of killing, but you cannot see the features of murder that entail wrongness of killing) and they are not verified by definition. They are not, therefore, facts about the world out there. They are no kind of fact or knowledge at all, but simply utterances that are relative to emotive responses in the same category as expressions of preference, attitude or feeling, as if we had trodden on a nail or eaten a delicious sweet. If I say something is good, I have warm emotions about that thing. If I say something is bad, I have cold feelings about it.

Emotivism is sometimes called the 'hurrah/boo' theory. To say generosity is good is to say 'hurrah to generosity'. The phrase 'lying is wrong' means 'boo to lying'. Ayer writes:

> 66 For in saying that a certain type of action is right or wrong, I am not making any factual statement, not even a statement about my own state of mind. I am merely expressing certain moral sentiments. And the man who is ostensibly contradicting me is merely expressing his moral sentiments. So there is plainly no sense in asking which of us is in the right. For neither of us is asserting a genuine proposition. 99
>
> A.J. Ayer, *Language, Truth and Logic*, 1936, pp. 107–8

Moral arguments are expressions of feeling. They are not even viewpoints or expressions of beliefs, although they are calculated to arouse feelings and stimulate action:

> 66 In fact we may define the meaning of the various ethical words in terms both of the different feelings they are ordinarily taken to express, and also the different responses which they are calculated to provoke. 99
>
> A.J. Ayer, *Language, Truth and* Logic, 1936, p. 106

Think question

Are moral statements simply expressive utterances or do they connect to truths about the world?

Synthetic

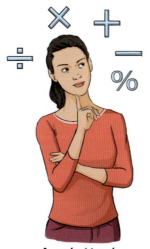
Analytical

Boo to bankers

How emotivism interprets moral expressions

C.L. Stevenson

The American philosopher C.L. Stevenson (1908–79) developed Ayer's thinking in his book *Ethics and Language* (1944). Ayer had classified moral statements as emotional expressions, but Stevenson linked them to attitudes.

People express a moral opinion not as an emotional response but as an expression of an attitude or a belief they have. Stevenson argued that moral judgements contain an element that expresses an attitude relative to a fundamental belief, and an element that seeks to persuade or influence others. Moral judgements express belief as well as approval or disapproval. If I say, 'This is good', I mean, 'I approve of this, approve of it too'. If I say abortion is wrong, I mean I believe abortion is wrong and I want you to agree with me. There is a persuading dimension to moral statements.

Stevenson appreciated the strong roots that underlie people's disagreements more fully than Ayer. Moral language is relative to the beliefs that people hold. While Ayer saw moral disagreements as arguments about preferences, Stevenson saw them as arguments about different beliefs. In fact, he thought moral disagreements were often differences of opinion about what to do, rather than genuine disagreements. People do not really disagree about whether it is right or wrong to steal, but they might disagree about the appropriate punishment (how to respond to the stealing).

Emotivism challenges the idea that the term 'good' represents any kind of fixed morality. Instead it is relativist, promoting the idea that there are no fixed morals.

Evaluating emotivism

Emotivism challenges the foundations of morality. Emotivists reject any sense that morality is beyond ourselves. Moral philosophy cannot commit us to any particular moral view. It cannot lead us to a conclusion; there is no 'therefore' or 'because' in moral debate. It is an interior, individual perspective of the world. A moral statement might mean nothing more than the kind of expression involved in a person preferring dark chocolate over milk chocolate. Attempts to portray morality as discernable in the natural order are mistakes. To emotivists, the claims of those who think morality is absolute, such as ethical naturalists, are mistaken. Emotivists maintain the ideas of a universal morality, such as those that Kantian ethics advances, are wrong. By implication, human rights, natural law, and attempts to quantify goodness in terms of human well-being, like utilitarianism, are all mistaken. If Bradley sought to incorporate morality into society, Ayer sought to eradicate any moral grounding from the social order entirely. Instead, he argued that moral utterances were entirely relative and dependent on emotions or beliefs.

In his book *A Short History of Ethics* (1995), Alasdair MacIntyre is not satisfied with emotivism. First, he questions 'emotive meaning'. He suggests that the thing that makes moral utterances a guide to our actions, what gives them meaning, is not so much whether they are factual or descriptive, but their importance or relevance to the people around them. To say your house is on fire means something very different if

See Chapter 2.3 of the AS and Year 1 book for a discussion of Kant's idea of a universal law.

you hear the news on holiday or if you hear it shouted while you are in your home in your bed – one contains a different demand or call to action than the other. The emotivists conflate meaning and use. They do not distinguish between statements that change significance when used differently. Second, MacIntyre argues that Stevenson paints a picture of a thoroughly unpleasant world in which everyone is trying to get ahead of everyone else by imposing their views on others. He also argues that Stevenson does not explain how the moral views are formed in the first place. Third, emotivism is, according to MacIntyre, opaque. It does not give any help in explaining how we can distinguish the feelings and attitudes that are moral from other feelings and attitudes we might have.

Discussing Meta-ethics

Does the definition of the word 'good' define the study of ethics?

The language used in moral questions and debates is not insignificant, as matters of morality inform law and policy. Moral debates are often linked to questions about people's suffering and questions about justice and rights.

Meta-ethics questions what is really meant by the word 'good'. When a moral judgement or statement is made, when something is said to be right or wrong, good or bad, to be done or not to be done, the words can mean quite different things to different people.

To make sense of any kind of moral debate, discussing what the speaker means by the words they use raises new questions about the issues. For example, the statement 'murder is wrong' might mean different things depending on whether you think 'wrong' means 'is disliked', 'is against the eternal rules' or 'is not in the interest of the majority'. I might feel compelled by the idea that there is some factual basis for morality. I might feel more inclined to be immoral if I believe morality is all just a matter of personal opinion. Or I might feel that if 'goodness' just means 'happiness' then perhaps we do not need goodness at all.

It can be argued that it does not really matter whether or not the language used points to anything fixed or absolute, as long as there is agreement among people about the general direction in which it points. As long as we share an understanding that, for example, morality is a matter of custom, what is important is understanding what those customs are and why they are important to people, not that we all mean exactly the same thing when we refer to 'good' and 'goodness'.

Perhaps there are other ways of talking about morality. Perhaps we can talk about it in terms of virtue, habit or practice, as Foot suggests, rather than a definition of 'good'. Maybe we should focus on how to

Apply your knowledge

16. What does it mean to describe ethics as sentiment?

17. What are the two kinds of facts about the world, according to Ayer, and why are moral statements not facts about the world?

18. Why is Ayer's theory known as the 'hurrah/boo' theory?

19. In emotivist terms, which of these statements are synthetic judgements, which are analytic judgements and which are moral (and therefore meaningless) judgements?

    a. The Pope is a holy man.

    b. The squirrel is behind the tree.

    c. An equilateral triangle is a three-sided polygon where all three sides are equal.

    d. A virgin has not had sex.

    e. Heaven is where we hope to go when we die.

    f. I must have left my mobile phone under his bed.

    g. You murdered my sunflower.

20. How does Stevenson differ from Ayer? Use the words 'belief', 'emotion', 'attitude' and 'expression' in your answer.

Apply your knowledge

21. Who from this chapter agrees with these statements and which do you find most convincing and why?

    a. Morals are prima facie duties, which we see at first appearance.

    b. Only things that can be verified through scientific and mathematic propositions are facts.

    c. Moral language is relative to the beliefs that people hold. If I say, 'This is good,' I mean, 'I approve of this, approve of it too.'

22. Consider the following sentences and explain how they are different:

    a. You ought not to take that dress because it does not belong to you.

    b. Thou shalt not covet thy neighbour's wife.

    c. Be good.

    d. To thine own self be true.

    e. First do no harm.

Think question

Is morality more than personal emotion?

flourish as human beings rather than on what it is wrong or right to do, and think about other features of moral decision-making like human motivation or conscience. Prichard offers other words like 'duty', 'obligation' and 'right', to use alongside 'good'. Do I have a duty to do what is good. Is it right to do your duty? Am I obliged to always do my duty? What about when obligations conflict and I have to choose? However, although these sorts of questions shed light on different dimensions of moral language reflecting choice, understanding, discernment, motivation and willpower, they do eventually come back to a question of defining 'goodness'.

Does ethical language have any factual basis? Is it objective, personally subjective or meaningless?

Meta-ethics questions the link between our ideas about right and wrong and reality. If you believe that the world contains no moral facts because facts are not things that can be moral, then you are saying something about the category of things that knowledge is and why it cannot include morals. Our approach to morality is affected by our attitude to the kind of things morals are. If you think that moral statements are things that, in general, we should apply consistently, then it follows that you should adopt moral statements that largely work all the time and you should encourage others to do the same.

Our view about the kind of thing a moral is affects how it might be used. For example, the American Declaration of Independence says that all are created equal and that these truths are self-evident, that they can be seen by all. The Universal Declaration of Human Rights proclaims that all are equal in dignity and have rights that signatories are compelled to affirm. Morality is clearly identifiable and objective in these documents.

The idea of objective moral truth is a powerful thing, with a capacity to command authority over all and provide assurances on what we should and should not do. If moral truth is objective, then we could be confident about how to live and the kind of laws we need. Rights could be more strongly defended; not simply as hopes or beliefs but as certainties about the world. This would also help confirm the sort of responses we have when we perceive something as abhorrent, like rape, child abuse and slavery – it is not just an opinion, but a moral fact.

Moore suggested that there must be some facts behind our moral utterances. He thought that if two people made opposing moral judgements, those judgements must be based on facts. If they were not based on facts, then the two people would not be disagreeing! However, Stevenson suggested that the two people could be disagreeing over beliefs, not facts. Morals may be down to subjective beliefs, perhaps informed by cultural differences. If morality is a matter of your beliefs and background, then what is morally 'true' is only really 'true for you'. If our morality is part of our individual view of the world, rather than anything shared or universal, then it has the advantage of being a reflection of what we individually and personally believe, but, on the other hand, it cannot bind other people. When it comes to laws and customs, it is not clear whether or not morality has anything to do with them. Nevertheless, Stevenson thinks our moral language has a purpose; it is an attempt to persuade other people to agree with our beliefs.

Subjectivism celebrates personal identity and individuality, but it is not so good for groups, communities and society. For example, when it comes to issues like female genital mutilation or forced marriage, we may find ourselves unable to agree a society-wide convention. We might find we disagree with each other about what is right or wrong. If morality is subjective, perhaps the only principle we can agree to is 'to thine own self be true'.

Perhaps we are kidding ourselves, giving morality a position of cultural importance. Perhaps our moral utterances are nothing more than emotional outbursts and have no meaning at all. We might feel something deeply one minute, but that feeling does not equate to any kind of fact or even reflect any kind of shared understanding; it is just a human response in a particular moment. If this is morality then it is not something that could confidently be relied upon for a system of justice and law-making and would make the need to form moral cultural traditions difficult to justify.

Do people just know in themselves what is good, bad, right and wrong?

How we know what is moral is a much-debated question, and whatever answer is given, further questions arise. Is it a kind of instinct, a sense, a feeling, an inner process of reason, a social habit or something else?

There is an experience of 'just knowing' when something is wrong, or just 'feeling' the injustice of a situation. We do not need a breakdown of the mental process because the sense of wrongness wells up within us. This is not something we need to be educated or trained in; it is something that we are born with, something that speaks to us. The problem is how we translate such an elusive thing into systems of rights and justice. When we try to do this we begin to discover that not everyone shares the same sense of wrongness. Some people commit acts we think are immoral. Do they not know the acts are immoral? If moral knowledge is something we 'just have' or 'just know' then how do we make sense of those who do not have it or do not know it or, alternatively, have a different moral compass.

Emotivists, like Ayer and Stevenson, do not think moral expressions reflect a kind of knowledge but merely an emotional response to something.

Apply your knowledge

23. Build the strongest naturalist case you can for evidence from the world pointing to morality. How convincing do you find it?

24. Some moral principles seem to be shared by many different thinkers. Consider the following quotes. How might they be evidence that the emotivists are wrong?

    a. 'Do unto others as you would have done unto yourself.' (This is the Golden Rule of the New Testament. Similar ideas are expressed in other religious texts from around the world.)

    b. 'Act only according to that maxim by which you can at the same time will that it should become a universal law' (Kant, *Groundwork for the Metaphysics of Morals* [1785], 1997, p. 44).

So moral thoughts do indeed come from within us, but they are not reliable facts. They are outbursts or expressions of belief. However, the problem with relying on this kind of thinking is that we can have very complex and contradictory feelings about things. Philosophers, like Ross, therefore think morality involves discerning between different moral duties and working out which is the right one to follow. And sometimes it is possible to make an error.

Some philosophers agree that moral utterances come from within us, but disagree about their status. They can be more than an individual's expression of belief. They could come from reasoned reflection on the world, as thinkers like Thomas Aquinas and Philippa Foot seem to suggest. Moral knowledge, in this case, is the product of wisdom or intelligence, and a reasoning process. In some way, information is received and processed, and a moral judgement is the result. Two problems can be seen with this perspective. First, moral judgements can produce feelings. A sense of moral injustice can create a powerful emotional response that is far from a cool, collected and reasoned judgement. Second, people can have strong views on morality that differ from those of others, suggesting that the logic or reasoning behind one perspective is not clear to everyone.

Perhaps moral knowledge is linked to human psychology, emotion, our personal histories, cultures and beliefs, or our spirituality in some way. This is not to say that these things have to influence our moral decision-making, just that we are all affected by these things and so we cannot be sure that they do not affect it. This is most clear with psychology, where things that have happened to us in the past might go on to shape how we respond to things in the future. But it is also true with spirituality and the beliefs people hold that there might be a different way of knowing through a link to an ultimate power, divine force or universal wisdom that connects to people in a way logical positivists would not understand or accept as possible. Perhaps knowledge is more mysterious than some people think.

The ultimate problem with relying entirely on an inner moral compass is that morality is fundamentally something that relates to other people. There is a social dimension to morality, in that morality is about interactions between, and attitudes towards, others, which means there really needs to be some way of agreeing a set of morals we can all live by. Relying on my inner feelings to justify the moral rules that everyone has to live by might not be very persuasive to others. A further problem is that the experiences and awareness that feed our understanding are things we feel within ourselves. So do we distinguish the moral elements from other elements of the reality we perceive? We might just know moral statement inside ourselves, but is that not true of all knowledge, feelings and preferences?

Apply your knowledge

25. Consider a moral dilemma you have faced, someone you know has faced or you have read about. Was there a role for intuition in the decision-making process?

26. To what extent can intuition be explained away by the emotivists?

27. Can we prove what is right and wrong by looking at the world, or do we have a sense of what is right and wrong?

Learning support

Points to remember

» Meta-ethics looks closely at what is meant by the language of ethics (words like 'good', 'right' and 'duty') and what these words actually refer to.

» Meta-ethics reveals different ways of understanding how we can (or cannot) access knowledge of morality.

» One way of interrogating the meta-ethics philosophers is to ask two questions: Do they believe morals are absolutely real or relative to something else? How do they think our perception of things that are true works?

» The naturalist thinks there is a perceivable scientific moral order of absolute facts in the world. There are absolute truths and we can detect them in the observable universe.

» The emotivist thinks that morality is relative to different emotive expressions, which do not correspond to anything other than the emotion. Emotivism is known as 'ethical non-naturalism' because it opposes naturalism's understanding of how things are known. It is linked to logical positivism, a broader philosophical movement associated with the Vienna Circle, that professed a particular understanding of the scientific way of knowing things.

» Intuitionists agree with emotivists that morals are not observable in the universe using our senses. However, the intuitionist believes that it is possible to perceive morality, but we use intuition rather than senses to perceive observable objects.

» Emotivists doubt that the intuitionist method of knowing reveals any fact, and they do not agree with what intuitionists think they know. Naturalists would agree with intuitionists that there is something to know but would disagree over the method intuitionists use to know it.

Enhance your learning

» To get a feel for the thinking that led to intuitionism, read G.E. Moore's *Principia Ethica* (1903). It is available online and Chapter II, which contains the key elements of Moore's thinking discussed in this chapter, is available at http://fair-use.org/g-e-moore/principia-ethica/chapter-ii.

» For a contemporary ethical naturalist, read Philippa Foot's work *Natural Goodness* (2001).

» The classic emotivist text is A.J. Ayer's *Language, Truth and Logic* (1936), which he wrote when he was a young man. It is bold and punchy, and Chapter 6 is most relevant.

» J.L. Mackie's *Ethics: Inventing Right and Wrong* (1977) is a classic book on ethics and the study of objectivism, absolutism, subjectivism and relativism. Part 1.3 is particularly relevant. Mackie is a contemporary relativist.

Practice for exams

At A level, essay questions invite you to demonstrate your knowledge and understanding of factual material (AO1) and also your critical ability in putting forward a coherent, balanced argument (AO2). You should aim to write essays that are persuasive responses to the question throughout, rather than writing a lot of description and then tacking an opinion on at the end of each paragraph.

How fair is the claim that ethical language is meaningless?

This question is asking you to decide whether ethical language, such as 'murder is wrong', has any real meaning, and you need to have an opinion about this issue that you can justify.

For high marks in AO1, you will need to recognise that this challenge to ethical language comes from the logical positivists, and from Ayer in particular. Show that you understand the challenge made and can explain clearly why some thinkers conclude that ethical language is meaningless. You will also need to demonstrate knowledge and understanding of different and opposing views, such as those of ethical naturalists.

Meta-ethics, as a topic, uses some specialist vocabulary, and you can enhance your marks in AO1 by using this accurately and with confidence.

For AO2, you need to present an argument that is clear and consistent throughout your answer. You might agree with the claim that ethical language is meaningless, in which case you should show why you think that counter-arguments are wrong. If you disagree with the claim, you should explain why you think it is flawed and why your own position makes more sense.

'Moral decision-making is just a matter of common sense – everyone knows right from wrong.' Discuss.

For this question, you need to decide whether it is true that 'everyone' knows right from wrong and that 'common sense' can resolve moral dilemmas. You might want to explore what 'common sense' means in this context, for example considering whether it refers to an emotional response or to intuition or conscience as a kind of 'inner voice'.

For high marks in AO1, you should demonstrate knowledge and understanding of different views of moral decision-making. You could refer to an emotivist perspective and to intuitionism, and show understanding of thinkers such as Ayer and G.E. Moore.

For AO2, you need to demonstrate your skills in critical evaluation and in offering a well-justified argument. Examples of real-life decision-making might help to clarify the points you make. You should aim for a consistent line of argument that leads to a sound conclusion.

Chapter 2.2

Conscience

Should we follow our conscience?
Does conscience connect us to moral knowledge?
*Is conscience mainly about a desire to please
and a fear of rejection?*

Key Terms

Ratio: the word used by Aquinas to describe reason, something which is placed in every person as a result of their being created in the image of God

Synderesis: for Aquinas, this means to follow the good and avoid the evil, the rule that all precepts follow

Id: for Freud, this is the part of the mind that has instinctive impulses that seek satisfaction in pleasure

Super-ego: Freud uses this word to describe the part of the mind that contradicts the id and uses internalised ideals from parents and society to make the ego behave morally

Ego: Freud uses this word to describe the mediation between the id and the super-ego

Conscientia: this is the name Aquinas gives to the process whereby a person's reason makes moral judgements

Vincible ignorance: this is how Aquinas describes a lack of knowledge for which a person is responsible, and can be blamed

Invincible ignorance: this is how Aquinas describes a lack of knowledge for which a person is not responsible, and cannot be blamed

Specification requirements

*   Aquinas' theological approach
*   Freud's psychological approach

Introduction

How do we determine what is the right thing to do? Do we act and then wait to see if we regret what we have done; wait to see if we feel guilty about what we did? Or do we have a sense that one course of action is right and the other is wrong, even if it is a struggle to do the right thing: 'For I do not do the good I want to do, but the evil I do not want to do—this I keep on doing' (Romans 7:19)? What is the cause of these feelings of guilt and obligation, and this sense of right and wrong?

Apply your knowledge

1. Find out and make a note of these passages where Paul seems to refer to conscience in the New Testament. Try: 1 Corinthians 8:10–12, 2 Corinthians 1:12, Romans 2:15, and Romans 7:15 and 18. To what extent do you agree with him and why?

2. Read these thoughts about conscience. Choose the one you find most stimulating or provocative and explain why you have chosen it:

   a. Martin Luther King Jr, in a speech made on 31 March 1968, said that there are times when you need take a position that is dangerous or unpopular because conscience tells you it is right.

   b. 'Conscience is the inner voice that warns us somebody may be looking' (attributed to Mencken, *A Mencken Chrestomathy*, 1949).

   c. 'The only tyrant I accept in this world is the "still small voice" within me. And even though I have to face the prospect of being a minority of one, I humbly believe I have the courage to be in such a hopeless minority.' (Mahatma Gandhi, *Young India*, 1922).

St Jerome (AD347–420) thought 'the spark of conscience' was the power to distinguish good from evil. Does it matter, then, if we do not follow our conscience? Some have refused to fight for their country because of conscience. Some have carried out acts of civil disobedience (they have broken the law) because of their conscience. Conscience can be disruptive, but it seems also to be a compelling dimension of the human experience that is somehow linked with moral integrity.

This chapter explores two different approaches to the concept of conscience. Thomas Aquinas' approach is theological. Drawing on many threads of ancient thought, Aquinas explains conscience as linking to the God-given gift of *ratio* (reason), moving the mind from knowledge of this world to some higher truth. He also links conscience with *synderesis*, a human inclination or habit towards good. Aquinas holds conscience to be incredibly important and argues that it is essential that a person follows their conscience. Humans may make mistakes, but if they follow their conscience responsibly, they cannot be blamed for their actions. Aquinas' account of conscience influences the official teaching of the Catholic Church and, therefore, many millions of Catholics today.

Sigmund Freud's approach to conscience is psychological. Freud sees all three of the elements of human psyche at work in what is commonly described as conscience: the impulse to seek satisfaction in pleasure (the **id**) on the one hand and the human tendency to act to please those in positions of authority (the **super-ego**) on the other, mediated by the **ego**.

In a speech made on 31 March 1968 Martin Luther King Jr said that people should act according to their conscience, even when their actions could be disliked or dangerous

Aquinas' theological approach to conscience

Ratio

Aquinas did not share the common belief that conscience is a special power or part of our mind that tells us what is right or wrong. He thought that to understand conscience you have to understand *ratio* (reason).

Humans have many special qualities that mark them out from other creatures, including imagination and intellectual ability. Humans can create ideas, pictures, music, stories and machines. They can learn to do complex and sophisticated things, like speaking languages, performing complex mathematical equations and sophisticated dances, and developing impressive levels of physical skill in sports.

St Augustine of Hippo (AD354–430) thought that reason, the intellect and the mind were all one power in human beings, but Aquinas

Thomas Aquinas (1225–74), author of *Summa Theologica*, 1265–74

distinguishes *ratio* (reason) as a separate thing. Aquinas believed that *ratio* distinguishes human beings from other animals. Of all creatures, only humans deliberate over moral matters and *ratio* is, therefore, a fundamental part of the created human being. It is a divine gift from God. The Bible refers to human beings made in the image and likeness of God (Genesis 1:27) and it is therefore, according to Christians, placed in every person.

Ratio is more than simply comprehending things, understanding them or perfecting them. I can comprehend the things I see before me; I can learn to master a particular skill, like singing a song. But this comprehension, this understanding or ability, is not *ratio*. *Ratio* moves us in our thinking from one thing to another. There is something progressive about it. It has some sort of direction linked to judgement. It is an act of working things out.

One ancient philosopher thought that opinions come from our imagination and the mind then judges the truth or error in the opinions to discover what is true. Aquinas, however, was inspired by Paul's letter to Romans (1:20), which suggests that we can move from the knowledge of this world to knowledge of the eternal world. *Ratio* (our ability to reason and to make moral judgements) connects us to the eternal realm, to the divine. People sometimes talk about having a powerful sense of the wrongness or rightness of something and Christians might describe this as a connection to a higher knowledge, some eternal or divine insight.

This means morality is not simply about doing that which is accepted by the many, what is culturally, socially or politically 'normal'. Recalling the crowd condemning Jesus, Pope Benedict XVI reflects on the dangers of following the crowd:

> 66 But at that moment they are caught up in the crowd. They are shouting because everyone else is shouting, and they are shouting the same thing that everyone else is shouting. And in this way, justice is trampled underfoot by weakness, cowardice and fear of the diktat of the ruling mindset. The quiet voice of conscience is drowned out by the cries of the crowd. Evil draws its power from indecision and concern for what other people think. 99
>
> Pope Benedict XVI, 'Good Friday Reflection on the Gospel', 2005

Hannah Arendt, writing about the Holocaust, argues that when the norms of society become profoundly immoral you must reject them. She argued that, in future, we need:

> 66 human beings [to] be capable of telling right from wrong even when all they have to guide them is their own moral judgment, which, moreover, happens to be completely at odds with what they must regard as the unanimous opinion of all these around them. 99
>
> Hannah Arendt, *Eichmann in Jerusalem, a report on the banality of evil*, 1994, pp. 294–96

If, as Zigmunt Bauman argues, morality 'may manifest itself in insubordination towards socially upheld principles, and in an action openly defying social solidarity and consensus' (Bauman, *Modernity and the Holocaust*, 1989, p. 177), then the moral instinct cannot simply be the

Think question

Does morality always come down to following one social convention or another?

Morality may manifest itself in insubordination towards socially upheld principles, and in an action openly defying social solidarity and consensus

reproduction of what is seen in front of you. This is where Aquinas' idea that in *ratio* there is a movement to something else, something higher, matters. It reaches beyond what is socially acceptable to a higher morality.

Synderesis

Aquinas thought that within each human person there is a principle called *synderesis*, that directs us towards good and away from evil. Aquinas noted that there is also sensuality within each of us, which tempts us towards evil, and which was operating in the Garden of Eden when Eve and Adam were tempted to eat the forbidden fruit. But, while he thought that both *synderesis* and sensuality are present in human beings, Aquinas was positive about the outcome of any conflict between them. He had a positive view of human beings' capability to lean towards the good and away from the selfish. *Synderesis* is a habit or a leaning, not a power, and humans can use ratio (the ability to reason and make moral judgements) to cultivate the habit of *synderesis*.

Synderesis is a habit directed towards the good

Go on, taste it

Word of God

Do not eat the fruit of the tree of knowledge

Can we resist temptations and instead form habits that are good?

Conscientia

Although some Christian writers had written about **conscientia** as a kind of spark of moral wisdom, Aquinas has a different understanding. For Aquinas, conscience is an act within a human person (a pronouncement of the mind) arising when the knowledge gained from the application of *ratio* to *synderesis* is applied to something we do. Conscience is 'reason making right decisions' (Thomas Aquinas, *Summa Theologica*, 1265–74, Part I–II); it is not a voice giving us commands.

> 66 Wherefore from this explanation of the name it is clear that conscience is an act. The same is manifest from those things which are attributed to conscience. For conscience is said to witness, to bind, or incite, and also to accuse, torment, or rebuke. 99
>
> Thomas Aquinas, *Summa Theologica*, 1265–74, Part I, Q79

According to Aquinas, therefore, man's reasoning is a kind of movement which begins with the understanding of certain things that are naturally known as immutable principles without investigation. It ends in the intellectual activity by which we make judgements on the basis of those principles.

Ignorance

Aquinas is clear that conscience is binding, even when it is utterly mistaken and directs awful misdeeds. To go against reason is always wrong, for, as Paul says, 'everything that does not come from faith is sin' (Romans 14:23). For Aquinas, coming from faith means coming from conscience, and that means coming from the application of *ratio*. This can sound as though Aquinas was a relativist. But he is not saying that whatever you feel to be good is in fact good and you should do it. He is saying that human beings should do what they think is right, and that human beings can, using reason, discern correctly what is right. He is also acknowledging that human beings make mistakes because the operation of *ratio* involves knowledge, and knowledge may be incomplete or erroneous.

For Aquinas, a responsibly informed action is not blameworthy, even though it may be wrong. A person can honestly do the wrong thing, whilst believing it is the right thing. This does not mean, however, that people are always blameless. A person might, through irresponsibility or even the temptation of sensuality, fail to educate themselves and may consequently act without the necessary knowledge.

There are two kinds of ignorance: **vincible ignorance** and **invincible** ignorance:

• Vincible ignorance is a lack of knowledge for which a person can be held responsible; they ought to have known better. Vincible ignorance is not an excuse and a person who demonstrates vincible ignorance is morally culpable for the acts carried out as a result. They cannot claim that 'conscience' justifies their action.

• Invincible ignorance is a lack of knowledge for which a person is not responsible. It is when a person acts to the best of their knowledge, having done all they can to reasonably inform themselves, but nevertheless gets it wrong and does not act in accordance with what is right and good. Aquinas does not believe that God will condemn humans for invincible ignorance. If they fear God and live according to their conscience, God, in his infinite mercy, will give them salvation even though they err.

Aquinas deliberately uses an unlikely scenario to make the point that human beings must do what their ratio tells them is right. He considers a situation where mistaken reason bids a man to sleep with another man's wife. This is clearly an evil act based on ignorance of the divine law, the commandment prohibiting adultery, that he ought to know. However, if the misjudgement comes about by thinking the woman really is his own wife, and if she wants him, then his will is free from fault. This example seems ludicrous, but Aquinas is deliberately trying to emphasise that a person is not blameworthy for invincible ignorance, for making a genuine mistake, even when the mistake involves breaking the commandment against adultery, an act that the Bible suggests should be punishable by death (Deuteronomy 22:22).

This powerful idea about the duty to follow conscience led a famous Catholic thinker to make another point that sounds curious. Cardinal John Henry Newman, in a letter to the Duke of Norfolk in 1846, wrote:

> **66** Conscience is the aboriginal Vicar of Christ [...] I shall drink – to the Pope, if you please, – still, to Conscience first, and to the Pope afterwards. **99**
>
> Cardinal John Henry Newman, 'Letter to the Duke of Norfolk, Section 5.' *Certain Difficulties felt by Anglicans in Catholic teaching II*, 1885, p. 249

Newman was not suggesting disrespect to the Pope, the highest of all bishops in the Catholic Church, but rather he was stressing that obedience to conscience is more important than anything else. The weight of moral responsibility in life falls on the individual. You should not surrender your moral responsibility to someone else. You cannot evade your duty to it by pleading that you are happy to do as you are told. The plea 'I was just following orders' is not enough.

The Catholic Church, following Aquinas' thinking on conscience, concludes:

> **66** Conscience must be informed and moral judgment enlightened. A well-formed conscience is upright and truthful. It formulates its judgments according to reason, in conformity with the true good willed by the wisdom of the Creator. The education of conscience is indispensable for human beings who are subjected to negative influences and tempted by sin to prefer their own judgment and to reject authoritative teachings. **99**
>
> *Catechism of the Catholic Church*, para 1783

Think question

Should we always follow our conscience?

123

Following conscience is the priority in moral action. Although it seems unlikely that anyone would believe a man who said he believed the woman he slept with was his wife when she was not, the point that is being made is that people make moral decisions when they have imperfect information. This is because human beings are finite creatures and can never have all the facts about a situation available.

People can feel deeply responsible for things they could not have foreseen. This does not mean they should surrender moral responsibility to others. It is not about simply obeying other people's rules. If you practice good habits and try to lean towards the good (*synderesis*), your reason (*ratio*) will help you act well. And if you try to gather knowledge to inform your decisions then your actions cannot be blameworthy (invincible ignorance) even if there are things you do not know. This is *conscientia* in operation.

Aquinas' theological approach to conscience is provocative. It challenges the notion that there is some sort of intuitive voice of morality (coming from God or from somewhere else) telling us what to do. Instead *ratio* (reason), *synderesis* (good habit or 'right' reason) and *conscientia* (moral judgement) are the essential components of moral decision-making. He acknowledges, pragmatically, that people make mistakes, but argues that a person should not be blamed for a genuine mistake arising from invincible ignorance. Note, however, that his basic positive view of human inclination towards the good is tempered by an awareness of the sensual temptations that draw people away from *synderesis*.

Aquinas' approach to conscience can be criticised for failing to take into account the social, political, environmental and economic pressures that affect a person's moral decision-making. Shame and guilt, regrets about past actions and a misplaced sense of duty are just some of the factors that affect our conscience and heavily influence our moral decision-making.

Apply your knowledge

3. Consider the following examples and decide whether they demonstrate vincible ignorance (the person should have known better) or invincible ignorance (the person should not be blamed as they could not have known the truth):

a. A head teacher employs a new teacher who goes on to abuse the children in their care. The head teacher did not request references or carry out criminal record checks before appointing the teacher. It later transpires that the new teacher had been banned from teaching as a result of a previous offence related to the abuse of children.

b. The mother of the birthday girl prepares a birthday tea, which includes chocolates with many different centres. One of the girl's friends becomes ill at the party. She has eaten a chocolate with a nut centre and has an allergy to nuts.

c. An arms manufacturer is approached by a foreign government wanting to buy weapons. The foreign government is currently fighting a war against a neighbouring country. The foreign government promises not to use the weapons against civilians, and the sale is completed. It later transpires that large numbers of civilians were killed by forces using the weapons that were sold.

4. What might a school for good conscience look like and what might a school for bad conscience look like? Consider the elements of *ratio*, *synderesis* and *conscientia* in conscience and the sort of curriculum and ethos each kind of school should have.

5. Do you think factors other than *ratio* (reason), *synderesis* (good habit or 'right' reason) and *conscientia* (moral judgement) might affect how a person feels they ought to act, and impact on 'conscience'? Consider social pressure from friendship groups and social media and parental expectations.

Freud's psychological approach to conscience

Sigmund Freud provides an alternative account of conscience in his books *An Outline of Psychoanalysis* (1940) and *The Ego and the Id* (1923). According to Freud, conscience is not based on rational decision-making, it is a product of psychological factors that influence human beings in ways that may or may not be healthy.

Freud developed the theory of psychosexual development. He argued that psychological development takes place in a series of fixed stages, and each stage is associated with a particular part of the body as the libido (sexual desire) focuses on that part of the body as a source of pleasure, frustration or both. According to Freud, the psychosexual stages of development are as follows:

Sigmund Freud (1856–1939)

- Oral (0–1 years): concerned with sucking and swallowing

- Anal (1–3 years): concerned with withholding and expelling

- Phallic (3–6 years): concerned with masturbation

- Latency (6 to puberty): concerned with the absence of sexual motivation

- Genital (puberty to adulthood): concerned with sexual intercourse.

Freud's theories about the genitals, especially the penis, are controversial. Freud thought that frustration in women was linked to penis envy. He also thought boys suffered from a fear of castration and had deep desires to replace their father so they could have exclusive possession of the mother (a phenomenon known as the Oedipus complex).

Much of Freud's thinking has now been challenged or rejected in the fields of psychiatry and psychoanalysis, in part due to a lack of evidence to support his notions. However, he raised the idea that there is an inner unconscious that interacts with our conscious awareness of our actions, which raises important questions about popular understandings of conscience.

Think question

Are human beings rational actors or are they driven by unconscious, primitive, instinctual desires?

Freud argued that the human mind is made up of the:

- *unconscious mind*: the repressed thoughts and feelings, including primitive desires, wish fulfilment, pleasure and dreams of gratification
- *preconscious mind*: the memories not readily available but accessible

> "The preconscious contains thoughts and feelings that a person is not currently aware of, but [...] It exists just below the level of consciousness, before the unconscious mind. The preconscious is like a mental waiting room, in which thoughts remain until they 'succeed in attracting the eye of the conscious.'"
>
> Sigmund Freud, 1924, *A General Introduction to Psychoanalysis*, trans. Joan Riviere, p. 306

- *conscious mind*: the thoughts a person currently has, which the unconscious mind cannot access.

The three aspects of the human personality (the id, the ego and the superego [sometimes called ego-ideal]) operate at different levels of the mind.

Think question

Could there be a link between the preconscious and unconscious and what philosophers sometimes describe as intuition?

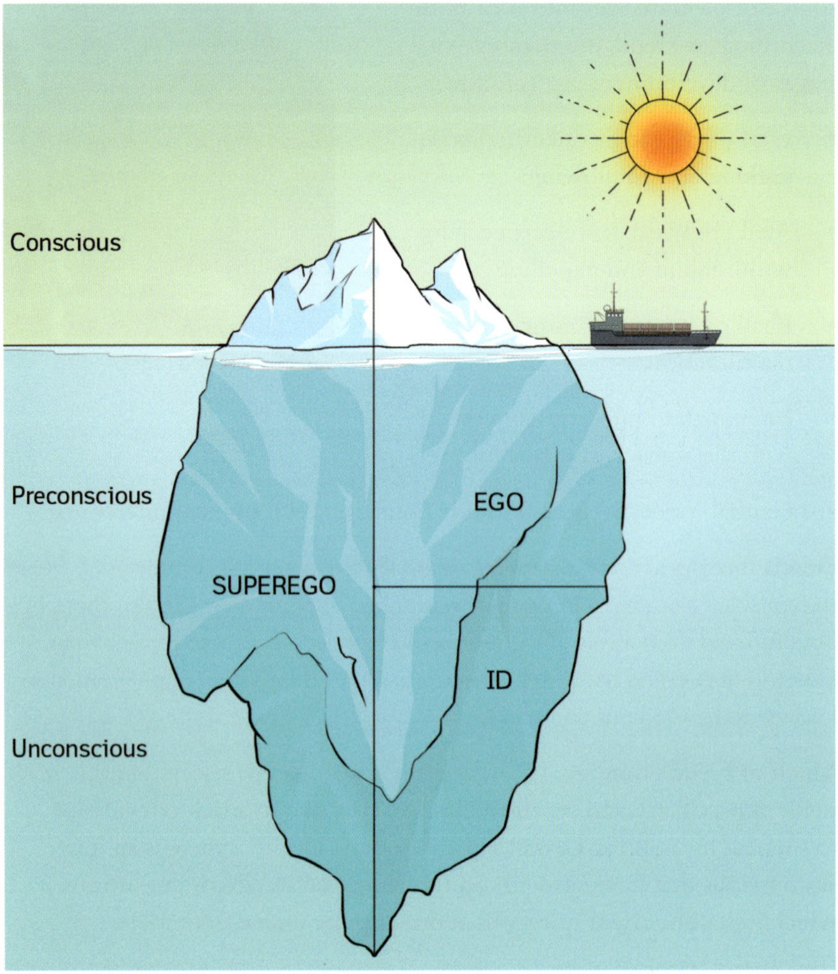

Freud's theory of the mind

The id

The id is an entirely unconscious aspect of personality that is present from birth. It is the central component of personality and it is powerful, instinctive and primitive. It is driven by the pleasure principle; it seeks immediate gratification. If the striving for immediate gratification fails to satisfy all wants, needs and desires, then anxiety and tension result. For example, the desire for food or drink to satisfy hunger or thirst is extremely strong and drives infants to cry when they want food or drink. Freud wrote, of the id:

> 66 It is the dark, inaccessible part of our personality, what little we know of it we have learned from our study of the dreamwork and of course the construction of neurotic symptoms, and most of that is of a negative character and can be described only as a contrast to the ego. We approach the id with analogies: we call it a chaos, a cauldron full of seething excitations. […] It is filled with energy reaching it from the instincts, but it has no organization, produces no collective will, but only a striving to bring about the satisfaction of the instinctual needs subject to the observance of the pleasure principle 99
>
> Sigmund Freud, *New Introductory Lectures on Psychoanalysis*, 1933, pp. 105–6

The id is a 'dark, inaccessible part of our personality' according to Freud

Libido is central to the human personality. Sexual pleasure and sexuality begins in early childhood, not at the onset of puberty as was, and sometimes still is, popularly thought. Children show an early interest in their genitals and form early sexual interests in other people. This is something that is commonly accepted by those who work in child development, even though it may sound a little disconcerting. For Freud, the libido drives the id to desire sexual gratification, and frustration ensues if that desire is not satisfied. When Freud wrote about sexual frustration, he used the term in a broad sense to refer to many different frustrations, including the frustration of not being able to go to the toilet or the frustration of not getting food or drink, as well as sexual frustration.

It is not always possible to satisfy all of the id's desires. For example, food may not be available, and hunger may go unsatisfied. Freud thought the id sought, therefore, to resolve the resulting tension by, for example, imagining food to try and satisfy hunger.

Think question

Are human beings ultimately always driven by desires?

Ego

It is not socially acceptable to seek immediate gratification for all of our desires, i.e. to act on all of the impulses of the id. If we did we would be lustful, greedy and angry. Children, therefore, learn to keep these desires in check. They are taught by their parents and by wider society what is, and is not, socially acceptable and they develop tactics to satisfy their desires in ways that do not disrupt society's rules. This mediation between the id and social

The ego reconciles the id and the demands of social interaction

norms is governed by the ego. The ego is driven by the reality principle. The ego reconciles the id, which otherwise drives us by the pleasure principle, with the demands of social interaction. Freud used the analogy of a horse and its rider to explain the relationship between the id and the ego.

Freud used the analogy of a horse and its rider to explain the relationship between the id and the ego. The rider (the ego) manages and guides the horse (the id)

Delayed gratification is one strategy used by the ego to manage the tensions caused when the id's desires are not immediately satisfied. The pleasurable activity is put off until a time and place when it will not be viewed as inappropriate.

A good conscience can, therefore, be seen as the effective operation of the ego over the id, where desires are achieved in such a way as to avoid censure and punishment from social authorities.

I feel hungry

The ego helps us to moderate our behaviour so that it is socially acceptable. In this way, our ego acts as our conscience

The super-ego (sometimes referred to as ego-ideal)

The super-ego is sometimes referred to as the ego-ideal. It is the last part of the human psyche to develop, around five years of age.

The super-ego is the repository of internalised moral standards of right and wrong that children acquire from their family and society. Early messages from authority figures establish a set of rules. Fulfilling these rules leads to a sense of pride and accomplishment, affirmation, approval and recognition. Failing to live up to these rules leads to criticism, punishment, guilt and remorse. The greater the extent to which the super-ego dominates over the ego, the greater the extent to which a person avoid actions that might result in them breaking the rules. This can lead to a person acting to please the external authority rather than finding a way to manage their desires in the least socially unacceptable way. If they do act on their desires, they will feel guilty. This, in turn, can interrupt the balance between the id and the ego and make it difficult for the ego to manage the id.

According to Freud, religious and moral feelings and conscience are related to the super-ego. When we talk about conscience we are not discerning the moral thing to do, we are feeling guilty because of the super ego. This may have nothing to do with the rightness or wrongness of our actions and everything to do with the feelings arising from the interplay between the id, the ego and the super-ego in our minds.

If the super-ego dominates the ego, it can lead to a person acting to please the external authority

Making sense of Freud's psychological approach to conscience

Barbara Engler and Bernado Carducci provide helpful explanations to make sense of Freud:

> **66** In discussing the id, ego, and super-ego, we must keep in mind that these are not three separate entities with sharply defined boundaries, but rather that they represent a variety of different processes, functions, and dynamics within the person **99**

Barbara Engler, *Personality Theories*, 2009, p. 43

> **66** With the ego placed in the middle, and if all demands are met, the system maintains its balance of psychic power and the outcome is an adjusted personality. If there is imbalance, the outcome is a maladaptive personality. For example, with a dominant id, the outcome could be an impulsive and uncontrollable individual (e.g., a criminal). With an overactive super-ego, the outcome might be an extremely moralistic individual [...]. An overpowering ego could create an individual who is caught up

in reality (e.g., extremely rigid and unable to stray from rules or structure), is unable to be spontaneous (e.g., express id impulses), or lacks a personal sense of what is right and wrong (e.g. somebody who goes by the book). 99

Bernado Carducci, *The Psychology of Personality: Viewpoints, Research, and Applications*, 2009, p. 85

Later psychologists developed Freud's theory with specific reference to conscience. They argued that conscience has a mature and an immature dimension.

The mature dimension is healthy and is identified with the ego's search for integrity. It is concerned with right and wrong, and acts dynamically and responsively on things of value. The mature conscience looks outwards to the world and the future, developing new insights into situations.

66 Conscience is thus [...] the voice of our true selves which summons us [...] to live productively, to develop fully and harmoniously. It is the guardian of our integrity. 99

Erich Fromm, *Man for Himself: An Inquiry into the Psychology of Ethics*, 1947, p. 159

The immature conscience comprises the mass of guilty feelings that humans acquire in their early years as their super-ego develops. These guilty feelings have little to do with the rational importance of the action the person is feeling guilty about. Rather, the immature conscience is acting out a desire to seek approval from others.

Conflict between the mature and immature dimensions of conscience emerges when people make moral decisions. On the one hand, I feel guilty about something because I was brought up to think it was wrong. On the other hand, I no longer believe it is wrong. The immature conscience urges us to conform to the will of the majority in order to live in harmony with other members of our social group, while the mature conscience is autonomous and encourages us to pursue individual self-fulfilment.

Discussing conscience

Comparing Aquinas and Freud

Aquinas and Freud both offer theories to explain conscience, and although one is theological and the other is psychological, both attempts are based on observations of the world. In Aquinas' case, he thought he could reason from his observations of the world. In Freud's case, his observations were based on his patients.

Apply your knowledge

6. Do you think parents have an undue influence on the choices their children make later in life? Can parental influence lead to a sense of guilt, regret or frustration in later life?

7. How might the stages of a person's psychological development in childhood influence their actions later in life?

8. Does the psychological explanation of conscience reduce the significance of people, like Martin Luther King Jr, who make conscious decisions to face personal danger because it is the right thing to do?

See Chapter 2.1 of the AS and Year 1 book for more about Aquinas' natural law.

On guilt

One way of thinking about guilt is that it is the conscience telling a person they have done wrong; it is the price of committing a sin. However, both Aquinas and Freud add different reflections to this simple account.

According to Aquinas, guilt is the gnawing sense that an action is not good, it is not in accordance with divine law. *Synderesis* indicates that things are not right, and guilt is the result. It would be wrong, however, to see Aquinas as advocating a tally system. He is not arguing that guilt registers sins that must be accounted for and God acts as some kind of sin accountant going through each instance of guilt and then making a judgement based on the overall 'score'. Guilt is not a mechanism for balancing the books. Rather, it helps God to restore a proper relationship with a person. The consequences of sin are damaging because they disrupt a person's relationship with God. For reconciliation to occur, guilt must be extinguished and good relations must be re-established. For Aquinas, it is God's grace that expels guilt from a person.

When a person makes a moral mistake through no fault of their own, and is not blameworthy, then they should not feel guilty. Despite their great sense of sinfulness, their guilt is misplaced because they are blameless. Misplaced feelings of guilt like this can disrupt a person's inner relationship with God.

Freud's approach to guilt is different, although there is a similarity with Aquinas in the disruption it causes. For Freud, guilt is a result of internal conflict in the mind; the struggle between what you desire and what you feel you should or should not do: 'The tension between the demands of conscience and the actual demands of the ego is experienced as a sense of guilt' (Freud, *The Ego and the Id,* 1923, p. 37). For Freud the inner turmoil of guilt can cause a person to do bad things. It is not, therefore, a consequence of wrongdoing, but a cause of future wrongdoing. Paul Strohm suggests Freud draws on Nietzsche:

....

66 Conscience [...] is not, as you may believe, 'the voice of God in man'; it is the instinct of cruelty, which turns inwards once it is unable to discharge itself outwardly. 99

> Friedrich Nietzsche, 'Why I Write Such Excellent Books',
> *Ecce Homo,* quoted by Strohm in *Conscience:*
> *a very short introduction,* 2011, p. 64

....

> **Think question**
>
> Is it possible for a person to feel guilt or shame for their actions in a way that is unjustified?

Freud himself said:

> 66 The more a man controls his aggressiveness, the more intense become the aggressive tendencies of the ego-ideal [super-ego] against his ego 99
>
> Sigmund Freud, *The Ego and the Id*, 1923, p. 53

Some later psychologists have distinguished between guilt and shame, suggesting that inner conflict can produce shame and it is shame that can be damaging to a person. Shame may be associated with things unconnected to moral actions, such as when a person loses their job through no fault of their own and feels ashamed to be unemployed, or a victim of rape feels a sense of shame and blames themselves, when it is the rapist who is to blame.

Both shame and guilt seem to be present in the story of the Garden of Eden in Genesis, a story that informed Aquinas' thinking about guilt and may also be interpreted from a Freudian perspective:

> 66 When the woman saw that the fruit of the tree was good for food and pleasing to the eye, and also desirable for gaining wisdom, she took some and ate it. She also gave some to her husband, who was with her, and he ate it. Then the eyes of both of them were opened, and they realized that they were naked; so they sewed fig leaves together and made coverings for themselves.
>
> Then the man and his wife heard the sound of the Lord God as he was walking in the garden in the cool of the day, and they hid from the Lord God among the trees of the garden. But the Lord God called to the man, 'Where are you?'
>
> He answered, 'I heard you in the garden, and I was afraid because I was naked; so I hid.' 99
>
> Genesis 3:6–10, New International Version

Both Freud and Aquinas see the link between guilt and desire. For Freud this was exclusively sexual, for Aquinas it embraced all sensual desires. For Aquinas, Adam and Eve gave in to sensual pleasures when they were tempted by the fruit of knowledge. As a result, they experienced guilt when they realised they were naked and had done wrong. From a Freudian perspective, the story illustrates the tension between desire for the fruit of knowledge encouraged by the id and then the sense of guilt at having done something that the authority figure (God) prohibited as a manifestation of the super-ego.

On the presence or absence of God within the workings of the conscience and super-ego

For Aquinas, knowledge in this world leads the human being to a higher knowledge, to the divine goodness of God's law. God has created human beings with *ratio* and *synderesis*. *Conscientia* is explained by this connection with God and God's law. In contrast, Freud makes no reference to God in his approach to conscience, and links religion to the kind of social authority that can cause the super-ego to become overactive.

However, the existence of God need not invalidate the psychological observations that Freud makes. Parallels can be drawn between Freud's description of a healthy personality, with the id, ego and super-ego in balance, and Aquinas' belief in the effective operation of reason and the cultivation of good character and good habits that it leads to.

Likewise, the psychological forces at work within a person need not invalidate the belief in reason or the possibility that reason connects to a divine law. You could even argue that imbalances in the relationship between the id, the ego and the super-ego interrupt the process of reasoning.

On the process of moral decision-making

For Freud, moral choices are choices that strike a balance between a person's desires and socially acceptable behaviour. For Aquinas, moral decision-making involves the application of *ratio*, *synderesis* and *conscientia* to bring about decisions that are good and not evil. Aquinas' approach sounds exclusively philosophical when compared to Freud's psychological account. Certainly there is no place for a connection to the divine in Freud's approach. However, Aquinas was aware of the presence of human emotions and the disruptive potency of what he called sensuality, which could direct human decisions away from the good. Both, therefore, have a sense of the possibility that decisions can be better or worse.

Aquinas was writing in the thirteenth century, long before the behavioural sciences and the social sciences emerged and began to study human behaviour, and human society and social relationships. Moral decision-making is now framed by many more insights than the theological ones that Aquinas explored when thinking about conscience. Perhaps, therefore, he is using theology to try to answer questions that, today, we would draw on other disciplines to help us answer.

A similar observation can also be made of Freud's approach, in that later psychologists have developed different thinking around moral decision-making and the interplay between the id, the ego and the super-ego. For instance, some think that, like the id, the ego is also present from birth and is, therefore, influenced by nature as well as by nurture. Criticisms have been made about Freud's reliance on his discredited theory of psychosexual development.

Think question

Does modern scientific understanding of human behaviour challenge both Freud and Aquinas?

Apply your knowledge

" Deep within his conscience man discovers a law which he has not laid upon himself but which he must obey. Its voice, ever calling him to love and to do what is good and to avoid evil, sounds in his heart at the right moment. [...] For man has in his heart a law inscribed by God. [...] His conscience is man's most secret core and his sanctuary. There he is alone with God whose voice echoes in his depths.

Moral conscience, present at the heart of the person, enjoins him at the appropriate moment to do good and to avoid evil. It also judges particular choices, approving those that are good and denouncing those that are evil. It bears witness to the authority of truth in reference to the supreme Good to which the human person is drawn, and it welcomes the commandments. When he listens to his conscience, the prudent man can hear God speaking.

Conscience is a judgment of reason whereby the human person recognises the moral quality of a concrete act that he is going to perform, is in the process of performing, or has already completed. In all he says and does, man is obliged to follow faithfully what he knows to be just and right. It is by the judgment of his conscience that man perceives and recognizes the prescriptions of the divine law:

Conscience is a law of the mind; yet [Christians] would not grant that it is nothing more; I mean that it was not a dictate, nor conveyed the notion of responsibility, of duty, of a threat and a promise. [...] [Conscience] is a messenger of him, who, both in nature and in grace, speaks to us behind a veil, and teaches and rules us by his representatives. Conscience is the aboriginal Vicar of Christ. "

Catechism of the Catholic Church, paras 1776–8

9. Identify the parts of the text that link directly to Aquinas' approach to conscience.

10. Identify where precisely Freud would want to add a different or contrasting perspective.

Is conscience linked to reason or the unconscious mind?

For Aquinas, *ratio* (reason) is the key factor in moral decision-making. *Ratio* helps a person to cultivate *synderesis* (good habit or 'right' reason) and move from knowledge to a moral decision; *conscienta* is a person's reason making moral judgements. Humans are reasonable beings (or they can be if well informed), and operation of their conscience is, therefore, a reason-oriented process. According to Aquinas, conscience is linked to and flows from reason.

In contrast, for Freud, conscience is not a conscious reason-oriented process. It is not about being well informed and trying to do things that lean towards the good because there is an unconscious and a preconscious dimension to the operation of the mind when it makes moral decisions. It will not matter that a person has the right knowledge and can use their reason to make a good moral judgement if their unconscious and preconscious mind leads them to act immorally. The interplay between the id, the ego and super-ego produce an account of morality that, therefore, has little to do with reason.

Despite the fact that many of Freud's theories have never been proven, psychoanalysts and psychiatrists continue to take the existence of the unconscious mind very seriously. Freud's theories, therefore, leave us needing a new explanation for human moral behaviour.

Psychological and behavioural sciences apply reason when they try to understand how factors such as environment, upbringing and socio-economic background affect human instincts and choices. Therefore, perhaps reason is a tool that human beings use to make sense of moral responses, and it helps people to understand and explain the moral choices they make.

Aquinas' idea that conscience is directly linked to reason is not accepted by all Christian thinkers. St Augustine of Hippo thought that conscience is the intuitive voice of God directing people to God's law in their hearts. Others have suggested conscience is a product of imagination or of opinions, and that there is divine influence over conscience through these human capacities. Perhaps, therefore, there is a spiritual dimension to conscience to which neither Aquinas nor Freud give credit.

Does conscience exist or is it an umbrella term covering various factors involved in moral decision-making?

There seems to be a popular feeling that conscience matters, however it is understood. People often refer to 'following their conscience' when they explain why they commit significant acts. Activists in many political movements (including the Suffragette movement in late nineteenth- and early twentieth-century Britain, the Black Consciousness Movement in twentieth-century South Africa, the Civil Rights movement in twentieth-century America, and environmental campaigners in the twenty-first century) resort to civil disobedience, to breaking the law on a point of principle, in order to change the status quo. People who refuse to serve in the armed forces because killing is against their principles are called 'conscientious objectors'. There is a sense that moral integrity is linked to conscientious action. The concept of conscience feels important because of the desire to explain moral action as something principled and arising from integrity. But is there one uniform concept of conscience or is it a term than encompasses lots of factors involved in decision-making?

While some thinkers, such as Augustine, argue that conscience exists as part of the human body, a message from God to the brain, some sort of intuition or insight, neither Aquinas nor Freud offer an account of conscience as a simple, disconnected thing. They both believed that multiple factors influence the moral decision-making process. For Aquinas, conscience involves *ratio* (reason), *synderesis* (good habit or 'right' reason) and *conscientia* (moral judgement), For Freud, conscience involves the operation of the id, the ego and super-ego at different levels of the mind.

Apply your knowledge

> ❝ The term 'the unconscious' is actually a mystification (even though one might use it for reasons of convenience, as I am guilty of doing in these pages). There is no such thing as the unconscious; there are only experiences of which we are aware, and others of which we are not aware, that is, of which we are unconscious. If I hate a man because I am afraid of him, and if I am aware of my hate but not of my fear, we may say that my hate is conscious and that my fear is unconscious; still my fear does not lie in that mysterious place: 'the' unconscious. ❞

Erich Fromm, *Beyond the Chains of Illusion*: My *Encounter with Marx and Freud*, 1980, p. 93

11. How does Fromm disagree with Freud?

12. How might Aquinas' thinking be integrated with Fromm's thinking?

13. Do you think conscience can be better explained by psychology, theology or spirituality? Explain your answer.

Yet it can be argued that there are many more factors that influence moral decision-making, including culture, environment, genetic predisposition and education. Conscience is not a simple, definable thing at all. This need not mean that conscience, conscientiousness and a sense of integrity do not matter, but rather the concept of 'conscience' is an umbrella term for a wide range of factors that influence decision-making and how humans feel about the decisions that they make.

Apply your knowledge

14. Marie has just started university and is living independently for the first time. Below is some information about Marie. Consider what Aquinas and Freud might make of each statement and how it might influence Marie's conscience and her moral decision-making.

   a. She had strict religious parents and a conservative upbringing.

   b. At an early age, she had a best friend at school who died tragically in a swimming accident.

   c. Her parents' business folded when she was a teenager and the family went through a period of being very poor.

   d. She experimented with soft drugs at school.

   e. She suffers from anxiety attacks and worries about her body shape.

   f. Her parents have high expectations of her and have taught her that she must work hard in order to do well in life.

   g. She has had two serious but not long-lasting relationships, neither of which her parents approved of, one with a boy and one with a girl.

   h. She has a tumultuous relationship with her father and, when she left for university, she was not on speaking terms with him.

   i. Her parents wanted her to do a Business Studies degree but she chose to study Performing Arts instead.

Learning support

Points to remember

» It would be easy to place Aquinas and Freud in opposition to one another and write essays that seek to show how one is correct and the other incorrect. However, it is important to remember that these thinkers are separated in time by over five centuries and had different sources of knowledge available to them. Both also try to give an account of conscience that is more sophisticated than the simple 'voice of God' explanation.

» Both Aquinas and Freud identified different factors that affect moral decision-making. These include *ratio*, the knowledge available and the extent to which a person inclines towards *synderesis* or sensuality in the case of Aquinas and the id, the ego and the super-ego in the case of Freud.

» Both Aquinas and Freud had a sense that developmental factors influence behaviour. For Freud, these were the psychosexual developments of the libido and the way it manages pleasure and frustration. For Aquinas, these were to do with the education of the conscience, the encouragement of good habits.

» The key area of divergence between Aquinas and Freud is whether conscience is, or is not, a product of conscious rational thought. Aquinas argues it is. Freud argues the preconscious and the unconscious play a significant role in moral decision-making. Despite this divergence, both thinkers believed that human beings can be badly affected by internal conflict and this can lead to bad decision-making. Freud saw how destructive internal conflict can be for a person, and Aquinas argued that human beings are happiest once reconciled to God.

Enhance your learning

» *Man for Himself: An Inquiry into the Psychology of Ethics* (1947) by Erich Fromm is an interesting account of psychology and ethics, See Chapter 4, part 2.

» You can read more about Freud in the *Internet Encyclopedia of Philosophy*: www.iep.utm.edu/freud.

» *The Ego and the Id* (German: *Das Ich und das Es*), a prominent paper by Sigmund Freud, is a study of the human psyche and Freud's theories of the id, ego and super-ego. It was first published in 1923.

» Aquinas' magisterial work *Summa Theologica* (1265–74) is available online in a number of places, including: www.newadvent.org/summa. Part 1.1, Q79 deals with a discussion of *ratio*, *synderesis* and *conscientia*.

» Paul Strohm's *Conscience: A Very Short Introduction* (2011) is an excellent short book on conscience. Chapter 1 offers a very good discussion of the background to the concept of conscience, including pagan and Christian elements of conscience, and Chapter 3 deals with criticism of theories of conscience, including Freud's theory of conscience.

» Sigmund Freud's *An Outline of Psychoanalysis* (1940) is the summary of his work and includes his thinking on the id, the ego and the super-ego.

Practice for exams

At A level, essay questions invite you to demonstrate your knowledge and understanding of factual material (AO1) and also your critical ability in putting forward a coherent, balanced argument (AO2). You should aim to write essays that are persuasive responses to the question throughout, rather than writing a lot of description and then tacking an opinion on at the end of each paragraph.

'Freud's understanding of conscience in terms of the super-ego is convincing.' Discuss.

This question invites a critical evaluation of Freud's opinions of the conscience.

For high marks in AO1, you need to demonstrate knowledge and understanding of the thinking of Freud in relation to the super-ego, explaining how it fits in with his views about the unconscious. If, in your argument, you plan to compare Freud with any other thinkers such as Aquinas, then you can score well in AO1 by giving accurate accounts of their thinking too.

For AO2 marks, you need to explain why you think Freud's account of the conscience is convincing or unconvincing. You might find some aspects of it more convincing than others. Make sure that the reasons for your opinion are clear and lead to a well-justified conclusion.

'Conscience is the voice of God working within us.' Discuss.

For this question, you need to consider the idea that the conscience is a God-given faculty and that it is a means by which God lets us know what is right and wrong.

To demonstrate knowledge and understanding and gain a high mark in AO1, you should show that you understand the views of different thinkers, such as Aquinas and Freud, and the reasons why they think that conscience does or does not come from God. You probably know quite a lot about these thinkers, so you will need to be selective in the examples you use in order to answer the question directly.

In your argument for AO2 marks, aim to support your opinions with reasoned argument rather than simply stating what you believe, as this will be more persuasive for your reader.

Chapter 2.3

Sexual ethics

Should sex require more than consent between those concerned?

Why should sex be exclusive within marriage?

Does sexual orientation have any bearing on the structure of modern marriage?

Key Terms

Cohabitation: an unmarried couple living together in a sexually active relationship. Sometimes known pejoratively as 'living in sin'

Consent: freely agreeing to engage in sexual activity with another person

Premarital sex: sex before marriage

Extramarital sex: sex beyond the confines of marriage, usually used to describe adulterous sex

Betrothal: traditionally the exchange of promises, which in earlier times marked the point at which sex was permitted

Consummation: an act of sexual intercourse that indicates, in some traditions, the finalisation of the marriage

Exclusive: a commitment to be in a sexual relationship with a person to the exclusion of all others. This is the opposite of an 'open marriage' or a 'casual relationship'

Homosexuality: sexual attraction between people of the same sex

Specification requirements

Consideration of the following areas of sexual ethics:

- premarital and extramarital sex
- homosexuality

The influence of developments in religious beliefs and practices on debates about the morality, legality and tolerability of these areas of sexual ethics

Application of the following theories to these areas of sexual ethics:

- natural law
- situation ethics
- Kantian ethics
- utilitarianism

For more about Freud's theory of psychosexual development, see Chapter 2.2.

Introduction

Sexual pleasure and satisfaction are often presented as the holy grail. They are used in advertising to sell products and often seen as a necessary ingredient in films. Some, such as Sigmund Freud, even argue that human sexuality is the defining feature of our personalities. As they say, sex is everywhere! Consequently, there are a multitude of personal moral issues and debates surrounding sexual ethics.

Two groups of ethical questions are considered in this chapter. The first is the extent to which sex should be connected to marriage. What are the ethical issues raised by sex before or outside marriage? Should sexual relationships be formally recognised by a public, legal marriage? Are sexual relationships a matter of law, of social norm or personal preference? The second is whether the only moral sexual relationships are heterosexual relationships. Are homosexual sexual relationships as moral as heterosexual relationships? Or are they immoral?

Social norms and laws about these questions have changed considerably in Western countries in recent decades. This is expressed through radical shifts in public attitudes to what is acceptable, and also through changes to the law. In the UK, **cohabitation** and having children outside of marriage is no longer stigmatised, while civil partnerships and same-sex marriages are now legal.

Religion remains a potent factor in debates about sexual ethics. Sex is referred to throughout the Bible. In the Hebrew scriptures, Abraham sires children with his servant Hagar and his wife Sarah (Genesis 16); in the face of a devastating famine, Ruth uses sex to seduce a landowner (Ruth 1–3); and adultery is prohibited in the Commandments. The New Testament contains similar problematic sexual dilemmas, including a woman who is in uncertain relationships with more than five men (John 4), a women condemned to stoning for adultery (John 8:1–11) and a question about divorce (Matthew 19:3–12/Mark 10:2–12). Paul is worried about sexual morality, especially fornication (sex between people who are not married to each other), in his First Letter to the Corinthians (1 Corinthians 6:9, 6:18, 7:2).

Many debates about sexual morality contain restatements or rejections of religious beliefs about marriage and sexual acts. This is true even when the debate itself does not have a religious basis. In a more secular world, society seems to have selected which principles of ethical sex it wants to keep from the past, and which it now wishes to set aside. For example, **consent** and exclusivity have become common shared values, but homosexual relationships are not viewed as immoral in the way they once commonly were, and legal and social controls around sex before marriage have been largely abandoned in liberal Western society.

Think question

In an age when Christian principles are being challenged by liberal thinking, what is right in terms of sex before marriage?

Premarital and extramarital sex

In ethics, **premarital sex** and **extramarital sex** raise questions around cohabitation (living in sin) and consensual sexual intercourse between people who are not married to one another (the sin of fornication). They relate to questions of divorce, adultery and remarriage, in that the Catholic Church believes marriage is indissoluble, so sex with someone other than your spouse after a divorce is considered to be adultery and fornication.

Premarital sex

Premarital sex refers to sex before marriage. It can happen on a casual basis, as part of a short relationship or as part of longer relationship. Sex before marriage and cohabitation has grown steadily. In the 1960s, fewer than 1 in 20 UK couples cohabited, but that has increased to more than half of all couples today. The introduction of the contraceptive pill in the 1960s has been credited with driving this social change, as removing the fear of unwanted pregnancy diminished the need to contain sex within marriage. In the 1960s, cohabitation commonly meant a short period when a couple lived together before they married or went their separate ways. Today cohabitation can occur as a long-lasting alternative to marriage, with or without children.

Historical research reveals findings that may surprise modern readers. In Anglo-Saxon England, spouses pledged themselves to one another in a **betrothal** ceremony, after which they could have sex, and the formal marriage followed later. In eighteenth-century England, half of brides were pregnant at their marriage ceremony, with sexual relations beginning after the betrothal but before the marriage. Marriage was expected to follow after betrothal, but women were vulnerable to abandonment. In Britain, the rise in the importance of female virginity at marriage was not just about Christian tradition. It was also due to the fact that male members of the British aristocracy wanted to know that the children born to their wives (i.e. the children who would become their heirs) were in fact their own.

Christian teachings traditionally view sex before, or outside of, marriage as a sin. The mainstream Christian understanding of sex places it firmly in the context of a bond of marriage between two people. Sexual intercourse in any other circumstance is, consequently, wrong. It is argued that premarital sex indicates a lack of moral discipline and poses a threat to the institutions of marriage and family. The community dimension of marriage is undermined by the lack of commitment inherent in cohabitation; cohabitation is seen as less stable than marriage.

These mainstream Christian views are informed by biblical references to marriage. In the following quote from Genesis, the Hebrew word 'cleave' is translated as 'become one flesh':

Christian teachings traditionally view sex before, or outside of, marriage as a sin

Think question

Does cohabitation show a lack of moral discipline, or does it show two people carefully considering their compatibility before making the commitment of marriage?

> ❝ That is why a man leaves his father and mother and is united to his wife, and they become one flesh. ❞

> Genesis 2:24, New International Version

This emphasises the spiritual, emotional, social and sexual purposes of marriage. Marriage and sexual union are part of God's plan. For the Catholic Church, the miracle at the wedding at Cana (John 2:1–11) in the New Testament confirms God's approval of marriage as a good thing and a sacrament, a sign of God's presence in the world (*Catechism of the Catholic Church*, para 1613). Marriage brings with it many benefits:

> ❝ This love is above all fully human, a compound of sense and spirit. It is not, then, merely a question of natural instinct or emotional drive. It is also, and above all, an act of the free will, whose trust is such that it is meant not only to survive the joys and sorrows of daily life, but also to grow, so that husband and wife become in a way one heart and one soul, and together attain their human fulfillment. ❞

> Pope Paul VI, *Humanae Vitae*, 1968, Chapter 9

However, Churches adopt differing approaches to the practical application of these traditional messages. The Catholic Church treats any act of sexual intercourse outside marriage as a 'free union', in which a couple have refused 'to give juridical and public form to a liaison involving sexual intimacy' (*Catechism of the Catholic Church*, para 2390). This exhibits an inability to make a long-term commitment, and is condemned as an offence against marriage.

> ❝ Some today claim a 'right to a trial marriage' where there is an intention of getting married later. However firm the purpose of those who engage in premature sexual relations may be, 'the fact is that such liaisons can scarcely ensure mutual sincerity and fidelity in a relationship between a man and a woman, nor, especially, can they protect it from inconstancy of desires or whim.' Carnal union is morally legitimate only when a definitive community of life between a man and woman has been established. Human love does not tolerate 'trial marriages.' It demands a total and definitive gift of persons to one another. ❞

> *Catechism of the Catholic Church*, para 2391

For the Catholic Church, premarital sex does not express fidelity, exclusivity and commitment and, consequently, it does not tolerate sex before marriage. People who engage in premarital sex are committing a grave sin and are excluded from sacramental communion until they have reconciled with a morally correct way of living.

Some Christian leaders have advocated recognising premarital sex differently, as a progression towards marriage rather than a rejection of marriage. The Church of England published a book, *Something to Celebrate: Valuing Families in Church and Society* (1995), in which the authors stated:

> 66 The wisest and most practical way forward therefore may be for Christians both to hold fast to the centrality of marriage and at the same time to accept that cohabitation is, for many people, a step along the way towards that fuller and more complete commitment. Such an approach has much to be said in its favour. 99
>
> General Synod Board for Social responsibility, *Something to Celebrate: Valuing Families in Church and Society,* 1995, p. 115

This was a response to a recognition that an increasing number of members of congregations were cohabiting. However, the suggestion was opposed by more conservative Church of England Christians in General Synod.

How Christian Churches respond to the growing norm of premarital sex is a difficult question. Some are trying to find an alternative to simply ignoring it or rejecting people who cohabit. Adrian Thatcher argues that Christians who believe all pre-ceremonial sex is immoral have wrongly assumed that the ceremony is a requirement of marriage (*Marriage After Modernity: Christian Marriage in Postmodern Times*, 1999, Chapter 4). Thatcher suggests there is a long tradition that locates the key point of commitment between two people as betrothal, when promises are made, not the marriage ceremony which happens later although a breach in betrothal was viewed as incredibly serious in the Christian tradition.

In Catholic thought, the sacrament of marriage is conferred by the couple onto each other, not by the priest or by the attending public; the couple marry each other. Nevertheless, the question is whether a commitment is made at betrothal. Betrothal did have a strong expectation of commitment, unlike casual cohabitation.

Think question

Should Christian Churches introduce a service of betrothal to mark the promise that two people make to each other?

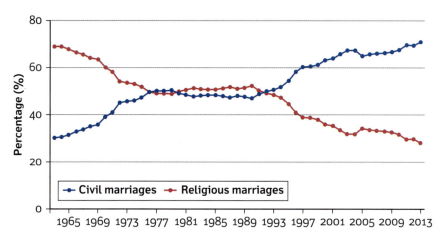

Marriages in England and Wales by type of ceremony, 1963–2013
Office for National Statistics

In Western countries, social attitudes and laws do not follow the Church's moral teachings. For instance, civil marriages now outnumber religious marriages in the UK and people wait longer before getting married, during which time cohabitation is increasingly normal.

Christianity seems to be taking two approaches to responding to this reality. One rejects the new social norms and asserts traditional sexual rules and binds members to follow them, even when the law does not. Another reinterprets sexual acts previously decried as sinful, and looks for ways to encourage a more positive engagement with people who are engaged in premarital sex, beyond excluding them from membership. This reinterpretation does not go so far as accepting casual sexual relationships outside marriage per se, but rather sees premarital sex as a step in the process towards marriage.

Extramarital sex

Extramarital sex can be understood in two ways: when a married person has sex with someone other than his or her spouse, or when a single person has sex with a married person.

Sex is associated exclusively with married relationships in Christian thought, and marriage binds a couple in a lifelong relationship. The Catholic Church holds that a valid marriage cannot be dissolved. It forbids divorce between two baptised Christians in a marriage that has been **consummated**, and it excludes from communion those who have been divorced and remarried. However, since the time of Vatican II Council (1962–5), there has been an in increase in the number of annulments (declarations that a true marriage was never present in the beginning), which has led some to argue that annulment is a tacit form of divorce.

Since the Reformation in the sixteenth century, Protestant Churches have, to different degrees, permitted divorce in exceptional circumstances. The Catholic Church holds that anyone remarrying after a divorce is having extramarital sex with their new husband or wife. The Church of England is more divided on the matter, but in theory it still forbids divorce.

> ### Think question
>
> Should Christianity learn from society on matters of premarital sex, or should society learn from Christianity? Might both learn from each other?

Marriage existed before Judaism and Christianity. However, from its earliest days, the Christian Church began the process of gradually claiming jurisdiction over marriage. The New Testament and other early Church decrees contain teachings that warn Christians away from adultery but allow remarriage after a spouse has been adulterous. In the tenth century, the Church assumed more power over the law of marriage and, henceforth, Christians were obligated to receive a Christian blessing when they married. The Catholic Church came to view marriage as a sacrament, and Protestant thinkers came to see it as a holy estate (a holy kind of relationship).

In *Sex, Gender and Christian Ethics* (1996), Lisa Sowle Cahill argues that Christianity's stance against divorce originated in an attempt to limit men's ability to manipulate marriage, women and children in the interests of power and wealth. Amongst the medieval tribes of western Europe, marriage was contracted in three ways: capture (abduction and rape), purchase and consent. Wealthy, powerful men had concubines (a concubine is a lower status woman who lives with a man as if she is his wife) as well as wives. Men having long-term relationships with several women at the same time (polygamy) was common. Adultery was a crime that virtually only women were accused of, and divorce was exclusively a male prerogative. In this context, the Church's ban on adultery made it impossible for men to have concubines, and the ban on divorce stopped men abandoning women. Arguably, the Christianisation of marriage made marriage more just, particularly for women, curtailing extramarital sex and the consequent negative outcomes for women and children.

As society becomes ever more secular once again, social attitudes towards sex are increasingly diverse. However, a study published in *The Lancet* in 2013, as part of the third National Survey of Sexual Attitudes and Lifestyles, reported that the number of people having sex under the age of 16 had not increased over the previous 25 years, and the proportion of people who disapproved of non-**exclusive** marriage (adultery) had increased amongst men (from 45 per cent to 63 per cent) and women (from 53 per cent to 70 per cent). The UK population is, therefore, reporting a more conservative attitude to some traditional aspects of sex and ethics, in particular around commitment and exclusivity in marriage – values that are central to Christian understandings of marriage.

A second area in which prevailing social attitudes and Christian beliefs coincide is around consent. Consent has long been an important factor in Christian marriage. Christian teaching maintains that marriage must be freely and willingly entered into. For instance, couples preparing for marriage are asked separately by a Catholic priest to confirm they are entering into the marriage freely. Consent is also a key concern in contemporary society. Sexual offences such as rape and forced marriage are commonly viewed as wrong.

The Christian Church gradually claimed jurisdiction over marriage

See Chapter 3.3 for a discussion of the traditional Christian teaching on the roles of men and women in the family and society.

Think question

Do sexual relationships need to be regulated to protect people?

Chapter 3.5 discusses secularisation in detail.

Apply your knowledge

1. How far, and to what extent, if at all, are each of the following values significant in relation to sexual intercourse: mutual consent, permanence, promise, pleasure, exclusivity.

2. Consider the following viewpoints. Make a Christian case for each of them and decide which is most compelling and why:

   a. Sex is permissible between freely consenting adults without any other condition.

   b. Sex is permissible after a couple are betrothed, but on the condition that marriage follows at some point.

   c. Sex is permissible only after a public marriage ceremony.

3. People who are married are not free to have sex with anyone other than their husband or wife because they have bound themselves to one person. Explore the importance of promise-keeping and exclusivity in marriage. Is it ever moral to have adulterous sex?

4. If churches recognised betrothal through a formal service, could sexual intercourse that takes place after the betrothal but before the formal marriage ceremony be considered in keeping with the Christian tradition?

Homosexuality

In recent decades, Western liberal democracies have witnessed a radical change in the legal frameworks relating to homosexuality

In recent decades, Western liberal democracies have witnessed a radical change in the legal frameworks relating to **homosexuality**. Sex between men was a crime in the UK in the first half of the twentieth century, and homosexuality was considered a mental illness for which appalling treatments were prescribed. In 1957, the Wolfenden Report recommended that homosexuality be decriminalised and Parliament implemented the recommendation by passing the Sexual Offences Act 1967, which made it legal for men aged 21 or over to have sex. The age of consent was lowered to 18 in 1994, and lowered to 16 (in line with the age of consent for heterosexual sex) in 2001. The first same-sex marriages in England and Wales took place on 29 March 2014, giving same-sex couples who choose to marry the same social recognition and legal protections long afforded to men and women in heterosexual marriages. Equality and human rights laws also protect people on the grounds of their sexual orientation. In recent years, this more tolerant approach has been extended to transsexual and transgender people, and people who seek not to be defined by binary gender distinctions.

Changes in the legal landscape have not always been mirrored by changes in social attitudes, however. The 1999 nail-bombing of a gay bar in Soho, London, illustrated the extent of the hostility felt by some towards the homosexual community, and the continuing existence of hate crimes against homosexuals and others in the LGBTQ+ communities is an indication of some social resistance to change. Some areas of public life, such as professional football, have been less than tolerant of homosexuality. This reflects an underlying cultural prejudice against homosexuality. And, as the British population becomes more diverse as a result of migration from parts of the world with strikingly different moral attitudes towards homosexuality, there is still a marked plurality to society's response to homosexuality: is it a socially acceptable moral norm or is it immoral?

Think question

Is equality the most important ethical principle in sexual ethics?

Christianity and homosexuality

Traditional Christian teaching views homosexuality as wrong for several reasons. There is no possibility of life arising from the sexual union of same-sex couples, so it is contrary to natural law and/or is seen to undermine the traditional idea of Christian marriage as being between a man and a woman for, in part, the purposes of bringing new life into the world. Same-sex marriages have not been permitted in many Churches and so any kind of homosexual sex has taken place outside marriage – which is sinful, just as all other forms of sex outside marriage are sinful.

There are specific scriptural sources that imply a divine command against sex acts between men. Leviticus says, 'Do not have sexual relations with a man as one does with a woman; that is detestable' (Leviticus 18:22) and it is punishable by death (Leviticus 20:13). Deuteronomy 23:17–18 prohibits the practice of shrine prostitution, where men and women are available to have sex with men for money. In Genesis 19:4–11, God destroys the city of Sodom, where licentious sexual acts, including male same-sex acts, were taking place. The story is often interpreted as showing God's displeasure with homosexuality.

In addition, Paul's letters have influenced Christian teaching. In Romans 1:21–31, St Paul writes of people giving themselves over to 'shameful lusts', the product of a 'depraved mind':

> 66 Even their women exchanged natural sexual relations for unnatural ones. In the same way the men also abandoned natural relations with women and were inflamed with lust for one another. Men committed shameful acts with other men 99
>
> Romans 1:26–27, New International Version

And, in a letter to the Corinthians Paul writes that 'men who have sex with men' will not inherit the Kingdom of God (1 Corinthians 6:9–11).

These texts have been used as a basis for the condemnation of homosexuality and homosexual acts: God commands that homosexual acts are wrong and, therefore, taking part in homosexual acts is sinful. There has also been a tendency to see homosexuality as a shameful condition of uncontrollable and unnatural lust (Romans 1:26–27), for which the sufferer should receive sympathy and be helped to find a cure.

There is, however, much disagreement over what these biblical passages mean and whether they should be interpreted as propositions or understood in the context in which they were written. Many of the homosexual acts described in the Bible are between men who are either already married and are, therefore, adulterous, or acts with prostitutes. The biblical texts do not describe relationships between two people in an exclusive committed relationship. In the ancient Greek world,

See Chapter 2.1 of the AS and Year 1 book for a discussion of the primary and secondary precepts of natural law.

men commonly had sex with other men in addition to the sexual relationships they had with their wives. The prevailing model for same-sex relationships in the Greco-Roman era also involved pederasty (sex between a man and a prepubescent boy). There is also an absence of any reference to lesbian relationships in the Bible. These sexual acts might well be described as immoral on the grounds of consent (children are too young to consent to a sexual relationship) or adultery, but it is arguably unwise to take these moral judgements out of the biblical context in which they were originally made and apply them to a very different time and culture to influence modern debates about homosexuality and ethics. The biblical texts may, after all, tell us more about the culture that the authors lived in than divine will.

Other Old Testament rules are not so emphatically enforced by Christians today. Gareth Moore writes that while Christians are happy to follow the law set out in Leviticus, which says that it is immoral for a man to lie with a man, they reject the passage later on that advocates beheading as a punishment. Christians also ignore the requirement in Leviticus 19:19 that forbids the wearing of garments made of two kinds of material. Moore argues that we are ignoring the laws that we find inconvenient while pursuing those that attack minorities that we do not like (Moore, *The Body in Context: Sex and Catholicism,* 1992, pp. 184–6). Moore thinks that Scripture is being used inconsistently to reinforce prejudices.

Peter Vardy notes that Paul's notion that homosexual acts are against nature, as they are impure acts, seems to contradict the general rejection of the Jewish view of impurity found elsewhere in the New Testament (Vardy, *Puzzle of Sex*, 1997, p. 207–8). However, Jesus tended to have more demanding standards than the Torah on moral matters and it is difficult to find evidence that Jesus would have supported a liberal view of homosexuality (House of Bishops Group, *Some Issues in Human Sexuality: A Guide to the Debate*, 2003, p. 146).

There is, consequently, debate in both the Anglican Church and Catholic Church about many aspects of homosexuality.

The Anglican Church and homosexuality

The Church of England opposes same-sex marriage, and requires gay and lesbian clergy who are in same-sex relationships to remain celibate. This position was defined in *Issues in Human Sexuality* (GS Misc 382, December 1991, www.churchofengland.org/media/445118/humansexualitych5.pdf), but divisions within the Church were later acknowledged in a *Report of the House of Bishops, Working Party on human sexuality* (GS 1929, November 2013, www.churchofengland.org/media/1891063/pilling_report_gs_1929_web.pdf).

The following extracts are from a Church of England discussion document about human sexuality:

66 'My partner and I started going to church […] It was Church of England with an evangelical feel to it – it was very lively and always full. At first we went on Sundays, then made ourselves known to the vicar and curate […] As we attended church and became friendlier with the people in it, the curate became aware that we were a couple. We talked to the curate about being baptized and he came to the house […] [H]e said he knew we were a couple, and that the vicar of the church would not allow us to receive communion. The curate produced a book which was basically how to become 'straight' […] Since then we have not attended church. The memory still hurts very much and we both feel very angry towards the church. Christians are supposed to be loving and non-judgmental. We still believe in God and Jesus but not in the way that the church teaches.'

★

'When I became a Christian, I began to believe it was wrong to be involved sexually in homosexual relationships and struggled to know how to tell my gay friends. We had always been close and supported each other. In fact, if it had not been for my Christian beliefs I would have been happy to continue my homosexual relationships. When I first became a Christian, it was not difficult for me to be celibate. And for this reason I felt that I could be quite open with other Christians about my homosexual past […] A few years later I did struggle with homosexual feelings and temptations, but by this time my faith was meaning enough to prevent me from abandoning Christianity and becoming involved in homosexual relationships again.'

★

'There have been many times when I've wondered whether I'd have become a Christian at all if I'd been heterosexual. Certainly, my experiences of God's grace could not have been the same if I'd been part of the heterosexual mainstream. My return to faith as an adult was entirely the result of another man falling in love with me.' 99

House of Bishops Group, *Some Issues in Human Sexuality: A Guide to the Debate*, 2003, p. 117–19, quoted in M. Hallett, *Out of the Blue*, 1996, p. 19

The ethical and theological questions around homosexuality and Christianity have led to heightened debates and tensions within many Churches, and the Anglican Communion is divided on the subject.

The Anglican communion is divided on the subject of homosexuality

The worldwide Anglican community has debated the issue of gay priests and gay marriage and commented that the ordination of 'practising homosexuals and the blessing of same-sex unions call into question the authority of Holy Scripture' (*The Kuala Lumpur statement on Human Sexuality, 2nd Anglican Encounter in the South,* 10–15 February 1997, Kuala Lumpur, Malaysia). However, Gene Robinson (b. 1947) was elected bishop of the Diocese of New Hampshire in the Episcopal Church in the USA in 2004. He was the first priest in an openly gay relationship to be consecrated bishop in a major Christian denomination. Nevertheless, in England, in 2003, Jeffrey John (b. 1953) became the first person in an openly same-sex relationship to be nominated as a Church of England bishop, but he withdrew his acceptance of the nomination due to the controversy it caused.

The Episcopal Church in the USA elected a bishop who is in an openly gay relationship

In *Some Issues in Human Sexuality: A Guide to the Debate* (2003, p. 306), the House of Bishops Group noted that the Church of England remained divided on homosexuality, noting real disagreements about:

- whether homosexual relationships can have ethical validity

- whether it is right to give a blessing to long-term same-sex relationships

- whether *practising* homosexuals are suitable for ordination

- whether the normal requirements of heterosexual monogamy are applicable to bisexuals

- whether a person's God-given sexual identity is determined by their physical nature or self-perception.

In 2017, the Bishops of the Church of England issued a statement called *Marriage and Same Sex Relationships after the Shared Conversations, A Report from the House of Bishops.* This reaffirms that marriage is between one man and one woman, although it also seeks to affirm the place of gay men and lesbian women in the Church and states that some penitence is appropriate for some of the treatment received by gay and lesbian people. It continues to affirm that a minister of the Church of England may not conduct a same-sex marriage although a minister may pray with the couple after a state ceremony. Clergy who are in same-sex relationships are expected to remain celibate. However, when the Bishops' proposal was put to a vote before General Synod, it was rejected. The Church of England remains divided on this issue.

The Catholic Church and homosexuality

The Catholic Church's teachings on homosexuality are summarised in the *Catechism of the Catholic Church* (paras 2357–9). The Catholic Church maintains that there is no sin involved in an inclination towards a member of the same sex, as such an inclination is not freely chosen and is a trial. Homosexual people should be treated with respect, compassion and sensitivity, and unjust discrimination should be avoided. The Catholic Church teaches that such people are called to chastity and with the help of friendship, prayer and grace will achieve Christian perfection.

Pope Francis has confirmed that he considers there to be no grounds for considering the recognition of homosexual unions:

> ❝ In discussing the dignity and mission of the family, the Synod Fathers observed that, as for proposals to place unions between homosexual persons on the same level as marriage, there are absolutely no grounds for considering homosexual unions to be in any way similar or even remotely analogous to God's plan for marriage and family. ❞
>
> Pope Francis, *On Love in the Family,* 2016

In their book *Catholics and Sex: From Purity to Purgatory* (1992), Kate Saunders and Peter Stanford argue that the words of some Catholic cardinals about homosexuals in the past fuelled intolerance. For example, in 1991, the Polish Cardinal Glemp referred to homosexuals as 'backyard mongrels'. In a similar vein, Arcigay, an Italian gay rights group, has linked the Church's teaching with violent expressions of intolerance. Arcigay estimates that, each year, between 150 and 200 gay men are murdered in Italy because of their sexual orientation (see www.religioustolerance.org). However, Pope Francis has said, 'If a person is gay and seeks God and has good will, who am I to judge?' (*The Guardian*, 26 June 2016), and has also argued that the Church should apologise for the harm it has done to gay people.

Pope Francis said, 'If a person is gay and seeks God and has good will, who am I to judge?'

Think question

Should Christianity adopt a more liberal Western view of homosexuality, or would that betray its sources of authority?

See Chapter 3.3 for more on the traditional Christian teaching about the roles of men and women in the family and society.

> ❝ [Gay people] should not be discriminated against. They should be respected, accompanied pastorally […] I think that the Church not only should apologise […] to a gay person whom it offended but it must also apologise to the poor as well, to the women who have been exploited, to children who have been exploited by (being forced to) work. ❞

Pope Francis, as quoted in *The Guardian*, 26 June 2016

Changing Christian moral thought on homosexuality

Some Churches have sought explicitly to welcome homosexual people. The United Methodist Church instructs that:

> ❝ We affirm that all persons are individuals of sacred worth, created in the image of God. All persons need the ministry of the Church in their struggles for human fulfillment, as well as the spiritual and emotional care of a fellowship that enables reconciling relationships with God, with others, and with self. The United Methodist Church does not condone the practice of homosexuality and considers this practice incompatible with Christian teaching. We affirm that God's grace is available to all. We will seek to live together in Christian community, welcoming, forgiving, and loving one another, as Christ has loved and accepted us. We implore families and churches not to reject or condemn lesbian and gay members and friends. We commit ourselves to be in ministry for and with all persons. ❞

The Book of Discipline of The United Methodist Church, 2012, 161G

Some Christian churches and thinkers have gone further, challenging the traditional condemnation of homosexuality. They maintain that the quality of the relationship (be it heterosexual or homosexual) is what determines its moral value. They dispute a biblical basis for Christian opposition to homosexuality and reject the natural law approach as unsound. They draw on the teaching in Genesis that all are made 'in the image of God' (Genesis 1:27). If God creates men and women as homosexuals, they argue, then that nature and inclination must be good. Otherwise, it would suggest that God intentionally creates disordered human beings.

In his book *The Body in Context: Sex and Catholicism* (1992), Gareth Moore argues that there is a Christian basis for an inclusive attitude towards homosexuals, because Christianity is a religion that positively seeks to make room for the marginalised and outcast in society (see 1 Corinthians 1:26–28). On the website www.religioustolerance.org, B.A. Robinson notes that liberal Christians within the Methodist Church consider gay and lesbian ordination and same-sex marriage as *civil rights* issues. If human rights are for all, then ordination and marriage should be available to gay people as well as heterosexual people. They maintain that homosexuality is normal and natural, and is not changeable or freely chosen.

On Saturday, 9 July 2016 the General assembly of the United Reformed Church of the UK empowered its ministers to conduct and register marriages for same-sex couples. Reverend John Proctor, General Secretary of the URC, said:

> 66 Today the URC has made an important decision – at which some will rejoice and with which others will be uncomfortable. Those of our churches who now wish to offer full marriage services to same-sex couples are free to do just that – and those churches who do not wish to are not compelled to. All are part of this denomination. This has been a sensitive issue for many in our churches. It has been important to take our time over the decision process, and to listen as carefully as we can to one another along the way. 99
>
> www.urc.org.uk/media-news/2084-the-united-reformed-church-votes-to-allow-the-marriage-of-same-sex-couples-in-its-churches.html#sthash.hfJ1UPlT.dpuf

Beyond the practical policy of Christian Churches, scholars are discussing the prospect of a more radical change in Christian thinking. Scholars, such as Richard Hay, have examined whether Acts 10–15 is relevant to the question of whether or not homosexuality should be accepted as a normal

Think question

Is it time for Christian Churches to change their responses to same-sex unions?

Apply your knowledge

5. Compare the different experiences of homosexual Christians quoted on page 149. What issues do they each raise?

6. Identify the different messages about homosexuality, homosexual acts, same-sex marriage and attitudes towards gay people contained in the quotes and references from Catholic teachings and the quotes by leading Catholics in this section.

7. Identify the different approaches to same-sex marriage and gay ministers taken by the different Protestant Churches referred to in this section.

8. Identify key Bible passages about homosexuality and explain how these passages can be interpreted differently.

Think question

Read Acts 10–15. Should Christian Churches treat homosexuals in the same way as the early Church treated gentiles?

part of Christian life. In these verses, Peter and Paul debate whether or not gentiles could become Christians without first becoming Jews. The decision to allow gentiles to become Christian without having to be circumcised and without following the traditional Jewish food rules became a turning point in the development of Christianity, which up until then had been a Jewish movement. Christianity radically reinterpreted the Hebrew Scriptures in this debate, making a significant and fundamental decision to set aside many aspects of Jewish law for new non-Jewish Christians. Jeffrey Siker concludes that it is appropriate to regard homosexual Christians in the same way as gentiles were regarded in the past and incorporate them fully into the Christian community (Siker, 'Homosexuals, The Bible and Gentile Inclusion' in *Theology Today*, 51, July 1994, pp. 219–34).

Secular thinking on sexual ethics

In time, the social protections provided by the Christianisation of marriage laws came to be viewed as social restraints on freedom by some. In *On Liberty* (a book written in 1859 with his wife, Harriet Taylor Mill), the philosopher, social reformer and libertarian J.S. Mill argued that individuals should be protected from unnecessary legal oversight (the tyranny of political power) and from the social attitudes of the masses (the tyranny of the majority), and should be free to behave as they choose to as long as no one else is harmed by their behaviour. Mill questioned, 'the nature and limits of the power which can be legitimately exercised by society over the individual', and argued that individuals who are different should be protected:

J.S. Mill (1806–73)

> 66 Protection, therefore, against the tyranny of the magistrate is not enough: there needs protection also against the tyranny of the prevailing opinion and feeling; against the tendency of society to impose, by other means than civil penalties, its own ideas and practices as rules of conduct on those who dissent from them; to fetter the development, and, if possible, prevent the formation, of any individuality not in harmony with its ways, and compel all characters to fashion themselves upon the model of its own. 99

J. S. Mill, *On Liberty,* 1859, Chapter 1, para. 5

Mill maintained that the prevention of harm was the only justification for restraining an individual:

> ❝ That the only purpose for which power can be rightfully exercised over any member of a civilized community, against his will, is to prevent harm to others. His own good, either physical or moral, is not a sufficient warrant. He cannot rightfully be compelled to do or forbear because it will be better for him to do so, because it will make him happier, because, in the opinions of others, to do so would be wise, or even right. These are good reasons for remonstrating with him, or reasoning with him, or persuading him, or entreating him, but not for compelling him, or visiting him with any evil in case he do otherwise [...] In the part [of life] which merely concerns himself, his independence is, of right, absolute. Over himself, over his own body and mind, the individual is sovereign. ❞
>
> J.S. Mill, *On Liberty,* 1859, Chapter 1, para. 10

Mill envisaged a free liberal society, and he was concerned at the extent to which religion forbids certain behaviours. For example, Mill sought to make artificial contraception available to the poor, something prohibited by Christian Churches at the time (and still prohibited by the Catholic Church today).

Yet, Mill was not casual in his attitude to sex. He was not opposed to marriage and, in fact, seems to have shared the concerns that drove the Christianisation of marriage laws, wishing to make marriage fairer. However, he did not believe that society and the Church had gone far enough and he fought for women's rights and gender equality. He believed marriage should be an equal partnership and he was particularly concerned that the legal, Christian conception of marriage placed constraints on women, oppressing them. In *The Subjugation of Women* (1869), he argued that society, often via the institution of marriage, relegated women to the status of slaves. He noted, for example, that divorce was used exclusively by men to rid themselves of their wives.

In modern times, many countries continue to regulate sexual relationships legally and, in many parts of the world, the laws arise out of Christianity's normalisation of monogamous marriage as the ideal relationship. There are, however, significant differences in the way sexual relationships were regulated in the nineteenth century, when Mill was writing, and the way they are regulated today. Not least, today a woman can file for divorce just as easily as a man, cohabitation and having children outside of wedlock is common, it is illegal to discriminate on grounds of sexuality, and same-sex marriage is legal. Nevertheless, open marriages (where a married couple agrees to engage in extramarital sex) are rare, and polygamous marriages (which involve marriage to more than one spouse) are illegal in the UK. At present, society continues to support the values of consent and exclusivity within sexual relationships, although not necessarily within the traditional concept of marriage between a man and a woman.

See Chapter 3.3 for more on the traditional Christian teaching about the roles of men and women in the family and society.

Think question

Do laws about sex protect against exploitation or do they limit individual freedom?

See Chapter 2.1 of the AS and Year 1 book for a discussion of natural law.

Catholic approaches to sexual ethics draw heavily on natural law

Amartya Sen (*Development as Freedom*, 2001) and Martha Nussbaum (*Creating Capabilities: The Human Development Approach*, 2011) go beyond the libertarian notion that the state and society should only intervene on matters that cause harm to others. They developed a capabilities approach to making sense of human development, focusing on the freedoms that human beings need for well-being. These include:

- having bodily integrity, including opportunities for sexual satisfaction

- having emotional attachments to things and people outside ourselves; to love those who love and care for us. This includes not having one's emotional development blighted by fear and anxiety.

If human well-being requires people to be able to have opportunities for sexual satisfaction and to love and be loved, then there is an ardent argument that human beings should be free to establish consensual sexual relationships with whomsoever they choose, as long as no one is harmed by those relationships. It then remains to decide what causes harm.

The application of ethical theories to sexual ethics

Natural law

Natural law ethics sees right and wrong as fixed things, in that they are linked to a view of the human being and what makes humans flourish. They do not change according to the situation or what might happen as a result, but are linked to some greater idea of an eternal law devised to help humans flourish. Acts are judged right or wrong in relation to the extent to which they meet their ultimate end. The process of judging what is right or wrong involves the use of reason, and reason leads us towards doing good. According to Aquinas, reason, reflecting on the world, reveals that certain primary precepts are good: protecting life, ensuring reproduction, education and loving God.

Catholic approaches to sexual ethics draw heavily on natural law: the creation of new life is central to the purpose of sexual intercourse and marriage, and the unifying aspect of lovemaking must not be separated from procreation.

> 66 The reason is that the fundamental nature of the marriage act, while uniting husband and wife in the closest intimacy, also renders them capable of generating new life – and this as a result of laws written into the actual nature of man and of woman. 99
>
> Pope Paul VI, *Humanae Vitae*, 1968, Chapter 12

Sexual relationships and sexual acts that cannot bring forth and nurture new life are, therefore, morally questionable.

> 66 The Church, nevertheless, in urging men to the observance of the precepts of the natural law, which it interprets by its constant doctrine, teaches that each and every marital act must of necessity retain its intrinsic relationship to the procreation of human life. 99
>
> Pope Paul VI, *Humanae Vitae*, 1968, Chapter 11

> 66 [A]n act of mutual love which impairs the capacity to transmit life which God the Creator, through specific laws, has built into it, frustrates His design which constitutes the norm of marriage, and contradicts the will of the Author of life. 99
>
> Pope Paul VI, *Humanae Vitae*, 1968, Chapter 13

These understandings guide the Catholic Church's approach to premarital, extramarital and homosexual sex. Sex is linked to new life, to stability, community and commitment. According to the Catholic Church, homosexual sex cannot bring forth new life, and bringing new life into the world outside of marriage does not ensure a child is nurtured in a stable, committed loving relationship. Homosexual sex, premarital sex, extramarital sex and sex using contraceptives are, therefore, morally wrong according to natural law because they do not support Aquinas' precepts, they are not good for sustaining a flourishing human society. Sex might feel good in these situations, but this is an apparent good, not a real good, because the primary purposes of sex are frustrated.

Approaches to sexual ethics based on natural law come under criticism. It is argued that the positive effects of a unifying sexual act between a loving couple are a good enough reason for sex without the need to focus on reproduction, especially in the modern age where women live longer and can therefore live more adult years being non-fertile than fertile. Sexual acts often cannot lead to reproduction: in the non-fertile part of the menstrual cycle, after the menopause, when one or both partners are infertile, or when the woman is pregnant. And, if reproduction is not an intrinsic purpose of sex, then natural law no longer opposes homosexual sex. If some human beings flourish in same sex relationships perhaps the precepts need to be reviewed?

In 'Homosexuality, Morals, and the Law of Nature', Burton M. Leiser argues that sexual acts may have multiple purposes and he questions why every sexual act should be required to simultaneously fulfill every purpose (*Ethics in Practice. An Anthology,* ed. LaFollette, 1997, pp. 242–53). Sexual organs are suited for reproduction and for the production of intense pleasure in oneself and others and, Leiser argues, if the purpose of sexual organs is only reproduction then marriage between elderly couples who cannot have children is unnatural. Condemning people for using their sexual organs to unite in pleasure reveals the prejudices and irrational taboos in our society.

Furthermore, an argument could be made that, under natural law, extramarital sex could be moral, as a way of resolving infertility. For example, in the Hebrew scriptures, Abraham sired a child by his servant girl Hagar when his wife, Sarah, was believed to be barren (Genesis 16). In this way, surrogate mothers offer the possibility of reproduction when infertility prevents it. Surrogate sex may be extramarital sex, but it is not necessarily against natural law. This is not a conclusion that Catholic thinking could reach.

Situation ethics

Joseph Fletcher uses examples of sexual ethics to illustrate when and how traditional ethical rules might be broken in situations where the most loving thing to do, in his view, justifies setting aside moral norms. He used the example of a woman who asked a guard to have sex with her and impregnate her so she could be freed from a prisoner of war camp, and the example of a spy who has to have sex with an enemy agent in order to bring a war to an end, to argue that, despite the fact that neither encounter involved a lifelong commitment or exclusive love, both could be seen as ethical in the circumstances. Fletcher's examples were criticised as being exceptional examples that were not a suitable basis for a general moral theory. But Fletcher proposed situation ethics as a method for making moral decisions in extraordinary circumstances where the usual moral rules did not seem to work. The question is, therefore, whether situation ethics can be applied to more day-to-day sexual moral choices.

Situation ethics focuses on the particular situation, the interests of the individual person, and love and justice and, might, therefore, permit the breaking of traditional moral rules around sex in day-to-day situations. It would seek a pragmatic approach to premarital and extramarital sex and same-sex unions, setting aside fixed moral truths in order to put the person and their relationships at the heart of each decision.

Situation ethics is ostensibly concerned with matters of selfless unconditional love (agape love) and, although this is not the same as erotic love, it is sensitive to deep love between individuals, even if that love does not manifest itself in the traditionally recognised form of deep love between a heterosexual married couple. Situation ethics would focus on the injustices in the way sexual relationships are regulated: the fact that heterosexual married couples are often viewed as the only form that a legitimate relationship can take would be viewed as unjust. If a same-sex couple can only find a meaningful relationship with one another then that, according to situation ethics, would be the end that justifies breaking rules on who can have sexual relationships. Similarly, an extramarital or a premarital sexual relationship might be viewed as good in some circumstances. For instance, a wife, whose husband has

> **Think question**
>
> What does natural law mean for women having sex after the menopause?

> *See Chapter 2.2 of the AS and Year 1 book for a detailed discussion of situation ethics.*

Situation ethics is always open to breaking traditional ethical rules, including sexual ethical rules, because decisions are made situationally, not prescriptively early onset Alzheimer's disease and is in a care home, may find comfort in an extramarital relationship while continuing to care for her husband. Situation ethics is always open to breaking traditional ethical rules, including sexual ethical rules, because decisions are made situationally, not prescriptively. It comes down to the situation at hand.

The difficulties with applying situation ethics to sexual ethics emerge when questions about other people affected are considered. Situation ethics puts the needs of the primary protagonists first, which makes it difficult for it to protect broader family interests and the interests of society as a whole. For example, parents who have extramarital affairs are putting the happiness of their husband or wife and their children at risk, undermining their own relationship with betrayal, and endangering the security of the upbringing of the children. It might be the most loving thing to do to allow premarital sexual relationships, but what happens if the female partner becomes pregnant and she and her child are abandoned by the male partner? There is, therefore, a danger to vulnerable people in the more sexually permissive society that situation ethics would encourage. If situation ethics cannot protect the vulnerable and the young from exploitation, then its claims to be about love and justice will not stand up to scrutiny.

Kantian ethics

Kantian ethics is based on the key ideas of Immanuel Kant. Freedom, or autonomy, is at the heart of Kant's ethics, placing consent at the heart of a Kantian approach to sexual ethics. The consensual promises made by two people getting married, to commit to each other permanently and exclusively, are very much in line with Kant's ethics. They focus on the worth of the two human beings involved and encourage them to be attentive to each other and not treat each other as a means to an end, for pleasure or social convenience. They also look forward to the kingdom of ends where people respect marriage bonds. In contrast, any sexual act that is not consensual, including sexual assaults like rape and forced marriage, would be prohibited. The human person is of the highest moral worth for Kant, and must be treated with dignity. Therefore, sex that objectifies a person and does not express the utmost consideration for them would be unethical because sexual relationships, like all relationships, must be based on equality.

Kantian ethics offers principles that can be used to formulate rules governing sexual behaviour. Traditional rules prohibited sex outside of marriage and homosexual sex. It is possible, however, that the Kantian principle of treating every human person with dignity would require all sexual relationships, including homosexual relationships, to be treated equally. Additional rules, based on Kantian ethics, might focus on the importance of mutuality, freely given consent, commitment and exclusivity. According to Kant, our actions must be universalisable (good for all people in all situations) and these principles can be applied to all relationships, irrespective of the gender of the participants in the relationship or whether the couple are married or not. Universalising reproduction as a requirement of sex would, however, make homosexual sex unethical.

> **Think question**
> Should sexual ethics be governed by principles that set rules, or principles that set rules aside?

> *See Chapter 2.3 of the AS and Year 1 book for a detailed discussion of Kantian ethics.*

Think question

a. What would Kant say about the boss who is pushing a junior member of staff into giving him sexual favours, or the wealthy person who buys sex from poor prostitutes?

See Chapter 2.4 of the AS and Year 1 book for a detailed discussion of utilitarianism.

Think question

b. Is deeper love a greater good than brief sexual pleasure? How might utilitarian thinkers respond?

Premarital and extramarital sex could be problematic from a Kantian perspective. Kant is concerned that human beings are not used, that they are always treated with dignity. Premarital and extramarital sex involve sexual relationships that are outside normative social rules. And, if you believe social rules exist to protect the vulnerable, sex not governed by those rules is more risky for some; it opens up the possibility that the person with less power in the relationship will be abused. Although allowing premarital sex and extramarital sex increases individual freedom, something Kant thought was important, it also increases the requirement for the individuals involved to conduct themselves ethically and take their moral duty towards others seriously, another central concern for Kant.

Utilitarianism

Utilitarian ethics seeks to maximise the greatest happiness for the greatest number. If happiness is equated with hedonistic pleasure, rather than a wider sense of well-being and happiness, then utilitarianism could be used to legitimise a free, unregulated approach to sexual behaviour. This is because giving people licence to have sex in and out of marriage and irrespective of sexual orientation can, arguably, maximise pleasure. However, free love can also lead to unhappiness, particularly if it results in the spread of sexually transmitted diseases, shallow or unfulfilling relationships, or unwanted pregnancies. Pleasure could quickly begin to cause unhappiness to many people.

However, Jeremy Bentham, the first utilitarian, had a wider conception of the greatest good than pure pleasure. He wanted greater well-being for everyone. Thus, marriage rules protect the poor by restraining the sexual behaviour of the powerful towards those with no social power. For example, women are protected by the public nature of marriage and the prohibitions against premarital and extramarital sex from men (who are generally more powerful in a patriarchal society) who might want to use them for personal pleasure.

Christian teaching tells us that reproduction is one of the main reasons for sex, and the rules against premarital and extramarital sex are designed to foster the best possible environment for bringing up children. Society as a whole needs children for the continuation of the species and for the care of the elderly. So, if the application of utilitarianism resulted in maximising pleasure, and everyone freely chose to use contraception and not have children, then society as a whole would suffer and happiness for the greatest number would not be achieved. Utilitarians might, therefore, argue for ethical rules about sexual behaviour that facilitate reproduction.

Although sexual identify is being understood, more and more, as something fluid, the majority identify as heterosexual. Utilitarians might, therefore, argue that homosexuality should be prohibited in the interests of the majority, especially if the majority view it as harmful to society. However, John Stuart Mill, a utilitarian who was also a libertarian, believed it was important to prevent mass social prejudice restricting the rights and happiness of individuals. His focus on qualitative measures of happiness, on measuring the worth of different pleasures and pains, would place the pleasure and happiness of the homosexual minority above the pain of those who oppose homosexuality and would prevent mob instincts governing the lives of those who are different.

Apply your knowledge

11. Identify how the key principles of the four ethical approaches apply to premarital, extramarital and homosexual sex and then use them to evaluate the morality of the following situations:

   a. A wife refuses to leave her wealthy, abusive husband so she can protect and bring up their children. She maintains a discreet sexual relationship with a dear friend and finds her only physical sexual happiness and solace in that relationship.

   b. A couple have been married for a long time and their life together is filled with friendship and companionship. However, he had a previous relationship with a woman he could never be with. He has secretly kept photographs and videos of their time together and frequently views them and thinks deeply about the closeness he had with her.

   c. A same-sex couple have lived together, unmarried, for many years. They present themselves as friends to the outside world, but they share a deeply committed sexual relationship in private.

   d. A holiday romance blossoms between two youngsters on family holidays overseas. Their families are from different parts of the world and from cultures that would never tolerate their marriage. They enjoy a brief passionate sexual relationship on holiday. They never meet again.

12. Copy and complete the following table to explain how each of the four ethical theories is applied to sex within marriage, premarital sex, extramarital sex and homosexual sex.

	Natural law	Situation ethics	Kantian ethics	Utilitarianism
Sex within marriage				
Premarital sex				
Extramarital sex				
Homosexual sex				

Discussing sexual ethics

Do religious beliefs and practices concerning sex and relationships have a continuing role in the area of sexual ethics?

To a greater or lesser extent, most societies and cultures are influenced by religiously framed ethical value systems and these affect the laws relating to marriage, divorce and homosexuality. This results in the criminalisation of extramarital and homosexual sex, and in Sudan, Iran, Saudi Arabia, Yemen, Mauritania, Afghanistan, Pakistan, Qatar, the UAE, parts of Nigeria, parts of Somalia, parts of Syria and parts of Iraq being gay or bisexual is punishable by death.

Many ethical values based on religious beliefs and practices correspond with modern secular ethical values. Although they may not be justified in the same way, they do share a common understanding of what is morally right. For instance, Christian rules about the importance and sanctity of marriage were, in part, developed to protect women from practices such as concubinage and to prevent women from being abandoned, often pregnant, after betrothal but before marriage. Christian marriage values consent, and the regulation of sexual relationships through marriage was an attempt to make sexual relationships more just. Ensuring sexual relationships are consensual and are just is important today amongst people with different and no religious beliefs. For example, in Personal, Social and Health Education classes teachers are encouraged to teach about the importance of consent in sexual relationships, and the law makes non-consensual sexual acts illegal. People need not share the religious beliefs that justify these values, but they may nevertheless conclude they are right.

However, in the UK, the link between Christian values and the law is coming under pressure. For example, the law no longer reflects the traditional Christian position towards homosexuality. Homosexual sex was decriminalised in 1967, the age of consent for homosexual sex is in line with the age of consent for heterosexual consent, and same-sex marriages are now legal. It can, therefore, be argued that there is no place for religious beliefs and practices concerning sex and relationships in the area of sexual ethics when the prevailing culture has a different understanding of how sex and relationships should be conducted.

In many parts of the world, homosexuals are oppressed and discriminated against, and even tortured and executed for crimes that are founded on religious beliefs. Often these religious beliefs are based on particular interpretations of sacred texts that may be challenged by other people practising the same religion, but are nevertheless widespread. In this context, involving religion in setting social norms for sexual ethics is problematic.

Ethics is not only concerned with how society as a whole behaves, it is also concerned with personal conduct. If religion is understood as a way of life that individuals choose to follow freely, then to ignore it in matters of sex would seem to relegate it to the margins of life which would be unacceptable because sex touches on the fundamentals of human nature, on human identity, human happiness and the future of humanity. There is, therefore, a juggling act for Christians when it comes to ethical obligations promoted by their religion but not supported by law or by the prevailing culture in which they live.

Think question

Which sexual wrongs require no more than moral condemnation and which require legislation to prohibit them?

Apply your knowledge

13. Which of the following statements do you find most convincing and which least convincing. Explain your answers.

    a. Christian marriage should be supported by the law, and the law should not undermine it.

    b. All the law should do is ensure justice and fairness in matters of sexual ethics. Religious views of sexual ethics are fine as personal principles, but they should not be integrated into the law.

    c. Different religions and other belief systems may express their views on social norms, but none should have privileged influence over what becomes the law.

    d. It is inevitable that beliefs, be they religious or philosophical, are going to influence the social norms of a society. What matters is that social norms are not harmful.

Should choices in the area of sexual behaviour be entirely private and personal, or should they be subject to societal norms and legislation?

Sex can be viewed as entirely personal. What goes on in a person's private life, how they express themselves and relate to others sexually, is, arguably, nobody's business but their own. Sex is, thus, freed from social obligations and constrained only by a person's individual sexual ethical code. From this perspective, rules that prohibit premarital sex, extramarital sex and homosexual sex are inappropriate.

However, sex is never exclusively private. Not only does a sexual 'relationship' involve another person, but, because human beings are sexual beings, the way people live their sex lives affects how they relate to wider society. A society that advocates extramarital sex, for example, would put marriages at risk, and marriage break-ups can have significant negative consequences for both the adults and any children involved. Wider society also plays a role in supporting particular sexual relationships through, for example, providing tax breaks to married couples. The link between sex and reproduction also adds an additional social dimension; the most private and intimate acts between people are also the way life and society is created. Therefore, sex is both private and public.

Most ethical theories suggest that sexual behaviour should be governed by societal norms and/or legislation. Utilitarians seek to maximise happiness for the greatest number of people, but are in danger of allowing the majority to determine rules that will bind some into unhappy situations, notably those who are homosexual. Libertarians want to free individuals from this kind of restriction, and Mill, a notable utilitarian libertarian, advances higher qualities of good as something that the majority must respect. He places the happiness of the minority above the pain of the majority in order to ensure that the rules do not condemn the minority to unhappiness. However, such freedoms might threaten social organisations. Kantians would want sexual relations to be governed by ethical principles and for any laws developed by society to be informed by those principles. For Kant, in contrast to legal rules, social rules may not always reflect the correct principles, but moral people should act as if they do (as if they lived in a kingdom of ends). Natural law would argue for the establishment of moral laws governing sex. Of the four ethical theories examined, situation ethics is the most permissive and accepting of the concept of sexual behaviour as private and personal because it was devised to permit the setting aside of social rules if that is the most loving thing to do.

Ethical theories offer ways of framing debates about sexual ethics, both in terms of what might be considered right and what might require legislation, but questions remain about whether any of them can help to fully resolve the issues surrounding premarital, extramarital and homosexual sex currently under debate in contemporary society.

Think question

Does privacy exist in the twenty-first century or is everything we do (including sex) public?

Apply your knowledge

14. Discuss the following points of view.

a. Without ethical constraints, without some sort of societal pressure, harmful sexual cultures will overwhelm society. Hardcore pornography, easily accessible via the Internet, depicts every sexual act imaginable. Magazines aimed at teenagers encourage them to think about sex as if it is a performance, pressuring them to perform in the right way, and the right way is any and every way. Women being raped and beaten are both crimes and a source of titillation in major movies. Girls are expected to 'do' things for their boyfriends. The idea of a mutually fulfilling relationship is lost in a sea of performance, pressure and exploitation, where ultimately the most powerful lord it over the less powerful. Considering sex as a purely private matter simply licenses the pornographer to make money, for the powerful to abuse the less powerful, and for the fashion and advertising industries to depict human beings in ever more unrestricted and objectified ways.

b. Sex is never free from social pressure. A thing that is personal and private is controlled by society, as those who seek to set the standard impose their own preferences as social norms. And so homosexuals are punished for their desires, and the patriarchy is bolstered as fathers hand their daughters over to their new husbands whom their daughters must honour and obey, men are given the right to divorce their wives but their wives are denied the right to divorce their husbands, and women denied access to contraception are enslaved by pregnancy. Sex must be freed from social controls so that it can be just and fair.

Are normative theories useful in what they might say about sexual ethics?

The four ethical theories considered in this chapter (situation ethics, natural law, utilitarianism and Kantian ethics) each provide ethical norms for addressing the ethics of sex.

Situation ethics provides a way of thinking about the morality of sex in extreme circumstances where it might be the most loving thing to do to break the prevailing social rules. It focuses on the individual, on the person or people involved in very specific, and potentially desperate, situations. It makes space for those who are different. Because it is designed to deal with exceptions, it does not clearly articulate how the social implications of sexual relationships could be addressed.

In contrast, natural law places the needs of the community and the importance of creating a good society above individual personal concerns. It offers an approach that is focused on establishing clear rules for society. It provides a system for making sense of all moral behaviour, yet is forgiving enough to recognise that human beings sometimes make mistakes when it acknowledges that people may do things wrongly believing they are right. However, natural law might be used in ways that narrowly define the purpose of human beings and can, therefore, be used to create rules that are too prescriptive in its search for uniformity.

Utilitarianism seeks the greatest happiness for the greatest number. This might encourage a free approach to sex if happiness is equated with pleasure, although it is arguable whether 'free love' necessarily produces the deep happiness that can be found in more meaningful, committed relationships. Utilitarians who seek to measure pleasure qualitatively would limit the extent to which the majority could control or limit the freedoms of the minority. Utilitarianism takes a societal view of morality, which perhaps makes it less useful when it comes to personal questions of sexuality.

Kantian ethics offers principles for every aspect of human life and seeks to ensure that social and legal rules take account of the importance of freedom and human dignity. Kantian ethics emphasises an individual's responsibility to act ethically and the need for a universal approach to morality. Kant's approach to ethics does not prescribe particular rules, it prescribes the principles that underpin those rules and is, arguably, the most adaptable of the four ethical theories as a result. It can inform both personal choices and law, and it recognises both the inherent value of the individual human life and also the importance of ensuring people live with each other and treat each other fairly.

Apply your knowledge

15. Consider the following principles for moral sexual relationships and identify which you think are essential and which are not. You could arrange them in a pyramid pattern with the most important principle at the top, the next two most important principles on the second row, the next three most important principles on the third row and so on.

   a. Government and society should refrain from interfering in personal matters as long as people do no harm.

   b. Sexual satisfaction is essential to physical and mental health and well-being.

   c. People should be free to form emotional attachments to whoever they want. Emotional development should not be blighted by fear and anxiety about whether or not society approves of the attachment.

   d. Sex should follow the intended plan of the creator, God.

   e. Sex should not involve any unjust harm (harm of a serious nature).

   f. Sex is only just when all concerned consent freely.

   g. Sexual relationships should be equal and mutual; one side should not be more powerful than the other.

   h. Sex should only take place in committed relationships.

   i. Sex should be left open to new life without using artificial contraception (artificial contraception is wrong).

   j. Sex should not be the product of unjust circumstances. For example, poverty should not force people into prostitution.

16. Explain why you have chosen your top three principles. Look back and see which ethical theories support your chosen principles.

Learning support

Points to remember

» Christians and Christian Churches offer different responses to questions of sexual ethics. Some are based on biblical interpretations and others are deduced from natural law. Some seek to assert traditional heterosexual marriage as the only space where moral sex can take place. Others disagree.

» Sexual ethics raises questions about the role of religion in establishing and maintaining social moral norms in secular societies, and also about which issues require legislation and which do not. A related issue is the question of what it means for a human being to flourish individually and what it means for communities to flourish, and, conversely what harms individuals and what harms communities.

» Premarital and extramarital sex raise questions about the values traditionally embodied in marriage: consent, fidelity, commitment, mutuality and equality. There is common agreement about the importance of these values, but differences in how some are applied.

» An additional factor is the extent to which there is a received wisdom about the way human beings should live their lives, and whether that wisdom is fit for purpose in present times. Different ethical theories offer different principles for judging whether a society is good and whether a human being is flourishing.

» Sexual relationships have not always been informed by what is often presented as traditional Christian ethics; religion has not always controlled marriage. However, the Christianisation of sexual relationships and marriage sought to make sexual relationships and marriage more just.

» More recently, Christianity has been seen as a cause of injustice, with its prohibitions against same-sex relationships.

Enhance your learning

» Pope Paul VI's *Humanae Vitae* (1968) is most famous for its condemnation of artificial contraception, but it also contains a concise account of the natural law ethical premises behind the Catholic Church's stance on marriage and sex.

» *Issues in Human Sexuality*, produced by the Church of England House of Bishops in 1991, outlines key issues relating to contemporary sexual ethics from an Anglican perspective.

» *Some Issues in Human Sexuality: A Guide to the Debate*, produced by the Church of England House of Bishops in 2003, is a wide-ranging study exploring many of the issues discussed in this chapter.

» Chapter 1 of John Stuart Mill's *On Liberty* (1859) sets out the key questions around the importance of individual liberty, the limits of government and societal pressures, and the harm rule.

» *Marriage after Modernity: Christian Marriage in Postmodern Times* (1999) by Adrian Thatcher explores Christian marriage from theological, historical and social scientific perspectives.

» *Theology and Sexuality: Classic and Contemporary Readings* (2002) by Eugene Rogers is an excellent collection of short chapters on topics including faithfulness, love, gay friendship and homosexuality from many different Catholic and Protestant perspectives.

Practice for Exams

At A level, essay questions invite you to demonstrate your knowledge and understanding of factual material (AO1) and also your critical ability in putting forward a coherent, balanced argument (AO2). You should aim to write essays that are persuasive responses to the question throughout, rather than writing a lot of description and then tacking an opinion on at the end of each paragraph.

How useful is utilitarianism in making decisions about the ethics of premarital sex?

For this question, you are being asked to apply the theories of utilitarianism to issues of sexual ethics.

In order to gain high marks for AO1, you should be able to show a thorough understanding of utilitarianism, for example demonstrating your understanding of different kinds of utilitarian theory. You also need to show that you understand the ethical issues raised by premarital sex.

For AO2, you need a clear line of argument. You are being asked how useful utilitarianism is in this context, so your answer should tell the reader whether utilitarianism is very useful, not useful at all, or useful to a certain extent. You might want to compare utilitarianism with another method of ethical decision-making as part of your argument.

'There is no need for religious rules about private sexual behaviour between consenting adults.' Discuss.

This question invites you to discuss whether religious beliefs should have an influence on sexual ethics.

For AO1 marks, you need to show knowledge and understanding of religious rules about sexual behaviour, for example rules about premarital sex, adultery and homosexuality. You should be able to explain the religious reasons for these rules.

For AO2, you should construct an argument to support your opinions about whether or not such religious rules are necessary. For example, you might think that sex is something private between the individuals concerned and does not need anyone else to make rules about it. Or you might think that religious rules are a useful guideline at times when people might not be thinking rationally. Or you might have a different opinion. Try to make sure that your essay is fair in its treatment of different opinions.

Studying developments in Christian thought

What questions does plurality and diversity of belief raise for any one religion?

How has the role of women changed in recent times and what are the implications for Christian thought?

Are better answers to the human condition offered by Freud and Marx than by Christian thinkers?

Study of developments in Christian thought in the second year of your A level focuses on an exploration of three powerful changes that have raised important questions for Christianity, Christian thinking and society at large.

The first two chapters in this section are an examination of the impact of religious pluralism on theology and society. The development of a modern, plural, diverse society has focused Christian thinking around its message, whether that message is exclusive or inclusive, and how Christianity makes sense of other religions. This has had an impact on inter-faith dialogue, leading to changes in the way sacred scripture is read. These discussions illustrate the key question for any religion: how does it make sense of itself in the modern world?

The next two chapters in this section explore the impacts of the changing place of women on society and the development of feminist thought on theology. Secular ways of thinking have challenged, and are continuing to challenge, traditional Christian ideas about the roles of men, women and the family in society, and Christian thinking is responding. In particular, feminist theologians have challenged the status quo, some rejecting Christianity and others suggesting ways in which it can be reformed.

The final two chapters in this section examine new theories that explain religion, and Christianity specifically, as a sociological or a psychological force. These theories challenge the role of religion in government and public life and have had an influence on theological thinking. In the chapter on the challenge of secularism, the psychological and sociological theories that provide a non-theological account of religion and question whether or not religion is of value in modern life are discussed. The final chapter in the book looks at the impact of Marxist thought in one theological area in particular: liberation theology. This radical theology asked questions about the extent to which theological thought should be based on people's experience of injustice and the extent to which Marxism explains the experience of the human condition.

Chapter 3.1

Religious pluralism and theology

If there is salvation through Christ, does this mean that other religions must be wrong?
Should Christians try to convert members of other faiths to Christianity?
Will genuinely good people who are not Christians be excluded from salvation?
Do all religions offer equally effective paths to God?

Key Terms

Exclusivism: the view that only one religion offers the complete means of salvation

Inter-faith dialogue: sharing and discussing religious beliefs between members of different religious traditions, with an aim of reaching better understanding

Theology of religion(s): the branch of Christian theology that looks at the relationship between Christianity and other world religions from a Christian perspective

Inclusivism: the view that although one's own religion is the normative (setting the standard of normality) means of salvation, those who accept its central principles may also receive salvation

Pluralism: the view that there are many ways to salvation through different religious traditions

Particularism: an alternative name for exclusivism, meaning that salvation can only be found in one particular way

Vatican II: the Second Vatican Ecumenical Council, held from 1962 to 1965 to discuss the place of the Catholic Church in the modern world

Noumena: a Kantian term to describe reality as it really is, unfiltered by the human mind

Phenomena: a Kantian term to describe reality as it appears to us, filtered by the human mind

Specification requirements

The teaching of contemporary Christian theology of religion on:

- exclusivism
- inclusivism
- pluralism

Introduction

From its beginning, Christianity has always existed as a religion alongside other world religions. When it first began, the earliest Christians developed their beliefs and traditions while living with people who believed in the Greek and Roman gods, with people who had Jewish faith and with people who had no religious beliefs of any kind. Jesus himself was Jewish, and his teachings often caused controversy amongst the local rabbis, with Pharisees and Sadducees asking him questions and trying to discover the extent to which Jesus' teachings were consistent with traditional Jewish beliefs.

After Jesus' death, the early Christians had to try and work out their place in the world. Many of the letters in the New Testament, written by early Christian leaders to new churches, deal with the extent to which Christianity should accept or reject the beliefs and practices of others. Was it acceptable for Christians to eat any kind of food, or should they follow the Jewish kosher food laws? Should Christians be circumcised, like Jews? What was a distinctively Christian style of worship, and should women be allowed to take part in it? Should they reject all of the beliefs around them as false, seeing truth only in Christianity, or did other religions also contain valuable truths and insights? Should they work to convert others to Christianity, or should they leave others to seek and follow whatever they felt to be true?

The first Christians saw themselves as having a unique kind of relationship with God, made possible through the death and resurrection of Jesus. They did not choose to become a branch of Judaism alongside others, but instead set out to preach the gospel ('good news') of Jesus Christ with the aim of changing people's minds and converting them to Christianity. They did not see Christianity as an extra option for those who preferred a different kind of worship, but saw it as holding the key to salvation. They thought that they should try to convert as many people as possible to the Christian faith as an urgent task because, otherwise, those people would miss the opportunity for salvation. The early Christians believed that Jesus would return to the earth very soon, probably within their own lifetimes, and that he would divide people into believers and non-believers. The Christian believers would be destined for heaven and the others for eternal damnation. Only conversion to Christianity could save people.

Apply your knowledge

1. Read the story of Peter's vision in Acts 10:9–16. What does this story show about Christian attitudes towards Jewish kosher laws?

2. Read Matthew 28:16–20, which is the last passage of Matthew's gospel. What does this passage teach about Christian attitudes towards converting others?

Apply your knowledge

At the time of Jesus, the holiest part of the temple was kept secret, hidden from the public by a heavy curtain. Only the High Priest could go there, into the presence of God.

3. Look up Matthew 27:51, Mark 15:38 and Luke 23:45. Find out what happened to the curtain that separated the people from God, at the moment of Jesus' death.

4. What do you think the gospel writers intended readers to understand about the death of Jesus by this event?

This **exclusivist** view, where it is believed that salvation can be gained only through Christian faith and not through other belief systems, has been a mainstream position for most of Christian history. However, in more modern times, especially since the latter half of the twentieth century, the relationship between Christianity and other world religions has become an important issue for discussion.

Is it true that Christianity alone holds the key to salvation? Are those who sincerely follow the traditions of the dominant religion of their non-Christian culture destined for hell, however much they try to devote themselves to God and to caring for others? Can any truth be found in the teachings of religions other than Christianity? What, if anything, can Christians learn by talking, listening and sharing their beliefs with people of other faiths; by taking part in **inter-faith dialogue**? Should Christians actively try to convert others to Christianity? If someone is sincerely good but not particularly religious, or even actively anti-religious, does that goodness count for nothing?

Theology of religion looks, from the viewpoint of Christianity, at issues of truth, belief, salvation and dialogue that arise from the fact that Christianity exists in a religiously plural world.

In his book *Christians and Religious Pluralism* (1982), the writer Alan Race identifies three broad perspectives that Christians might adopt when understanding their relationship to believers of other faiths. Race calls these perspectives 'exclusivism', '**inclusivism**' and '**pluralism**'. He uses the term 'exclusivism' to encompass those views that hold that there is no salvation outside explicit commitment to the Christian faith. 'Inclusivism' is used to refer to those who agree that Christianity is the key to salvation, but think that it might be possible for non-Christians to be saved by Christ even if they do not recognise Christ as such. 'Pluralism' is the term used for views that hold that there are many different paths to salvation and that truth and salvation can be found in many different religious traditions and contexts.

Since Race wrote his book, other models in the theology of religion have also been explored. For example, in his book *Introducing Theologies of Religions* (2002), Paul F. Knitter set out a system with four different ways of looking at the relationship between Christianity and other world faiths.

As with all attempts to classify views into different categories, there are some thinkers who do not quite fit under one label and might, for example, be considered to be largely exclusivist or to have elements of pluralism in their thinking.

Think question

If Christian beliefs are true, does that mean that all non-Christian religious beliefs must be false?

One way of classifying different viewpoints in the theology of religion is to divide people into exclusivists, inclusivists and pluralists

The teaching of contemporary Christian theology of religion on exclusivism

'Exclusivism' is the name given to the belief that salvation can only be found through Christianity and that other religions cannot lead people to the right relationship with God. Most Christians believe that Christ's sacrificial death on the cross was a unique event of cosmic significance. The Christian exclusivist position claims that Jesus Christ, the Son of God, brought salvation to the world once and for all. Only through hearing the gospel and responding to it by faith in Christ can a person be saved. For some Christians, this includes going through the rite of baptism as a symbol of being cleansed from sin and reborn into Christian life as a new person. Salvation requires giving up one's old way of life and beginning a new one centred on Christ and his church. Christ did not come simply to add another option to the many different routes to heaven, but provides a pathway to God that cannot otherwise be found.

Some people who hold this view prefer the term '**particularist**', finding it less negative in tone than 'exclusivist', which might appear to convey hostility, arrogance or lack of respect for others.

Exclusivists believe that there is only one true religion

'Narrow' and 'broad' exclusivism

Exclusivism, or particularism, is a classification that covers a range of different views.

Some Christians have a narrowly exclusivist view, holding that salvation is available only to people who belong to their own particular denomination within Christianity. For example, some Christians who take the words of the Bible literally might make a distinction between what they call 'Bible-believing Christians' and others, and might claim that only those who have the same view of scripture as their own are 'true' Christians destined for heaven. Augustine in the fourth century and Calvin in the sixteenth century both took very narrow exclusivist views, believing and teaching that God elects through grace only a small number of Christians for heaven, so that simply belonging to the Christian religion and adopting Christian beliefs is not a guarantee of salvation. God chooses whom he will save and people cannot force God's choice.

See Chapter 3.2 of the AS and Year 1 book for more information on Augustine and Calvin's narrowly exclusivist view of election to heaven.

Some Catholics take the view that salvation is only for those who are baptised into the Catholic Church and who regularly receive the Eucharist only at those Masses celebrated by Catholic priests. The Church still officially teaches this. For a long time the motto '*extra ecclesiam nulla salus*', which translates as 'there is no salvation outside the Church', illustrated the exclusivist position taken by the Catholic church. However, attitudes began to change after **Vatican II**. Vatican II, more formally known as the Second Vatican Ecumenical Council, was a long series of meetings held between 1962 and 1965 in which leading figures in the Catholic Church discussed the role of the Church in the modern world, including its relationships with other Christian denominations and its relationships with other world religions. It led to a more outward-looking Catholicism with views that were not as narrowly exclusivist as before.

This teaching from the Catholic Church's document *Lumen Gentium* illustrates this change in approach:

> 66 Christ, the one Mediator, established and continually sustains here on earth His holy Church, the community of faith, hope and charity, as an entity with visible delineation through which He communicated truth and grace to all.
>
> This Church constituted and organized in the world as a society, subsists in the Catholic Church, which is governed by the successor of Peter and by the Bishops in communion with him, although many elements of sanctification and of truth are found outside of its visible structure. 99
>
> *Lumen Gentium*, 1964, Chapter 8

Within Christian exclusivism is the broader view holding that all people who accept Christ through faith are saved, regardless of the kind of Church to which they belong or the style of worship they prefer.

Some exclusivists hold that truth can be found in other religions, but it is only partial truth, which is not enough for salvation. They believe that salvation can only be found through Christianity.

The writer Gavin D'Costa divides exclusivists into two groups: those he calls 'restrictive-access exclusivists' and those he calls 'universal-access exclusivists' (D'Costa, *Christianity and World Religions*, 2009, pp. 25–33). Restrictive-access exclusivists are those who follow a similar view to John Calvin and who hold that salvation is only for those who hear and respond to the gospel during their earthly lives, before death. God saves only those whom he has chosen. Universal-access exclusivists are those who hold that Christ's salvation is offered to all and that it is the will of God that everyone should come to love him. Some universal-access exclusivists, most notably those in the Catholic tradition, draw attention to the possibility of salvation after death that is part of the concept of purgatory.

As a Catholic theologian, D'Costa takes this second, universal-access position. One of the biblical texts he uses in support of his views is 1 Timothy 2:3–6:

See Chapter 3.2 of the AS and Year 1 book for a discussion of the Catholic doctrine of purgatory, which includes the idea that people can continue to develop their relationship with God after death.

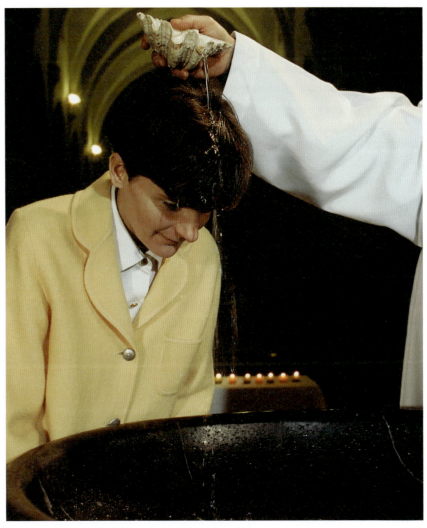

Many exclusivist Christians believe that people can only be saved if they make a deliberate personal commitment to Christ

> 66 This is good, and pleases God our Savior, who wants all people to be saved and to come to a knowledge of the truth. For there is one God and one mediator between God and mankind, the man Christ Jesus, who gave himself as a ransom for all people. This has now been witnessed to at the proper time. 99
>
> 1 Timothy 2:3–6, New International Version

D'Costa uses this passage to emphasise that although there is, in his view, only one exclusive way to salvation, nevertheless it is the will of God that this one route should be available to everyone and is offered to everyone.

Hendrik Kraemer

One well-known Christian exclusivist was Hendrik Kraemer (1888–1965), who was a leading figure in the Netherlands in the movement to bring different Christian denominations together (the ecumenical movement). His book *The Christian Message in a Non-Christian World* (1938) was very influential for Christian missionaries working in non-Christian countries, as he emphasised that non-Christians cannot achieve salvation through their own faith systems but have to convert to Christianity. Kraemer argued that God's revelation can be seen by others outside the Christian faith. For example, they can understand the existence and creativity of God through human reasoning and through observing the beauty and order of nature. However, he claimed, salvation can be found only in Christianity and not through any other religion, however well-meaning its followers might be.

One of Kraemer's arguments was that it does not make sense to look at religions other than Christianity and pick out the beliefs and practices that seem to be the most Christian as if they are points of contact. This is because religions are whole belief systems and ways of life, which have to be considered in their entirety. So, for example, finding that Confucianism, Hinduism and Buddhism, like Christianity, also teach 'always treat others as you would like them to treat you' does not demonstrate that these religions and Christianity are linked. Kraemer writes that religion 'is not a series of tenets, institutions, practices that can be taken one by one as independent items of religious life' (Kraemer, *The Christian Message in a Non-Christian World*, 1938, p. 40). Kraemer argued that all world religions have to be evaluated as whole systems and cannot be taken apart and considered in a piecemeal way. The religion as a whole either accepts the salvation offered by Christ or it does not; there is no middle ground or 'partial truth' to be found.

Exclusivism in the thinking of Karl Barth

The Protestant theologian Karl Barth (1886–1968) is well known for expressing views about the essential importance of Christ for human salvation. Most scholars classify him as an exclusivist thinker, although there are interesting arguments that suggest alternative classifications for Barth's thinking.

Barth believed that people cannot know God through their own efforts, but that God chooses to reveal himself through Jesus Christ, through the Bible and through the teachings of the church. One of Barth's distinctive messages was his 'theology of the Word', in which he asserted that knowledge of God can be found only where God chooses to reveal it through his word. The opening of John's gospel, on which Barth based his theology of the Word, reads:

> 66 In the beginning was the Word, and the Word was with God, and the Word was God. He was with God in the beginning. Through him all things were made; without him nothing was made that

Kraemer argued that religions should be considered as a whole, not piece by piece

Think question

Do you agree with Kraemer's argument? Could the same argument be made for political systems?

See Chapter 3.3 of the AS and Year 1 book where there is a discussion of Karl Barth's teaching that true knowledge of God can be found in God's revelation through Christ.

has been made. In him was life, and that life was the light of all mankind. The light shines in the darkness, and the darkness has not overcome it.

There was a man sent from God whose name was John. He came as a witness to testify concerning that light, so that through him all might believe. He himself was not the light; he came only as a witness to the light.

The true light that gives light to everyone was coming into the world. He was in the world, and though the world was made through him, the world did not recognize him. He came to that which was his own, but his own did not receive him. Yet to all who did receive him, to those who believed in his name, he gave the right to become children of God – children born not of natural descent, nor of human decision or a husband's will, but born of God.

The Word became flesh and made his dwelling among us. We have seen his glory, the glory of the one and only Son, who came from the Father, full of grace and truth. **99**

John 1:1–14, New International Version

Barth used this idea of Jesus as the living Word of God in developing his theology. He argued that this Word consists of three forms. The most important form is Jesus Christ, present from creation and made known to humanity through his life, death and resurrection. Barth thought that Jesus was the Word of God in human form, teaching and exemplifying God's love to humanity. The second form is the Bible, which is not the Word of God in a literal sense but is what he called a 'witness' to the revelation of God in Christ. The third form of the Word is the church's teaching, bringing the Christian message to people and spreading the gospel so that everyone has the chance to hear and respond to it. The Bible and the church become the Word of God when God chooses to use them to reveal himself. For Barth, Jesus Christ himself is the only totally reliable way to genuine knowledge of God, because Jesus is fully and uniquely the way in which God has chosen to make himself known.

Barth writes:

Barth's Theology of the Word underpins his views on the relationship between Christianity and other world religions

66 God created the world for no other reason than to enter into covenant fellowship with it in the incarnation, death and resurrection of Jesus Christ. **99**

Karl Barth, 'Church Dogmatics IV/1'. In *The Doctrine of Reconciliation*, Part 1, trans. G. W. Bromiley, 1956, p. 50

See Chapter 3.2 of the AS and Year 1 book where there is discussion of Christian views that hold that it is possible for a person to make a choice to accept the Christian message after death.

For Barth, then, God's self-revelation through Jesus Christ was and is unique. God cannot be found through human efforts, even if people are very sincere in trying to find him through their own beliefs and traditions, and through leading morally good lives according to whatever understanding of morality they might have. God can be known only through Christ.

Some people argue that Barth's theology is not entirely exclusivist. He does emphasise the centrality of Christ in salvation as the self-revelation of God. However, he also emphasises that God can and does reveal himself when he chooses, which could leave open the possibility of God choosing to reveal himself in other ways.

Inclusivism in Christian theology

The term 'inclusivism' in the theology of religion is used for the range of views that take a middle path between exclusivism and pluralism. Some thinkers are uncomfortable with a view that salvation is totally impossible outside the Christian church, but they want to maintain that Christianity holds the truth and do not want to go as far as suggesting that any other path to God is equal to that of commitment to Christianity.

Like exclusivist and pluralist views, inclusivism also describes a range of different positions. Some inclusivist thinkers accept the idea that salvation is still possible for the individual who turns to a Christian faith only after death. They argue that the end of human life is not the end of the opportunities to hear and respond to the gospel – perhaps God gives people a chance, after death, to repent and turn to him before entering heaven.

Many inclusivists adopt the idea that God's omnibenevolence leaves open a possibility of salvation even for non-Christians. They suggest that non-Christian religions hold a degree of truth and that God in his wisdom will make allowances for those who sincerely choose to follow him but are doing so in the context of the wrong religion.

Some inclusivists take the view that truth found in religions other than Christianity is the work of Christ, even though people might not recognise it as such and might attribute this truth to a different understanding of God. They might call Christ other names, but still be following him and accepting him even though they have given him a different label and do not know that he was to be found in Jesus of Nazareth.

Karl Rahner and the 'anonymous Christian'

Karl Rahner (1904–84) was a Catholic theologian who was extremely influential during the twentieth century and was one of the leading voices in the discussions of Vatican II. His name has come to be associated with inclusivism as a position in the theology of religion. In his book *Theological Investigations* (1967), he set out his thinking on the relationship between Christianity and other world religions and on questions about whether non-Christians could be saved.

Rahner explained that Christianity has a unique position in being the religion that is founded on God's ultimate act of revelation, when God came to earth in the person of Jesus. No other religion offers the salvation through Christ that is found in Christianity. Rahner described Christianity as the 'absolute' religion, seeing it as normative, in the sense that it sets the standard by which other religions should be measured. However, he went on to explain that an understanding of Christianity as absolute seems to exclude from salvation anyone who lived before Jesus came to earth, and anyone who has not been able to hear about God's revelation through Christ. For Rahner, this exclusion did not seem to be compatible with an omnibenevolent and all-wise God.

Religions other than Christianity, therefore, must have some means of aiding their followers towards the saving grace offered by God. It must be the case, Rahner argued, that God in Christ is able to offer salvation to those who, through no fault of their own, have not been able to respond to God in the Christian message, so Rahner rejected the exclusivist idea that there can be no salvation outside Christianity. He thought that there could be a kind of partial truth in other world religions, whose followers do not know about Jesus. Once someone who belongs to a religion other than Christianity has heard about the salvation offered through Christ, then that person should become a Christian in order to be saved, as there would no longer be any excuse for rejecting the gospel.

Rahner rejected the idea that all religions are in some ways equal as paths to God. Christianity holds the truth, in his view, but the grace of God makes allowances for those who have not been able to access this truth. God in Christ can save people even if they do not realise that it is Christ who is saving them. People can devote their lives to the service of others without realising that in doing so, they are following Jesus' example.

The document *Lumen gentium* ('A Light to the Nations') was one of the principal achievements of Vatican II, and it teaches that those who, through

Rahner was a leading figure in discussions about how Catholic Christianity should work in the modern world

Rahner argued that religions other than Christianity might hold a partial truth

....

66 no fault of their own, do not know the Gospel of Christ or His Church, but who nevertheless seek God with a sincere heart, and moved by grace, try in their actions to do His will as they know it through the dictates of their conscience – those too may achieve eternal salvation 99

Lumen gentium, 1964, Chapter 2.16

....

Rahner's thinking on inclusivism as a Christian response to world religions is often credited as being influential in bringing the Catholic Church to this view.

Hendrik Kraemer, the exclusivist thinker, argued that non-Christian religions are little more than misguided attempts by some people to try and find the truth for themselves. Non-Christian religions are, for Kraemer, cultural constructs rather than responses to the revelation of God in Christ. Rahner, however, disagreed and thought that non-Christian religions can hold some degree of truth. To support his argument, he used the example of figures from the Old Testament who are praised for their faith in the Bible, but who obviously were not in a position to respond to the message of Christ because they lived before Christ. Abraham, Moses and Job, for example, are seen as exemplars of people who had faith in God and sustained their faith through difficult times. They were aware of the grace of God and dedicated their lives to God, but were unaware that this came through the revelation of God in Christ, who would come to earth after their lifetimes. Job, for example, spoke of his confidence in God in terms that Christians might see as referring to Jesus, even though Job himself did not know this:

Rahner used the term 'anonymous Christians' to describe people who were living good lives and who could be saved even if they did not explicitly express Christian belief

66 I know that my redeemer lives,
and that in the end he will stand on the earth. 99

Job 19:25, New International Version

Rahner used these Old Testament examples to argue that the Bible supports the view that people who do not know Christ can have genuine faith in God, and that God recognises this. Rahner called such people 'anonymous Christians'. They do not call themselves Christian, they have not been baptised and they do not go to church or read the Bible; but in the decisions that they make and the attitudes they adopt, they are turning to Christ without knowing it and they are not excluded from salvation.

Exclusivists often refer to biblical passages to support the view that there can be no salvation for non-Christians, but inclusivists also find support for their position in the Bible. For example, in Paul's letter to the Romans, he writes:

66 (Indeed, when Gentiles, who do not have the law, do by nature things required by the law, they are a law for themselves, even though they do not have the law. They show that the requirements of the law are written on their hearts, their consciences also bearing witness, and their thoughts sometimes accusing them and at other times even defending them.) This will take place on the day when God judges people's secrets through Jesus Christ, as my gospel declares. 99

Romans 2:14–16, New International Version

This passage might be used to support the idea that non-believers can still have an intuitive sense for Christ, even if they do not recognise it as such, and that God will treat them with justice.

Another passage that can also be interpreted as representing an inclusivist view comes from the parable of The Sheep and the Goats in Matthew's gospel, where Jesus is talking about those who help the poor, visit people in prison and look after the sick:

> 66 He will put the sheep on his right and the goats on his left.
>
> 'Then the King will say to those on his right, "Come, you who are blessed by my Father; take your inheritance, the kingdom prepared for you since the creation of the world. For I was hungry and you gave me something to eat, I was thirsty and you gave me something to drink, I was a stranger and you invited me in, I needed clothes and you clothed me, I was sick and you looked after me, I was in prison and you came to visit me."
>
> 'Then the righteous will answer him, "Lord, when did we see you hungry and feed you, or thirsty and give you something to drink? When did we see you a stranger and invite you in, or needing clothes and clothe you? When did we see you sick or in prison and go to visit you?"
>
> 'The King will reply, "Truly I tell you, whatever you did for one of the least of these brothers and sisters of mine, you did for me."' 99
>
> Matthew 25: 33–40

The passage can be interpreted as saying that any people who treat others with altruistic love are working for Christ, whether or not they realise it.

Rahner's inclusivist thinking has not been universally accepted by the Catholic Church. Hans Urs von Balthasar was a colleague of Rahner's and a fierce critic of the idea of the 'anonymous Christian'. Von Balthasar's writings emphasise what he saw as the absolute centrality for human salvation of Jesus' crucifixion and resurrection. He reminded his readers of Saint Cordula, who knew that the Huns were attacking and at first went and hid from them. Then she remembered that death was not final, came out of hiding, affirmed her faith and was martyred for it. Von Balthasar argued that the Church should not go into hiding in the modern secular world or present a watered-down version of the Christian message in order to appease people of other faiths or of no faith; it should instead be able to stand out in the open and be courageous in its claims that salvation is to be found only in Christ.

Think question

Do you think people can have an intuitive understanding of the Christian life even if they have never heard of Christianity?

Apply your knowledge

6. Some people argue that an inclusivist position is demeaning to the faith of someone from a non-Christian religion, by saying to them that, even if they think they are following their own religion, they are really following Christ without knowing it. Do you agree with this criticism? Give reasons for your answer.

7. Do you think someone can have a Christian morality without the Christian beliefs that motivate it? Explain why, or why not.

8. Do you think an inclusivist position is preferable to an exclusivist position for Christians? Explain why, or why not.

Pluralism as a response to questions of the theology of religion

Pluralists believe that different religions can all be paths to salvation or enlightenment

The term 'pluralism' is used for a range of positions which hold that many different religious traditions can have value and the potential to lead their followers to salvation, enlightenment or whatever people choose to call it. Pluralists tend to argue that different religions share the same ultimate goal. The beliefs and practices associated with different religions arise because of human culture, and the differences are only superficial. The religions all offer paths to the same destination, so people should not feel that they have to convert each other to the 'true' religion as there are many different ways for people to make their way to God, or Reality, or whatever term might be used.

The parable of the blind men and the elephant is often used by pluralists to support their views. This is a parable that originated in India, where blind men (or sometimes men in the dark) encounter an elephant. Each feels a different part: the trunk, the tusk, the ear, the flank and so on. Each, therefore, has a different understanding of what the elephant is like, and the men argue. However, they are all encountering the same elephant.

John Hick's pluralist views

One strong advocate of the pluralist view of the relationship between Christianity and other world religions is John Hick (1922–2012). Hick was an evangelical Christian as a young man, firmly convinced of the truth of Christianity and of the need to convert others to the Christian message of salvation through Christ. However, when he worked in Birmingham he was impressed by the faith and the service to others of people he met who belonged to other religions, for example Sikhs, Hindus and Muslims. He noticed in many of them their commitment to prayer, their family values, their willingness to work together to help disadvantaged people and their genuine devotion to living godly lives. For Hick, this raised serious questions. Was it really true that a God of love would condemn such people and deny them salvation, just because their cultural heritage was such that they were looking to serve God in a religion other than Christianity?

Hick writes:

> 66 As soon as one does meet and come to know people of other faiths a paradox of gigantic proportions becomes disturbingly obvious. We say as Christians that God is the God of universal love, that he is the creator and Father of all mankind, that he

wills the ultimate good and salvation of all men. But we also say, traditionally, that the only way to salvation is the Christian way. And yet we know, when we stop to think about it, that the large majority of the human race who have lived and died up to the present moment have lived either before Christ or outside the borders of Christendom. Can we then accept the conclusion that the God of love who seeks to save all mankind has nevertheless ordained that men must be saved in such a way that only a small minority can in fact receive this salvation? **"**

John Hick, *God and the Universe of Faiths*, 1993, p. 122

Hick suggested that there was a need for what he called a 'Copernican revolution' in theology. Copernicus caused a huge shift in the way scientists of his day understood the universe, by proposing that the Earth was not at the centre but that it was one of a number of planets that orbited the Sun. Copernicus met with resistance, but once people accepted that the Sun was at the centre and not Earth, other astronomical observations began to make a lot more sense. Hick used this Copernican revolution in the way people thought about the planets as an analogy for what he believed was the right direction for theology. Instead of seeing Christianity as a normative absolute, and measuring other religions against Christianity, Hick thought that people should put God, or 'Reality', at the centre. Christianity is then seen as one of the 'planets' alongside others, all of which have a common centre.

Hick used the philosophy of Immanuel Kant in formulating his pluralist theology. Kant drew a distinction between the '**noumenal**' and the '**phenomenal**'. The noumenal world is a world of things as they really are, whereas the phenomenal world is the world as it appears to us. We filter our experiences of the world and interpret them, not always consciously, so that the act of knowing something gives us a phenomenal understanding. We see things from a perspective, as they relate to us and as we can understand them, rather than as they are in themselves. Kant thought that the nature of God belongs in the noumenal world. We are not capable of knowing God as he really is, because of our finite minds. We are only capable of making a limited attempt at knowing God, relating him to ourselves and who we are.

Hick argued that religion is a human, phenomenal attempt to understand and relate to God. All religions are human constructs, where we filter what we can understand of God in accordance with our own contexts and cultural upbringing. Every religion, according to Hick, falls short of the truth because none is capable of a noumenal understanding of God. This is why religions can have different and sometimes contradictory beliefs.

For Hick, Christianity should not be understood as 'the truth'. In his view, it has its flaws, just as every religion does. Hick recognised that his position on the theology of religion meant that he had to rethink how

Apply your knowledge

9. Find out more about Copernicus' breakthrough in science, which was supported by Galileo. Why do you think the Church was resistant to the idea that the sun is at the centre of the universe?

Hick argued that religion comes from flawed human attempts to connect with 'the Real'

Hick argued that religious belief and practice are based on human culture. Different ways of worship are all attempts to approach the same reality

Hick's theology involved an Irenaean response to the problem of evil, allowing for universal salvation. See Chapter 1.6 of the AS and Year 1 book for a discussion of the Irenaean response to the problem of evil.

Christianity should be understood. He came to the conclusion that the truth-claims of Christianity, such as that Jesus was God incarnate (God made flesh), that Jesus rose back to life after death and that Jesus' mother was a virgin when she conceived Jesus through the Holy Spirit, were not cognitive claims about literal facts but should be understood as myth. These claims are, in Hick's view, pictorial ways of expressing the human relationship with what he calls 'the Real', and should not be understood as historical truth. Once they are understood as myth, differences between the truth claims of different religions become different symbols, each meaningful in their own contexts rather than contradictory.

Hick believed that a God of love would not organise the universe in such a way that salvation was limited to only some people. His pluralism also involves an understanding of life after death in which everyone has the opportunity to continue the journey towards 'the Real' in a post-mortem existence.

The relationship between Christianity and other religions in the thinking of Raimon Panikkar

Raimon (or Raimundo) Panikkar (1918–2010) had a different kind of pluralist view from that of Hick. Panikkar explicitly did not think that there are many different truths or that the world's religions are different ways of expressing one truth. Instead he talked about the need for openness, rather than making any claims to know what 'the truth' is or where it might be found.

Panikkar came from a mixed-faith family – his father was an Indian Hindu and his mother was a Spanish Catholic. So he grew up feeling equally at home in both religious traditions. He grew up in Spain and went to a Catholic school. He visited India to study for the first time in 1954 and was quoted in the *New York Times* as commenting, 'I left Europe as a Christian, I discovered I was a Hindu and returned as a Buddhist without ever having ceased to be a Christian' (*New York Times*, September 2010). This visit marked a turning point for him. He met and studied with several Christian monks who had embraced the spiritual richness of India and who were trying to live according to Christian principles within the cultural context of Hindu and Buddhist beliefs and practices. Panikkar was deeply impressed by the ways in which these thinkers had overcome differences between faiths, and in particular he adopted their commitment to the Hindu concept of Advaita, which looks to the essential sacred unity of all things. Because he had grown up in the Catholic faith, Panikkar had a deep knowledge of the work of Thomas Aquinas, which he compared with Hindu sacred texts and teachings.

Panikkar did not claim to have uncovered a truth about the one and only correct way to understand the relationship between different world faiths, but instead emphasised the mystery of the divine. He talked about the need to discover truth by living it, choosing actions and words with a vision of harmony between people, and trying to find the essential nature of what it means to be human in the presence of the divine without destroying different cultural traditions and diversity. He talked of trying to find his religious identity by losing it, not holding on stubbornly to traditions of the past but letting go of them and treating life as a searching pilgrimage. Panikkar did not simply advocate showing respect for religious traditions other than one's own. He thought it was necessary to respect the freedom of God, or of whatever one understands to be the divine, to work in ways that go beyond human attempts to define it and make it into a system of doctrines.

John Hick saw the Christian understanding of Jesus as mythical, in which Jesus was a symbolic way of understanding God that had developed in the Christian tradition but which needed to be seen as limited by human flaws. For Hick, the Christian myth of God in Christ was not the only way of understanding God. Panikkar took a somewhat different view. He often spoke and wrote of 'Christophany', which means Christ being made plain to human consciousness. Panikkar saw Christ not as a specific individual, but as a name for God showing himself to people. 'Christ', for Panikkar, is the word Christians use for God making himself known; other religions have other words for it. Panikkar thought that Christophany was not limited to the figure of Jesus of Nazareth. Christ, in the sense of God making himself known, can be found in other religious traditions apart from Christianity, although it would be called something else and not 'Christ'. For example, in the Hindu tradition, *ishwara* is a concept that refers to a personal God or supreme soul or spiritual inspiration, through which people can have personal encounters with the divine.

> ## Think question
>
> What do you think Panikkar meant when he said he tried to find his religious identity by losing it?

Panikkar thought that God can make himself known in religions other than Christianity

Panikkar saw religious pluralism as a spiritual attitude rather than an intellectually reasoned position

In some ways, Panikkar's thinking is similar to that of Rahner, who believed that someone could be an 'anonymous Christian' by recognising the truth of Christianity without putting Christian labels onto that truth. The title of Panikkar's book, *The Unknown Christ of Hinduism* (1965), certainly has echoes of Rahner's 'anonymous Christian' idea. However, Rahner understood Christianity to hold more truth than other religions, whereas Panikkar thought that this was putting a limit on God's freedom to make himself known however he wishes. Panikkar argued that Christians have choices: they can bring their own understanding of Christ to other people and other religions and try to get others to see Christ their way, or they can recognise the unknown, mysterious dimension of Christ revealed in many different contexts and work towards developing in themselves a receptive attitude of love. Panikkar saw the second of these two choices as being the more Christian.

Like many thinkers, Panikkar is quite difficult to classify. Often he is designated as a pluralist, as he believed that the truth can be found in many contexts and that Christ can be revealed in whatever way God chooses. However, he did not like being called a 'pluralist', as he thought the title suggested that he had taken up an intellectual position on the relationship between Christianity and other religions, whereas he believed that religious pluralism is a spiritual position rather than a position based on intellectual reasoning.

Discussing religious pluralism and theology

If Christ is the 'truth', can there be any other means of salvation?

The exclusivist position in the theology of religion holds that, because Christ is the truth, there can be no other means of salvation. Exclusivists often use a quotation from John's gospel to support their position:

> 66 Jesus answered, 'I am the way and the truth and the life. No one comes to the Father except through me.' 99

> John 14:6, New International Version

They argue that the Bible reveals that there is only one way to salvation, which is through Christ. Another argument offered is that Christ's death on the cross had a once-for-all cosmic significance. Jesus did not come to earth and suffer and die simply to provide an extra alternative route to salvation, but was the fulfillment of God's plan, enabling people to become reconciled with God by atoning for their sins brought into the world by Adam.

Exclusivists also argue that it is irrational to hold the view that more than one religion can be true, because they teach different things. All of the religions could be wrong, but they cannot all be right. Islam, Judaism and Christianity, for example, are strictly monotheistic, whereas Hinduism contains a range of beliefs including the idea that there are many deities, and significant branches of Buddhism do not teach a belief in God at all. Christianity claims definitively that Jesus was the Son of God, whereas Judaism and Islam teach that he was not. They cannot all be right.

Exclusivists recognise that a relativist position is fashionable in the modern world, with respect and 'tolerance' for the beliefs of others being seen as a virtue to be encouraged. Being 'judgemental', in the sense of telling others that they are wrong and should follow your views instead tends to be frowned upon. However, exclusivists argue that people should not be led by political correctness and a fear of offending

Apply your knowledge

10. What do you think are the key similarities and differences between Hick's view and Panikkar's view?

11. Which, if either, of these views do you find more persuasive? Give reasons for your answer.

Think question

Do you think that Christian missionary work fails to respect people's rights to hold their own opinions? Give reasons for your answer.

others on matters of ultimate truth. The Christian message, they claim, is not a matter of personal taste but is of vital importance for everyone's eternal soul and, therefore, it is necessary to make it plain to non-Christians that they are wrong because of the dangers of following a non-Christian path. Missionary work and trying to convert others to Christianity is a duty, not a sign of arrogance.

Inclusivism and pluralism undermine the work of those who have given their lives for the Christian faith; if Christianity is only one of many routes to salvation, then it is pointless for people to sacrifice their lives as witnesses to Christianity.

However, some critics of an exclusivist position point out that revelation requires interpretation. There are uncertainties about which are the very words spoken by Jesus and which are part of the gospel writers' crafting of the narrative of Jesus' life in order to communicate the Christian message. There are uncertainties about how different parts of the Bible should be interpreted, with the result that even within Christianity there is not total agreement about exactly what is 'the truth'. The evidence for only one right viewpoint is thin and requires faith, making it difficult to justify to people of a different faith, who make similar claims for their own revelation.

Probably the strongest criticism of exclusivism is that it makes God seem unfair if only those who believe the Christian gospel are to be saved. Some people have much easier access to the Christian message than others. Even with today's technology and easy access to information, there may still be people who have never heard of Christianity, or they might have heard of it but be totally immersed in the religion of their own culture. Someone who has been brought up in a Christian family, in a country where Christianity is the dominant religion, is likely to find it far easier to accept Christianity than someone whose family follows a different faith or no faith at all. In addition, there is the problem of those who lived before Jesus and never had the opportunity to be saved by faith in Christ; the problem of those who have severe learning difficulties such that they cannot understand the Christian message; and the problem of those who live such short lives that they do not have the chance to choose to be Christian. For inclusivist and pluralist Christians, the idea that a God of love would deny people salvation, including those who had genuinely tried to find him within their own tradition, is unacceptable.

William Lane Craig (b. 1949), a Christian philosopher and theologian, proposed an interesting way of overcoming this difficulty with exclusivism, by making reference to the omniscience of God. For Craig, God's perfect knowledge includes what is known as 'middle knowledge'. This means that God not only knows what is in every person's heart, so that he can judge them on the basis of their faith as well as their actions; God also knows, with perfect knowledge, what people would have done if they were in different circumstances. God's 'middle knowledge', according to Craig, enables God to know whether people would have believed the Christian message if only they had the chance to hear it. There is no possibility that God could unfairly deny salvation to some people, because God is never unfair and God knows what decisions they would have taken about faith in Christ. If some people never have the opportunity to hear the gospel, then that is because God already knows that they would not have taken any notice of it even if they had heard it. It also enables God to judge correctly the souls of babies and children whose lives are too short for them to make a firm commitment to Christ, because God knows what they would have chosen if they had lived to adulthood.

However, critics of William Lane Craig point out that if God does have this 'middle knowledge' and uses it to judge whether or not someone is saved, then there is little point in Christians trying to convert others; it also calls into question the extent to which people have genuine free will. God would be able to judge non-Christians on the basis of what they would have done had they heard the gospel, which, it can be argued, takes away the urgency of Christian mission.

The inclusivist might answer the question of whether Christ is the only 'truth' by saying that Christ is the only means of salvation, but that people do not necessarily have to be aware that they are following Christ in order to be saved. They could be 'anonymous Christians'. Jesus' death and resurrection made salvation possible for everyone, whether they know it or not; Christ is the only truth but people do not have to know the truth in order to be saved. Brendan Sweetman gives an analogy to clarify this idea:

> 66 Suppose that in a particular city engineers put fluoride into the water, and that this leads to the people in the town having healthier teeth. These facts are true not just for those who believe that there is fluoride in the water, and that it leads to healthier teeth, but even for all those who deny one or both of these facts. All that matters is that one drink the water! This is analogous to the way in which the Christian inclusivist thinks that the death and resurrection of Jesus makes salvation possible for all, as long as they live the right kind of life and genuinely seek out God. It does not matter whether they believe in Christianity, or whether they believe that Jesus lived but did not rise from the dead, or whatever. All that matters (metaphysically) is that Jesus did rise from the dead, and that this act made salvation possible for all, irrespective of one's particular religion. 99

Brendan Sweetman, *Religion, Key Concepts in Philosophy*, 2007, p. 154

One of the difficulties with an inclusivist position is that it becomes unclear whether or not missionary work is a good idea. If people can be saved whether or not they explicitly accept Christian doctrines and beliefs, perhaps there is no need to try and convert them.

Think question

Should people be judged according to what they would have done in different circumstances, even if they never did it? For example, if someone would have saved a baby from a burning building if they had been there at the time of the fire, but never actually did so, should that person still be regarded as a hero?

Apply your knowledge

12. What do you think of the idea that someone can be following Christ without realising it? If people are accidentally following Christ, should they be judged in the same way as people who make a deliberate choice to follow him? Give reasons for your answer.

13. Some people argue that only God can judge who is saved and who is not, so there is no need for people to have exclusivist, inclusivist or pluralist opinions about it. What do you think of this point of view?

See Chapter 3.2 of the AS and Year 1 book where there is a discussion of the doctrines of election taught by Augustine and Calvin, where only a limited number of people would be saved.

A pluralist response to this issue would involve questioning whether Christ is 'the truth' in a unique way, and in a cognitive way. In other words, a pluralist would question the idea that 'Jesus is the truth' is a statement of fact rather than a statement about a preferred way of looking at things. Christian pluralists might argue that Christ is 'a truth', rather than 'the truth', and would support the view that salvation is possible outside the Christian faith. However, this position has its difficulties. It is difficult to see how 'Jesus Christ is the Son of God' could be just as true as 'Jesus was not the Christ and was not the Son of God'. Pluralists have to resort to a different view of religious truth-claims, saying that they are not necessarily cognitive but have some other function instead. The truth-claims could, for example, be mythological or symbolic ways of communication rather than factual statements.

Does it make sense to claim that a loving God would ultimately deny any human being salvation?

For Hick and many other Christian pluralists and inclusivists, the idea that some people will be denied salvation, especially if they are genuinely trying to lead a holy life, is incompatible with belief in a God of love. They argue that God could have revealed himself in different ways to people in different times and cultures, and that God is free to make himself known in whatever way he wishes. God's omniscient will means that he never makes mistakes in judging people's actions and beliefs and always acts with perfect love, justice and mercy, forgiving sins and making sure that everyone ultimately ends up saved.

Other Christians, however, argue that if a relationship with God is to be meaningful, then it must come from a person's conscious decision to have that relationship. People must be free to choose not to have a relationship with God and not to be saved. People have to be free to make a choice about Christianity, and decide whether to believe the gospel, follow the beliefs of another religion instead or reject religion altogether. A God of love would not force someone's choice by imposing salvation on all, whether they want it or not.

Some Christians, such as Augustine and Calvin, have argued that salvation is only for the elect, the few whom God chooses for eternal life in heaven. They believe that everyone is tainted with the original sin of Adam and Eve, so that no one at all deserves salvation. For them, it is a sign of God's supreme love and grace that he offers salvation to anyone.

Many Christians argue that God is a God of justice, as well as a God of love. They argue that God makes the opportunity of salvation available to everyone, as Christ died for everyone and accepts everyone who believes in him. However, if people do not want to take up this opportunity, then they have chosen their own fate and cannot blame God for the consequences of their choice. It could be argued that it would be unjust of God to give salvation to everyone, even those who reject him and those who commit terrible crimes, alongside those who have dedicated their lives to Christianity and to helping others.

It could also be argued that if salvation is ultimately given to everyone, then it makes religion rather pointless. It means that Jesus died on the cross for no reason, because everyone would have been saved anyway and there are many alternative paths to God. It means that making a commitment to Christianity, or to any other religion, is unnecessary, and leading a morally good life is not important if everyone receives salvation whether they believe or not.

Does Christian belief include the view that all good people will be saved?

Many people struggle with the idea that well-meaning, kind, honest people who are not Christians will be denied salvation. There are many examples of men and women who have sacrificed their lives for others, or who have done huge amounts for charity, or who have fought against injustice in world-changing ways but who have not explicitly claimed to have Christian beliefs. Will God refuse them salvation, but still give it to others who profess Christian belief and go to church but do a lot less to help others?

The relation between beliefs and actions in Christianity has caused controversy ever since Christianity began. In the New Testament, early Christians can be seen to be debating 'faith and works'. Is it faith that brings people to salvation, or is it their deeds?

Some passages of the Bible suggest that Christian faith alone is both necessary and sufficient for salvation:

> 66 For God so loved the world that he gave his one and only Son, that whoever believes in him shall not perish but have eternal life. For God did not send his Son into the world to condemn the world, but to save the world through him. Whoever believes in him is not condemned, but whoever does not believe stands condemned already because they have not believed in the name of God's one and only Son.' 99
>
> John 3:16–18, New International Version

> 66 And God raised us up with Christ and seated us with him in the heavenly realms in Christ Jesus, in order that in the coming ages he might show the incomparable riches of his grace, expressed in his kindness to us in Christ Jesus. For it is by grace you have been saved, through faith—and this is not from yourselves, it is the gift of God—not by works, so that no one can boast. 99
>
> Ephesians 2:6–9, New International Version

Apply your knowledge

14. Do you think it is possible for God to be perfectly loving and perfectly just at the same time? Give reasons for your answer.

15. Do you think it would be more just of God to save everyone, or more just to save only those who have made the effort to follow him in their earthly lives? Give reasons for your answer.

These passages and others can be used to make the claim that the Bible supports Christian exclusivism. No one is good enough to deserve salvation; everyone is guilty of sin, both because of the original sin of Adam and Eve and because humans are fallible creatures who always fall short of God's standards. Being 'good' cannot bring a person to salvation; salvation is freely offered to those who accept Christ explicitly and accept the grace of God, who forgives the sins of all who have Christian faith.

However, other passages emphasise the need for people to do the right things in order to be saved, and they do not always mention faith. In the Old Testament, for example, the prophet Micah sums up the things God asks of his followers:

66 He has shown you, O mortal, what is good.
And what does the Lord require of you?
To act justly and to love mercy
and to walk humbly with your God. 99

Micah 6:8, New International Version

The parable of the sheep and the goats, in Matthew's gospel, shows the Son of Man (which Christians understand to be Jesus) judging people, not on the basis of their faith but entirely on their actions and their treatment of the poor, the sick, strangers and those in prison. Such passages could be used to support Christian inclusivist or pluralist positions, arguing that the Bible teaches that God will judge people on the basis of their actions rather than on their adherence to particular doctrines.

In addition, there is a famous passage in the New Testament where the writer argues that faith and good deeds have to go together:

66 What good is it, my brothers and sisters, if someone claims to have faith but has no deeds? Can such faith save them? Suppose a brother or a sister is without clothes and daily food. If one of you says to them, 'Go in peace; keep warm and well fed,' but does nothing about their physical needs, what good is it? In the same way, faith by itself, if it is not accompanied by action, is dead.

But someone will say, 'You have faith; I have deeds.'

Show me your faith without deeds, and I will show you my faith by my deeds. You believe that there is one God. Good! Even the demons believe that—and shudder.

You foolish person, do you want evidence that faith without deeds is useless? Was not our father Abraham considered righteous for what he did when he offered his son Isaac on the altar? You see that his faith and his actions were working together, and his faith was made complete by what he did. And the scripture was fulfilled that says, 'Abraham believed God, and it was credited to him as righteousness,' and he was called God's friend. You see that a person is considered righteous by what they do and not by faith alone. **99**

James 2:14–24, New International Version

The message here seems to be that faith is incomplete without the moral actions that it inspires. The example chosen is that of Abraham, who lived before Jesus and so did not have explicit faith in Christ and yet was still 'considered righteous'. This passage would not support a pluralist position, but it could be used to support Christian inclusivism.

An issue that arises in the debate about whether all good people are saved is that of whether all religions, or even all people, have the same fundamental moral code. Inclusivists and pluralists often argue that it would be unjust of God to condemn the morally good non-Christian, but this carries the assumption that there is the same moral code inside Christianity as there is outside it. In practice, this assumption is questionable. Different people have different ideas about morality and what constitutes a 'good person'. For example, some people might admire a conscientious objector in wartime for his pacifist principles and refusal to kill, while others might condemn him as a coward who will not defend the weak. Even within one religion, although there are many moral rules that are common to all mainstream traditions, there can also be some significant differences of opinion, for example about the moral acceptability of homosexual relationships. Furthermore, if non-Christians have essentially the same moral code as Christians, so that they could be living a 'Christian' life in spite of lacking explicit Christian beliefs, this suggests that acceptance of the central messages of Christianity does not make much difference to a person's moral behaviour.

Does theological pluralism undermine central Christian beliefs?

One of the strongest objections to pluralism is that it seems to undermine central Christian beliefs. It presents a serious challenge to the belief that Jesus' death and resurrection were unique events through which God made salvation possible. It begs the question: which Christian beliefs are to be considered 'central', and which, if any, can be regarded as expressions of culture and tradition rather than 'the truth'?

In his book *God and the Universe of Faiths* (1993), Hick lists aspects of traditional Christianity that he felt were 'either quite untenable or open to serious doubt' (p. 92). These aspects include:

- the idea that there are divinely revealed truths

- the idea that god created the universe out of nothing

> ### Apply your knowledge
>
> **16.** Would you agree that it is possible for people to live morally good lives without being at all religious? Give reasons for your answer.
>
> **17.** Do you think it is possible for someone to have Christian faith but not make an effort to live a morally good life? Give reasons for your answer.
>
> **18.** How far does religious belief make a difference to someone's moral code? Do we all have the same basic morals whether we are religious or not?

- the doctrine of the Fall

- the idea of Christ coming to save people from their fallen state

- the idea that the death of Jesus paid a necessary price for human sin

- the doctrine of the Virgin Birth

- the belief that Jesus performed miracles that suspended the laws of nature

- the belief that Jesus' dead body was resurrected from the grave and returned to earthly life

- the belief that people must have explicit faith in Christ to be saved

- the belief that the point of death 'fixes' someone's eternal destiny

- the belief in heaven and hell.

Hick thought that all of these ideas need to be understood as non-cognitive, mythological ways of expressing the human relationship with God, and cannot be taken literally. The list made his critics wonder whether anything was left of Christianity at all. Hick's view demands a radical understanding of the Bible as full of symbol and myth rather than as a book of divinely revealed truth.

Not all pluralists would go as far as Hick in rejecting the literal truth of so many traditional Christian ideas. However, it is difficult for a pluralist to assert that salvation can be found in all religions while still holding on to many traditional Christian doctrines.

Hick argued, however, that doctrines such as those he lists are not central to a relationship with God, but are examples of religious beliefs and practices that belong in the realm of the phenomenal rather than the noumenal. They arise out of human attempts to express their search for God in their different cultural contexts, through the use of symbol and myth. For Hick, the central Christian belief of the love of God is not lost or undermined by a pluralist position. Instead, in his view, the central Christian belief in a God of unconditional love is undermined by the phenomena of traditional Christian doctrine.

Some writers have criticised Hick because he explains that human religion is phenomenal and flawed, and that we are unable to see things as they really are, but then proceeds to tell us how things really are when he argues that all religions essentially lead to the same end goal. It is as though he is claiming insight of a 'bird's-eye view' kind which is hidden from everyone else. His critics argue that the Bible contains God's revelation and can be trusted more than Hick's assessment of reality.

Panikkar's version of pluralism might be considered less undermining of traditional Christian beliefs, as he emphasises God's revelation in Christ and he does not suggest discarding any traditional Christian doctrines. However, Panikkar's encouragement to people to be open to the truths of other religions might be seen to undermine the doctrine that there is no salvation outside the Christian church.

> **Think question**
>
> If all of the traditional ideas listed by Hick are taken out of Christianity, do you think there is anything left? If so, what is it?

Learning support

Points to remember

» The 'theology of religion' addresses questions about the relationship between religions, and whether if one religion is true the others must therefore be false.

» Different positions within the theology of religion are classified in different ways. Dividing them into exclusivism, inclusivism and pluralism is just one way of classifying them.

» Within each category, there are a range of views and different responses to the questions that the theology of religion raises.

» Often, individual thinkers are hard to classify under one particular label. Some people are largely exclusivist but have some inclusivist beliefs for example.

Enhance your learning

» Brendan Sweetman's *Religion: 'Key Concepts in Philosophy'* (2007) is an engaging and accessible book. Chapter 8 is especially relevant to the topic of the relationship between world religions.

» *God and the Universe of Faiths* (1993) details John Hick's pluralist position. Chapters 1, 9 and 10 are most relevant. It can sometimes be demanding to read, but it is worth the effort.

» John Hick's *The Rainbow of Faiths* (1995) also explains Hick's views about different world religions and their relationship.

» Chapter 17 of *Christian Theology: An Introduction* (2010, 5th edition), Alister McGrath's scholarly and very clear text, explores different perspectives in the theology of religion.

» In Chapter 5 of *Christianity and World Religions* (2009), Gavin D'Costa presents a clear case for an inclusivist Catholic point of view, while discussing different possibilities.

Practice for exams

At A level, essay questions invite you to demonstrate your knowledge and understanding of factual material (AO1) and also your critical ability in putting forward a coherent, balanced argument (AO2). You should aim to write essays that are persuasive responses to the question throughout, rather than writing a lot of description and then tacking an opinion on at the end of each paragraph.

To what extent does a theologically pluralist approach undermine the central doctrines of Christianity?

This question asks you to consider whether a pluralist view undermines Christianity, and if so, how far it does so. Therefore, you need to form an opinion about this.

You could think about which doctrines of Christianity you think are 'central'. You might want to consider whether, if it did undermine Christianity, that would be unacceptable, or perhaps a good thing.

For high marks in AO1, you need to show a solid knowledge and understanding of religious pluralism as a theological position. Try to make reference to scholarly thinkers, and give their views a critical commentary in order to score well in AO2.

'Non-Christians who live morally good lives and genuinely seek God can be considered to be "anonymous Christians".' Discuss.

This question refers to the views of Karl Rahner. You need to be able to show knowledge and understanding of his inclusivist views and their influence on the Catholic Church to gain high marks for AO1. For AO2, you need to give a reasoned argument supporting or criticising Rahner's ideas about 'anonymous Christians'. You might want to compare Rahner's views with those of other thinkers, for example Barth and/or Hick. Make sure that you give an assessment of Rahner's views rather than just explaining them.

Chapter 3.2

Religious pluralism and society

Can members of different religions live and work peacefully together?

How have Christians responded to living in multi-faith communities?

What is inter-faith dialogue and what does it achieve?

How far, if at all, can Christians engage in dialogue with other faiths without compromising their own faith?

Should Christians try to convert members of other religions, and people of no faith, to Christianity?

Key Terms

Multi-faith societies: societies where there are significant populations of people with different religious beliefs

Encyclical: an open letter sent to more than one recipient

Missionary work: activity that aims to convert people to a particular faith or set of beliefs, or works for social justice in areas of poverty or deprivation

Synod: the legislative body of the Church of England

Social cohesion: when a group is united by bonds that help them to live together peacefully

Specification requirements

- The development of contemporary multi-faith societies
- Christian responses to, including:
  - responses of Christian communities to inter-faith dialogue
  - the scriptural reasoning movement

Introduction

One of the most important issues for Christians living in the twenty-first century is how they should relate to people who follow non-Christian religions or who have no religious belief.

The UK has become religiously diverse, and although Christianity is still the predominant religion, significant proportions of the population practise other religions or reject religion entirely. People are encouraged by modern society to tolerate and respect the religions of others, to welcome diversity and to embrace everyone's freedom to have their own beliefs, tastes and opinions.

However, this atmosphere of tolerance can put Christians in a difficult position. Sometimes they are left wondering whether it is appropriate and acceptable for them to share their faith openly with others or to try to convert other people to Christianity. Occasionally incidents reach the news headlines, for example when someone chooses to wear a crucifix necklace in the workplace or publicly criticises homosexuality by making reference to the Bible. Modern society in the UK seems to hold the view that religious belief is a personal matter that should not be on public display in case it offends the rights of others to have different beliefs. Christians might feel that they are not able to say that they think other religions are wrong, for fear of being considered arrogant or judgemental or discriminatory.

The Christian Churches have attempted, in various ways, to address the difficulties for Christians of living in a **multi-faith society**. For example, the Catholic Church and the Church of England have issued statements giving guidance to their members about living a Christian life and speaking about Christianity with members of other faiths. Some Christians have also become involved in the more formal practices of inter-faith dialogue, where they meet with members of other faith communities for discussion in an effort to achieve better understanding.

The development of contemporary multi-faith societies

In the past in the UK, most people lived in communities that were almost exclusively dominated by Christianity. Big cities often had areas that hosted a small Chinese or Jewish or Muslim community. Samuel Pepys records visiting a London synagogue in 1663 and being fascinated by the celebration of the festival of Simchat Torah. Pepys clearly knew nothing about this festival and its tradition of following the commandment to rejoice in the Law. He watched the congregation take the Torah scrolls out of the Ark and carry them around the synagogue in celebration, and he wrote of his experiences in his famous diary:

> 66 Thence home and after dinner my wife and I, by Mr. Rawlinson's conduct, to the Jewish Synagogue: where the men and boys in their vayles, and the women behind a lattice out of sight; and some things stand up, which I believe is their Law, in a press to which all coming in do bow; and at the putting on their vayles do say something, to which others that hear him do cry Amen, and the party do kiss his vayle. Their service all in a singing way, and in Hebrew. And anon their Laws that they take out of the press are carried by several men, four or five several burthens in all, and they do relieve one another; and whether it is that every one desires to have the carrying of it, I cannot tell, thus they carried it round about the room while such a service is singing. And in the end they had a prayer for the King, which they pronounced his name in Portugall; but the prayer, like the rest, in Hebrew. But, Lord! to see the disorder, laughing, sporting, and no attention, but confusion in all their service, more like brutes than people knowing the true God, would make a man forswear ever seeing them more and indeed I never did see so much, or could have imagined there had been any religion in the whole world so absurdly performed as this. 99

Diary of Samuel Pepys, Wednesday 14 October 1663

Pepys' experiences of encountering a religion other than Christianity were unusual. Most of the population never came into contact with someone who was from a different ethnicity or who belonged to a religion other than Christianity. In rural towns and villages, there might be some people who went to church while others went to chapel (and some did not go anywhere), but there was little awareness of different religious beliefs beyond knowing about the different denominations of the Christian church. Schools educated children in Christianity, but not in the beliefs of any other religion. Laws and customs were based in the traditions of Christianity and people were routinely baptised into the Christian church, had Christian marriages and funerals, and were buried in the local churchyard.

The UK has not always been a predominantly Christian country. Before the Romans came to Britain, local religious practices centred around agriculture, fertility and ancestor worship. Christianity, like other religions in Britain, arrived in the country from elsewhere. It was introduced by the Romans, and it coexisted alongside traditional religious practices until about the seventh century when Christian missionaries established Christianity as the primary faith of the British.

Multi-faith societies are those in which there are significant populations of people from different religious backgrounds. In the West, multi-faith societies began to develop as travel and communications developed. It became possible for people to move to new areas for work, while still keeping in touch with family at home. People from rural areas sometimes

Over time the UK has developed to become a multi-faith society

Bevis Marks synagogue in London is the oldest synagogue in the UK, dating from 1701. It was built to serve a community of Sephardic Jews from Spain and Portugal who moved to London to escape persecution

moved to the cities to find employment and came into contact with a wider variety of people than they had been used to. International migration became an option, with families moving from one country to another to find a better quality of life, or because life in their home country was unsafe or unsustainable. For example, Jews came to Britain with William the Conqueror, who valued their commercial skills. Much more recently, Hindus, Muslims and Sikhs arrived from Uganda in 1972 when Idi Amin expelled the Asian population. Naturally, when people arrive in a foreign country to start a new life, they often want to live among people who are related to them, or at least among people who share their language and beliefs, as well as wanting to live where they can find accommodation and work. Therefore, rather than spreading evenly across the country there are communities that have a higher concentration of Sikhs or Muslims, Hindus, Buddhists or Jews. The first Sikhs to come to the UK to seek work in the 1950s tended to settle in London, Birmingham and West Yorkshire, for example, while there are significant Jewish populations in Manchester, North London, Hertfordshire, Gateshead and Leeds.

The answers to the question 'What is your religion?' in the 2011 census illustrate the multi-faith nature of the UK today. Significantly, on his sixtieth birthday in 2008, Prince Charles made a statement indicating his wish that if and when he becomes king, he should be known not as 'Defender of the Faith' (a title given to the monarch since the reign of Henry VIII), but as 'Defender of Faith'. He wanted it to be known that he recognises the multi-faith nature of the UK and that he is keen to defend the rights of everyone to hold their own faith, whatever it might be, rather than being the defender of Christianity in the face of other belief systems.

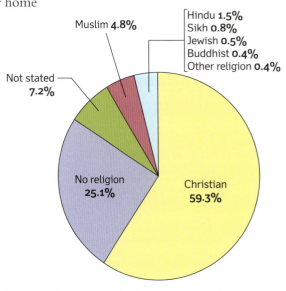

The 2011 England and Wales census asked people 'What is your religion?' This pie chart shows how people responded

Think question

What do you think are the implications of Prince Charles wanting to be 'Defender of Faith' rather than 'Defender of the Faith'? Does his choice undermine Christianity?

Prince Charles visiting the Hindu temple in Neasden, London

Migration, travel and developments in communication have made people much more aware of the existence of belief systems that differ from their own

Even for those in the UK who do not live in multi-faith communities, there is now a much greater awareness of the diversity of beliefs in the world. Foreign travel for work and holidays brings people into contact with different religious beliefs and cultural traditions, often including a need to learn about the beliefs and customs of others in order to respect local etiquette. Methods of communication, such as books and newspapers, television and the Internet, have made it much easier for people to gain insights into the lives and cultures of other people. In the late nineteenth century, for example, Eastern religion caught the imagination of the British when a scholar called Max Müller translated the sacred texts of Hinduism into English in 50 volumes called *The Sacred Books of the East* (1879–1910). People who were previously unaware of Hindu spirituality were able to read holy texts, and subsequently there was a rise in the popularity of practices such as meditation and increased interest in ideas such as reincarnation.

Today, many communities in the UK have multi-faith populations, even in rural areas. People live alongside others of different religious beliefs, sharing the same schools, workplaces and public facilities. There are also many inter-faith marriages and partnerships, which join together two different traditions in one family. In school, children learn about the different major world faiths, the supermarkets stock festival foods for both Christian and non-Christian religions, hospitals, airports and some cities have multi-faith prayer areas, and most people have friends and colleagues from religious backgrounds that are different from their own. In addition, atheism and agnosticism have become entirely socially acceptable, with many people openly rejecting the claims of religious believers. As a result, Christians are challenged not only by the religious beliefs of others but by those who disagree with any form of religion.

What challenges do encounters with different faiths present for Christianity?

For Christians, religious diversity can provide positive opportunities for learning, sharing common values, adopting new ways of thinking and developing relationships. Christians can work with their non-Christian neighbours to set an example of co-operation, helping to dispel prejudice and promote peace. Encounters with people whose religious beliefs are non-Christian encourage many Christians to think more deeply about their own faith. When they encounter people whose beliefs are different from their own, they have to think about what it is that they are accepting and rejecting, what reasons they might give for holding their views, and how they might defend Christianity in the face of criticism. Some people find this challenge very rewarding, because it means they cannot just go through the routines of Christian practice unthinkingly but have to spend some time working out exactly what Christianity means to them as individuals. They enjoy the opportunity to find out about the faith and practices of others, to get to know their neighbours better and to form interesting new friendships.

However, some Christians are concerned that a multi-faith environment might be damaging for Christianity, undermining the uniqueness of its message by suggesting that salvation through Christ is only one way to heaven amongst many routes. Some Christians are worried that living in a multi-faith society can encourage their children to become interested in following false beliefs and practices, as they might become attracted to a different religion. Some are uneasy about the popular insistence on tolerance and respect for the faith of others, where sharing a Christian faith with others is seen as judgemental or arrogant, at the expense of the Christian mission.

> ### Think question
>
> What do you think are the advantages and disadvantages for Christians of sending their children to Christian faith schools?

The responses of Christian communities to inter-faith dialogue

What is inter-faith dialogue?

Inter-faith dialogue is sometimes known as inter-religious dialogue, or inter-belief dialogue in order to include those whose beliefs are non-religious. It is about communication between people of different beliefs in order to build relationships, break down stereotypes and prejudices, and promote peace and understanding. Inter-faith dialogue aims to achieve mutual respect and co-operation, where people get together to talk about beliefs they hold in common. They also identify points on which they differ and that can cause tension, and they try to understand each other's point of view even if they do not agree with it. It is not about trying to convert people from one faith to another or demonstrating that one belief system is superior to another, but about coming to a deeper understanding of one's own faith while learning about, and from, the beliefs of others.

Inter-faith dialogue is about people of different religious beliefs coming together and trying to develop a deeper understanding of each other's faith

Think question

How far, if at all, can inter-faith dialogue be compatible with an exclusivist view of Christianity? Refer back to Chapter 3.1 for a reminder about exclusivist views of Christianity.

Sometimes inter-faith dialogue is understood as having four strands to it. The Church of England document 'Sharing the Gospel of Salvation' (2009, point 97) identifies these as:

1. 'the dialogue of daily life', in which people strike up informal conversations about their differing religious beliefs

2. 'the dialogue of the common good', in which adherents of different faiths work together to benefit the community

3. 'the dialogue of mutual understanding', in which people get together for formalised debates, such as in the Scriptural Reasoning movement

4. 'the dialogue of spiritual life', in which people of different religious beliefs meet together for prayer and worship.

Inter-faith dialogue is not something new as people have always talked about their beliefs with others who hold different opinions. However, as societies have become more diverse, inter-faith dialogue has become something that different religious communities have adopted more formally, making special efforts for the leading figures in a religion to enter into discussions with those from other religions rather than just waiting for individual conversations to happen naturally. Sometimes, particular trends have sparked renewed interest in inter-faith dialogue, such as changes in the ethnic population of a city when immigrants arrive, or world events such as the attack on the Twin Towers in the USA on 11 September 2001.

In 1972, Idi Amin expelled Asians from Uganda. The sudden growth of Britain's Asian population as a result led to calls for more inter-faith dialogue to help Christians understand and welcome their new neighbours

In his book *The Future of Christian Theology* (2011), David Ford draws attention to two strands in history that have led to new directions in inter-faith dialogue: the twentieth-century Holocaust, and the rise in tensions between Islam and the West at the beginning of the twenty-first century.

The events of the Holocaust, in which six million Jews were among the many people killed by the Nazis, forced many Christians to think again about their relationship with Judaism. Germany was traditionally a Christian country and yet many of the population had enthusiastically supported Nazism in its prejudice and persecution of Jews. The role of the Church in Nazi Germany has been the subject of a lot of historical debate, but Christians could not escape the fact that the Church held at least some degree of responsibility for presenting Judaism as a 'failed religion', whose followers had gone in the wrong direction because they had failed to recognise Jesus as the fulfilment of the Old Testament. Christianity often presented itself as the religion that had superseded Judaism, understanding Judaism as a religion that once had the purpose of preparing the way for Christianity but which was no longer important. Although there were some Christians who resisted Nazism and risked their lives to oppose it and to help the Jews, there were also many others who did nothing or else actively supported anti-Semitism.

The uneasy relationship between Christianity and Judaism after the war, once many of the horrors of anti-Semitism had come to light, led to an effort at inter-faith dialogue initiated by Jewish rabbis and scholars from around the world. In a document called Dabru Emet ('Speak the truth'), Jews invited Christians to a discussion. They highlighted the ideas that Jews and Christians share the same God and seek authority from the same scriptures, and that Jews and Christians needed to work together for peace. They drew attention to the importance of Judaism in the world and the contribution it had made to cultures and economies. The discussion that followed Dabru Emet led to several conclusions, including the need for Christians and Jews to continue to communicate and work together and the requirement that this co-operation should become a normal part of Jewish and Christian life.

The second event in inter-faith dialogue to which David Ford draws attention is the issuing of a letter in October 2007, from leading Muslim scholars and teachers to the Christian churches. The letter, known as 'A Common Word Between Us and You', pointed out the passion Muslims and Christians share for worshipping one God and putting love for one's neighbour into practice. There was no attempt in the letter to pretend that Muslims and Christians have no differences, but it asked each religion to look more deeply into its own faith and the demands that it makes of its adherents. The letter concentrated on the central messages of the scriptures of both religions and looked at the responsibilities both religions have for working for everyone's good. It emphasised the need for Muslims and Christians to live up to their own teachings. This letter, like the Jewish Dabru Emet, called for a continuing and ongoing dialogue between Muslims and Christians in order to find ways to engage with each other.

Apply your knowledge

Abhishiktananda (also spelled Abishiktananda), formerly known as Henri le Saux, was one of the pioneers of inter-faith dialogue between Hindus and Christians. Find out about his thinking and the work he did to develop a greater understanding between Christians and Hindus. Try to find out about the aims of the Abhishiktananda Centre that was set up after his death.

1. Why did Abhishiktananda think that it was important for Christians and Hindus to engage in dialogue?

2. Why might some Christians be critical of Abhishiktananda's views?

3. Do you think that Christians should support this kind of inter-religious dialogue? Give reasons for your answer.

Inter-faith dialogue does not only take place between Christians and other religions. There have also been many interactions between Sikhs and Muslims, for example, where believers have been working towards reaching a greater understanding of how they can use both their similarities and their differences to address social issues as well as religious ones.

The Catholic church and inter-faith dialogue: 'Redemptoris Missio'

In the Catholic Church, there is a tradition of Papal **encyclicals**, which are letters sent from the Pope to leaders of the Church. These encyclicals address significant issues in the life of the Church and its relationship with modern society and are used for guidance and consultation about Catholic doctrines. Because they are formal letters from the Pope, they are believed to have enough authority to be the final word on issues where there is some disagreement.

Pope John Paul II (1920–2005) issued an encyclical called 'Redemptoris Missio' in 1990. This was intended to revisit some of the key Catholic teachings and issues that had arisen during the discussions of Vatican II in the 1960s. The title 'Redemptoris Missio' translates as 'The Mission of the Redeemer', and the subject matter of the encyclical was the place of Christian **missionary work** in a multi-faith world. The Pope recognised that relations between religions had moved on since Vatican II, and he wanted to make sure that Catholic teaching about mission remained clear and up to date.

The encyclical makes it plain from the outset that Christian mission to non-Christians remains essential. The Pope states that Jesus Christ is the one saviour and that Christ is the only way in which God is revealed to the world. Christians have always been, and should continue to be, empowered by the Holy Spirit to bring others to the Christian faith. He makes reference to the Bible to support his point:

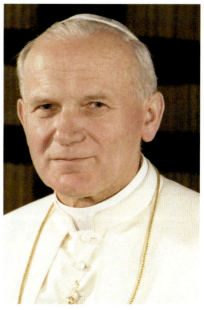

John Paul II wrote 'Redemptoris Missio' to encourage the Catholic Church to persevere with Christian mission in a multi-faith world

> 66 For when I preach the gospel, I cannot boast, since I am compelled to preach. Woe to me if I do not preach the gospel! 99
>
> 1 Corinthians 9:16, New International Version

However, while maintaining the view that missionary activity is urgent and important, the Pope also recognises that, in a multi-faith world, Christian mission can be seen in a negative way, as intolerant or condemnatory of other religions. The purpose of the encyclical is to show how Catholic Christians can be missionaries for their faith while still respecting religious and cultural diversity and people's freedom of choice. Catholic Christians can recognise and learn from the good in the faith of others and at the same time seek to bring them to Christianity.

Think question

Do you think it is possible for meaningful inter-faith dialogue to take place alongside Christian mission?

One section of 'Redemptoris Missio' is subtitled 'Dialogue with our brothers and sisters of other religions'. In this section (55–7), the Pope considers how inter-faith dialogue might work alongside the missionary requirement for Christians to encourage others to turn to Christ and be baptised into the Christian Church.

He begins by saying that inter-religious dialogue should be seen in the context of Christian mission, as a part of it and 'one of its expressions' rather than in opposition to it. The Pope says that God wishes to share his revelation and love with all people, even if they belong to other religions, which might contain 'gaps, insufficiencies and errors'. He explains that although inter-religious dialogue and Christian mission can work together, the two should not be confused as each has its own distinctive nature and aim.

Pope John Paul II writes that:

> 66 the Church gladly acknowledges whatever is true and holy in the religious traditions of Buddhism, Hinduism and Islam as a reflection of that truth which enlightens all people 99
>
> 'Redemptoris Missio', 1990, point 55

But he asserts that Christians still have a duty to emphasise that the way to salvation is through Jesus Christ. Even if there might be salvation through God's grace for people who belong to other religions, this does not cancel out the need for a call to Christian faith and baptism into the Church, which the Pope sees as the will of God for all people. He writes:

> 66 Dialogue should be conducted and implemented with the conviction that the Church is the ordinary means of salvation and that she alone possesses the fullness of the means of salvation. 99
>
> 'Redemptoris Missio', 1990, point 55

He refers to the Bible to show that Christianity is unique in offering the means to salvation, quoting from a speech by Peter the apostle following a miraculous healing:

> 66 then know this, you and all the people of Israel: It is by the name of Jesus Christ of Nazareth, whom you crucified but whom God raised from the dead, that this man stands before you healed. Jesus is
>
> 'the stone you builders rejected,
>
> which has become the cornerstone.'

'Redemptoris Missio' addresses the issue of how Christians should practice their faith and share their beliefs in a multi-faith society

> Salvation is found in no one else, for there is no other name under heaven given to mankind by which we must be saved. **"**

Acts 4:10–12, New International Version

Although he is insistent that Christianity alone has the 'fullness' of God's revelation, the Pope underlines the need for respect in inter-religious dialogue, saying that it should be based on 'hope and love' and that Christians should use it with the aim of uncovering universal truths. He draws attention to the power and freedom of the Holy Spirit to reveal God in all kinds of contexts, and sees dialogue as an opportunity for the Church to examine its own identity as well as an opportunity for Christian mission. When dialogue is conducted with honesty and humility it can overcome 'prejudice, intolerance and misunderstandings'.

This section of 'Redemptoris Missio' concludes with the recognition that dialogue can take many forms, whether it is between academics and experts, religious officials or non-expert religious believers. The Pope emphasises that dialogue can be practised by all members of the Church, although not necessarily in the same way. People can demonstrate their Christian faith and spiritual values in the ways in which they conduct their daily lives and interact with their neighbours. He writes that Christian mission can often be difficult and misunderstood, but that it is important to persevere with it: 'Dialogue is a path toward the kingdom and will certainly bear fruit, even if the times and seasons are known only to the Father'.

The Church of England debated the role of Christian mission in a religiously diverse context

The Church of England and inter-faith dialogue: 'Sharing the gospel of salvation'

In 2006 Paul Eddy, a member of the Church of England, put a question to the **Synod** of the Church of England, asking them to debate it and to give Church members some clear guidance. He wanted to know where the Church of England felt it stood on the question of whether or not it should be trying to convert people of other faiths to Christianity. He thought that Christians had become too fearful of giving offence, to the extent that they no longer proclaimed that Jesus Christ was the way to salvation, but instead kept quiet and went along with the idea that everyone should be free to have their own beliefs and not be challenged. Mr Eddy argued that there was a need for the Church of England to make a statement about whether Christians in a religiously diverse country should claim publicly that salvation could be found only in Christ. The document 'Sharing the Gospel of Salvation' came about as an outcome of this discussion and was published in 2010.

'Sharing the Gospel of Salvation' reaffirms the Christian message that God's plan for the salvation of the world is uniquely achieved in Jesus Christ. The Church of England, therefore, has a mission to be a witness to this, with each individual Christian being encouraged to live as a Christian disciple, which always involves sharing faith with others.

The document reminds Christians of the history of Christianity in Britain and that their own faith and traditions are the result of the missionary efforts of others. It also reminds them that Christian mission through the ages has not always lived up to the teachings of the Bible, when it has become entangled with political dominance and been guilty of cultural insensitivities. It warns against treating Christian mission as a kind of marketing exercise, where non-Christians are seen as 'targets' rather than as individuals. However, the document makes it plain that Christians should not be intimidated by the fear of getting it wrong and should make an effort to be open about their Christian beliefs and to talk about them honestly. They should remain aware that when other people do convert to Christianity, it is because of the work of God and not because of their own achievements in 'making a sale'. Christians should share their faith by living for the good of others rather than just by telling people what they believe; but at the same time, when they are working for others and trying to put Jesus' teachings into practice, they should not be afraid to be open about the Christian beliefs that inspire their good works.

One of the issues addressed in the document is the problem of finding the right ways to share beliefs about the uniqueness of Christ with people who already belong to one of the other major world religions. 'Sharing the Gospel of Salvation' reaffirms Christian beliefs about the oneness of God, using biblical references to support the view that there is only one true God and that Jesus came to earth as God incarnate. It claims that this one God offers salvation to everyone, whether or not they know it, and that Christians are called to bring others to an explicit faith in Jesus Christ and to encourage them to be baptised into the Christian Church.

The Church of England recognises that there are very substantial communities of non-Christian religious believers in some areas of the country and that this raises issues for the parish churches there. It advises Christians to 'go beyond tolerance into positive engagement and dialogue and change (tolerance having unfortunate overtones of indifference).' In other words, Christians should not merely put up with living among members of other religions but should make an effort to engage with them and find opportunities to talk with them.

The document draws on the experience of Christians who live in richly diverse parts of the UK to give some guidance on good practice. It reminds people to think about the commandment, 'Always treat others as you would have them treat you', and encourages Christians to be sensitive to others' feelings and to be aware that most people do not like to be pressurised into changing their views. It also reminds people

Apply your knowledge

6. Do you think that religious people should be free to try to convert others when they are in the workplace? Give reasons for your answer.

7. What might a Christian say if they were accused of showing a lack of respect for other people's opinions and beliefs by attempting to convert others?

8. Why do you think the Church of England warns its members against taking a 'marketing' approach to Christian mission?

Think question

What do you think might be the particular problems for Christian churches in communities where the majority of the population follows a different faith?

that conversion to Christianity from a different world faith can be very difficult, causing hurt to family members, and risking estrangement and sometimes even danger. Christians should, therefore, be prepared to let people take their time. They should be open to explaining what their Christian faith means to them and should feel able to say, 'I wish you could see things the way that I do,' but they should also be willing to listen and to learn about different faiths. Importantly, it stresses that Christians should not make claims about the darkness and hopelessness that they think awaits those who seek God in non-Christian ways, but that they should leave ultimate judgement to God.

The Scriptural Reasoning Movement

The Scriptural Reasoning Movement aims to deepen understanding of different religious traditions by studying holy scriptures together

'Scriptural Reasoning' as a movement began amongst Jewish scholars in the USA. It was initially called 'Textual Reasoning', and it was a forum for Jewish academics to meet together in a university context to study together. They looked at the sacred texts of Judaism and shared the expertise of Jewish philosophers, historians, linguists and spiritual leaders. There was nothing unusual about this; biblical study has been an important part of Jewish life throughout the religion's history. However, in the mid-1990s some Christians from the UK approached the group and asked if they could join it as listeners, hoping to increase their own understanding of the scriptures and of Judaism. The resultant conversations were very lively and engaging, to the extent that it was decided the meetings should become a regular inter-faith forum. Rather than discussing general inter-faith issues, the focus was very much on scripture, looking at different ways in which sacred texts could be interpreted and applied. Muslims were also invited to join because of the common roots shared by Judaism, Christianity and Islam. The three religions are known as 'religions of the book' because they all have holy scriptures that they consider to be revelatory and authoritative. As the movement has grown, it has welcomed people of all religions.

Scriptural Reasoning has become part of the Cambridge Inter-Faith Programme. Participants from Christianity, Islam and Judaism meet together to read passages from their sacred texts that address different themes, such as education and learning, clothing and modesty, what it means to be a created human, and the role of fasting in spirituality. They look together at passages from the Bible and from the Qur'an that address the chosen topic. They discuss the wording of the texts, talking about how the texts shape and influence their understanding, and how they think the texts should be applied in contemporary society.

The movement stresses that its goal is not achieving agreement, but to get beyond the superficial. Rather than assuming that there are some beliefs that are common across the religions, the discussion looks more deeply into the different ways that apparently similar beliefs are understood in their own contexts. The participants tell each other about their central values and beliefs, listen to each other and ask questions. The idea is to foster a spirit of openness and honesty, where it is permissible to disagree while remaining respectful and friendly. Those who take part in the debates find themselves looking at their own assumptions and digging more deeply into their own traditions, asking themselves why they interpret their texts in the ways that they do. When they hear people of other faiths looking at things differently, it encourages them not to assume that their own strategies for interpreting scripture are the only right ways.

The movement aims to present an opportunity for committed religious people to engage in debate and in inter-faith dialogue without undermining or threatening anyone's particular beliefs. The ways in which passages are read is not prescribed, which allows participants to work within a style that is appropriate to their faith. However, the texts are read in English and not in the original languages, to enable everyone to join in. Hospitality is one of the key features of the Scriptural Reasoning Movement, and different faith groups take it in turns to host meetings, or the meetings are held in a neutral space so that everyone feels comfortable.

There is an agreement that Scriptural Reasoning meetings should not be places where people feel under pressure to change their beliefs. Participants in the groups need to agree that their meetings should not be used as a context for missionary work, and that they should not try to convince the other people to accept their way of looking at things, although they can make their love for their scriptures apparent and should not feel that they have to compromise. Participants are also discouraged from trying to speak for their entire religion, so they try not to say, 'Christians believe…' or, 'Muslims understand…', but instead contribute as individuals, saying what they personally take the scripture to mean.

The Scriptural Reasoning Movement aims to help an understanding of different and conflicting religious truth claims. There are clear points of difference in the teachings of world religions: Muslims, for example, claim that Muhammad was the final prophet of God, whereas Christians claim that Jesus revealed the final and complete truth. Christians claim that God is one but in three 'persons', namely the Father, the Son and the Holy Spirit, which is known as the doctrine of the Trinity. Jews and Muslims disagree with the idea of God as a Trinity.

Studying religious scriptures together allows for discussion of these differing truth claims. Different individuals can explain their own understanding of the claims and show how their scriptures have formed their beliefs. It is not expected that people from different faith backgrounds will come to an agreement on points of conflict, but it is hoped that they will reach a better understanding of the other's point of view and will find respectful ways of voicing their disagreements so that communication can continue.

Apply your knowledge

9. What do you think might be the positives and the negatives of the Scriptural Reasoning Movement?

10. Why do you think that the Scriptural Reasoning Movement does not allow people to try and convert each other at its meetings? Do you think this is a good rule? Give reasons for your answer.

11. Many Christians believe that the Jewish Bible (the 'Old Testament') has authority, but they do not have the same beliefs about the Qur'an. How might different opinions about the authority of different texts have an effect on Scriptural Reasoning meetings?

12. Visit the website of the Scriptural Reasoning Movement and look at some of its resources to get an idea of how different scriptures address similar topics.

See Chapter 1.2 for more about truth-claims in religious language.

Discussing religious pluralism and society

Has inter-faith dialogue contributed practically towards social cohesion?

'Social cohesion' has become a popular term in the twenty-first century. It is used to describe a society in which people have a strong sense of belonging, where people feel that they can communicate easily with each other, where they share moral values and where they feel fairly treated. Socially cohesive groups are seen to be better at achieving common aims and tend to be more peaceful, although they can also be exclusive of other societies that are different from their own. When there is little social cohesion, some groups within a society tend to feel marginalised or oppressed, and this can lead to hostility and sometimes violence. Outbreaks of rioting in some towns and cities in the UK, such as Oldham, Bradford and Brixton, have led politicians to look at ways to promote social cohesion. The emergence of some politically and religiously extremist groups has also resulted in renewed attempts to find ways in which British society can be more cohesive.

Social cohesion is very difficult to measure. Although there are indicators, such as crime statistics, to determine the prevalence of rioting, criminal damage or hate crime, it is hard to know accurately how people feel about their communities, and harder still to make judgements about the causes of the feelings and the effectiveness of efforts to improve social cohesion.

It could be argued that inter-faith dialogue has been largely ineffective in contributing to social cohesion. One reason for this might be that not everyone agrees with it. For example, many Christians think that members of other faiths should be persuaded to adopt Christianity as the one true religion, and are uncomfortable with the idea that different beliefs should be respected and tolerated without there being any missionary effort to bring people to Christ. A substantial group of Catholics, for example, disagreed with the emphasis in Vatican II on developing inter-faith dialogue, arguing that there is only one true Church and that inter-faith dialogue falsely suggests that other religions are worthwhile and might also lead people to salvation. With this disagreement within Christianity about the role of inter-faith dialogue in Christian life, it could be argued that inter-faith dialogue has brought about less cohesion rather than more, by causing divisions within religions while not succeeding in healing rifts between different faiths.

A different argument might be that a lack of social cohesion stems largely from material inequality. This is a point that is raised in the Church of England document 'Sharing the Gospel of Salvation' (point 57). Relationships between different world religions have a limited effect on social cohesion because the problems that divide societies come about because of inequalities in housing, employment, income and education. When people see themselves as being excluded from having the material goods that other groups can access easily, from public decision-making and from employment, this can lead to social disorder, racism and other kinds of crime. Hostility between people of different religious beliefs often arises because there is already a lack of social cohesion; hostility between people of different religious beliefs is a symptom of poor social cohesion rather than its cause.

People are unlikely to feel a sense of loyalty and solidarity with their city or their country if they see themselves as powerless or as victims of injustice. Improving relationships between members of different religious faiths could be seen as important, in that efforts at social cohesion always work better if communication is encouraged, but inter-faith dialogue is very limited in what it can achieve while there are huge gaps in the material conditions of different groups of people in a society. Also, religion is becoming less important to many people. It no longer holds the power it once held to direct public opinion. Whether religious people communicate well or not might be of little interest to many, making the instigators of inter-faith dialogue powerless to effect very much change in society.

However, it could be argued that inter-faith dialogue has had a positive effect on social cohesion. Inter-faith groups and events have increased in popularity over the last hundred years. There are regular dialogues between members of different faith communities, special events where they work together and pray together, and numerous societies and projects that have grown out of a desire to promote understanding and tolerance between religious believers of different persuasions. David Ford points out the ways in which Jewish and Christian inter-faith dialogue has offered new possibilities for the relationship between the two religions:

66 [It] allows for retrieving the past differently and for dialogue and collaboration that opens up new ways forward together. The trust is that there are genuine Jewish and Christian resources for a better future and that these are best activated through engagement before God between living members of both communities. 99

David Ford, *The Future of Christian Theology*, 2011, p. 136

Another argument that might be put forward is that social cohesion is not the main aim of inter-faith dialogue. Inter-faith dialogue is essentially a religious undertaking for spiritual purposes, where people are seeking truth. It is easy to equate efforts at inter-faith dialogue with the assumption that all religions are different cultural ways of expressing the same ideas and moral codes. If inter-faith dialogue is intended to demonstrate that underneath the surface, religious beliefs are all the same, then perhaps social cohesion might be seen as its primary aim, but this is not what inter-faith dialogue is about. It encourages discussion of points of difference and conflict just as much as discussion of points of similarity.

Think question

What do you think should be the main aim of inter-faith dialogue?

Should Christian communities aim to convert people from other faiths?

Most Christians believe that it is part of every Christian's duty to bring people to share their faith in Christ. The New Testament stresses the importance and urgency of Christian mission. Jesus gives his followers a commission to spread the Christian message throughout the world:

> **66** Therefore go and make disciples of all nations, baptizing them in the name of the Father and of the Son and of the Holy Spirit **99**
>
> Matthew 28:19, New International Version

Christians believe they should try and bring others to Christ because they want to share what they consider to be a life-transforming faith that opens the doors to eternal salvation. It is not just a desire that others should share their taste, but a sense that people are missing out on something of ultimate importance. The Papal encyclical, '*Redemptoris Missio*', talks of everyone having the right to hear the Christian message, and that it is not enough for Christians simply to try and live in harmony with others but not make efforts to bring them to Christ.

> **66** Nowadays the call to conversion which missionaries address to non-Christians is put into question or passed over in silence. It is seen as an act of 'proselytizing'; it is claimed that it is enough to help people to become more human or more faithful to their own religion, that it is enough to build communities capable of working for justice, freedom, peace and solidarity. What is overlooked is that every person has the right to hear the 'Good News' of the God who reveals and gives himself in Christ, so that each one can live out in its fullness his or her proper calling. **99**
>
> '*Redemptoris Missio*', 1990, point 46

The Church of England has the same view. However, it does point out the potential practical difficulties of Christian conversion for people whose families and traditions belong to a different world faith, and it advises sensitivity.

Converting others to Christianity comes from an exclusivist view of the relationship between Christianity and other world religions. If someone believes that there is only one way to salvation, which is through explicit acceptance of Christianity, then it will be important to them to try to convert people to accepting this truth. However, an inclusivist view will consider that salvation could be possible within a different religious tradition. For example, if sincere Muslims or Sikhs were genuinely trying

Exclusivist Christians see a need to convert others to Christianity, but inclusivist and pluralist views might think it less important: see Chapter 3.1.

to serve God through prayer and care for other people, then perhaps they could be considered 'anonymous Christians', living Christian lives without knowing they were doing so. It might, then, be unnecessary to pressurise them into becoming Christians because it could be possible for them to achieve salvation within their own religious context.

Those who have pluralist views, believing that Christianity is one path to God and other religions are equally valid, will not see any need for Christians to try to convert others. If every religious tradition is shaped by culture and there is no single 'truth', and if an all-loving God will grant salvation to everyone universally, then it is not necessary for people to try to change each other's religious beliefs.

To what extent does scriptural reasoning relativise religious beliefs?

Some people might argue that the Scriptural Reasoning Movement suggests that, fundamentally, all religions are working together towards the same end even though there are differences in detail. Therefore, it could be seen to 'relativise' religious belief; in other words to dismiss the idea that one religion holds the truth and instead suggests an 'each to his own' kind of mentality, where Christianity is for those who like that kind of thing and other religions are equally valid alternatives. Looking at scriptures together and discussing them carries the assumption that everyone's holy scriptures have something to offer and are worth studying. An exclusivist Christian, such as Karl Barth, would probably disagree, reasoning that God is fully and exclusively revealed in Christ and in the Christian Bible, and that the teachings of other religions are false, except where they agree with Christian teaching. Exclusivists might argue that instead of studying the scriptures together, Christians would do better to point out the uniqueness of the Christian message and warn people that non-Christian religions lead away from the truth.

Supporters of scriptural reasoning might respond by arguing that their movement does not relativise religious belief, but instead encourages differences of opinion and argument. It does not pretend that all religions are basically doing the same thing, but openly and fearlessly confronts the points of tension and the contradictions between different belief systems. It encourages its participants to reach a firmer understanding of their own faith and allows for the strong possibility that people will come away from meetings all the more convinced of the truth of their own religious tradition, without any sense of compromise. It does not tell people what to conclude.

Religious pluralists, such as John Hick, might argue that if scriptural reasoning does relativise religious belief, that is not a bad thing but a realisation that religion is a human construct and that no religion can claim to have a monopoly on the truth. Pluralists might suggest that scriptural reasoning could lead people to the insight that different religious beliefs and practices are relative, and that they are all responses to the same reality but shaped by different cultural contexts and traditions.

> **Think question**
>
> What do you think might be the major difficulties for someone who wanted to convert to Christianity but whose family were firm believers in a different faith?

Should Christians have a mission to convert those of no faith?

Trying to convert people with no faith to Christianity is somewhat different from trying to convert people who already have their own religious beliefs.

When someone is already a member of a different faith community, conversion to Christianity can bring with it a whole lot of social difficulties and tensions, including a sense that the converts have betrayed their culture and disrespected the rest of their community. People of no faith are unlikely to encounter the same problems if they choose to become Christian, although there might still be tensions with other family members who find religious belief alien to their way of thinking. Sometimes people have no faith simply because religious belief has never been a part of their upbringing and they feel they can manage perfectly well without it. Others have strong feelings against religion, perhaps believing it to be outdated and superseded by science or believing it to be a source of conflict and bloodshed.

Christians who seek to convert those with no faith have to take into account that there is a wide spectrum of views and that they will need to be able to defend their beliefs against criticism. For example, they might need to be prepared to explain how Christian belief can fit in with a scientific understanding of the world. Or they might need to have some response to questions of why a God of love would allow innocent people to suffer.

Christians who take an inclusivist view might think that those who genuinely seek God in the context of a different world religion could be considered 'anonymous Christians' and, therefore, mission might not be an urgent necessity. However, they might think that people with no faith have a much greater need to be encouraged to know God.

Traditionally, Christians understand themselves to have a mission to those of no faith, as well as to anyone else who is not explicitly Christian. The Catholic Church, the Church of England and many other Christian denominations encourage their members to act as ambassadors for Christianity and make deliberate attempts to convert non-believers. Often, Christians try to do this in ways that are non-confrontational. For example, they may run weekday coffee shops on church premises where people drop in for refreshment and may have their attention drawn to church events and community activities at the same time. They might also offer 'Alpha courses', which are introductions to Christianity for people who want to explore what Christianity means. Non-Christians are invited to these, but the courses are not forced on them. It tends to be the manner in which mission is conducted that influences whether or not people find it objectionable. Most people of no faith do not have a problem with religious believers, except when they try to force their opinions on them in a strident manner.

Apply your knowledge

13. **a.** What do you feel if someone with views that are different from your own tries to convert you to their taste in music, their politics or their religious beliefs (or lack of belief)?

    b. Do you think that all people have a right to their own opinions without others trying to change their minds? Should you challenge people's beliefs if they are misinformed or racist or sexist?

14. Should religion be regarded as a special case, where it is never right to challenge someone's faith even if you could challenge some of their other opinions? Give reasons for your answer.

Learning support

Points to remember

» When writing about inter-faith dialogue, it is important to recognise that it has not all been initiated by Christians and does not always involve Christianity. There have been many attempts between non-Christian religions to engage in dialogue in order to deepen mutual understanding.

» Remember that within the Christian tradition, and also within the traditions of other world religions, not everyone thinks in the same way. Try to avoid writing about 'the Christian view' of initiatives such as inter-faith dialogue, as there is a range of different opinions about it.

Enhance your learning

» Chapter 7 of *The Mystery of Salvation* (1995), written by The Doctrine Commission of the Church of England, gives a formal account of the Church of England's position on the relationship between Christianity and other religions.

» David Ford is one of the leading figures in the Scriptural Reasoning Movement in the UK. His book *The Future of Christian Theology* (2011) is academic but accessible. Chapter 7 is called 'Inter-faith blessing' and is about Ford's understanding of the need for inter-faith dialogue and what he thinks it can achieve.

» Pope Paul VI's *Nostra Aetate, Declaration on the Relation of the Church to Non-Christian Religions* (1965) is a formal statement from Vatican II, which is useful to read to gain some context for an understanding of the encyclical '*Redemptoris Missio*'.

» '*Redemptoris Missio*' is available online and is useful to read to get a sense of how the Catholic Church's position on other religions fits with the rest of the Pope's message about mission.

» 'Sharing the Gospel of Salvation' is available online and traces the history of Christian relationships with other religions as well as making a statement about the Church of England's position on multi-faith diversity.

» 'Meeting God in Friend and Stranger' (2010) is a Bishops' Conference document from the Catholic Church which sets out the Catholic position on inter-faith dialogue in a clear and straightforward way.

Practice for exams

At A level, essay questions invite you to demonstrate your knowledge and understanding of factual material (AO1) and also your critical ability in putting forward a coherent, balanced argument (AO2). You should aim to write essays that are persuasive responses to the question throughout, rather than writing a lot of description and then tacking an opinion on at the end of each paragraph.

'Christians should seek to convert others to Christianity at every opportunity.' Discuss.

This is the kind of question where the statement you are asked to discuss takes a view that is at one extreme. You need to decide whether your own view is at the other extreme (Christians should never seek to convert others), or whether it is somewhere in the middle (Christians should seek to convert others, but only in some circumstances or only up to a point), or whether you agree with the statement.

Use your knowledge and understanding of different views in order to support the arguments you make rather than presenting different opinions uncritically. You need to be able to justify your own point of view with sound reasoning.

Discuss critically the view that inter-faith dialogue is of little practical use.

For this question you need to consider what the aims of inter-faith dialogue might be, and what kind of 'practical use' inter-faith dialogue might be expected to have.

In order to demonstrate your knowledge and understanding, you should be able to give some examples of inter-faith dialogue in practice, but be careful to ensure that your essay presents an argument and not merely description and explanation. You might want to argue that inter-faith dialogue does, or does not, contribute to social cohesion or better mutual understanding between people of different faiths. You might want to argue that inter-faith dialogue is intended to be more spiritual than practical.

Chapter 3.3

Gender and society

How has Christianity traditionally understood gender roles for men and women?

Can Christianity be compatible with secular views of gender?

How has Christianity responded to the challenges presented by contemporary secular views of gender and family life?

Can biblical and church teaching about family life and gender roles be relevant for modern society?

Key Terms

Feminism: the name given to a wide range of views arguing for, and working for, equality for women

Gender biology: the physical characteristics that enable someone to be identified as male or female

Gender identification: the way people perceive themselves in terms of masculine, feminine, both or neither

Gender expression: the ways in which people behave as a result of their gender identification

Socialisation: the process by which people learn cultural norms

Patriarchal society: a society that is dominated by men and men's interests

Specification requirements

The effects of changing views of gender and gender roles on Christian thought and practice, including:

- Christian teaching on the roles of men and women in the family and society
- Christian responses to contemporary secular views about the roles of men and women in the family and society

Introduction

The relationships between contemporary society, Christianity and gender are very complex. There are many different kinds of society, many different beliefs and attitudes within Christianity, and many different ways of understanding the whole concept of gender.

Christianity has traditionally taught that men and women were created by God to have different, complementary qualities. It teaches that marriage is ordained by God so that men and women can live together as couples and raise children together. The Bible teaches that within a marriage, a man should be in charge and his wife should submit to his authority.

However, these views have been challenged. **Feminists** argue that women should have the same rights and freedoms as men. They object to the idea that men have a natural authority over women. Christianity is sometimes blamed for perpetuating injustice by giving support to the idea that women need not be treated as well as men. Secular society also presents challenges to traditional Christian teaching with rising divorce rates, a growing acceptance of same-sex relationships and a growing number of children being born to parents who are not married.

Christians have responded to such challenges in a range of ways. Some Christians are keen to defend the traditional views of heterosexual marriage and clearly defined gender roles. Others want to reconsider Christian teaching to make it more inclusive of different genders and different kinds of families Some thinkers have rejected Christianity altogether because they see its teaching on gender as incompatible both with contemporary society and with the rights of women.

> **Think question**
>
> Do you think Christianity should change in order to keep up to date, or should it work to maintain traditional values?

Changing views of gender and gender roles

One of the most significant changes in society since the First World War has been a change in the way people view gender. Traditionally, men have held the power in Western society. Gradually, often through the efforts of feminists, women's rights have increased, and today many people do not accept the view that men have a right to be in charge just because they are men.

Biological sex and gender

Many people use the words 'gender' and 'sex' as if they mean the same thing when talking about the distinction between male and female. However, there is a difference between biological sex and gender. Someone's biological sex is determined by physical attributes such as chromosomes, sex organs and hormone levels. The word 'gender', however, refers to a more sophisticated relationship between someone's physical

Biological sex is different from gender, and many people argue that gender is cultural rather than natural

Apply your knowledge

1. **a.** What do you think parents might do if they want to bring up their child in a gender-neutral way?

    b. What effects do you think attempts at a gender-neutral upbringing might have on a child?

2. At a playgroup for under-fives, often (but not always) the boys will play with the toy vehicles while the girls play with the dolls or the dressing-up clothes. Do you think that girls and boys are born with tendencies to be interested in different things (by nature), or do you think this is learned behaviour (by nurture)? How would you support your opinion?

3. Which characteristics, if any, would you think of as typically feminine, and which as typically masculine?

characteristics (their biological sex or '**gender biology**'), the way people perceive themselves (their '**gender identification**') and the ways in which they choose to behave (their '**gender expression**'). Gender identification and gender expression are often heavily influenced by the ways society expects its members to behave and feel.

Gender can be related to sexuality but it does not determine sexuality. For example, a biological man who identifies as male and expresses himself in traditionally masculine ways is not necessarily going to be heterosexual, and a biological man who expresses himself in ways that are traditionally seen as feminine is not necessarily homosexual.

Lots of people find that their gender aligns comfortably with their biological sex. For example, they have female physical characteristics, they feel feminine and identify as female, and they adopt the kinds of behaviours that their society sees as appropriate for females. Others do not have the same experience. They might, for example, have biologically female physical characteristics but feel masculine and identify as male, and they might want to behave in ways that their society sees as masculine. Alternatively, they might have biologically masculine physical features but not identify as exclusively male or female, and they might choose to express their gender however they like, regardless of the labels society chooses to give to behaviours such as the wearing of make-up.

Most people are born with a distinctive biological sex, which is obvious from the moment they are born and often also obvious before birth (i.e. during pregnancy). A small number of babies are born with ambiguous biological sex, where their bodies have some male and some female physical characteristics, and then the parents have to decide whether to raise the child in the gender of boy or girl, or whether to aim for a gender-neutral upbringing.

In the view of many people, but not all, gender is something that is acquired. From a young age, people learn about the expectations associated with being a boy or a girl, and they develop their gender identification and expression through **socialisation**.

'Socialisation' is a term used by sociologists, anthropologists and others to refer to the lifelong process by which we learn the norms of our society. Our parents, siblings, peer group and other members of our society all contribute to our socialisation. This is how we learn all of the spoken and unspoken rules of the culture in which we live, such as what to eat and how to behave when eating it, which words can be used in which kind of company, how children should behave towards adults and how to co-operate with others. In Western society, socialisation traditionally puts a lot of emphasis on learning to make a distinction between male and female. As soon as a baby is born, the parents announce 'it's a boy' or 'it's a girl', and this is understood to be much more important than any of the baby's other characteristics.

Greetings cards congratulating parents on the arrival of their new baby are often decorated in blue for a boy and pink for a girl. Shops offer different ranges of clothing for boys and girls, even when they are newborn. These sometimes have decorations on them that hint at the gender roles expected of the baby. For example, a baby boy's sleep suit might have trains or dinosaurs in strong primary colours such as red or royal blue on it, whereas a sleep suit for a baby girl might be decorated with flowers or butterflies in softer colours such as pink and yellow. Throughout childhood, there are constant reminders of our gender, whether or not it is directly relevant to what we are doing. We might call up the stairs to our children, 'Boys! Dinner's ready!' or say, 'Good girl for remembering to clean your teeth', even though the child's gender has no bearing at all on the subject of the conversation. In English, we use pronouns for people to denote their gender, saying 'he' or 'she' so that our listeners always know whether the person we are referring to is male or female. We have gendered words for family members such as 'auntie' and 'uncle'; we are expected to tick one of two boxes to tell other people our gender when we are filling out forms; we learn to address people formally by gendered titles such as Mr and Mrs – for women, these formal titles include letting everyone know whether or not they are married. Our use of language is gender-binary – in other words, it implies that there are two and only two distinct genders, and that people are either one or the other.

Children's toys are often marketed with a heavy bias towards gender, with merchandise labelled separately 'toys for boys' and 'toys for girls', although there is resistance to this from some consumers. In an effort to avoid restricting children's aspirations through stereotyping, schools make an effort to use textbooks and story books which show that girls can enjoy science or be engineers and that boys can write poetry or be nurses. But in spite of these conscious efforts to overcome gender stereotyping, it is still common to hear teachers telling children to 'ask your mum to sew your name into your PE kit' without acknowledging that an adult carer of any gender might equally be able to sew. Traditional views of gender are deeply embedded in Western culture.

> **Think question**
>
> About 90 per cent of parents today want to know the sex of their baby before it is born, i.e. during pregnancy. Why do you think they want to know the baby's gender in advance of the birth?

The idea that there are two distinct genders is heavily embedded in Western culture

Children are taught from a young age that boys and girls are expected to be interested in different things

By the time we have grown into adult life, we have a strong sense of what is expected of us as male or female. Although, increasingly, some people challenge traditional gender roles, it is nevertheless the case that when young people reach an age when they can choose their school subjects, significantly more boys than girls pick sciences and more girls than boys pick languages and arts. The gender gap widens in further education and is even more distinct in the world of employment.

Patriarchy and feminism

Most societies in the world are patriarchal, which means that men tend to dominate social structures and domestic relationships. Men hold most of the positions of power in government and in the workplace, men create the laws, and men are seen as the 'head of the household' at home. In a **patriarchal society**, men have more power than women, and more wealth. Patriarchal societies tend to be organised in ways that are primarily for men's benefit, and in ways that enable men to hold on to power. They also tend to offer ways of looking at the world that are largely from a male perspective, expressed through male voices. For example, in a patriarchal society, the historical events that are considered worth remembering are generally men's stories and achievements rather than women's.

It is an 'accepted truth', in patriarchal societies, that men are stronger than women and that men and women have different aptitudes which make them better suited to different roles in public and private life. For example, men are seen as more rational whereas women are thought of as more emotional. This has been used as an argument for allowing men to make the important decisions involved in governing, voting and running companies, while women are seen as more suited for caring roles such as looking after young children and the elderly. Such roles are seen as better suited to women because they make the best use of a woman's allegedly softer and more compassionate nature.

However, such ideas have been challenged and continue to be challenged. The 'feminist movement' is a term used to encompass a range of different beliefs and ideologies that share the aim of improving rights and opportunities for women. Feminism became a significant movement in the nineteenth and twentieth centuries, but it can trace its roots back much further. There have always been women who have resisted being cast into traditionally subordinate roles and who have refused to express themselves in ways their societies have considered appropriate for women. One of the best-known early feminist texts was written by Mary Wollstonecraft in 1792 and was called *A Vindication of the Rights of Woman*. In it, Wollstonecraft set out an argument for educating both women and men to the same standard.

Feminism is the name given to a wide range of beliefs that seek freedom for women. It used to be known as the 'women's liberation movement' (often shortened to 'women's lib') because of its emphasis on removing

Apply your knowledge

Some feminists argue that the 'fact' that men are physically stronger than women has become accepted only because men have decided how strength is to be measured. Physically, men can exert greater force, lift heavier weights and run faster than women. But female babies have a higher chance of survival than male babies if they are born prematurely, and women tend to live longer than men. Also, according to the American Psychological Association, girls have outperformed boys in all school subjects for at least a hundred years.

4. What do you think would be a fair way to measure which gender is strongest?

5. Do you think physical strength is the best way of deciding which gender, if any, should have most control in society? Give reasons for your answer.

the restrictions that a patriarchal society places on women and allowing them the same freedoms that men enjoy. Sometimes the history of feminism is divided into three 'waves'. 'First-wave feminism' is the name given to the movement that worked primarily for women's rights to vote and began in the late nineteenth century. 'Second-wave feminism' began in the 1960s and took on wider issues, including issues surrounding women's sexual health and reproduction, such as contraception and abortion, as well as the issues of domestic violence and rape, and equality in the workplace. 'Third-wave feminism' refers to movements that began in the 1990s and continue to the present day. Third-wave feminism calls into question the whole notion of gender roles as well as aiming to be inclusive of women of all ethnicities, sexualities and backgrounds, as a reaction to the challenge that earlier versions of feminism concentrated too much on the voices of affluent heterosexual white women in Western society.

Feminism is a diverse movement that works for equality for women and has made important changes to Western society

During the twentieth century, there were significant changes in UK law that enabled women to have more freedom. Women were not allowed to vote on an equal footing with men until 1928 (by 1918 some women over the age of 30 were given the vote, but not everyone was allowed to vote). Reliable birth control was not readily available until the early 1960s. Before the contraceptive pill, most women were married in their early twenties and were expected to stay at home and raise a family. When the contraceptive pill was introduced, it was originally prescribed for older married women who already had as many children as they could manage. It was not until 1974 that family planning clinics were allowed to prescribe the pill as a contraceptive for single women. This was controversial at the time because it was thought that it would encourage sex outside marriage, if single women had control over their own fertility and could have sexual relationships without the fear of pregnancy. Abortion was illegal until 1967. It was only in 1970 that women were legally entitled to be paid the same as men for the same work (before that, it was legal to pay men more than women even when they were doing exactly the same job).

Changes in freedoms for women also happened in other countries. For example, in France, a married woman could only be employed to work outside the home if she had her husband's permission, and this restriction was not lifted until 1965.

Feminism is not a single ideology, it is a broad term encompassing many different strands. For example:

- Liberal feminism is the name given to feminism that seeks equality for women by campaigning for changes in the law, for example by staging protests against rape or for equal pay.

- Radical feminism takes the view that women cannot be liberated within a capitalist patriarchal society, and it advocates a total uprooting and rebuilding of society.

- Marxist feminism sees women's struggle for freedom through the lens of Marxism, so women's oppression is understood as a symptom of the oppression that occurs when there is private ownership of the means of production (such as factories and farms).

- Black feminism, post-colonial feminism and indigenous feminism are all strands of feminism that aim to give voices to, and further the interests of, non-white women in their own cultural contexts.

- Ecofeminism emphasises a connection between women and the natural world, seeing a relationship between care for the planet and freedom for women, and placing blame for damage to the planet on patriarchal capitalism.

- Separatist feminism seeks freedom for women in isolation from men, seeing heterosexual relationships as inherently disempowering for women (in other words, there is something in heterosexual relationships that always puts women at a disadvantage). Separatist feminism is closely related to lesbian feminism, which promotes same-sex relationships for women.

The diversity of opinions and aims within feminism makes it impossible to single out 'the feminist view' on many issues. In the context of Christianity, there are some feminists who argue that changes need to be made within the structure of Christian practice, worship and leadership in order to give women more equality with men. Some argue that religious worship should focus on God as feminine, using the language of motherhood rather than the language of fatherhood. There are others who argue that Christianity and other religions are entirely incompatible with feminism, because religion is a social construction that is heavily intertwined with patriarchy, and they argue that feminists should abandon religion altogether.

See Chapter 3.4 for a more detailed discussion of gender and feminist theology.

Different views of male and female gender roles

The question of gender roles and gender equality is addressed in many different ways by different people.

The view that men and women are not equal

Some people believe that men and women are not equal, and that men are better than women in every way. This is a view that dates back at least to the time of Plato and Aristotle. Plato believed, along with the rest of his generation, that women were inferior to men. In the context of life after death and rebirth into this world, Plato wrote:

> 66 It is only males who are created directly by the gods and are given souls. Those who live rightly return to the stars, but those who are cowards or lead unrighteous lives may with reason be supposed to have changed into the nature of women in the second generation. 99
>
> Plato, *Timaeus*, c.360BC

In other words, being born a woman is seen by Plato as something that unfortunately happens to men who did not get it right the first time. However, Plato did support the idea that women should be treated more fairly, and in his book *Republic* (c.380BC), where he discusses his views on the ideal society, he recommends that women should not be treated as the possessions of men.

Aristotle's opinions of women have been highly influential on Western thought, partly because they seemed to be supported by science (or what was accepted as science in Aristotle's time, the fourth century BC). Aristotle argued that women are naturally inferior to men, and therefore it is right that men should rule women and women should submit to men. He drew his conclusions from observation, so by looking at the way women in his society behaved, he decided what was 'natural'. According to Aristotle's understanding of biology, reproduction happens because of the male ability to produce semen. He did not know about the female ability to produce eggs and thought that women were just on the receiving end of a life-giving force produced by men. He observed that women were unable to produce semen and from this concluded that women were equivalent to an infertile man, seen by Aristotle as 'defective'. For Aristotle, the male is active in reproduction and the female is passive. Aristotle writes that women are:

> 66 more mischievous, less simple, more impulsive […] more compassionate […] more easily moved to tears […] more jealous, more querulous, more apt to scold and to strike […] more prone to despondency and less hopeful […] more void of shame or self-respect, more false of speech, more deceptive, of more retentive memory […] also more wakeful; more shrinking, more difficult to rouse to action 99
>
> Aristotle, *History of Animals*, c. 400BC, 608b, 1–14

Aristotle writes that women are naturally inferior to men and, therefore, it is naturally best that men should govern women, just as non-human animals are governed by humans:

> 66 It is the best for all tame animals to be ruled by human beings. For this is how they are kept alive. In the same way, the relationship between the male and the female is *by nature* such that the male is higher, the female lower, that the male rules and the female is ruled. 99
>
> Aristotle, *Politica*, 1254b 10–14

Aquinas, in the thirteenth century, took a similar line. In *Summa Theologica* (1265–74) (for example in his discussion of Part II.I, Q92), he argued that women are inferior to men in physical strength and also in intelligence.

Following Aristotle, Aquinas also used the word 'defective' of women when comparing them to men. He thought that women were created by God to be inferior to men as part of the natural variety and order of the world; they had always been that way, it was not just the result of the sin of Eve. God made women to be subordinate to men, according to Aquinas, and it was natural and right that men should have authority over women in everything.

Despite his view that women are inferior to men, as a Christian, Aquinas noted that there is a special high place in heaven for women such as the Virgin Mary and the women who waited at the foot of the cross when Jesus was crucified, and he commended them for their love of God.

The view that men and women are equal in worth

Another possible view which many people have is that men and women are equal in worth but different in their skills and aptitudes. This is a mainstream view that has traditionally been held by Christians, although in Western society it is not as popular as it once was. According to this point of view, all people are equally valuable (in Christian terms, all are equally valuable in the sight of God) but men and women have different, complementary characteristics, which equip each gender for different, complementary roles. It is argued that there are occupations which are better suited to men, such as firefighting or the armed forces, and occupations which are better suited to women, such as nursing and primary-school teaching. From this perspective, neither gender is explicitly considered better than the other. This is a position taken by some feminists, who do not claim that there is no difference between men and women beyond biological difference, but claim instead that women's special skills should be recognised and celebrated as equal with men's rather than seen as second-rate.

Some Christians argue that the different skills men and women have mean that women should not be priests or have other positions of authority in the Christian Church. In particular, they should not take

Aristotle and Aquinas were both instrumental in popularising the view that women are inferior to men

Apply your knowledge

6. Aristotle and Aquinas have been blamed by feminists for introducing into Christianity an unequal and repressive ideology, based on poor scientific theory. How fair is this accusation, in your view?

Think question

Do you think that there are some jobs that are better suited to people of one gender? For example, do you think that women should fight alongside men in the armed forces?

roles where they are representing Christ, such as in the blessing of the Eucharist (Holy Communion). The Catholic Church and the Orthodox Church, for example, do not ordain women to the priesthood, arguing that Jesus chose only men to be his disciples. They also argue that God chose to come into the world as a man, not as a woman, and therefore only a man, not a woman, can represent him in the sacraments. However, other Christian denominations, such as the Church of England and the United Reformed Church, have ordained women as well as men, arguing that God calls people to the ministry without gender discrimination.

The view that women are superior to men

Some people challenge the idea that feminism has to be about seeking equality with men, but instead think that women should aim higher. Some argue that when women seek equality with men, they are being far too unambitious. For example, the feminist theologian Mary Daly (1928–2010) argued that women's abilities and knowledge are superior to those of men, and that women ought to govern men as this would result in a more peaceful society and would also be better for the environment. She is best known for her books *The Church and the Second Sex* (1968) and *Beyond God the Father* (1973), in which she tackled issues of gender and patriarchy within the Christian tradition.

The view that gender is a matter of choice

Some people challenge the whole idea that there are 'masculine qualities' and 'feminine qualities'. They argue that designating some qualities and behaviours as masculine and others as feminine is entirely artificial, determined by the cultural norms of society rather than by nature. Women can be aggressive, powerful, rational or mathematical, just as men can be submissive, weak, compassionate, emotional or artistic. People are individuals with their own personalities. It only appears that some qualities are more prevalent in men and others in women because society encourages and reinforces rigid rules of gender expression.

Boys are taught from a young age not to cry when they are hurt, and they are encouraged to be physically strong and adventurous. Girls are taught to take an interest in their own appearance (and society often dictates what should be considered attractive and unattractive about a woman's appearance). They are encouraged to show disgust at dirt and mud and to play imaginative games involving childcare and fashion. However, these behaviours are not intrinsically male or female, they argue; they are cultural norms that are impressed on people from a young age through socialisation.

Some people who challenge the notion of masculine and feminine qualities also challenge the whole idea of gender as binary (with only two options: 'male' or 'female'). They prefer to think of gender as a spectrum and as a matter of choice, where all individuals have the right to decide how they identify and express themselves, and have the right to change their minds about their gender.

This point of view is sometimes extended to include the idea that it makes no sense to talk of 'women's experience' as if there is something singular about it that can be defined. There is too much diversity between women in terms of culture, ethnicity, age and social class for there to be a single phenomenon of 'women's experience'. An affluent white woman in the UK is unlikely to share many experiences with a black woman living in poverty in Somalia. Even physically female experiences, such as menstruation and childbirth, are going to be experienced in very different ways over time and across the world, so it is unhelpful to classify them together as 'women's experience'.

Traditional Christian teaching on the roles of men and women in the family and society

There is not one unanimous 'Christian view' on the roles of men and women in the family and in society. There is a range of different views and responses, just as there is a range of Christians each with their own gender biology, identity and expression.

However, there is traditional Christian teaching on the roles of men and women in the family and in society, which is based on teachings found in the Bible. This teaching is that God created men and women in order that they should have different, complementary roles. Some Christians consider this teaching sets an ethical standard that is appropriate for all time, whereas others think it needs to be reinterpreted to keep Christianity relevant for modern society.

The book of Genesis is often used to support the view that men and women, although equally valued by God, were always intended to have different roles. In the book of Genesis, the first creation story tells how God creates humanity 'in his own image', and this phrase is applied to both men and women:

> 66 So God created mankind in his own image,
> in the image of God he created them;
> male and female he created them. 99
>
> Genesis 1:27, New International Version

This text suggests that both male and female in some sense reflect the nature of God, and there is no hint here that one sex is superior to the other. However, in the second creation story, the male is created first and the woman second, in order to be the man's companion and his 'helper':

> 66 But for Adam no suitable helper was found. So the Lord God caused the man to fall into a deep sleep; and while he was sleeping, he took one of the man's ribs and then closed up the place with flesh. Then the Lord God made a woman from the rib he had taken out of the man, and he brought her to the man. 99

Genesis 2:20–22, New International Version

The second Genesis story has often been used to justify the view that the proper role of a woman, and especially a wife, is as a companion for a man. As the story continues, the two people are tempted to turn away from God, and it is the woman who is the first to succumb to temptation and eat the forbidden fruit:

The Genesis story of Eve eating the forbidden fruit first has often been used as evidence that women make bad decisions and need to be governed by men

> 66 Now the serpent was more crafty than any of the wild animals the Lord God had made. He said to the woman, 'Did God really say, "You must not eat from any tree in the garden"?'
>
> The woman said to the serpent, 'We may eat fruit from the trees in the garden, but God did say, "You must not eat fruit from the tree that is in the middle of the garden, and you must not touch it, or you will die."'

'You will not certainly die,' the serpent said to the woman. 'For God knows that when you eat from it your eyes will be opened, and you will be like God, knowing good and evil.'

When the woman saw that the fruit of the tree was good for food and pleasing to the eye, and also desirable for gaining wisdom, she took some and ate it. She also gave some to her husband, who was with her, and he ate it. **"**

Genesis 3:1–6, New International Version

This passage is sometimes used to support the belief that women are weaker willed than men and more likely to give in easily when challenged. It is also used to support the view that men should take the lead in decision-making and should not allow their opinions to be swayed by women.

In the New Testament, there are letters to newly formed Christian churches in which the writers give teaching, encouragement and advice to churches in different places, such as Ephesus, Rome and Galatia. Some of the letters are written by Paul (whose dramatic conversion to Christianity is described in the Acts of the Apostles) and some are by other writers.

In these letters, advice is given on the roles of men and women in a household. In the first century, it was common for people writing about politics or ethics to include some ideas about household management, as the family was seen as central to the well-being of society as a whole. If people ran orderly households then wider society would also be more stable. The household included husband and wife, children and servants, and the writers of the New Testament letters sometimes included advice for all the different members of a household. Part of their motivation might also have been to demonstrate that Christianity was peaceful and not a dangerous and subservient movement. It was important that Christians should be seen to be respectable members of society.

The letter to the Ephesians is an example of a New Testament letter that gives teaching about the roles of men and women in a household. Like other New Testament teachings on the subject, it is quite conservative in its tone, keeping closely to the cultural norms that were considered to be good ethics in first century society, in both Christian and non-Christian households. Society was patriarchal, the father was the head of the family and he had complete rule over the rest of the household. The author of the letter to the Ephesians writes:

" Wives, submit yourselves to your own husbands as you do to the Lord. For the husband is the head of the wife as Christ is the head of the church, his body, of which he is the Savior. Now

Think question

Do you think that the Genesis story demonstrates that women are naturally weaker than men?

Apply your knowledge

10. Look up these passages from the New Testament:

    a. Colossians 3:18–25 and 4:1. What advice is given here to different members of a first-century household? Do you think this is good advice? Give reasons for your answer.

    b. 1 Peter 2:18–25 and 3:1–7. In 1 Peter, the writer explains the reasons for the advice he is giving by making reference to Christian beliefs. What are the Christian reasons he gives to justify his advice to slaves and to wives?

11. Some Christians argue that, in a relationship, it is better to have someone who is in charge, so that if there are disagreements, one partner has the casting vote and the argument is over quickly. How far would you agree with this idea?

as the church submits to Christ, so also wives should submit to their husbands in everything.

Husbands, love your wives, just as Christ loved the church and gave himself up for her to make her holy, cleansing her by the washing with water through the word, and to present her to himself as a radiant church, without stain or wrinkle or any other blemish, but holy and blameless. In this same way, husbands ought to love their wives as their own bodies. He who loves his wife loves himself. After all, no one ever hated their own body, but they feed and care for their body, just as Christ does the church—for we are members of his body. 'For this reason a man will leave his father and mother and be united to his wife, and the two will become one flesh.' This is a profound mystery—but I am talking about Christ and the church. However, each one of you also must love his wife as he loves himself, and the wife must respect her husband.

Ephesians 5:22–33, New International Version

In this passage, the traditional gender roles of a patriarchal society are emphasised. The husband should be in control, and other members of the household, including the wife, should submit to his authority. Any ethics advice from the era would say the same thing. However, in this biblical letter, there is a development of this relationship to show how it should work in a Christian context. The writer draws an analogy between the relationship between a husband and a wife and the relationship between Christ and the Church. The wife should accept the authority of her husband in the same way that the Church accepts the authority of Christ. But it is not a one-way relationship. The husband should also love his wife in the way that Christ loves the Church. Christ, according to the writer, sacrificed himself for the Church and through his sacrifice allowed the Church to be holy, and in the same way the husband should be self-sacrificing for his wife.

The passage uses the imagery of the Church as the 'body of Christ', and describes how a husband should love his wife to the same extent that he loves his own body. The writer quotes from Genesis to remind the reader that a husband and wife have become 'one flesh', and therefore the respect a man has for himself is dependent on his showing love for his wife. Recognising that the woman is in a disadvantaged position in a patriarchal society, the instructions to show self-sacrificing love are for the husband; the wife is simply advised to show her husband respect.

This passage places Christian marriage and the Christian household in the context of living under the authority of Christ. The couple is reminded that their personal relationships, as well as every other aspect of their lives, are to be conducted in ways appropriate for people who are part of the body of Christ (the Church).

Think question

Do you think that this biblical passage requires the wife to respect and submit to her husband regardless of whether he treats her with love or not?

Biblical teaching about the roles of men and women causes some controversy in Christianity. Some argue that the Bible has authority as the Word of God and should be accepted at face value. If contemporary society disagrees with some of the teachings of the Bible, then contemporary society needs to change. The Bible teaches, quite consistently, that a man should be the head of the household and chief decision-maker and that his wife should be obedient to him and support him. This view is sometimes known as 'biblical patriarchy', where the Bible is cited as justification for the man having complete authority in the home.

However, other Christians argue that biblical directions about how to run a household were written for a historical context very different from our own. Religious ethics and practices do not develop in a vacuum but within a social context, and when people no longer live according to the customs of the first century, rules about gender roles need to be reconsidered along with other outdated rules such as how to treat slaves and witches. The view that, in a Christian marriage, the husband and wife should be mutually respectful and supportive without either dominating the other is known as 'Christian egalitarianism'.

Christian responses to contemporary secular views about the roles of men and women in the family and society

Modern secular society presents many challenges to Christian belief. Traditional Christian ideas about gender and about the roles of men and women in society are challenged when people question patriarchy and demand equal rights and freedoms for women. They are also challenged when people live in non-traditional families, which do not fit the pattern of married father and mother and their children.

Motherhood and parenthood in *Mulieris Dignitatem*

Pope John Paul II wrote an open letter in 1988 on the subject of the dignity and rights of women, called *Mulieris Dignitatem*. This letter was intended to clarify the Catholic position on issues raised by feminism, in response to accusations that the Church was sexist and that it promoted injustice by denying women the same rights as men. In the letter, the Pope wrote about the particular skills and qualities of women, and drew attention to the examples of Christian devotion set by female European saints. His position on gender roles was that men and women have different, complementary characteristics given to them by God, and he wanted to emphasise that a woman's role as a Christian is a role that is to be respected.

The Pope wrote that the turning point of human history happened when God came to earth as Jesus Christ, and that this was made possible because of a woman, Mary, who freely chose to take on the role of mother of the son of God. When the angel Gabriel appeared to Mary, she recognised the call to service and responded to it. He wrote that, on the character of Mary, two 'particular dimensions of the fulfilment of the female personality' are exemplified: virginity and motherhood (Pope John Paul II, *Mulieris Dignitatem*, 1988). Through the miraculous grace of God, Mary was able to be both a virgin and a mother.

In point 18 of the letter, the Pope writes:

> 66 Motherhood is the fruit of the marriage union of a man and woman, of that biblical 'knowledge' which corresponds to the 'union of the two in one flesh' […]. This brings about – on the woman's part – a special 'gift of self', as an expression of that spousal love whereby the two are united to each other so closely that they become 'one flesh'. 99
>
> Pope John Paul II, *Mulieris Dignitatem*, 1988, point 18

In *Mulieris Dignitatem* the Pope explains that motherhood enables a woman to be self-giving as she has a 'special openness' to the new person that will be her child. The Pope writes that women are 'naturally disposed to motherhood' both physically and psychologically, and that this is a gift from God. Although parenthood is shared by both the husband and wife, 'he owes a special debt to the woman'. A woman's personality is such that she is more capable of attending to the needs of others than a man is. However, the Pope also writes that the child's upbringing, 'should include the contribution of both parents', although he does not say whether this should be an equal contribution.

Mulieris Dignitatem (1988) was written to reaffirm Christian beliefs about the dignity of women

In point 19 of the letter, the Pope reflects on the examples of womanhood given in the Bible. He repeats the word 'passive' used by Aristotle and Aquinas to say that a pregnancy is something that takes place in a woman rather than being something that a woman actively does, but nevertheless motherhood involves creativity. He draws attention especially to Mary, the mother of Jesus, saying that through her obedience to God's will, God begins a new relationship with humanity. In this way, women safeguard and pass on the word of God, because every human being comes into the world through the 'threshold' of motherhood.

He writes that the pain of childbirth experienced by women is the result of original sin, but it also allows women an insight into the mystery of the suffering of Christ. Women, according to the Pope, are better able to cope with suffering than men, but are also more sensitive. He lists some of the ways in which women suffer, especially when their children are ill or 'fall into bad ways', and also mentions women who are lonely or have

Think question

a. Do you think that *Mulieris Dignitatem* (1988) implicitly suggests that women who are unable to have children are in some sense less successful than women who are mothers?

Apply your knowledge

12. Some people argue that women cannot have the dignity and respect claimed for them by Catholicism unless the Church also allows women to have access to artificial contraception. To what extent would you agree with this claim?

Think question

b. In some infant baptism services, the baby is welcomed into the 'Church family'. What do you think the word 'family' means in this context?

to make a living on their own. However, the suffering of childbirth is immediately forgotten (according to this letter) with the joy of receiving a newborn child into the world.

Although other Christian denominations might not express their views in the same way as the late Pope, Christianity teaches that women have a special dignity because of their capacity for motherhood and their unique ability to bring the next generation into the world. Christian teaching reminds people that women are not to be treated in a degrading and disrespectful way because no one would be here at all without the existence of motherhood.

Christian views about different types of family

One of the challenges that secular society presents to Christianity concerns the notion of family. Traditional Christian teaching often assumes that a family consists of two parents, one of whom is male and the other female, and their children. This picture of a 'normal' family has been much exploited by advertisers, who for many years showed their products being used in scenarios in which a father went off to work as chief breadwinner while his wife busied herself with the domestic chores and childcare. Contemporary modern society has challenged this stereotype and advertisers today sometimes acknowledge that some families have one parent, that many women work outside the home and many men do domestic chores.

The concept of family is difficult to define, as the word can have different meanings in different contexts. Consider, for example, the difference between 'extended family' and 'immediate family'. People who consider themselves part of the same family might not necessarily be related. For example, an unmarried couple might each have children from previous relationships who all live together in the same house. Or someone who is estranged from their own relatives might join a different family and live with them without being related to them. Sociologists and anthropologists understand the function of the family as a social unit that provides protection and socialisation for its members. Family members share tasks such as earning money, preparing meals and raising children.

A family with two heterosexual married parents and their children is the ideal in Christianity, but in reality there are many different kinds of family and there always have been. Some people have children before marriage, or without ever getting married; some people are widowed or separated or divorced and have to raise children on their own; some people do not want to have children or are unable to have them. Throughout history, some families have included children who are adopted because their biological parents are unable to look after them, or several generations of a family live together. In recent years, same-sex couples have been able to live together more openly, sometimes with children. The increase in divorce and the reducing popularity of marriage has meant that a high proportion of families in the UK are not the traditional kind.

Christianity teaches that marriage is the best context for raising a family. The majority of Christians understand this to mean heterosexual marriage. According to Christian doctrine, marriage is ordained by God. In other words, it is not just a social convention but it is something that God designed and intended when humanity was created. In some Christian denominations, such as the Catholic Church, marriage is seen as a sacrament, which means it is an outward visible sign of the grace of God. Marriage is understood to be a special relationship given to humanity as a gift from God. Christians are encouraged to enter into marriage only after serious thought, in the knowledge that they are making a lifelong commitment to another person and that God is joining them together.

Secular society presents several challenges to Christian beliefs. Divorce is accepted in some Christian denominations, but not all. For example, the Catholic Church holds that marriage is a sacrament that cannot be undone. Although it recognises that some marriages become irretrievably damaged, it does not recognise the possibility of divorce. Human beings do not have the power to dissolve a marriage. Catholicism does not insist that a married couple live together, but it will not recognise civil divorce and will not allow people who have been divorced to marry new partners in a church. Many other Christian denominations take a different view, emphasising the importance in Christianity of forgiveness and opportunities to make a fresh start. They often allow the parish priest or minister to make a decision about whether to conduct a service of marriage between people who have previously been divorced.

Most non-religious feminists believe that women should have access to both contraception and abortion in order to have the choice of avoiding or terminating unwanted pregnancies. However, artificial methods of contraception are not acceptable to the Catholic Church, and many Christians disagree with abortion, seeing it as the destruction of a sacred human life. Christian teaching emphasises that sexual relationships should take place within marriage and that children are a gift from God, whereas non-religious people and some Christians might consider this old-fashioned, restricting of the rights of adults to enjoy sexual freedom.

For many Christians, homosexual relationships are 'unnatural'. Some Christians accept homosexuality and are happy to support homosexual friends in their relationships but feel that 'marriage' is the wrong word to use for a legally binding commitment between a same-sex couple. They argue that marriage is ordained by God to be between a man and a woman. However, other Christians are happy to accept marriage between same-sex couples in the same way that they accept heterosexual marriage. They argue that all love comes from God and that couples should be encouraged and supported by the Christian community if they want to make public commitments of faithfulness to each other in marriage.

See Chapter 2.3 for a discussion of how verses from the Bible are used to support the view that homosexuality is wrong.

Apply your knowledge

13. What do you understand by the term 'family'? Can someone be a family member if they are not related to you?

Discussing gender and society

Should official Christian teaching resist current secular views of gender?

Some people argue that Christians have a responsibility to defend traditional biblical ideas about gender roles and family life. Christians believe that the Bible has authority as the word of God, although there are differences of opinion about what this means in practice. Biblical teaching is consistent in saying that God deliberately created two distinct sexes, male and female, and that each gender was created for different purposes. Christians might cite research studies that support the idea that children are happiest and achieve better at school if they come from stable families with two parents, and if they have both male and female role models in their lives. Secular views of gender that are at odds with traditional Christian teaching could be considered destabilising, depriving children of the security offered by clear gender roles and an established hierarchy in the family.

Others argue that there is a need for Christianity to take notice of challenges to traditional gender roles. It has been argued by many feminists that Christianity perpetuates injustice by forcing women into a position of subservience, and some Christians see this as a fair criticism and work to improve the lives of women in their own societies and around the world. The Christian ethical principles of agape and of treating others as you would like to be treated yourself could be employed to support the view that Christians have a duty to make society fairer, which could include challenging patriarchy and insisting on more freedoms for women.

The resistance from some Christians to same-sex marriage could be seen as upholding Christian virtues and maintaining the sanctity of marriage as a gift from God in the joining of a man and a woman. Christians are sharply divided on the issue, with some wanting Christian Churches to conduct same-sex marriages on an equal footing with heterosexual marriages, while others see it as condoning sin and undermining the idea of marriage as a sacred gift.

Some argue that if Christianity is to appeal to future generations, it has to take notice of the views of contemporary society and adapt to the modern world; it cannot hang on to old-fashioned and repressive gender inequalities. However, others argue that Christianity sets high standards of moral behaviour that should not be undermined. It can be argued that perhaps a religion that fits comfortably with secular thinking offers nothing distinctive and is not worth following.

Have secular views of gender equality undermined Christian gender roles?

Gender equality is an important issue for many people in the modern world, and it is especially important for women. People are very aware

Apply your knowledge

14. How far, if at all, do you think Christianity should adapt its teachings to keep them in line with changes in public secular opinion?

15. Do you think that gender equality is incompatible with traditional Christian teaching? Give reasons for your answer.

of sexist stereotyping and make efforts to ensure that girls as well as boys have access to a full range of educational opportunities. Women today are able to turn to the law for help if they suffer discrimination in the workplace. Gender equality also affects men, allowing them rights such as paternity leave and sometimes better access to their children if they divorce. More men feel able to take career breaks in order to raise small children, as this is no longer seen as an exclusively female role, and more women feel able to return to work after having a baby without being accused of neglecting their maternal responsibilities. Baby nappy-changing facilities in public places are no longer always restricted to mothers, and pre-school playgroups are often more welcoming to fathers, grandfathers and male childminders than they once were. There is still considerable gender inequality, but many people in modern secular society agree that continued efforts should be made to treat men and women equally.

This movement towards gender equality could be seen as undermining traditional Christian gender roles. For example, many couples, including Christians, no longer accept the view that the man is the head of the household and that his wife should obey him in everything. It could be argued that this is a good thing, giving greater freedoms to both women and men, who no longer feel that they have to fit into predetermined ideals of female and male. Christians could argue that the main message of Christian teaching about gender is a message of mutual love and respect under God, and that patriarchal guidelines in the Bible can be disregarded as belonging to a different era.

However, some see secular views of gender as a threat to Christian morality. Secular views on artificial contraception, abortion and same-sex marriage are seen as particularly dangerous, because they appear to disrespect God's gifts of the conception of children and the sanctity of marriage.

To what extent is motherhood liberating or restricting?

Some people claim that, for a woman, becoming a mother is the ultimate fulfilment of female potential. Motherhood enables women to put into practice their skills of nurturing, patience, feeding, care and compassion. The Papal letter *Mulieris Dignitatem* (1988) explores what this can mean in the context of Catholic Christianity, where motherhood gives women the opportunity to fulfil their potential in the creation and nurturing of another human being. Motherhood can give women the opportunity to develop their best characteristics and gain a new and dignified status in the family and in the community.

Others, however, have not shared this view of motherhood. The feminist writer Simone de Beauvoir (1908–1986), for example, wrote in the 1940s about the ways in which motherhood forces a women to suspend her own interests and personality in order to take care of her children. She wrote that women have motherhood forced upon them and that it leaves

> ### Apply your knowledge
>
> **16.** It could be argued that if people dismiss biblical teaching, supporting patriarchy as old-fashioned and irrelevant to the present day, this starts a 'slippery slope' and allows people to dismiss other Christian moral teachings too, such as the commandment not to steal. Do you think this is a fair point? Give reasons for your answer.

them crushed, unable to develop as individuals while their children are young, and then left empty and without purpose once their children grow up and leave home. At the time, de Beauvoir's work was considered to be startlingly unconventional, but it struck a chord with many women in the days before there was readily available contraception. De Beauvoir was born into a Catholic family but became outspokenly atheist. Her work *The Second Sex* (1949) is considered to be one of the classics of feminist literature.

The sociologist Ann Oakley (b. 1944) also wrote about the negative side of motherhood. As part of her research, she interviewed women and gave their accounts of their lives in their own words, describing how they felt about housework and motherhood. She concluded that a woman's feeling that she needs to become a mother is not biological but is entirely the result of socialisation: there is no such thing as a 'maternal instinct'. Oakley wrote about the ways in which women feel powerless during childbirth, when medical experts (usually men) take over and start treating them as 'cases'. She described the frustrations that women feel when they have to stay at home while their children are young. Many of Ann Oakley's readers described a sense of relief at realising that other women did not always find motherhood easy.

For most women, perhaps, motherhood is both liberating and restricting. It could be argued that motherhood is not the same for any two women, nor even the same for one woman from one day to the next. Experiences will vary widely, depending on a woman's relationship with her partner if she has one, her physical and mental health and that of her child, whether she has enough money and whether her extended family supports her. Many women find that motherhood is both far better than they expected it to be and also far worse. Labelling motherhood as 'liberating' or 'restricting', 'dignified' or 'demeaning' fails to take into account the many different facets of parenthood as well as the uniqueness of each mother–and–child relationship.

Is the idea of family entirely culturally determined?

In the social sciences, including sociology and anthropology, the family is studied as a 'social institution'. In other words, it is seen as a pattern of behaviour that is well-established in a society and which performs a function that is valued by that society. The family is a social unit in which each member has a role and gains a sense of belonging. In families that work well, everyone feels protected and supported. The family performs functions such as the care of young children and the elderly. It allows some members of the family to work outside the home for long hours to earn money while other members of the family perform domestic tasks, and everyone shares the benefits of the wage and of the clean home.

The family can be seen as entirely culturally determined, which means that its structures are created by the wider society in which it operates. For example, in an industrialised society, people tend to live in smaller

> **Think question**
>
> How do you think that fatherhood compares with motherhood? Does it depend on the individual, or is being a father easier or more difficult than being a mother?

family units because different people do different kinds of work in different parts of the city or the country. It is unusual in the UK for one household to contain several generations as well as uncles, aunts and cousins. Instead, a parent or parents live with their children in one house, and other family members live in another small family unit somewhere else. Adult children tend to leave their parents' house and live independently once they are earning enough money to do so. In a more rural society, people tend to live in larger family units. All of the men might go out hunting together and all of the women might share the work of caring for the children, growing domestic crops and preparing food. Many societies divide work according to gender, both outside and within the family unit.

Most sociologists see human behaviour as being shaped entirely by the society to which people belong. Socialisation shows us the cultural norms of our own society, so we grow up knowing what is expected of us and we usually accept it without thinking too deeply about it. In the UK today, it is normal behaviour for young adults to find a partner and to set up home together. Someone aged 15 would be considered too young to move out of their parents' home to live with a partner, and someone aged 40 who still lives with their parents is considered unusual. In other countries, social norms are different.

In contrast, Christianity teaches that the family is not something that has been created and shaped by human society. It teaches that family is created and shaped by God. God decides, when he creates humanity in the book of Genesis, to make a male and a female who should become lifelong partners and give each other mutual support. God sets rules about the correct behaviour for different family members, teaching through the Bible how different genders should take different roles, how parents and children should relate to one another and how household servants should be treated.

The belief that the family is created by God rather than by society has implications. If the family is solely a social institution, created and shaped by cultural norms, then there is nothing wrong with ideas about what constitutes a 'normal' family changing as society changes. For example, if society changes its view about homosexual relationships and this is reflected in the structure of some families, there is nothing wrong with this; the new family structure is simply a reflection of prevailing culture. If society gives women equal rights with men in the workplace, family life might change so that it is acceptable for a woman to go out to work while her partner stays at home to raise the children, or she might decide to employ someone to look after her children while she works, or choose not to have any children. And, again, there is nothing wrong with this because it reflects the society in which she lives.

However, if marriage and the family is created by God, then it has a different status. It can be seen as a gift or a sacrament, and as an ideal way of life. It can be argued that the rules God has given for the conduct of family life are for all time and should not change along with societal changes. Christians could consider heterosexual marriage and hierarchical family life as something that should be preserved and defended against the challenges of contemporary culture.

Apply your knowledge

17. **a.** What evidence might a sociologist provide to demonstrate that the family is culturally determined?

    b. What evidence might a Christian provide to demonstrate that the family is ordained by God?

    c. Which kind of evidence do you think is stronger? Give reasons for your answer.

18. Could the family be both ordained by God and culturally determined, or are the two ideas incompatible? Give reasons for your answer.

19. Do some research to explore some alternatives to family life, such as kibbutzim and communes. What do you think are the advantages and disadvantages of communal living?

Learning support

Points to remember

» Remember that feminism is very diverse. Feminists do not all share the same opinions or the same visions for the future.

» Christianity is also very diverse. Although some Christians are traditional in their thinking, others are more liberal.

» Issues of gender can be controversial and cause strong feelings. When you are writing about them, remember to keep your arguments fair and balanced. You can express strong opinions, but make sure that you present counter-opinions fairly.

Enhance your learning

» In order to increase your knowledge and understanding of feminism, you could research the lives and ideas of some well-known feminist thinkers. Mary Wollstonecraft, as an early writer about feminism, is interesting to read. Emmeline Pankhurst, Elizabeth Cady Stanton, Simone de Beauvoir and many others have fascinating stories that are well worth exploring.

» Rosemarie Tong's book *Feminist Thought* (2013) is a very thorough introduction to the history and diversity of feminism, although it is written at a level appropriate for academics. Chapter 1 explores the history of liberal feminism in bringing about changes to the law.

» There are some short, clear and accessible sections in Alister McGrath's book *Christian Theology* (5th edition, 2010). See p. 88–9 and p. 336–7, which give a brief introduction to the challenges posed to Christianity by feminist thought.

» Chapter 8 of Neil Messer's *SCM Studyguide to Christian Ethics* (2006) considers the implications for Christian ethics of feminist ideas about equality and gender. This is an accessible book that makes useful links between different parts of this A level course.

» Ephesians 5:21–33 is an example of biblical teaching about gender roles within a family. Passages on a similar theme can be found in Colossians 3:18–25 and 4:1, 1 Peter 2:18–25 and 3:1–7 and Titus 2:1–10.

» Ursula King (ed.) *Religion and Gender* (1995), is written for university students, but it covers a wide range of themes that could be interesting reading for people who wish to study the topic further.

» There are many interesting novels that explore the nature of gender identity and expression, sometimes in the context of religion. For example, Jeanette Winterson's *Oranges Are Not the Only Fruit* (1985) tells the story of a young girl struggling with her gender identity and sexuality in the context of a hyper-religious family. *Middlesex* by Jeffrey Eugenides (2003) is a fictional story of a person born with an ambiguous biological sex.

Practice for exams

At A level, essay questions invite you to demonstrate your knowledge and understanding of factual material (AO1) and also your critical ability in putting forward a coherent, balanced argument (AO2). You should aim to write essays that are persuasive responses to the question throughout, rather than writing a lot of description and then tacking an opinion on at the end of each paragraph.

'In a Christian society, men should have authority over women.' Discuss.

For this question, you are invited to consider whether a Christian society should also be a patriarchal society.

For high marks in AO1, you should demonstrate knowledge and understanding of Christian teaching about gender roles of men and women, and you should be able to support them with reference to sources of wisdom and authority, such as the Bible and the teachings of Christian Churches. You should also show knowledge of alternative views, such as the views of feminists.

For AO2 you need to construct and sustain an argument. Remember that the question is asking about a 'Christian society' so you need to think about whether a society could have equality between genders and yet still be Christian.

With reference to *Mulieris Dignitatem*, discuss critically the view that motherhood gives women a liberating dignity.

This question asks you to consider the view that there is something special and dignified about motherhood, which is liberating for women. It asks for reference to *Mulieris Dignitatem*, which means that you should show familiarity with the teaching in this document. You should have studied sections 18 and 19 and will not be expected to know what is in the rest of the document.

For high marks in AO1 you should demonstrate knowledge and understanding of the view that motherhood is considered by the Catholic Church to be one of the ways in which women can fulfill their potential and be self-giving. You should also show knowledge of other points of view, such as that of Simone de Beauvoir.

For AO2 you should 'discuss critically' different ways of looking at the idea of motherhood as liberating and dignified, which means that you should have an opinion on the different perspectives you present and should be able to point out what you consider to be their strengths and weaknesses.

Chapter 3.4

Gender and theology

Should the Christian God be depicted in female terms?
Can Christianity be saved from sexist patriarchy?
Can a male Messiah save womankind?

Key Terms

Post-Christian theology: religious thinking that abandons traditional Christian thought

Reform feminist theology: religious thinking that seeks to change traditional Christian thought

Davidic Messiah: a Messiah figure based on the kingly military images of the Hebrew scriptures (the Old Testament)

Servant king: an understanding of the Messiah that focuses on service rather than overlordship

Sophia: Greek for 'wisdom', personified in female form in the ancient world

Thealogy: studying God based around the goddess ('thea' is Greek for 'goddess')

Specification requirements

The reinterpretation of God by feminist theologians, including the teaching of Rosemary Radford Ruether and Mary Daly on gender and its implications for the Christian idea of God

Introduction

Feminism is a movement that challenges the view that men are superior and dominant and women are inferior and passive. Some feminists seek to reverse this and express female dominance, but many argue for an equality between men and women.

Feminist theology questions:

- the justification of male dominance and female subordination in theology

- the exclusive use of male language for God

- the view that men are more like God than women

- the view that only men can represent God as leaders in Church and society

- the view that women are created to be subordinate to men and if they reject this they are sinning.

Most of the theologians and philosophers named in books about theology are men, because men have dominated academic writing about theology and philosophy. However, in recent decades, male domination of society and culture has been challenged. Twentieth-century female theologians have questioned the influence and impact of the cultural legacy of patriarchy, not just on practices such as exclusively male priesthoods or a belief that the divinely ordained role of women is a subordinate one to men, but on the development of Christian thought from its origins in a patriarchal ancient world.

Daphne Hampson, a feminist theologian, wrote:

66 Feminism represents a revolution. It is not in essence a demand that women should be allowed to join the male world on equal terms. It is a different view of the world. This must be of fundamental import for theology […] As women come into their own, theology will take a different shape. 99

Daphne Hampson, *Theology and Feminism,* 1990, p. 1

Some feminist theologians suggest that the patriarchal understanding of Christianity is mistaken and that a better, truer, non-sexist interpretation can be found. Others believe Christianity needs to be reinterpreted without the patriarchal elements, cleansed of their distorting influences. Another group believes Christianity may be intrinsically sexist and so flawed that it should be discarded, along with all the sexist practices and beliefs associated with it.

This chapter considers two key feminist theological thinkers:

- Mary Daly (1928–2010) was an American radical post-Christian feminist theologian, who argues that the idea of a patriarchal fatherly God is the foundation of a sexist culture of denigration and violence towards women, and an unholy trinity of rape, genocide and war.

- Rosemary Radford Ruether (b. 1936) is an American feminist scholar, a Catholic theologian and an advocate of women's ordination in the Catholic Church. She is a critic of aspects of traditional Christian theology but she continues to reform it, arguing that it has been distorted by patriarchal traditions.

Apply your knowledge

1. Christianity as a religion is patriarchal. Discuss with reference to these pictures.

Mary Daly and the unholy trinity of rape, genocide and war

Mary Daly (1928–2010)

Mary Daly was a radical feminist **post-Christian theologian** writing in the second half of the twentieth century who argued that men have, throughout history, sought to oppress women and that religion is used as a tool to enforce this oppression. She argued that women need to get beyond religion – a statement that is both provocative and controversial.

Daly was inspired by Nietzsche:

> 66 Whenever man has thought it necessary to create a memory of himself, his effort has been attended with torture, blood, sacrifice. 99
>
> Friedrich Nietzsche, *The Genealogy of Morals,* 1887, pp. 192–3

Daly argued that female oppression is a product of the cultural and historical impact of Christianity's unholy trinity of rape, genocide and war. One patriarchal divine person (God) combines sexism, racism and classism to create a three-headed monster that has to be fought.

The biblical and popular image of God is as the great patriarch in heaven, who rewards and punishes, and dominates the imagination. In the human imagination the symbol of 'God the Father' has spawned the mechanisms for the oppression of women. God has his heaven, his people and his nature of things in which society and the universe is male dominated. The husband, dominating the wife, represents God himself. If God is male then male is God. This distorts the spirituality of nature, where the divine is not limited to maleness.

Patriarchal religion perpetuates these sexual role delusions, calls them natural and bestows supernatural blessings on them. Daly criticised so-called fathers or experts in the Christian tradition for their anti-feminism. She noted that

If God is male then male is God

Tertullian (an early Christian theologian) saw women as 'the devil's gateway', responsible for the Fall and the reason God needed to send Jesus to die to save everyone. Augustine suggested women were not made in the image of God; Aquinas suggested women were misbegotten males; and Martin Luther suggested that God created Adam lord of all, but Eve spoiled this. Daly criticised the idea that the role of the Christian woman is to be a mother, and the argument that women cannot be ordained because Jesus was male.

She believed that 'God the Father' is inadequate, and the maleness of God should be removed: God should be castrated. She argued that women need to use language in a new way because the old language is androcentric (man-centred). She believed that women need a new spirituality.

Daly was critical of modern theologians, arguing that male superiority reinforces male superiority. She accused Bonhoeffer of insisting that women should be subject to their husbands, and she accused Barth of claiming that a woman is subordinate to a man who is her head (her senior authority). She criticised Pope Pius XII for suggesting women's true liberation does not come from formalistic or materialistic equality with men, but in the recognition of the vocation of a woman to become a mother, something specific to women.

Daly was also critical of the situation ethics of Fletcher. Situation ethics is a male-made theory and part of the thinking of patriarchy's dominating elite. It takes a personalist, individualistic approach to ethics, denying the communal dimension required for the liberation of women. For Daly, the entire system of ethics and theology is the product of males, and they tend to serve the interest of the sexist patriarchal society overtly, explicitly oppressing women in the process.

See Chapter 2.2 of the AS and Year 1 book where Fletcher's situation ethics is discussed in detail.

Rape

According to Daly, a 'rapism' is a culture of rape. It is a symbol of all violent oppression which builds and ultimately connects together to create a society that encompasses, for example, the nuclear arms race, racism, man-made poverty and ecological disaster. The mentality of rape creates a pervasive culture of violence that is difficult to break out of. The leaders of society (Daly called them 'sovereigns of sado-society') use culture, religion, politics, the professions and the media to erase female power and imprison women in a state of the grateful dead. Patriarchally possessed sleeping women have forgotten the reality of the gross inequality that Daly called 'gynocide' and have become divided against each other. (See Daly, *Beyond God the Father: Toward a Philosophy of Women's Liberation*, 1973.)

Daly did not view rape only in theoretical terms. She identified systematic acts of physical violence towards women: rape, genital mutilation, foot binding, widow burning and hysterectomy. Daly argued there is a connection between the mentality of rape and the phenomenon of war. She identified accounts of conflicts in which rape was a product of war, including, for example, the rape of hundreds of thousands of Bengali

Think question

What examples from culture glorify or exemplify male violence against women?

women by West Pakistani soldiers in 1971 and the dreadful stories of women raped to death by soldiers. Daly then pointed to the link between rape and war in the Bible, where Moses is enraged after a campaign against Midian because the commanders had spared the lives of all women:

> 66 Now kill all the boys. And kill every woman who has slept with a man, but save for yourselves every girl who has never slept with a man. 99
>
> Numbers 31:17–18, New International Version

Daly also drew attention to the example from Judges, where scoundrels arrive at a house demanding to abuse a guest staying there and the host offers his daughter as a substitute for the guest:

> 66 Look, here is my virgin daughter, and his concubine. I will bring them out to you now, and you can use them and do to them whatever you wish. But as for this man, don't do such an outrageous thing. 99
>
> Judges 19:24, New International Version

The scoundrels refuse this offer so the guest offers his concubine as a replacement and the visitors rape her to death through the night.

Daly did not limit rape to men who literally commit the act of rape. She described as 'arm chair rapists' those who vicariously enjoy stories of rape through pornography or who metaphorically rape women by looking at pornography, using it to enhance their sense of power over women (Daly, *Beyond God the Father: Toward a Philosophy of Women's Liberation*, 1973, p. 117). In this way, television reinforces the self-destructive mechanisms of patriarchy.

Genocide

Rape is the cultural manifestation of a sexual caste system. Daly argued that there is a worldwide phenomenon of a sexual caste, a hierarchy that gives males and females unequal power. This exploitative sexual caste system is perpetuated by the consent of the victims (females) as well as the dominant sex (males) through sex-role socialisation, as girls and boys learn how to be members of the society in which they live. This conditioning process begins at birth and continues throughout our lives. It is constantly reinforced through our experiences at home, at school and at work, through the information we learn, the entertainment we absorb, the adverts that we see and hear, and our interactions with public institutions.

Daly believed there is a deep link between rape and genocide (the deliberate killing of a large group of people). Male sexual violence forms the basis of military interests. Rape objectifies all those who can be cast

Think question

What examples of sex-role conditioning can you identify in life?

into the role of victims of violence. Rape makes the raped person the objective victim of the rapist; the raped person stops being an individual and becomes part of a group of raped people. Rape is a primordial act of violation, but it is more than just an act on an individual. It is an act of one group against another, of male against female, and therefore an expression of the thinking of the dominant group that is perpetrating the rape.

Daly made a link between the kind of groupthink that the Nazis used against those they subjugated and the groupthink of the Catholic Church, where there is a collective focus on sameness in contrast to, and against, those who are 'other' or different. She then made a link to the Jewish origins of Christianity, where the people of Israel are chosen to be apart from others. This is highly controversial, because it highlights aspects of Jewish identity as a causal factor in genocide at a time when the term 'genocide' was related almost exclusively with the Holocaust. For Daly, there is something wrong with the groupthink that is found in Christianity and the Church that is responsible for the patriarchal culture she opposes.

War

The third element of Daly's unholy trinity is war. She argues that war was an inevitable result of the male-dominated politics of the nineteenth and twentieth centuries. The horrors of war are associated with manly and adventurous virtues, with men doing courageous and powerful acts of violence in order to defeat the enemy. The language of violence is hidden by technical language; phrases like 'collateral damage' used to cover up the fact that the lives of innocent people are expendable. Daly believed that language has been corrupted when the killing of born humans in conflict is called 'just', and the killing of unborn humans during an abortion is called 'unjust'. War is defended by what Daly called a 'phallic morality' and a 'phallic mentality' (Daly, *Beyond God the Father: Toward a Philosophy of Women's Liberation,* 1973, p. 121). Women, she argued, need to seek liberation from this moral hypocrisy.

This liberation, according to Daly, requires women to be radically deviant in the face of patriarchal expectation. This means they must reject all moral standards because they have been constructed by men and used, by men, to subjugate women. The injustices and inequalities that oppress women are bound up in these male moral standards. A full-frontal assault on patriarchy requires complete demolition of the expectations placed on women.

66 The beginning of liberation comes when women refuse to be 'good' and/or 'healthy' by prevailing standards. To be female is to be deviant by definition in the prevailing culture. To be female and defiant is to be intolerably deviant. This means going beyond the imposed definitions of 'bad woman' and 'good woman,' beyond the categories of prostitute and wife. This is equivalent to assuming the role of witch and madwoman. 99

Mary Daly, *Beyond God the Father: Toward a Philosophy of Women's Liberation,* 1973, p. 65

Daly's liberation is no less than a total revolution of the moral and social standards and order of the time. According to Daly, Christianity is a key element in sustaining and shaping these moral and social standards. The incarnation of Christ is the 'symbolic legitimation of the rape of all women and all matter' (Daly and Caputi, *Webster's First New Intergalactic Wickedary of the English Language,* 1987). The underlying culture of rape, genocide and war is, therefore, impregnated in Christianity itself and is so fundamental to it that to change the culture means leaving Christianity.

Spirituality experienced through nature

Daly argued that the maleness of God needs to be overturned. The special sacred men's club of male mothers (priests) who control the spiritual moments of life through their positions of religious authority have locked women into an Eden, which must be shattered. Similarly, traditional holy places (buildings built and managed by men) are not suitable as centres of spirituality. Sacred space is a moving thing, part of a movement to freedom for both men and women. Daly uses the word 'quintessence' to describe the being in which we live, love and create (Daly, *Beyond God the Father: Toward a Philosophy of Women's Liberation,* 1973, p. 118). Quintessence is the highest essence, the spirit that permeates all nature, giving life and vitality to the whole universe. Quintessence can be damaged or partly blocked by many things, including violence, pornography and poverty, but it can be rediscovered in nature. Daly argued that there should be a turning away from the maleness of God and the fixed nature of sacred places towards the spirit of quintessence, which is found in the whole universe in nature.

Apply your knowledge

2. What might Daly say about the story of the rape of Tamar?

Then Amnon said to Tamar, 'Bring the food here into my bedroom so I may eat from your hand.' And Tamar took the bread she had prepared and brought it to her brother Amnon in his bedroom. But when she took it to him to eat, he grabbed her and said, 'Come to bed with me, my sister.' 'No, my brother!' she said to him. 'Don't force me! Such a thing should not be done in Israel! Don't do this wicked thing. What about me? Where could I get rid of my disgrace? And what about you? You would be like one of the wicked fools in Israel. Please speak to the king; he will not keep me from being married to you.' But he refused to listen to her, and since he was stronger than she, he raped her. Then Amnon hated her with intense hatred. In fact, he hated her more than he had loved her. Amnon said to her, 'Get up and get out!'

2 Samuel 13: 10–14, New International Version

3. Explain what Daly might say about this hymn:

Majesty worship His Majesty
Unto Jesus, be all glory,
Power and praise
Majesty, Kingdom authority
Flow from His throne,
Unto his own, His anthem raise.

From the hymn *Majesty* by Jack Williams Hayford

In the 1970s, there was renewed interest in pagan spirituality and nature worship, and Daly's theories reflect this. She called on women to ignore the oppressive taboos of patriarchy and connect with their wild side, embracing paganism and eco-feminist witchcraft.

Challenging Daly

There are those who challenge Daly's interpretation. Simon Chan argues that the Christian idea of fatherhood, as it is embodied in the Trinity, is unique. The Apostles' Creed says: 'I believe in God, the Father Almighty, the Maker of heaven and earth, and in Jesus Christ, his only Son, our Lord' (Paul Victor Marshall, *Prayer Book Parallels,* Volume 1, 2000, p. 171). This relational concept of God (God as God the Father, God the son and God the Holy Spirit) is quite different from a simple 'God is a male' idea. It has a dynamic element of multiple persons in a relationship.

A second aspect of the Christian idea of fatherhood, which Daly glosses over, is the way in which God is a heavenly father for all. The Christian God is in a relationship with all human beings and the concept of universal fatherhood expresses that relationship. This concept of fatherhood also includes a creative element: God as creator of all. Daly may be right about the cultures that have developed around this concept, but perhaps the concept offers more than she gives it credit for.

Chan also argues that using male language for God does not create masculine qualities for God. He notes that Isaiah 54:5–7 refers to God as the husband who acts with 'deep compassion', and deep compassion is not a stereotypical masculine characteristic.

> 66 The term father, then, excludes not feminine qualities, but rather the idea of a distant and impersonal deity, which is precisely the picture of the supreme being still seen in many primal religions. 99
>
> Simon Chan, 'Why We Call God "Father": Christians Have Good Reasons to Resist Gender-neutral Alternatives.' *Christianity Today,* 13 August 2013

The feminist theologian, Elisabeth Schüssler Fiorenza (b. 1938), suggests an alternative reading of the biblical texts and the sexism present in them. She argues that the Bible supports women's struggle against patriarchal biblical sexism because it contains examples that directly challenge patriarchal norms, such as the passages where Jesus breaks sexists customs (Matthew 26:6–13, Mark 5:25–34 and John 4: 1–42). For Fiorenza, Daly's approach to interpreting the Bible is mistakenly narrow.

Rosemary Radford Ruether

Rosemary Radford Ruether (b. 1936) is a **reform feminist theologian**. She argues that Christianity has become distorted by patriarchal traditions and is

Apply your knowledge

4. Does male language inevitably imply masculine stereotypes?

5. Is there alternative non-gendered language that could be used for God to capture the dynamic of the Trinity and its relationship with humanity? Suggest an alternative and explain its advantages and disadvantages.

6. Choose two examples of biblical passages that could be used to challenge established patriarchal norms of the time and explain why you have chosen them.

in need of reform as a consequence. She has similarly strong views about the impact of patriarchy on Christianity. She describes herself as an eco-feminist, advocates for women's ordination and campaigns for the Catholic Church to change its view on abortion. She believes the Catholic Church's teaching on these issues has been influenced, and distorted, by patriarchy. She also believes that patriarchy has shaped Christian thought about God, and this, too, needs to be challenged.

Jesus' challenge to the male warrior-Messiah expectation

The Hebrew scriptures (the Old Testament) views the Messiah as God's chosen (anointed) one. He is a future king, a son of David, who will be restored to Israel and will deliver the people from bondage through battle, and restore Israel as an autonomous power. This **Davidic Messiah** is a conquering warrior who liberates people from their enemies and reigns over them in a new kingdom. Because of his righteousness and his special relationship with God, God's favour and the well-being of his people are assured. The Messiah is both chosen by God (Son of God) and is a representative of his people before God (Son of Man).

There is, therefore, a maleness associated with Christ: 'the Messiah can only be imagined as a male' (Ruether, *Sexism and God-talk: Toward a Feminist Theology*, 1983, p. 110).

However, Ruether argues that Jesus was not the traditional warrior Messiah that was expected. The traditional Messiah is in no way an incarnation of the divine or a redeemer, one who forgives sins through redemptive self-sacrifice. 'He is expected to win, not to suffer and die' (Ruether, *Sexism and God-talk: Toward a Feminist Theology*, 1983, p. 110).

The future that Jesus brings is not the military victory of the male Messiah. Jesus rejects the nationalist–revenge mythology of the Davidic Messiah, and envisions a time on earth when basic human needs are met, and all people dwell in harmony with one another and with God without the need for a strong, domineering leader to protect them.

> **❝** Jesus' vision of the Kingdom is neither nationalistic nor other-worldly. The coming Reign of God is expected to happen on earth, as the Lord's Prayer makes evident (God's Kingdom come, God's will be done on earth). It is a time when structures of domination and subjugation have been overcome, when basic human needs are met (daily bread), when all dwell in harmony with God and each other (not led into temptation but delivered from evil). **❞**
>
> Rosemary Radford Ruether, *Sexism and God-talk: Toward a Feminist Theology*, 1983, p. 120

Think question

Are men closer to being god-like than women because the Messiah was male?

Jesus is a **servant king**, focusing on serving his people rather than ruling over them, attending to the poor and the dispossessed rather than the highest in the social order. He is critical of Jewish authorities and critical of reigning powers. He argues against those in positions of religious power at the time, including the Temple authorities (Matthew 21:12) and the local religious lawyers and experts who are referred to as hypocrites (Matthew 6:5). He dismisses the power of the Roman ruler Pontius Pilate (John 19:11) and warns his disciples about lording power over others (Matthew 20:25). He washes the feet of his disciples (John 13:1–17) and says leaders must be servants of their people (Luke 22:24–30). Ultimately, Jesus gives up his life for others.

> Jesus revises God-language by using the familiar Abba for God. He speaks of the Messiah as servant rather than king to visualize new relations between the divine and the human. Relation to God no longer becomes a model for dominant-subordinate relations between social groups, leaders, and the led. [...] Relation to God liberates us from hierarchical relations and makes us brothers-sisters of each other. Those who would be leaders must become servants of all.
>
> Rosemary Radford Ruether, *Sexism and God-talk: Toward a Feminist Theology*, 1983, p. 136

People are freed not through acts of military bravery, but by following the servant king and becoming servants of God:

> By becoming a servant of God, one is freed from bondage to all human masters. Only then, as a liberated person, can one truly become 'servant of all,' giving one's life to liberate others rather than to exercise power and rule over them.
>
> Rosemary Radford Ruether, *Sexism and God-talk: Toward a Feminist Theology*, 1983, p. 121

Although Christianity has a male symbol for the idea of Messiah, Ruether argues that the Messiah concept should not contain the Davidic military Messiah idea, but should instead represent the self-sacrificing, redeeming, servant Messiah who is connected to the female notion of wisdom. Christianity should not bundle the maleness of the historical Jesus and the maleness of the Davidic military Messiah into the Christian concept of Messiah. To do so, she argues, displaces the female from the concept of God.

Jesus is a servant king, focusing on serving his people rather than ruling over them

See 'Jesus the liberator' in Chapter 3.4 in the AS and Year 1 book for a detailed discussion of Jesus' challenges to religious and political authority.

Apply your knowledge

7. Ruether argues that Jesus was not a Davidic Messiah. Aspects of the Davidic Messiah can be seen in Zechariah 9:9 and 12:10 in the Hebrew Scriptures (Old Testament) and these verses seem to have echoes in Mark 11:7–9 (an early gospel) and John 12:12–18 (a later gospel). Ruether thinks the Davidic association grew in the early Church and influenced the writing of the gospels, especially John. Look up all three texts. How might they show the development of the male Davidic Messiah influencing early Christianity?

8. What are the differences between a victorious military kingly Messiah and a servant king?

9. Link the following references to the key arguments that Ruether makes about the kind of Messiah Jesus is and the kind of Messiah Jesus is not: Mark 10:35–40, Luke 22:24–30, John 13:1 and John 12:12–15. Use these references to make a case in support of Ruether's kind of Messiah.

God as the female wisdom principle and Jesus as the incarnation of wisdom

'Sophia' is Greek for 'wisdom', and in the ancient world wisdom was personified in female form as a goddess. Reuther argues that early Christians continued to refer to 'Sophia' as divine wisdom. In Scripture, divine wisdom was referred to in female terms (Proverbs 9:1); God is associated with wisdom, and wisdom is female (see 'The Book of Wisdom' in the *New Jerusalem Bible*, 1990). However, Christianity has merged the notion of a divine wisdom, that unites the cosmos with the divine, into the notion of a messianic king, who brings a new age of redemption. In the process, the idea of female wisdom has become obscured behind the patriarchal veil of the male Messiah, Jesus.

> 66 Does not wisdom call out?
> Does not understanding raise her voice?
> At the highest point along the way,
> where the paths meet, she takes her stand;
> beside the gate leading into the city,
> at the entrance, she cries aloud 99
>
> Proverbs 8:1–3, New International Version

'Divine wisdom' is the same, theologically speaking, as 'the Son of God', Ruether argues, pointing to Paul who links wisdom and Christ, 'but we preach Christ crucified [...] Christ the power of God and the wisdom of God' (1 Corinthians 1:23–24). She continues:

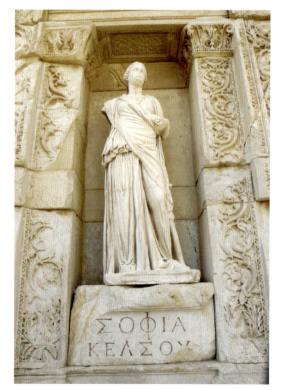

The personification of 'wisdom' (in Greek, 'Σοφία' or 'Sophia') at the Celsus Library in Ephesus, Turkey

> ❝ Theologically, Logos [the Word before he was made man in Jesus] plays the same cosmological roles as Sophie as ground of creation, revealer of the mind of God, and reconciler of humanity to God ❞
>
> Rosemary Radford Ruether, *Sexism and God-talk: Toward a Feminist Theology,* 1983, p. 154

For Ruether, divine wisdom is closely linked to Jesus Christ and wisdom is referred to in female terms. The Messiah (the Word of God, Jesus) is not, therefore, simply a male part of God but is also the incarnation of wisdom, which is female.

Ruether, who describes herself as an eco-feminist, goes so far as to refer to God as 'Gaia'. Gaia is the name of the ancient Greek goddess of the earth and, therefore, links divinity with the earth. In doing so, she is not abandoning the Christian notion of God, and does not think God is Gaia. Rather, she is trying to recover a concept of God that she believes is found in Christianity in the ancient notion of Sophia, but which has been suppressed by patriarchal ideas about maleness.

Ruether is seeking to recover a full account of human nature and a fuller picture of the divine by balancing male and female in our understanding of human nature and God. She believes this produces a truer reflection of *imago dei,* the belief that human beings are in the image and likeness of God.

Challenging Ruether

Some, such as Simon Chan, argue that you cannot rewrite the Christian story to give more prominence to women because it is the story itself that shapes Christian identity. Belief in the concept of the Trinity (of God as Father, Son and Holy Spirit) is central to Christianity, and key parts of the Christian liturgy rely on this identity language. The Anglican *Alternative Service Book 1980* addresses God as, 'Almighty God, our heavenly Father', and its Eucharistic prayers invoke a 'holy Father, heavenly King, almighty and eternal God'. The phrase 'almighty Father' is also part of the Catholic Church's Eucharistic prayer: 'Through him, with him and in him, in the unity of the Holy Spirit, all honour and glory is yours, Almighty Father, forever and ever.' Chan argues that to rewrite these central prayers to downplay 'maleness' would be wrong.

Christianity, according to Chan, should resist the temptation to abandon the male language for God. He accepts that feminine images are used to describe God's love, such as the frequent images of God protecting and comforting his children (for example Isaiah 66:12–13 and Hosea 11:1–4), but he notes that God is never called 'mother' and that this was unique in ancient times. Most other ancient religions had a goddess at their centre sometimes alongside a male god, including the goddess Asherah in Canaan, the goddess Isis in Egypt and the goddess Tiamat in Babylon.

Apply your knowledge

10. Create a diagram that shows the similarities between the biblical quotes that refer to wisdom and the attributes Christians apply to Jesus.

'Divine wisdom' is the same, theologically speaking, as 'the Son of God'

See Chapter 3.4 of the AS and Year 1 book for a definition of logos.

Think question

God is neither male nor female, so should images of God reflect this androgynous nature?

Apply your knowledge

11. Explain the following arguments used to counter feminist theology and suggest how feminist theologians might respond:

   a. 'If the maleness of Jesus is lost, the historicity of the figure of Jesus will be undermined.

   b. Male language for God is part of Christian identity and Christian worship and should be used by Christians.

Many of these goddess-worshipping cultures were also patriarchal, and not equal or matriarchal. Chan argues, therefore, that using female language for God does not make a society less patriarchal, and using male language for God does not cause a society to become patriarchal. He comments that:

> Even today, many societies devoted to goddess worship remain oppressive toward women. Devotion to the goddess Kali in Hinduism, for instance, has never resulted in better treatment of women, even among Kali devotees.
>
> Simon Chan, 'Why We Call God "Father": Christians Have Good Reasons to Resist Gender-neutral Alternatives.'
> *Christianity Today*, 13 August 2013

Discussing gender and theology

How do Daly's and Ruether's feminist theologies compare?

It is certainly possible to make arguments supporting the charge that patriarchal authority dominated and belittled women in traditional Christianity. The place of women in Christianity is, arguably, defined by three figures: the seducing temptress, Eve, the penitent prostitute, Mary Magdalene, and the Virgin Mother, Mary. Artists often give the face of Eve to the serpent responsible for the sinful temptation of Adam, suggesting perhaps that not only was the serpent female but that women are responsible for tempting men away from the true path. There is an inference that female sexuality is part of the source of the sin that came into the world at the Fall. In the New Testament, women are depicted as needing to turn away from their sexual desires and become penitent prostitutes, and the Virgin Mother is upheld as an impossible inspiration for earthly women. Such interpretations are possible.

Feminists argue that the ancient patriarchal tradition reaches the present. In some churches women are prohibited from entering the area around the altar (a prohibition that stems from the ancient belief that women are unclean when they bleed during their periods), and some Churches insist on an exclusively male priesthood. Ultimately, men seem to be closer to God than women because the male authority figures have encouraged the domination of the concepts of a male God and a male Messiah. Perhaps, therefore, Daly's account that Christianity is irretrievably patriarchal and misogynistic and must be abandoned is correct.

Some interpretations blame the Fall on Eve and, by extension, on women as a whole

In comparison, Ruether argues that Christianity is not intrinsically patriarchal and can be, and should be, changed. Christianity can be 'saved' from patriarchy. She identifies alternatives to the male-centric view of Christianity, both in the origins of traditional Christianity, where divine wisdom is female, and also in the practices of some mystical traditions that have maintained conceptions of God that include the female. Ruether also highlights that, by speaking with women and spending time with women, Jesus did not embody the patriarchal culture of the time in which he lived. Women were among his followers and the first people to see him risen were women. The gospel writers record that men did not believe the women who saw Jesus after the Resurrection, suggesting that the writers were conscious of the patriarchal culture of the time.

For Ruether there has been a 'patriarchalization of Christology' (Ruether, *Sexism and God-talk: Toward a Feminist Theology,* 1983, p. 125) which was due, in part, to the establishment of the Christian Church as the imperial religion of the Roman Empire, but it can be undone. The fact that some Churches are working to break away from the dominant patriarchal ideology (for example, the Church of England now ordains female priests and female bishops) indicates that Ruether may be right and change may be possible. What is needed, she argues, are theologies that link Christ and the Spirit (Ruether calls these 'Spirit Christologies'), which see the prophetic spirit of Jesus as continually present in the community and continuously revealed through the prophetic words of men and women of every age. This makes change more possible.

Post-Christian theologians like Daly are free of the authorities of Christianity. They create new symbols and traditions based on their new perceptions of ultimate reality. It remains to be seen whether what they offer will develop into long-lasting spiritual/religious traditions that are both sustainable and free from patriarchy.

Reformist feminist theologians, like Ruether, try to carry out a radical feminist transformation of Christianity. Their task is to change Christianity. Whilst there have been developments in some Churches, notably within Protestant Christianity in terms of women's ministries, Catholicism and conservative evangelical forms of Christianity continue to hold fast to the centrality of male ministries and can show reluctance towards using female language for God.

Apply your knowledge

12. To what extent might the following events be signs that reformist feminist theologians are succeeding?

a. In 2015, Libby Lane was consecrated as the first female Church of England bishop. The Right Reverend Libby Lane was made Bishop of Stockport after the Church formally adopted legislation to allow women bishops, following several decades of argument over women's ordination. There remains opposition to women's ordination in the Church of England.

b. In 2016, Pope Francis appointed a commission of six men and six women to study the issue of women deacons and their ministry in the early Church, at the request of the International Union of Superiors General, an organisation for the leaders of women's religious orders around the world. The Pope said that while his understanding was that the women described as deacons in the New Testament were not ordained as male deacons are today, it would be useful for the Church to clarify this question.

Is Christianity essentially sexist?

Unlike other religions of the time, which depicted the divine as male and female, Christians in the time of the early Church referred to God in mainly male terms. For example, a letter by Paul to the Christian community in Corinth contains the following quote:

> 66 the head of the woman is man […] For man did not come from woman, but woman from man; neither was man created for woman, but woman for man. 99

1 Corinthians 11:3–9, New International Version

Some thinkers have come to conclude, therefore, that Christianity is sexist and, as a result, not worthy. Daphne Hampson (b. 1944), a post-Christian theologian, argues that Christianity and feminism are essentially incompatible: you cannot be a Christian and a feminist. Hampson thinks God could not have been revealed at a particular time to a particular culture or group of people and in the particular male form of Jesus Christ. God must reach out to all people at all times. Some myths are morally sexist and rather than trying to reinterpret them in light of feminism, it is simply better to discard them. It is better to interpret the love of God in ways that do not carry the sexism found in the Christian story, with its male Messiah, male apostles and male-dominated Church. Hampson thinks that patriarchal religion must be overcome. It is far better to ground religious belief in our experience than in tradition, and our experience points to an equality between the sexes that Christianity fails to deliver.

However, some feminist theologians do not think that Christianity is essentially sexist, arguing that your perspective on this issue depends on how you interpret the Bible. For instance, Paul also wrote, 'There is neither Jew nor Gentile, neither slave nor free, nor is there male and female, for you are all one in Christ Jesus' (Galatians 3:28). Fiorenza thinks Christians read the Bible through different lenses:

1. For some, the Bible is divine revelation of timeless truth (Scripture says… therefore…). If scripture is read in this way, then it seems to be sexist.

2. Others seek a historical framework to understand what the actual facts were and, thereby, read the sexism in a historical context.

3. Some view the Bible as both divine revelation and a historical framework, and seek interpretation through a dialogue between these factors and people. The Bible reflects aspects of the sexist culture of the time, but it also contains moral messages that challenge the sexism of the time.

4. Another approach is to liberate the process of interpreting the Bible from those who have power in society and give it to those that have traditionally been silenced. This means allowing different people with different voices to read and make sense of the Bible, not just male members of the clergy or male theologians.

Fiorenza notes that people like Daly and Hampson have developed a criticism of both the male-dominated interpretation of the Bible and of the Bible itself. However, Fiorenza suggests that women need to understand how the Bible supports women's struggle against patriarchal biblical sexism. While sexist attitudes can shape the interpretation of the Bible, the Bible can also inspire anti-sexist attitudes with, for example, passages where Jesus breaks sexist customs such as those that involve not touching women (Matthew 26:6–13 and Mark 5:25–34) or speaking to them (John 4: 1–42). Fiorenza remains a Catholic and believes that there is a continuity in the religious tradition; that a feminist theologian need not reject or break away from the Christian tradition, but can work to better understand the Christian message, free from sexism.

Apply your knowledge

13. Discuss the following points of view:

    a. The Bible reveals an equality that the Churches have lost sight of.

    b. Christianity is full of sexist myths and these myths need to be set aside, even if that means setting aside Christianity.

    c. The Word of God inspires people to challenge the sexist attitudes that frame religion.

14. Parts of the New Testament suggest women may have played leading roles in the early Church.

When they came back from the tomb, they told all these things to the Eleven and to all the others. It was Mary Magdalene, Joanna, Mary the mother of James, and the others with them who told this to the apostles. But they did not believe the women, because their words seemed to them like nonsense. Peter, however, got up and ran to the tomb. Bending over, he saw the strips of linen lying by themselves, and he went away, wondering to himself what had happened.

Luke 24:9–12

On the Sabbath we went outside the city gate to the river, where we expected to find a place of prayer. We sat down and began to speak to the women who had gathered there. One of those listening was a woman from the city of Thyatira named Lydia, a dealer in purple cloth. She was a worshiper of God. The Lord opened her heart to respond to Paul's message. When she and the members of her household were baptized, she invited us to her home. 'If you consider me a believer in the Lord,' she said, 'come and stay at my house.' And she persuaded us.

Acts 16:13–15

John 4:4–26 and Mark 16:9–11 also suggest Jesus transgressed traditional rules on the treatment of women and identified specific women as people who brought others to believe in him.

How might these texts be linked to the discussion about Christian sexism? What might they indicate?

Can a male saviour save women?

See Chapter 3.4 in the AS and Year 1 book for a discussion on whether or not Jesus was human.

Traditional Christian belief holds that the death of Christ and his descent into hell was to ensure that the divine experienced all aspects of death so that all could be saved. Jesus offers salvation to all, and this is not limited by gender. The debate about whether Jesus was fully human resulted in a decision that he was both fully human and fully divine. The Church Fathers eventually concluded that the doctrine of the salvation of humanity required that Jesus was really human, rather than only partly human, for human beings to be fully saved. In theological terms, then, female salvation is assured.

However, some early Church Fathers debated whether the 'all' included women, because many of them believed that women, as the descendants of Eve, were guilty of the sin of Eve and could not, therefore, be saved. And, to get around the problem that the sin of Eve was responsible for the problem that the Messiah had to come and save people from, some suggested that, at the resurrection, women would be half male and half angel.

Jesus was male, not female. He was a male form of the human being, not a female form. Does this mean salvation can only be offered to men? This is not the traditional Christian theological understanding. It is more important that God became human, than God became male.

Daly argued that the idea of a uniquely male saviour is one more legitimisation of male superiority. It is simply not imaginable that the divine would take on female flesh, so patriarchal is the culture that produced Christianity. As a consequence, far from Jesus being a figure of salvation for women, he is a figure of male domination and enslavement.

In contrast, feminist theologians like Fiorenza argue that women living in patriarchal societies can take strength from the depictions of Jesus engaging with women, enabling women to be at important events in his ministry and speaking with them as he speaks to men. Jesus can offer a vision of salvation for women enslaved by patriarchal societies today, and his voice against the patriarchy can be viewed as all the more potent because he is a man. Jesus Christ is a figure of prophecy, promoting change to make the world more just, and this includes more equal and less sexist.

Apply your knowledge

15. Read the following extracts and consider the extent to which each one offers a satisfactory response to Daly's view that a uniquely male saviour legitimises male superiority.

Indeed, if one can say that Christ comes to the oppressed and the oppressed especially hear him then it is women within these marginal groups who are often seen both as the oppressed of the oppressed and also as those particularly receptive to the gospel. The dialogue at the well takes place not just with a Samaritan, but with a Samaritan woman [...] Among the poor it is widows who are the exemplars of the most destitute; among the moral outcasts it is the prostitutes who represent the bottom of the list. This is not accidental. It means that, in the iconoclastic messianic vision, it is the women of the despised and outcast peoples who are seen as the bottom of the present hierarchy and hence, in a special way, the last who shall be first in the kingdom.

Rosemary Radford Ruether, *To Change the World: Christology and Cultural Criticism*, 1981, p. 53

The women around Jesus, it is argued, actually understood his significance more easily than the male disciples and tended to his needs more than his male colleagues were able to. They remained faithful when others fled. Jesus reached out to women and they to him in a mutual embrace of recognition and respect. It is this image that Indian women theologians find most powerful. It is this Christ who they hope will stem the tide of dowry brides, temple prostitution and widow burning. It is perhaps only this Christ who can begin to balance the morality rate, which reflects the fact that far more female babies die from neglect than should be the case. [...] It is the male Christ who acted against 'male culture' who gives hope to many women in India. The message of women's dignity is more powerfully heard when spoken by a man within that culture.

Lisa Isherwood, *Introducing Feminist Christologies*, 2001, p. 22

Can only women develop a genuine spirituality?

Spirituality is notoriously difficult to define and it is impossible to do so adequately here. However, there is a clear implication from the feminist critique of Christianity that the spiritual culture of Christianity and the image of the divine has been influenced by patriarchy, by maleness. This raises the question of whether there can be something of the divine, something spiritual, that is feminine or female. Is a female understanding of spirituality or a female expression of spirituality possible? Can females be spiritual beings?

If spirituality is understood in the way feminist writers treat it, then several possibilities emerge. Thinkers like Daly believe that the only authentic women's spirituality is that which abandons all Christian trappings, is freed from patriarchal constraints and rejects traditional morality. Those who seek to remain within the traditional Christian tradition point to the strong tradition of great female contemplatives and the female notions of divine wisdom in the Bible as a model for female spirituality.

In the foreword to her book *Beyond God the Father: Toward a Philosophy of Women's Liberation* (1973), Daly writes about a flourishing new women's spirituality, a resurgence of 'gynergy'. This, she argues, is more than simply a replacement of 'God' by 'Goddess', more than a transsexual operation on the patriarchal God. It involves a profound psychic and social change. It requires a rediscovery of old words that have lost their power under the phallocentric rule of men: spinster, webster, weird, hag, witch, sibyl, muse and, of course, goddess. As the use of these words has waned, the spiritual power of females has also withered, but it is possible for women to rediscover these words and break out from their man-made mind-moulds. Goddess images inspire creative activity, in the work of weaving or the dragon-identified passions of rage and lust for nemesis. Goddess names call for action, movement, change.

There must be a transformation through self-realisation. Women must dare to realise their elemental woman-bonding powers, and break away from the propaganda of patriarchy found in fairy tales, popular songs and films, which replicate the godfather, son and holy ghost theology that represses women. Then, Daly argues, there is a possibility of an authentic female spirituality.

> 66 The sources of authentic hope are to be found within Wild women – Self-proclaimed Witches/Hags who choose the creation of our own space/time as a primal expression of intellectual/emotional vitality, knowing that without this we will suffocate in the ranks of the living dead. 99
>
> Mary Daly, *Beyond God the Father: Toward a Philosophy of Women's Liberation*, 1973, p. xxi

Daly's radical perspective of women's spirituality is sometimes referred as '**thealogy**' ('thea' is Greek for 'goddess'):

> 66 Goddess thealogy, like feminist theology more generally, begins in women's experience. Goddess thealogy often begins with an individual women's dissatisfaction with the male imagery of biblical religion. Her experience of the goddess, which may have come to her through reading, dreams, ritual or meditation, becomes authoritative for her. 99
>
> Carol Christ, 'Feminist Theology as Post-traditional Thealogy'. In Susan Frank Parsons, ed. *Feminist Theology,* 2002, p. 83

Others offer a less-radical, but no less genuine, vision of female spirituality.

There have been many female contemplatives. Teresa of Avila (1515–82) is just one example:

> 66 It pleased our Lord that I should see the following vision a number of times. I saw an angel near me, on the left side, in bodily form. This I am not wont to see, save very rarely […] In this vision it pleased the Lord that I should see it thus. He was not tall, but short, marvellously beautiful, with a face which shone as though he were one of the highest of the angels, who seem to be all of fire: they must be those whom we call Seraphim […] I saw in his hands a long golden spear, and at the point of the iron there seemed to be a little fire. This I thought that he thrust several times into my heart, and that it penetrated to my entrails. When he drew out the spear he seemed to be drawing them with it, leaving me all on fire with a wondrous love for God. The pain was so great that it caused me to utter several moans; and yet so exceedingly sweet is this greatest of pains that it is impossible to desire to be rid of it, or for the soul to be content with less than God. 99
>
> Teresa of Avila

Women are also depicted as spiritual beings in Christian art.

The Coronation of the Virgin by Diego Velázquez

Some Christian movements became dissatisfied with what Ruether calls the 'masculinist Christ and clerical Church'. She notes that these movements began to 'dream of a new dispensation of the divine in which women will represent new, not yet imagined dimensions of human possibility and divine disclosure' (Ruether, *Sexism and God-talk: Toward a Feminist Theology,* 1983, p. 132). Ruether thinks that women bring a new perspective to spirituality that complements the spirituality that men can offer.

Daly would go further and argue that only women have the opportunity to develop a genuine spiritual identity. Christianity is so patriarchal that it is devoid of spirituality. Men, who are embodied by the 'masculinist Christ and clerical Church', are, therefore, unable to be spiritual beings, such is the patriarchal influence (Ruether, *Sexism and God-talk: Toward a Feminist Theology*, 1983, p. 132). In this sense, only women, who have broken away from traditional Christianity, can be truly spiritual.

Apply your knowledge

16. Consider the following viewpoints, choose one and make a case for it over the others.

    a. The only authentic women's spirituality is that which abandons all Christian trappings, is freed from patriarchal constraints and rejects traditional morality.

    b. Christian spirituality for women can best find its expression in the great female Christian contemplatives.

    c. Women can find genuine spirituality by balancing goddess spirituality and the Christian tradition.

17. Is spirituality better served if inclusive language is used in scripture and liturgy?

    a. Compare Rite 1 Eucharist Nicene Creed: Jesus Christ came down from heaven 'for us men and for our salvation' with Rite 2 Eucharist Nicene Creed: Jesus Christ came down from heaven 'for us and for our salvation' (*Book of Common Prayer*, 1979, p. 326, p. 328 and p. 358).

    b. Compare John 6:35 in the Revised Standard Version of the Bible (1952), 'I am the bread of life; he who comes to me shall not hunger, and he who believes in me shall never thirst' with the New International Version (1978), 'I am the bread of life. Whoever comes to me will never go hungry, and whoever believes in me will never be thirsty.'

18. Consider whether the language used during services seeks to express accurately the will of God, to make people feel included or something else.

Can the Christian God be presented in female terms?

Catholic Christianity in the twentieth century emphasises the traditional doctrine that God is neither male nor female:

> 66 In no way is God in man's image. He is neither man nor woman. God is pure spirit in which there is no place for the difference between the sexes. But the respective 'perfections' of man and woman reflect something of the infinite perfection of God: those of a mother and those of a father and husband. 99
>
> *Catechism of the Catholic Church*, para 370

The Catholic Church cites a number of Bible passages in support of this conclusion: Psalm 131:2–3, Isaiah 49:14–15, Isaiah 66:13, Jeremiah 3:4–19 and Hosea 11:1–4.

Nevertheless, the vast majority of depictions of God (as God the father and as Jesus) are male, and Ruether comments that:

> 66 Male monotheism has been so taken for granted in Christian culture that the peculiarity of imaging God solely through one gender has not been recognised. 99
>
> Ruether, *Sexism and God-talk: Toward a Feminist Theology*, 1993, p. 151

Think question

a. Given that God is neither male nor female, should there even be a question about whether God can be depicted as a woman or as a man?

b. Are debates about male and female relevant today, when gender and identity is more fluid and less fixed?

However, it can be argued that people are too literal when they make sense of biblical language. God the father is often depicted as an old male, even though God is not 'old' in the sense that a human being grows old, and not a male father in the sense that a human father is the male parent of his son. Nevertheless, depictions of the crucified Jesus as a woman cause controversy.

Phyllis Trible (b. 1932), who comes from a Southern Baptist background, thinks we can 'depatriarchalize' readings of the Bible; that it is possible to remove the overly male interpretations. She argues that the Christian tradition uses the feminine to describe God in the Old Testament more often than is usually thought. In Numbers 11:12 God is portrayed as mother and nurse of her wandering children. In Isaiah, God cries out like a woman in child birth (Isaiah 42:14) and she (God) is a comforting mother (66:13). Trible thinks that the Bible has been misinterpreted in a patriarchal way, and a better understanding shows that God can be depicted in a female terms because female qualities are referred to in the Bible, as well as, and alongside, male qualities.

Apply your knowledge

19. Which do you find most convincing and why?

a. The Bible mainly talks about God in male terms and Jesus described God as Abba Father. Christians should follow the example of Jesus. It would be confusing for people to depict God as a woman.

b. Depicting God as a woman is no more objectionable than depicting God as a white male. The fact that some Christians do not like female depictions of God shows they are sexist.

c. We should not depict God as either male or female because God is neither male nor female.

Learning Support

Points to remember

» Theologians writing about issues of feminism in Christianity can be broadly grouped into those who think Christianity is inextricably connected to sexism and must be abandoned, those who think Christianity can be reformed and the sexism removed, and those who think Christianity has been misunderstood. Mary Daly is part of the first group, Rosemary Radford Ruether is part of the second group.

» Debates in feminist theology centre on biblical interpretation and an examination of the roles of men and women in the rituals of Christian life. Questions of salvation, the nature of the Messiah and the treatment of women in the Bible link to the way Churches are organised and how Christians worship.

» The question of the maleness and femaleness of God is closely linked to the language and imagery in the Bible and also the theological role of figures like the saviour, Jesus the male Messiah, and God the Father.

» The views of feminist theologians have not gone unchallenged and some argue that their critique of Christianity is based on misunderstandings and on misinterpretations of the Bible.

Enhance your learning

» In the introduction and Chapter 2 of *Texts of Terror* (1984), Phyllis Trible discusses the biblical texts that seem to reflect negative sexist attitudes and, in particular, the story of a royal rape.

» Mary Daly's book, *Beyond God the Father: Toward a Philosophy of Women's Liberation* (1973) is provocative, powerful and controversial reading. Chapter 4 explores the need to end the traditional patriarchal system of values and challenge them with something quite different.

» Chapter 9 of Rosemary Radford Ruether's *Sexism and God-talk: Toward a Feminist Theology* (1983) focuses on the aspects of Ruether's thinking explored in this chapter.

» Rosemary Radford Ruether's article 'The Emergence of Christian Feminist Theology' helpfully summarises feminism and feminist theology. It can be found in *The Cambridge Companion to Feminist Theology* (2002), edited by Susan Parsons.

» Luke 24:9–12 presents an interesting feature of the resurrection stories of the New Testament and the role of women as the first witnesses to the resurrection. At the time, women were not considered reliable witnesses in a court of law. The fact that the New Testament has women as the first messengers of the Gospel is interpreted by some as an indication that the events really happened (this is not how the story would have been told if it was made up) and also a pointed challenge to the idea that men are the authority on the Good News.

» Acts 16:13–15 is an account of a leading figure, who seems to have been an authority in the early Christian community acting as a minister in some way, and who is a woman. It is often used in debates about the role of women in the priesthood and about women in positions of authority in the Church.

Practice for exams

At A level, essay questions invite you to demonstrate your knowledge and understanding of factual material (AO1) and also your critical ability in putting forward a coherent, balanced argument (AO2). You should aim to write essays that are persuasive responses to the question throughout, rather than writing a lot of description and then tacking an opinion on at the end of each paragraph.

'Christianity should be abandoned by feminists because it is essentially sexist.' Discuss.

For this question, you need to think about whether Christianity is so sexist that it cannot be compatible with feminism, and if this means that feminists should abandon Christianity altogether.

For AO1 marks, you need to demonstrate your knowledge and understanding of the reasons why people might accuse Christianity of sexism, as well as the views of different writers on the subject, such as Mary Daly and Rosemary Radford Ruether. You could demonstrate your knowledge of key vocabulary by using terms such as 'patriarchy'.

For AO2, you need to explore a range of different possible opinions in formulating your argument. For example, you could consider the view that Christianity is right to be male dominated and that people should abandon feminism rather than Christianity. You could take the view that it is unfair to call Christianity sexist. You might think that Christianity is male dominated but that this can be changed without abandoning Christianity altogether. Or you might have another opinion.

Try to make your essay balanced by giving a fair hearing to views that differ from your own, as well as explaining why you think your own opinions are more convincing.

Discuss critically the view that only women can develop a genuine spirituality.

This question invites discussion of what is meant by 'genuine spirituality', with a consideration of whether gender is a significant factor in spirituality.

For high marks in AO1 you could show knowledge and understanding of different thinkers, for example you could show knowledge of Mary Daly's feminist approach to spirituality and of the writings of some Christian women such as Teresa of Avila.

For AO2, you need to consider whether the view that only women can develop a genuine spirituality is correct. For example, you might want to argue that the Christian ideal of putting selfish desires last and giving commitment to serving others is much more accessible for women if men have been used to thinking of themselves as leaders and authorities. You might want to argue that Christianity teaches that everyone, whatever their gender, is a recipient of the universal love of God and can respond to God. You might think that Christianity should be abandoned and that spirituality is not something that people should aim to develop.

Whatever your point of view, try to establish a consistent line of argument throughout your essay.

Chapter 3.5

The challenge of secularism

Is Britain a Christian country?
Should public life permit expressions of religion and belief?
How should Christianity respond to the growth of the non-religious?

Key Terms

Secularism: a term that is used in different ways. It may mean a belief that religion should not be involved in government or public life. It may be a principle that no one religion should have a superior position in the state. It often entails a belief in a public space and a private space, and that religion should be restrained from public power

Secularisation: a theory developed in the 1950s and 1960s, developed from Enlightenment thinking, that religious belief would progressively decline as democracy and technology advanced. Sociologists now doubt such a linear decline

Secular: not connected or associated with religious or spiritual matters. Used colloquially in widely differing ways by atheists, pluralists and those who are anti-religion. Historically, the term was used to distinguish priests who worked in the world (secular priests) from those who belonged to religious communities, such as monasteries

Wish fulfilment: according to Freud, wish fulfilment is the satisfaction of a desire through a dream or other exercise of the imagination

Specification requirements

The rise of secularism and secularisation, and the views that:
- God is an illusion and the result of wish fulfilment
- Christianity should play no part in public life

Introduction

Ethics, the philosophy of religion and Christian theology, offers approaches for exploring and questioning religion. However, other disciplines also provide tools to scrutinise religion. In the modern age, the disciplines of psychology and sociology offer insights asking new questions, which can be drawn together as a single topic, the challenge of **secularism**.

The role of religion in Western Europe has changed and continues to change. Christianity used to pervade British culture in ways that are no more. At the start of the twentieth century, 80 per cent of UK marriages were solemnised in church, but by the end of the century that figured dropped below 40 per cent. The number of people belonging to a church, attendance at church, and participation in Sunday school all show dramatic reductions.

Steve Bruce, a sociologist of religion, describes Christianity in Britain as a pale shadow of its former self. Bruce thinks religious belonging as a majority practice has drained away, and religious belief is following. In the early years of the twenty-first century, a growing number of British people declare themselves of no religious belief. Within a few years, Bruce thinks that total Christian membership will have dropped below 10 per cent of the total population. This questions the place of religious institutions in public life and culture.

There are many possible causes for these trends. For many in Western Europe, religion has become a largely private matter, an expression of individual preference. This is often described as '**secularisation**', a theory linking a decline in religion to modernisation. A **secular** view of life separates public life and private life. Religion and belief (which may be controversial or unreasonable) reside in the 'private space', leaving the 'public space' free for views and practices that can be justified by reason alone. In this context, 'public' refers to the people as a whole, to what is common to our local communities and our national community, including government decisions at local and national level and the law.

Jose Casanova identifies three ways in which people talk about secularisation:

....

> 1. … [T]o the decline of religious belief and practice in modern society. Some suggest this is a normal universal, human development process.

For many people in Western Europe, religion has become a largely private matter

Think question

Should there be a division between public space, which is free from religion, and private space, where religion is permitted?

2. ... [T]he privatisation of religion, something which again is seen as a normal situation and something required for living in a modern liberal democracy, where religion *should* be private and *should not* be seen in public (for instance in the wearing of symbolic clothing in places of work).

3. ... [T]he secular separation of spheres of state, economy, science, which are set free from religious institutions as a new norm (for instance the religious sponsorship of state funded schools). **99**

Jose Casanova, 'Rethinking Secularization: A Global Comparative Perspective.' *The Hedgehog Review,* spring/summer, 2006, p. 7

The differences between these three ways in which people talk about secularisation are illustrated through the question, 'Is Britain secular?' If secular refers to a decline in religious belief, then perhaps it is secular because, according to the 2014 British Social Attitudes survey, more people claim to be non-religious than Christian. If secular refers to keeping religion out of public life and culture, then perhaps Britain is *not* secular because major national events, such as Remembrance Day, involve religions and religious organisations are permitted to support public services (for example, churches sponsor schools). If secular refers to the nature of government, then perhaps it is *not* secular because there is a strong link between the establishment and Christianity: the Queen is the head of state and the head of the Church of England, and Bishops of the Church of England sit in the House of Lords.

A number of vocal public figures who are prominent atheists (called the 'new atheists' by Tina Beattie), such as Richard Dawkins, Steven Fry and Philip Pullman, have challenged the traditional presence of Christianity in English culture, and its influence over moral matters in law, such as euthanasia and homosexuality.

Some sociologists of religion, such as Paul Heelas and Linda Woodhead, identify a growth in alternative spiritualities as Christianity declines. In the UK, as the sacred landscape is changing and the traditional bond between Christianity and British culture is dissolving. Spirituality, on the other hand, seems to be flourishing, with sociologists observing a considerable increase in, and acceptance of, alternative spiritual practices such as mindfulness (a practice based on Buddhist techniques), which some businesses offer to their employees to help them manage stress.

Thinkers, including Karl Marx, Sigmund Freud and Richard Dawkins, have argued that religion is something entirely of the human mind, that there are no spiritual realities outside us. Meanwhile, science and social science have

Think question

When discussing 'secular' do you think about the faith of the people, the presence of religion in cultural and public life or the separation of religion from government?

changed the understanding of the world and human life, providing rational accounts of life.

In the 1960s, sociologists suggested that Western Europe would lead the way in secularisation and the rest of the world would follow. And while it is certainly true that the process of setting aside dictatorship and absolute monarchy in preference of democracy has led to an increase in freedom in religion and belief and a decline in the relationship between religion and government around the world, it is simplistic to argue that the world is secularising in the way Britain has. For example, the vast majority of the world's population still claim adherence to a religion, and there has been an upsurge in religious adherence in former Soviet countries since the decline of communism. Meanwhile, the story in the UK is not one of simple decline. Immigration has brought new religious populations into the UK. Whilst Anglican numbers decline, Catholic numbers remain relatively unchanged, and the number of Pentecostal Christians and Muslims has grown. Western governments are confronting foreign policy challenges in which religion is a key factor, and religion is now more prominent in the media than in recent decades.

Charles Taylor suggests that, in our secular age, the presumption that a government will be Christian, and so will the state and the people within it, has been replaced with a plural religious situation (Taylor, *A Secular Age*, 2007). Shmuel Eisenstadt, an Israeli sociologist, describes the present time as one that perceives 'multiple modernities' (Eisenstadt, 'Multiple Modernities'. *Daedalus*, vol. 129, 2000, p. 1) where there is a diversity of societal patterns with many secularities. Religion is declining, present, absent and resurgent in different ways and in different parts of the world. The assumption that countries would all follow the Western European model of modernisation is mistaken, he argues. Put more simply, 'to say the least, the relation between religion and modernity is rather complicated' (Peter L. Berger, ed., *The Desecularization of the World: Resurgent Religion and World Politics*, 1999, p. 3).

Britain may feel much less religious, but the world feels much more religious

See Chapter 3.2 for further discussion about religious pluralism and society.

Britain is becoming more atheist just as the world becomes more religious

Apply your knowledge

Forty years ago, there was a widespread belief that religion was a spent force in the Western democracies, having been confined to the private sphere and destined to be eliminated altogether by the forces of science, reason and secularism. However, in the last three decades religion has been catapulted back into public consciousness, not least by acts of violence, extremism and various forms of fundamentalism. This has generated considerable public debate about the potentially harmful effects of religious faith. Is it irrational to believe in God? Is religion simply so much mumbo-jumbo? Does religion justify violence? Does it turn good people into fanatics and extremists?

Tina Beattie, *The New Atheists*, 2007, p. 1

1. Read and write/discuss your response to the quote above.
2. Discuss the contradictions and complications that flow from these realities:
   a. Traditional religion in Britain is declining.
   b. Religion in the world as a whole is growing.
   c. Religion is more prominent in politics and the media.
   d. There are strong public atheistic views.
   e. Alternative spiritualities are increasing.

God is an illusion and the result of wish fulfilment

Religion as an illusion: Freud

Sigmund Freud is regarded as having contributed to the change in Western thinking about religion. He offered an explanation for the existence of religion that differs from the explanations found in theology, ethics and philosophy. His alternative account comes from the theories he developed about how the human mind works.

Freud denounced religion as a lie:

> " The whole thing is so patently infantile, so foreign to reality, that to anyone with a friendly attitude to humanity it is painful to think that the majority of mortals will never be able to rise above this view of life. "
>
> Sigmund Freud, *Civilization and its Discontents*, 1930, p. 74

> " The religions of mankind must be classed as among the mass delusions. "
>
> Sigmund Freud, *Civilization and its Discontents*, 1930, p. 81

Religious beliefs are a psychological invention that exist to protect us from nature and fate

Although he was clearly fascinated with religion and its appeal, Freud believed that religion and modern religious beliefs are a delusion that exists to protect us from nature and fate. According to Freud, religion is a product of **wish fulfilment**. The experience of vulnerability and helplessness that humans experience as children is made more tolerable by the invented belief that there is a purpose to life, with a moral code advanced by a higher wisdom, and that any injustices in this life will be corrected in the next. Human beings personify the things they want to influence, so a deity or divine force is invented to replace the sense of uncertainty with something controllable.

Religion also represses human desires, particularly desires that are destructive to society, such as sexual violence, theft and murder. The Commandments illustrate this with their emphasis on not killing, not stealing, not committing adultery and so on.

66 Life in this world serves a higher purpose; no doubt it is not easy to guess what that purpose is, but it certainly signifies a perfecting of man's nature. It is probably the spiritual part of man, the soul, which in the course of time has so slowly and unwillingly detached itself from the body, that is the object of this elevation and exaltation. Everything that happens in this world is an expression of the intentions of an intelligence superior to us, which in the end, though its ways and byways are difficult to follow, orders everything for the best – that is, to make it enjoyable for us. Over each one of us there watches a benevolent Providence which is only seemingly stern and which will not suffer us to become a plaything of the over-mighty and pitiless forces of nature. Death itself is not extinction, is not a return to inorganic lifelessness, but the beginning of a new kind of existence which lies on the path of development to something higher.

And, looking in the other direction, this view announces that the same moral laws which our civilizations have set up govern the whole universe as well, except that they are maintained by a supreme court of justice with incomparably more power and consistency. In the end all good is rewarded and all evil punished, if not actually in this form of life then in the later existences that begin after death. In this way all the terrors, the sufferings and the hardships of life are destined to be obliterated. Life after death, which continues life on earth just as the invisible part of the spectrum joins on to the visible part, brings us all the perfection that we may perhaps have missed here. 99

Sigmund Freud, *The Future of an Illusion*, 1927, p. 25

Freud argues that religious ideas are highly prized because they provide information that humans crave about things that cannot be discovered through a study of reality. This affects how religious people look on those who do not share their ideas: 'Anyone who knows nothing of [religious ideas] is very ignorant; and anyone who has added them to his knowledge may consider himself much the richer' (Freud, *The Future of an Illusion*, 1927, p. 25). Religious beliefs and teachings demand to be believed because they were believed by our ancestors and passed down to us and, historically, societies severely punished those who challenged them. As a result, Freud argues that there are many problems with the claims made in the name of religion. He writes:

> 66 The proofs they have left us are set down in writings which themselves bear every mark of untrustworthiness. They are full of contradictions, revisions and falsifications, and where they speak of factual confirmations they are themselves unconfirmed. 99
>
> Sigmund Freud, *The Future of an Illusion*, 1927, p. 27

According to Freud, religion assuages infantile fears we have of things we cannot change, and represses negative human behaviours. Discarding theological, philosophical and ethical explanations of religion and observing it as part of his study of the human mind, Freud believed religion is unhealthy. It is a cultural carrier for much negative information, dividing people and causing conflict as non-believers, people who do not have the religious knowledge that believers have, are seen as inferior. Freud is also concerned about the psychological impact that religiously framed ideas have on the mind. He can see that religion is produced by uncertainty and anxiety about things beyond our control, but it creates something unreliable and unhealthy.

Apply your knowledge

3. Freud argues that religious belief is designed to help us deal with things that are beyond our control. Identify two things that Freud is referring to and explain how religion helps us to deal with them. Consider, for instance, human fallibility and mortality and Christianity's theological responses.

4. Find historical or contemporary examples of religious people looking negatively on those who do not have their religious knowledge. Consider:

   a. examples of hostility between religious groups

   b. examples of religious people judging and condemning 'non-believers'.

5. Is Freud's account of religion consistent with Christianity?

   a. Look at the different features of the long Freud quote on p. 272 (from p. 25 of *The Future of an Illusion*) and label them with theological Christian beliefs including belief in the Last Judgement, heaven and hell, beliefs about calling/discipleship and beliefs about the Commandments.

   b. Does Freud's account appreciate the recognition of lamentation and suffering in the Bible? Is his account of how Christian belief supposedly 'solves' the problem of suffering adequate? Read Lamentations 1:16, Jeremiah 31:15, and the book of Job (especially 31:1–40) and think about these questions.

Richard Dawkins (b. 1941)

Religion as something for children to escape from: Dawkins

Richard Dawkins is a scientist who has articulated a vociferous critique of religion, and his criticism draws on a range of social and cultural observations and interpretations of religion.

> 66 There is something infantile in the presumption that somebody else (parents in the case of children, God in the case of adults) has a responsibility to give your life meaning and point. […] Somebody else must be responsible for my well-being, and somebody else must be to blame if I am hurt. Is it a similar infantilism that really lies behind the 'need' for a God? 99
>
> Richard Dawkins, *The God Delusion*, 2006, p. 404

Dawkins thinks that life should be meaningful without reference to religion. The human need for God is infantile and an adult should be able to find meaning in life from sources other than religion. Religion is repressive, he suggests, identifying religious dress codes as an example of the way in which religion represses women. The burka not only ensures female submission, it is also a metaphor for the impact that religion has on reducing our ability to perceive and understand things. While religion narrows our perception, science widens it. And religion not only dims our view of the world, it is also the cause of conflict. Dawkins suggests that conflicts between Catholics and Protestants in Northern Ireland and those between Sunni and Shi'a Muslims in the Middle East exemplify the problem.

Religion is something that everyone needs to escape from, but Dawkins is particularly concerned about the indoctrination of children by religion, as well as other harm that religion can bring upon children. He is concerned that in bringing children up as religious, by labelling them as religious, harm is being done. He uses extreme examples to illustrate theses dangers.

Dawkins cites instances in the nineteenth century of children of Jewish parents being kidnapped by priests and raised as Catholics (usually by Catholic nursemaids) after secret baptisms. In *The God Delusion* (2006) Dawkins uses these examples to illustrate 'the religious mind', a mind in which the sprinkling of water over the head of a baby can totally change that baby's life in a way that takes precedence over the consent and wishes of parents and children, and over everything that ordinary common sense and human feeling would see as important. Dawkins argues that the idea that an uncomprehending child can be regarded as Jewish or Christian is absurd, something that comes about when a mind is 'hijacked by religious faith'. He also refers to the sexual abuse of children by

Christian ministers, and identifies the abuse and brutality of the Christian brothers in Ireland and the sadistic cruelty of nuns in many of Ireland's girls' schools.

However, Dawkins' concern is not just with specific examples such as these, but with the general practice of religious parents bringing up their children as religious, and the state's acquiescence in allowing children, who are not of the age of consent, to be considered religious (as they are in some school admissions processes). For Dawkins, bringing up a child as a Catholic is a form of long-term psychological abuse. He describes conversations with a women who had been a victim of sexual abuse as a girl but found the abuse of the fear of going to hell was an even greater harm than the sexual violence.

The power of belief to abuse is far greater than the impact of physical abuse, Dawkins argues. He cites the example of a Hell House, devised by a pastor in Colorado, where children were scared witless by what might happen to them after they die. Actors played out the sins of abortion and homosexuality and then the sinners were tortured and punished in hell by a devil-like figure. This can leave profound scars on a person's psyche.

Dawkins argues that Christianity is replete with messages of these kinds of extremes, and he references Mark 9:43–44 which mentions the cutting off of offending hands, as an example. He quotes Nicholas Humphry's Amnesty Lecture of 1997:

> 66 I am talking about moral and religious education. And especially the education a child receives at home, where parents are allowed (even expected) to determine for their children what counts as truth and falsehood, right and wrong.
>
> Children, I'll argue, have a human right not to have their minds crippled by exposure to other people's bad ideas – no matter who these other people are. Parents, correspondingly, have no God-given licence to enculturate their children in whatever ways they personally choose: no right to limit the horizons of their children's knowledge, to bring them up in an atmosphere of dogma and superstition, or to insist they follow the straight and narrow paths of their own faith.
>
> In short, children have a right not to have their minds addled by nonsense, and we, as a society have a duty to protect them from it. So we should no more allow parents to teach their children to believe, for example, in the literal truth of the Bible or that the planets rule their lives, than we should allow parents to knock their children's teeth out or lock them in a dungeon. 99

Nicholas Humphrey, 'What Shall We Tell the Children?' Amnesty Lecture, 21 February 1997

The power of belief to abuse is far greater than the impact of physical abuse

Apply your knowledge

6. Should the state protect children from any harmful ideas their parents have? Consider the following practices that could be considered harmful: circumcision, healing children using exorcism, requiring children to confess their sins to God for forgiveness, teaching children that there is a hell where sinners are punished and where they might go.

7. How should the state protect children from their parents? Consider the following methods for protecting children from their parents: controlling all education, prohibiting home schooling, prohibiting underage children taking part in religious rituals, removing children from their parents in some cases, using religious education lessons to warn children about the dangers of religion.

275

Religion and belief as a source of well-being

Freud and Dawkins both argue, in different ways, that religion and religious belief harm the human mind and that people would be happier without Christianity. As a consequence, they present arguments for restricting parental control over the upbringing of their children.

However, there are scientists who argue that some beliefs can be shown to be good for people. Jo Marchant, a science journalist, suggests there is compelling evidence for positive medical and psychological benefits arising from some beliefs. In *Cure: A Journey into the Science of Mind Over Body* (2016), she does not seek to defend religion but explores how a range of practices and beliefs (many of which are found in religion and include social gatherings, belief in a loving God, time of prayerful stillness and silence, and being part of something bigger) bring about physiologically measurable benefits to the participants. For example, she cites a scientist who studied loneliness and found that social connections and a belief in the transcendent were important features for living happier and longer lives, and that these features are prominent in religious believers. After interviewing scientists and doctors who provided compelling evidence, Marchant writes that 'feeling part of something bigger may help us not only to deal with life's daily hassles but to defuse our deepest source of angst: knowledge of our own mortality' (Marchant, *Cure: A Journey into the Science of Mind Over Body*, 2016). Belief has a positive effect on people's mental and physical well-being. She concludes:

Feeling part of something bigger may help us not only to deal with life's daily hassles but to defuse our deepest source of angst: knowledge of our own mortality

> 66 There are powerful evolutionary forces driving us to believe in God, or in the remedies of sympathetic healers, or to believe that our prospects are more positive than they are. The irony is that although those beliefs might be false, they do sometimes work: they make us better. 99
>
> Jo Marchant, *Cure: A Journey into the Science of Mind Over Body*, 2016

Marchant is not necessarily disagreeing with Freud's analysis of the reason why people are religious, but the scientists she interviewed come to a radically different conclusion to the one that Freud reached.

Christianity should play no part in public life

The idea of a separation between the private and the public is essential in some secular traditions, especially those associated with the French revolution, which saw the abolition of the monarchy and the removal of religion from established positions of power in France. French secularity (*laïcité*) means the absence of church (or religion) in government and state: the absence of religious involvement in government affairs, the prohibition of religious influence over public matters, and the absence of government involvement in religion including any sense that the government should determine the religion of the people. In France, *laïcité* resulted in the removal of state-funded Christian schools, although the French government continues to provide tax relief to Catholic private schools It has also led the French government to ban people from wearing religious symbols and religious clothing in public spaces.

This concept of the separation of Church and State is found in the constitutions of other countries, including the USA and Turkey (although the situation in Turkey seems to be changing). The key idea is that religion should have no bearing or influence in the public world. It is not quite that the government is neutral in matters of religion, but there is a belief that government decisions affecting public services, including state-funded schools, and matters of law should be based on a democratic and non-religious foundation.

Not all secular forms of government follow the French model. For example, the Netherlands adopted a policy of pillarisation. 'Pillarisation' refers to the politico–denominational segregation of a society. Throughout much of the twentieth century, Dutch society was divided 'vertically' into different Christian denominations, and social and educational services were provided according to denomination. Each pillar has its own newspapers, political parties, trade unions, schools, universities, etc. This formal structure is no longer as evident as it was, but its effects can be seen in a society in which religion is present in public life and where different groups of people have strongly different attitudes towards religion.

The separation of Church and State in the UK

Debates about the place of religion in public life are present in the UK, with disagreements taking place over whether people should be allowed to wear religious symbols and religious dress in the workplace, the extent to which people have a right to assert their religious beliefs when running a business, and the extent to which religion should play a part in education. This has led to legal disputes, that show the different ways in which religious freedoms and religious beliefs are protected and limited by the law.

Think question

a. In a world where new technologies have eroded the sense of a private personal world, does the private space articulated by a separation of Church and State still exist?

Think question

b. Should society tolerate different visions of human flourishing? What does this mean in practice for businesses and the workplace?

Apply your knowledge

8. Consider these two legal cases.

Eweida v United Kingdom [2013] ECHR 37

Nadia Eweida, a Christian, worked for British Airways. In October 2006, she was asked to cover up the Christian cross necklace she was wearing outside her uniform as it was in contravention of BA's uniform policy for jewellery. She refused and was placed on unpaid leave. She planned to sue the airline for religious discrimination. BA was accused of double standards, as Sikh and Muslim employees were permitted to wear religious dress at work. The National Secular Society argued that staff handling baggage should not wear jewellery over their uniforms, and Nadia Eweida should not try to evangelise in the workplace. In the end BA decided they would allow employees to wear a symbol of faith on a lapel pin or chain.

a. Should religious dress be permitted in the workplace?

b. Should customers accessing services offered to the public be exposed to religious imagery?

Lee v McArthur & Others [2016] NICA 39

Gareth Lee, a gay activist, ordered a cake from Ashers, a bakery in Northern Ireland that was run by Karen and Daniel McArthur, who are both Christians. He wanted the cake decorated with the words 'Support Gay Marriage'. The McArthurs thought it would be sinful to write these words and refused to make the cake. Gareth Lee sued them under equality legislation. Gareth Lee's case was supported by the Equality Commission for Northern Ireland and the McArthurs were supported by a Christian organisation. The McArthurs lost the case and were ordered to pay Lee £500.

c. Should Christian businesses be obliged to provide services that they view as sinful, but which are legal?

d. Should a gay customer always be entitled to services offered to any other member of the public?

e. What should a secular society value more, pluralism or an absence of religion in the public sphere?

Should religion and belief be tolerated in public life?

Education and schools

In England, churches are by far the biggest sponsors of schools. More than 1.8 million children are educated in Church of England and Catholic schools in England. Some organisations, such as the British Humanist Association (BHA), campaign against schools with a religious character:

> 66 We aim for a secular state guaranteeing human rights, with no privilege or discrimination on grounds of religion or belief, and so we campaign against 'faith' schools, and for an inclusive, secular schools system, where children and young people of all different backgrounds and beliefs can learn with and from each other. We challenge 'faith' schools' admissions, employment and curriculum policies, as well as the privileged processes by which new 'faith' schools continue to open. 99
>
> The British Humanist Association, https://humanism.org.uk/ campaigns/schools-and-education/faith-schools

For the BHA, a secular state should not fund schools with a religious character. It should not give schools permission to recruit pupils on the basis of religion, or hold acts of worship or prayer in school lesson time. It argues that this segregates children into different religious groups, creating a sense that people of different religions live parallel lives, and increasing intolerance.

Dawkins is likewise worried about the involvement of religion in schools. He suggests that religious fundamentalism subverts science, replacing an evidence-based approach to understanding the world with superstition, which leads to the fundamentalists missing the engrossing and fascinatingly beautiful truths of evolution and science. 'Fundamentalist religion is hell-bent on ruining the scientific education of countless thousands of innocent, well-meaning eager young minds' (Dawkins, *The God Delusion*, 2006, p. 323). He is concerned that teaching that evolution is one theory alongside other theories, such as creationism, in science classes fails to give credit to the evidence that supports evolution and places a literal, geological interpretation of the Bible above more robust scientific accounts. Dawkins is also more generally concerned that religious schools are teaching children 'from their earliest years, that unquestioning faith is a virtue' (Dawkins, *The God Delusion*, 2006, p. 323).

The debates around religious schools are fierce and complex. In England, the school system was established by Christian Churches long before the national government was prepared to ensure education for all children. The relationship between Christianity and education is, therefore, deep-rooted and this has led to what is called a 'heritage argument' in defence of religious schools. Churches built schools for the poor in England, and indeed continue to own a lot of school property, and so removing schools from Church control would be an act of robbery. Additional arguments are that such schools give parents who want an education framed by a

Think question

Does teaching children in mixed groups make them tolerant and respectful of each other?

religious ethos the choice to have such schooling, and that a plural and diverse society should have plural and diverse kinds of schools.

Furthermore, it is not clear that religious schools are necessarily less diverse than non-religious schools when the measure is ethnicity. Catholic populations in England often have a greater proportion of poorer migrant families, and the resulting school populations may have richly diverse cultural and linguistic traditions as a result. Moreover, religion is not the only factor that segregates school pupils in England. Socio-economic and cultural factors can also result in poor integration.

The claim that 'separate' schools produce children who are less open to living in religious diverse societies and who are more prejudiced against people from other religious backgrounds is not supported by sound empirical evidence according to researchers at the Warwick Religions and Education Research Unit. Professor Leslie Francis of the University of Warwick, UK, suggests there is evidence that young people who are themselves committed to Christianity are more, not less, open to people from other religious backgrounds, and that there are often more committed Christian students in Church schools than in other schools. As a consequence, there is a more positive attitude towards religious diversity in Church schools. He observes that what is different in Church schools is the greater concentration of Christian students, but there is no evidence that schools themselves contribute to the more positive attitude towards religious diversity in these schools. The difference comes from the students' personal beliefs.

Although some forms of religion do seek to indoctrinate or brainwash people, the testimonies of many scientists are evidence that it is not correct to assume religion and faith necessarily closes down thinking, particularly scientific thinking. To take just one example: Francis Collins

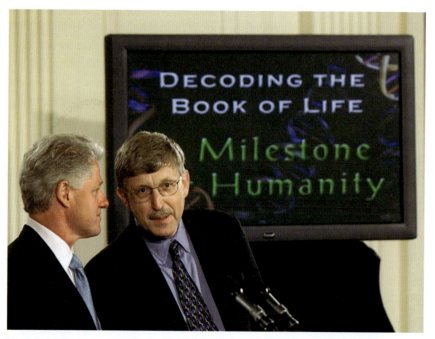

Does belief necessarily hold back scientific thought? President Bill Clinton recognising Francis Collins for his work leading the team that mapped the human genome

was born in 1950 and is an American physician-geneticist who has made important discoveries about disease genes and led the Human Genome Project. At university he described himself as an atheist, but his work with dying patients led him to question his views. He explored arguments for and against God in cosmology and re-examined his religious beliefs and, ultimately, became a Christian. Collins is an interesting contrast to Dawkins, as both are scientists interested in genes.

Critics of Dawkins note that his arguments against religious schools stem from a view of religion that is narrowly fundamentalist and extreme. If religion equates only to fundamentalist extreme belief, then religious schools would have serious questions to answer because they would limit children's ability to develop the skills of reason and logic. However, if religion is viewed as a cultural phenomenon, that is associated as much with identity and cultural practices as with belief, then the Dawkins argument is significantly weakened. Dawkins rejects this critique, suggesting that 'liberal' religion simply makes way for religion, and literal belief (which narrows thinking) is at the heart of religion. However, if a secular state is defined, not as a de-religionised space, but as a radically plural space containing many communities, many voices, multiple modernities, where different groups can experiment with different models of the good life, then shouldn't schools reflect that diversity?

Charles Taylor argues, in 'The Politics of Recognition' (*Multiculturalism: Examining the Politics of Recognition*, eds. Gutmann and Habermas, 1994), that there should be recognition that societies are increasingly multicultural. Every person should be recognised for their particular identity rather than living in a way that leads to a loss of distinctiveness and individual peculiarities. No culture, including an atheistic one, should impose itself on others because this causes minority cultures to diminish and vanish. All people need recognition and all people deserve equal recognition. In this context, schools with a religious character could nurture cultural diversity and prevent identities from disappearing. They may be viewed suspiciously in an atheistic secular society, but could be a sign of a plural, liberal secular society.

Schools with a religious character could be seen as helping to nurture cultural diversity

'It is no accident that the introduction of universal compulsory state education has coincided in time and place with the secularization of modern culture.' So begins Christopher Dawson's essay 'The Challenge of Secularism' (http://www.catholiceducation.org/en/education/catholic-contributions/the-challenge-of-secularism.html), in which he argues that secular education systems are problematic. Dawson points out that, where education systems have been dominated by a consciously anti-religious ideology, as was found in communist countries, religion became endangered. In other words, a professed neutrality towards religion in secular education revealed a programmatic intention to remove it entirely. Removing religion from culture, art, architecture and music not only deprives religion of a means of outward expression, it also deprives people of the ability to make sense of their own culture given the extent to which culture is steeped in religion.

Should economics drive the aims of education?

Apply your knowledge

9. Consider and discuss the relative strengths and weaknesses of the following points of view:

   a. Religious belief is a threat to children's development, so religion should be kept out of schools.

   b. Secular societies should only have atheistic schools based on ideas of human flourishing that do not come from religion.

   c. Schools in a secular society should include those that support diverse cultural identities, promoting different visions of the good life and allowing choice.

Should schools be controlled by the government, with education designed to serve a particular government agenda, such as an economic one? Or should they stand as a place to critique and challenge societal norms? Professor James Conroy argues that religious schools have an important role in a liberal democratic state. He suggests religious schools perform a 'liminal function' that serves to test the perspective of human flourishing that is offered by the liberal democratic state in state–run schools (Conroy, *Betwixt and Between: The Liminal Imagination, Education and Democracy*, 2004, p. 143). They exist to counter the general view that the market should define human flourishing and determine the aims of education, that individual people are little more than cogs in the machine of the economy. They instead propose an idea of the other that transcends capitalism. 'The student is not a resource for a nation, or one who is to be cultivated within a consumer teleology' (Conroy, *Betwixt and Between: The Liminal Imagination, Education and Democracy*, 2004, p. 195). Religious schools allow parental choice and provide counterbalances to any single driving influence in education.

Government and state

The British monarch, currently Queen Elizabeth II, is also the Head of the Church of England and, by ancient tradition, Defender of the Faith (*Fidei Defensor*), a title awarded to Henry VIII by the Pope after Henry wrote a book about the sacraments and before he broke with the Church of Rome. There are also Anglican Bishops in the House of Lords, the upper chamber of Parliament.

Some argue that the continued involvement of Anglican Christianity in the law-making process is not in keeping with the times and does not represent the diverse nature of the population of the country, which contains people of many religions and people of no religion. Religion and government should be separated entirely because, continuing to place the Church of England at the heart of government effectively excludes citizens who are not Anglican. In contrast, supporters of the status quo argue that other faiths are not excluded from the House of Lords. The Chief Rabbi has a seat in the House of Lords, representing British Jews, and although the Archbishop of Westminster refused an offer of a seat, the Duke of Norfolk traditionally represents Catholics. Members of other faith communities are also represented. Nevertheless, the Church of England does have a large number of seats in the House of Lords.

Both France and the USA have a formal separation between religion and government. In France, the concept of *laïcité* ensures that religion is absent from government and the state. For example, although Catholicism has a strong cultural tradition in France, marriages take place in civic institutions and any religious ceremony that takes place as part of the celebration is entirely separate. This is very different from the situation in the UK, where it is possible for a religious minister and a religious service to fulfil the state's legal function and contract marriages.

The relationship between the Church of England and the State in the UK can be viewed as benign, but the fusion of religion and government has had a turbulent history. For example, in Japan during the Second World War, the Japanese Emperor was viewed as a God, and a military cult drew together nationalism, religion and political leadership to such an extent that, when Japan was defeated, the Americans forced the emperor to publicly declare he was not a god.

Prince Charles has said that, when he becomes king, he would like to become 'Defender of Faith' rather than 'Defender of the Faith' in recognition of the diversity and plurality of religion and belief in the UK today. This kind of secularism keeps religion at the heart of the State but embraces all religions and beliefs rather than singling out one religion or denomination. Canada is another country that includes religion in public life, and it has the same head of state as the UK.

The relationship between religion and the State can be understood by looking at these two images:

Think question

Would it be better for the UK to have a head of state who defends faith and belief of all kinds rather than one particular faith, should the head of state be an example as someone who takes commitment to religion and belief in one tradition seriously, or should mention of religion be absent from the role of head of state?

The photograph on the left shows officers of the state enforcing a no-burkini rule on a French beach. Some have argued that this shows that there is anti-religious or anti-Muslim sentiment at the heart of French government. It depicts a non-inclusive secularity that seeks to remove religion from the public space.

The photograph on the right shows two beach volleyball players playing by the same rules but expressing their differing beliefs and values through their clothing. It shows an inclusive secularity where public plurality is possible.

The inclusive secularity seen in the second photograph is also evident in the workings of the National Health Service in the UK. Doctors may, as a matter of conscience, refuse to participate in medical procedures, such as abortions, transfusions or transplants, if they believe the procedures are incompatible with their religious beliefs.

> 66 You may choose to opt out of providing a particular procedure because of your personal beliefs and values, as long as this does not result in direct or indirect discrimination against, or harassment of, individual patients or groups of patients. This means you must not refuse to treat a particular patient or group of patients because of your personal beliefs or views about them. And you must not refuse to treat the health consequences of lifestyle choices to which you object because of your beliefs [...] Whatever your personal beliefs about the procedure in question, you must be respectful of the patient's dignity and views. 99
>
> General Medical Council, *Personal Beliefs and Medical Practice*, 2013

In democracies, the relationship between religion, government and state is also affected by the public's appetite for political leaders expressing their religious beliefs. When Tony Blair was Prime Minister, his special adviser Alasdair Campbell once famously told a reporter, 'we don't do religion', to ensure the questioning stayed away from the prime minister's religious views. However, more recent prime ministers have been keen to refer to their faith, including Gordon Brown, who often referred to himself as the son of the manse (a house where non-conformist ministers live), and Theresa May, who has commented that her faith helped her make difficult decisions.

Rowan Williams, former Archbishop of Canterbury, distinguishes between programmatic secularism and procedural secularism ('Secularism, Faith and Freedom', Rome Lecture, 23 November 2006). Programmatic secularism assumes any public expression of faith is offensive, and any presence of religion in public life is part of an attempt by religion to take control and remove opposing views. As such, the public space should be cleared of religion to be 'neutral'. Williams thinks this 'neutrality' is false as it ultimately silences certain voices in favour of a particular ideology, which claims to be neutral but is fact nothing of the sort. In contrast, procedural secularism permits as many public voices as possible, of all kinds and including religious voices, without privileging any of those voices. This ensures a crowded and argumentative, plural and diverse, public square, which requires the law to mediate, broker or balance and manage real differences ('Secularism, Faith and Freedom', Rome Lecture, 23 November 2006).

Think question

a. Is there is a difference between the formal separation of religion and State, and politicians expressing their religious beliefs publicly?

b. Should politicians refer to their religious beliefs in their public work?

Apply your knowledge

10. Consider advantages and disadvantages of:

a. government that is formally separated from religion

b. government that reflects the religions and beliefs of the people living in the country

c. government that reflects the single biggest religion in the country.

The failure of the secularisation thesis

Many social scientists, philosophers and theologians have concluded that secularisation theory (the theory that religious belief would progressively decline as democracy and technology advanced) is based on some mistaken assumptions that the change was inevitable. Luke Bretherton offers a visual depiction of an ordinary London journey that illustrates the complexity of trying to describe the modern world with the language of 'secular':

> **❝** I take the number 207 bus up the Uxbridge Road. On the bus is an extraordinary array of cultures, religions and nationalities, many of which are reflected in the shops and religious institutions we pass by on the street. To take a survey along one of these bendy buses would be to encounter Poles, Ukrainians, Latvians, Nigerians, Ghanaians, Somalis, Ethiopians, Lebanese, Algerians, Afro-Caribbeans, Zimbabweans and many more besides. Some are Christians, some Muslim, some Rastafarians, and some mind their own business. In among the *London Lite* newspapers you will see the Bible and the Qu'ran being read as well as texts from the Mind, Body, Spirit section of the bookshop. Here is the reality of multi-cultural, multi-faith London in full bloom. And we travel together, whether we like it or not, through a combination of the market and the state symbolised in our common dependence on the good offices of Transport for London, another public–private partnership. **❞**
>
> Luke Bretherton, 'Post Secular Politics? Interfaith Relations and Civic Practice'. *The Lambeth Inter-Faith Lecture*, King's College London, 4 June 2009, p. 1

The theologian David Ford (*The Future of Christian Theology*, 2011) asks how we should describe the present, the kind of scene Bretherton describes. Is it a modern age, a postmodern age, a secular age or a post-secular age? Is it secular and religious or none of these? In Britain, an increasing number of people describe themselves as not religious, but globally more people than ever link themselves to a religion, as Bretherton's London bus illustrates.

Peter Berger, an early contributor to the secularisation theory, has since retracted his earlier conclusions:

> 66 Modernization necessarily leads to a decline in religion, both in society and in the minds of individuals. And it is precisely that key idea that turned out to be wrong. To be sure, modernization has had some secularizing effects, more in some places than others. But it has also provoked powerful movements of counter-secularization. Also secularization on the societal level is not necessarily linked to secularization on the level of individual consciousness. 99
>
> Peter L. Berger, ed., *The Desecularization of the World: Resurgent Religion and World Politics*, 1999, pp. 2–3

A secular state is not necessarily atheistic but may be filled with believing people

In other words, a secular state is not necessarily atheistic but may be filled with believing people. For example, the USA remains just as religious now as it did a century ago, even though it is officially a country in which Church and State are separated. Up until recently, Turkey was an avowed secular state with a 99 per cent Muslim population.

Berger thinks that the assumption that we live in a secularised world is false. He says that, with some exceptions, notably Western Europe, the world today is as furiously religious as it ever was, and in some places more so than ever. The whole body of literature by historians and social scientists that is loosely labelled 'secularisation theory' is, as a result, mistaken.

David Ford suggests we need to stop thinking about the development of the world in linear terms that are bound to start from one point (such as a religious approach to life) and finish at another point (an enlightened atheistic approach to life). He thinks the 'unpredictability of a drama' is a better metaphor, as we do not know what is going to happen throughout the world and there seem to be quite different ways of being modern.

David Ford and Jose Casanova are both critical of the idea that a secular atheism is unquestionably good. They note that atheist ideologies, such as fascism, communism and capitalism, have sought to write religion out of the script of human civilisation and in some cases have used brutal methods to eradicate religious populations.

Discussing the challenges of secularism

Are spiritual values just human values?

Are the values that Christianity offers society anything more than human values? A strong case can be made that compassion, forgiveness, justice and peace are all essential human values. To be compassionate or loving reassures others and creates a positive experience of life. Forgiveness is necessary to help human beings overcome their failures, while justice is also important to ensure that people who make mistakes are dealt with fairly. Peace enables societies to flourish, while war disrupts and destroys life. To advance a moral code based on these values keeps a society from falling into brutal chaos. Such a code can be articulated without recourse to belief in the afterlife, belief in a loving God or a saviour Lord. Arguably then, these values are human not Christian.

However, not all Christian values are so easily explained in this way. Self-sacrifice (of one friend for another, of a mother for her child, of a soldier for his platoon) and unconditional love (which motivates nurses to travel to Ebola-stricken regions of the world to help those who are suffering) are less easy to explain in purely rational terms.

The Christian value of loving your enemy and those who are different is counter-intuitive; it contradicts feelings of self-interest and safety. It is easier to reject the foreigner or the stranger (because they are not known, not understood, and possibly not safe) than it is to welcome, trust and befriend them. Conversely, it is much easier to protect and defend those who are like us than those who are not. Loving your enemy expresses a commitment to a greater vision, something beyond the self.

Perhaps, therefore, spiritual values are better than human values in that human values are part of the physical, sensual, morally corrupt human world, and spiritual values are pure, perfect and untainted. Universal human rights are a human-designed value system, and are often presented almost as an alternative to religion. They are founded on a belief in the ultimate worth of human beings, in their intrinsic dignity. Yet human beings can behave immorally both individually (people lie, kill and steal) and collectively (people are consuming the earth's resources to meet their short-term needs without adequate thought for future generations). This suggests that the Universal Declaration of Human Rights is based on an unfounded belief that human beings have some kind of ultimate worth. Can any human-designed value system avoid a paradox such as this?

Or perhaps it is not possible to separate human values and spiritual values: spiritual values are *just* human values because human values are *just* spiritual values. Within Christianity there is the idea that God becomes incarnate; he becomes a human being and that in encountering human beings, especially human beings in need, one is encountering God. It is easy to interpret passages from the Gospel that talk of this as simple metaphors for 'treat others as if they were God', but in the incarnation something more profound takes place. There is a revaluation of humanity moving from sin to salvation. In becoming human, God reclaims and reasserts the worth of humanity. Arguably there is, therefore, no contradiction between spiritual values and human values because, in the incarnation, the dualism that divides the sacred from the profane, the divine from the human, is rejected. God represents them both.

> ## Think question
> Can self-sacrifice be explained as a human value or does it point to something beyond a particular person?

> *See Chapter 3.4 of the AS and Year 1 book for a discussion about Jesus' divinity.*

Apply your knowledge

11. Consider the extent to which values are:

    a. basic beliefs (such as a belief in the goodness or sinfulness of human beings)

    b. principles (such as 'do unto others as you would have done unto you')

    c. virtues or behaviours (such as courage or honesty)

    d. hopes or aspirations (such as world peace or unity).

12. Discuss which of the following you find most interesting and/or problematic.

    a. Values are things that people who hold different theological or spiritual beliefs share in common, such as justice or democracy.

    b. Values are bound up with beliefs and belong to particular traditions, such as sacrificial love (agape) or the need for forgiveness. They cannot easily be shared by people who believe different things because they express theological or spiritual ideas.

    c. Values can be quite different sorts of things that can be difficult to make sense of.

Is Christianity a major cause of personal and social problems?

Christianity can be seen as having a negative influence on society. It can be seen as patriarchal and sexist in the way in which it depicts women narrowly and limits their life chances. For example, traditionally, only men have been allowed to take on leadership roles within Christian Churches and women have been defined exclusively in terms of motherhood.

Christianity can encourage infantile and 'unscientific' views of the world. For example, Dawkins points to the role he says Christianity has played in the criminalisation of homosexuality (which was illegal in the UK until 1967). He points to the 'American Taliban' (evangelical Christians who say that Aids is God's punishment on homosexuals) as an illustration of how upsetting ideas can be developed through religion (Dawkins, *The God Delusion*, 2006, p. 237). The problem for society, he argues, is that an absolutist faith finds other belief systems and other ways of behaving incomprehensible, and exercises influence over the law to criminalise anything that differs from the moral absolutes it offers.

Do these photos provide an answer to the question, 'Is Christianity a major cause of personal and social problems?'

An absolutist faith also has a negative influence on society in the area of the sanctity of human life and the attempts to restrict or limit women's access to abortion, Dawkins suggests. He offers up the example of George W. Bush. While Governor of Texas, Bush oversaw more than a third of the executions that took place in the USA at the time, while simultaneously preventing medical research on embryonic life. Dawkins sees applying the death penalty on the one hand, while preventing scientific research that might alleviate suffering on the other, as an example of the damage religious absolutism causes to society. Dawkins notes that Mother Teresa of Calcutta said in her Nobel Peace Prize acceptance speech that abortion is the greatest destroyer of peace, and he points to the distorted stories and untruths that anti-abortion campaigners use to persuade people to join their opposition to legal abortions.

The difficulty with the argument that Christianity is the major cause of religious and social problems is that multiple examples are used to make a general point about Christianity, or religion more widely. And a wide range of alternative examples can be used to present the counter-argument. What about the examples of religious leaders who spearheaded social change?

- In the nineteenth century, Christian churches established schools for the poor in England.

- Anglican Bishops were instrumental in the decriminalisation of homosexuality in the 1960s, at a time when other parts of the British establishment resisted change.

- Many prominent civil rights activists who played a leading role in challenging segregation in the USA, such as Martin Luther King Jr, were religious.

- Many of the food banks run by volunteers throughout the UK today were set up and are now run by Christians and local churches.

Each example can be used to support Christianity or religion in general, but it is not clear how to judge which examples in tit-for-tat debate should be given most weight in order to help us come to a conclusion.

A further problem centres on how this debate frames the concept of religion and Christianity. It can be argued that one side draws on examples of what might be called 'bad religion' or 'bad Christianity', while the other side draws on examples of 'good religion' or 'good Christianity'. The proponents of one particular viewpoint choose the most extreme examples to support their argument. Perhaps this is because the kinds of examples that best represent the everyday behaviour of religion and the religious, Christianity and Christians, make the arguments less powerfully: members of local churches visiting the lonely or bringing them together in knitting groups or for harvest lunches; offering a mechanism for regular contact with others in a social setting

Think question

When evaluating religion, should we focus on the ideas it has, the institutions it forms or the people it attracts as followers?

and providing emotional support; giving time and resources to local charitable activities.

There is a difficulty in talking about 'what Christianity does'. Does this mean 'what (some) Christians do', or 'what (some) Christian institutions do', or 'the impact that (some) forms of Christian thought might have'? Making a link between people's actions, the rules and systems of institutional bodies, and the systems of thought within them can be difficult, especially when it refers to a movement, such as Christianity, that takes on multiple cultural forms around the world.

Apply your knowledge

13. How should we evaluate Christianity?

  a. We should judge it by the actions and personalities of (some/many) Christians.

  b. We should judge it by the systems and rules of (some/many) Christian institutions.

  c. We should judge it by the theories about the influence and impact of Christian thought.

14. Discuss these views:

  a. On balance, Christianity is more trouble than it is worth.

  b. To try and give a single judgement about something as complex as religion is impossible.

  c. Christianity is as flawed and as holy as human beings.

Do secularism and secularisation offer opportunities for Christianity to develop new ways of thinking and acting?

In *The Future of Christian Theology* (2011), David Ford argues that the beginnings of secularism led to an important development in Western European thinking: the advent of the idea of state tolerance. The Thirty Years' War (1618–48) consisted of a series of terrible conflicts in central Europe fuelled by religious difference. The experiences during the war led people of different religious beliefs to see a value in what Ford calls 'minimal secularism', which allowed different communities to live in peaceful toleration of one another. A concept of the public good that was not threatened by religious conflict and that made space for religious minorities was born.

This occurred alongside the development of a new understanding of government, in which it was no longer the case that kings would govern over their people forever. Democracy, and the organisations that facilitate it and the organisations that flourished as a result of it (parliaments and the rule of law, charities, trade unions, professional associations and universities) ushered in the modern age.

However, this 'secular settlement', found in many Western countries, has not existed unchallenged. There have been repeated attempts to assert new kinds of religion: the 'religion' of imperialism fuelled the First World War and the 'religions' of nationalism and fascism fuelled the

Second World War. Communism is also a belief system that sought to impose its ideology at the expense of what we more traditionally think of as religion.

Yet the story of religion is not all about society changing to accommodate religion, or society acting to eradicate religion. Some scholars argue that religion should, and does, change in response to the society that it encounters:

> 66 Practice changes, of course, over time, sometimes slowly, sometimes swiftly. And changed practice can lead to changed belief. Scriptural passages can get new interpretations. And if they can't adapt, they're often abandoned. That passage in the Psalms about how blessed you will be if you dash Babylonian babies on the rocks; the passage in First Peter about how slaves should submit themselves to their masters, however cruel – these we can usefully look away from. St Paul's powerful move was to hold on to the Jewish scriptures while instructing the followers of Christ that they could ignore large parts of them because they were only binding on the Jews. In short, if scriptures were not subject to interpretation (and thus to re-interpretation) they wouldn't continue to guide people over long centuries. When it comes to their survival, their openness is not a bug but a feature. A burden, perhaps, but also a blessing. 99
>
> Kwame Appiah, 'Mistaken Identities: Creed, Country, Colour, Culture'. *Reith Lectures 2016*, Lecture 1

> ### Think question
>
> If religion makes itself 'acceptable', does it lose that which makes it 'religious'?

Militant forms of both religion and secularism are prominent. Since 2000, France has progressively moved to prohibit religious dress in public places, while Turkey is in the process of removing bans on religious dress in public. At the same time, terrorist atrocities are carried out in the name of extreme and militant forms of religion. Secularisation theory proposed that religious institutions would adapt to the secular world and decline, but Peter Berger thinks the reverse is true:

> 66 What has in fact occurred is that, by and large, religious communities have survived, even flourished to the degree that they have not tried to adapt themselves to the alleged requirements of a secularized world. To put it simply, experiments with secularized religion have generally failed; religious movements with beliefs and practices dripping with reactionary supernaturalism have widely succeeded. 99
>
> Peter L. Berger, ed., *The Desecularization of the World: Resurgent Religion and World Politics*, 1999, p. 4

David Martin notes that since the 1980s there has been a steady global upsurge in conservative Protestant Christianity, which parallels an upsurge in conservative Islam. He writes:

> 66 The advance of conservative Evangelicalism has been most evident in what used to be called the Third World, especially Latin America and sub-Saharan Africa, but it is also notable in the Philippines, the Pacific rim (above all Korea), and China. Sizable conversions have occurred in parts of Eastern Europe, notably Romania. And Evangelical religion can clearly claim to be the liveliest sector in the developed 'Western' world, whether we speak of Britain, Holland, The United States, or Australia. 99
>
> David Martin, 'The Evangelical Upsurge and its Political Implications'. In *The Desecularization of the World: Resurgent Religion and World Politics*, ed. Berger, 1999, p. 37

Apply your knowledge

15. Consider the following viewpoints and build your own argument to support one of them over the others.

    a. 'Real' religion is always counter cultural, so always a challenge. That is the point.

    b. Religion that tries to be like non-religious society ends up being non-religion.

    c. Religion needs to update itself. It should look to the future as much as the past.

The emergence of secularism and secularisation brought an end to the concept of Christendom: the idea that there was a group of states in Europe where the vast majority of the population were Christians of the same denomination and other Christian denominations and religions were, at worst, persecuted or, at best, marginalised from public life. Instead a minimal secular society emerged, where religion and government were separated and religious differences were tolerated. Arguably this is good for both religion and government: it helps to protect religious authority from the potentially corrupting influence of political power and it helps to prevent government persecution of religious minorities. However, the continued development of the secular state has led religion, in recent times, to reassert itself and re-emphasise its traditional, more conservative, forms.

Looking ahead, Christianity is perhaps at a crossroads. On the one hand, it could become firmer in its convictions and stand in opposition to the secular world, taking strength from the growth in religion around the world. Alternatively, it could try to incorporate modern ideas, changing and growing within a secular world.

Is Christianity a significant contributor to society's culture and values, and should it be?

Today, British society has many features of Christianity present. The Head of State (the Queen) is the Head of the Church of England, and national holidays are linked to Christian festivals at Easter and Christmas. Most oaths taken in court are taken over the Christian Bible or an alternative sacred text. The anthem 'Jerusalem', a short poem by William Blake set to music by Sir Hubert Parry, is amongst the music played at the Last Night of the Proms. We remember our war dead on Remembrance Sunday, and the service at the Cenotaph involves leading figures from different religious communities. The nation's flag has a Christian cross at its centre.

Should Christianity still be linked to the cultural and constitutional life of the country?

There are regular debates about whether it is appropriate for BBC Radio 4 to broadcast a daily act of worship on longwave, or whether the monarch should be head of the Church of England. These are not just debates about what makes good radio and what makes a good constitution. They point to an underlying question about whether Christianity does, and should, influence the culture and values in our society.

Richard Dawkins, a vociferous critic of religion, is a strong defender of the study of the Bible in schools. In a section of a book called 'Religious Education as a part of Literary Culture', he writes of the outstanding literary merit of the King James Bible of 1611, of the sublime poetry it contains, and the influence it has had on the arts, music and language for centuries. Many phrases we commonly use today can be traced back to the King James Bible, including: 'physician heal thyself', 'lost sheep', 'prodigal son', 'doubting Thomas', 'den of thieves', 'good Samaritan', 'fight the good fight', 'I wash my hands of it' and 'to everything there is a season'. Biblical literacy is, therefore, essential to a full appreciation of English literature, and an atheist world view is no justification for cutting the Bible or other sacred books out of education. Dawkins extends his comments about the sacred texts to the cultural traditions of religions in general. As one of the greatest modern critics of religion, Dawkins seems clear that Christianity is a significant contributor to society's culture and values, although he sees this narrowly, in terms of respecting Christianity's legacy.

Acknowledging Christianity's role in the historical development of our culture and values is not, however, the same as giving religion a superior role in their future development. To describe the United Kingdom of Great Britain and Northern Ireland as a Christian country often raises criticisms that this flies in the face of the evidence. However, if by 'Christian country' we mean a country with a Christian-infused culture, rather than a believing society, these criticisms may be tempered. Yet, the cultural changes that have taken place as a result of migration and religious pluralism in recent decades mean that Christianity is no longer the sole, or even the dominant, influence on our culture and values. Popular music, for example, has many diverse influences. Therefore, it is questionable whether Christianity should rightfully continue as a significant contributor to society's culture and values.

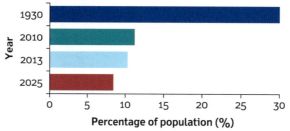

Membership of Christian churches in the UK, 1930–2025

Source: www.faithsurvey.co.uk

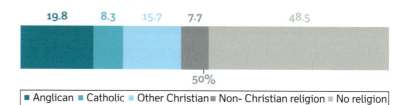

Religious affiliation in 2014, as a percentage of the total population, according to the British Social Attitudes Survey

Source: St Mary's University, Twickenham, London; www.theguardian.com/world/2016/may/23/no-religion-outnumber-christians-england-wales-study

Apply your knowledge

16. Consider the issues and the considerations below. Choose two issues and develop arguments to support them, drawing on the considerations to help you.

Issues:

a. Religious Education should give more time to Christianity.

b. All schools should have a daily act of worship of a mainly Christian character.

c. State holidays should follow Christian festivals.

d. The head of state should remain the head of the Church of England.

Considerations:

i. The UK has a Christian heritage, which has influenced the country's culture, art, music and law.

ii. Christianity is the biggest religion in Britain.

iii. People of no religion outnumber Christians in England and Wales.

iv. Freedom of religion and belief means that no one religion should be given superiority over another.

v. Identify one other consideration you can think of.

Learning support

Points to remember

» The words 'secular' and 'secularism' can mean different things, so when talking about a secular society, consider the possibility that it may refer to:

  ○ a society where people have largely abandoned religious beliefs

  ○ a society where the law and government do not allow religious expression in a public space

  ○ a society where the law and government do not give any advantage to any one religion but support a plural and diverse religious and cultural population, including diverse religious expressions of religion and belief, in the public space.

» Scholars in the 1950s and 1960s thought that religion around the world would decline as democracy and technology advanced, in the same way that it was declining in the UK. Now many reject this theory of secularisation, arguing that the decline is neither linear nor consistent. Some democracies, such as the USA, remain as religious as they were in the early 1900s, whilst the UK is experiencing a significant reduction in the number of people declaring a religious association.

» Understanding the concept of public space (a shared space for government, public services and law) is important in making sense of 'a secular society'. The key issue is the extent to which the public space should permit the expression of one, many or no religions and beliefs, and what 'expression' means in this context.

» Christianity has responded to the challenge of secularism in two contrasting ways: in some countries, as in the UK, Christianity has become part of a multi-religious society; in other countries, such as the USA, there has been an upsurge in traditional religion as the number of Latin American Christians increases.

Enhance your learning

» In *The Future of an Illusion* (1927) Sigmund Freud explores his concerns about the damage that religion and belief does.

» In *The God Delusion* (2006), especially Chapter 9, Richard Dawkins discusses his concerns about the impact of religion on children. The book is a worldwide phenomena. Christian theologians Alister McGrath and Joanna McGrath wrote a short response called *The Dawkins Delusion?* (2007).

» David Ford's work, *The Future of Christian Theology* (2011), is readable and accessible. It summarises social scientific evidence and arguments about secularism, and explores Christian responses to it. Chapters 3 and 6 are particularly pertinent.

» The British Humanist Association gives an account of humanism and has many essays on religion and belief in public life and especially faith schools: https://humanism.org.uk.

» For a Catholic response to secularism read Christopher Dawson. 'The Challenge of Secularism' in *Catholic World* (1956), also online at www.catholiceducation.org/en/education/catholic-contributions/the-challenge-of-secularism.html.

» The rise of the 'nones', people of no religion, is the focus of social scientific study. Search 'rise of the nones' online for access to interesting studies.

Practice for exams

At A level, essay questions invite you to demonstrate your knowledge and understanding of factual material (AO1) and also your critical ability in putting forward a coherent, balanced argument (AO2). You should aim to write essays that are persuasive responses to the question throughout, rather than writing a lot of description and then tacking an opinion on at the end of each paragraph.

How fair is the claim that Christianity has a negative impact on society?

This question invites discussion of the challenge that Christianity does more harm than good in society.

For AO1 you need to be able to show an understanding of the reasons people might present this challenge. For example, they might think that Christianity encourages sexism or is divisive or homophobic. They might think that belief in God is infantile or that religious belief hinders scientific progress. You might be able to refer to specific thinkers who present different challenges. You also need to show knowledge and understanding of counter arguments, for example the argument that Christianity has been the driving force for social changes such as education and many aid agencies.

For AO2 your argument should assess the strength of the challenge and reach a well-justified conclusion.

'Christian values are more than just basic human values: they have something distinctive to offer.' Discuss.

For this question, you need to think about how 'Christian values' might be understood. You need to consider whether there are basic human values that we all share regardless of our religious beliefs, and if so, whether these correspond exactly to Christian values or whether Christianity offers something distinctive.

For high marks in AO1, you should be able to give examples of Christian values and secular values, and demonstrate knowledge and understanding of the reasons for holding such values. You could make use of your knowledge from the ethics part of the course.

For AO2 you need to present an argument and support it with sound reasoning. Try to illustrate your argument with examples. If perhaps you wanted to argue that Christian values are not always the same as human values, you could give an example of where a Christian has disagreed with the rest of their society perhaps in wartime or on civil rights issues.

Chapter 3.6

Liberation theology and Marx

Should Christian theology begin with information or action?

Are the stories of liberation and salvation in the Bible about heaven or revolution in this world?

Should Christian theology be informed by all experience of human life and human thought?

Key Terms

Exploitation: treating someone unfairly in order to benefit from their work or resources

Alienation: the process of becoming detached or isolated

Capitalism: an economic system in which the means of production are privately owned and operated for profit, in contrast with communism where trade and industry is controlled by the state

Conscientisation: the process by which a person becomes conscious of the power structures in society

Basic Christian communities: Christian groups that gather together to try to directly resolve difficulties in their lives

Structural sin: the idea that sin is not just a personal action, but something that can be brought about through unjust organisations and social structures

Preferential option for the poor: the idea that Jesus Christ stood with the poor and oppressed, and that the Church should focus on the poor and oppressed and stand in solidarity with them

Specification requirements

The relationship of liberation theology and Marx, including:

- Marx's teaching on alienation and exploitation
- liberation theology's use of Marx to analyse social sin
- liberation theology's teaching on the 'preferential option for the poor'

Introduction

Liberation theology is a theological movement that starts with action rather than belief. It focuses on the experiences of the poor and interprets Christianity as a response to poverty and other examples of **exploitation** and **alienation**. Bringing about the Kingdom of God and salvation are not just events that happen after death; they are part of a physical struggle in this world to make the lives of the poor better.

Liberation theology is linked to Karl Marx's analysis of **capitalism**. Marx argues capitalism created a world in which wealth and power are concentrated in the hands of the few at the expense of the many.

Liberation theology has been criticised for its reliance on Marxism, a non-Christian explanation of human experience, but it has also contributed to a renewed emphasis on the importance of the poor in Christian thought.

What is liberation theology?

For many centuries theology was studied in seminaries and universities. From a liberation theology perspective, this is all wrong. Theology should not be exclusively academic. It should start with people's lives.

Liberation theology is a theological movement that began in 1964 when young Catholic theologians met in Petropolis in Brazil and pledged themselves to finding the truth of the Christian message in the poverty of Latin America. It therefore began as both an intellectual movement and a practical movement, among those who worked with the poor. The group included two people who became leading liberation theologians: Jon Sobrino and Gustavo Gutiérrez.

Gustavo Gutiérrez (b. 1928) is a Peruvian theologian, Dominican priest and one of the principal founders of liberation theology in Latin America

Jon Sobrino (b. 1938) is a Jesuit Catholic priest and theologian, known for his contributions to liberation theology

Liberation theology drew on the work of Paulo Freire who, in *Pedagogy of the Oppressed* (1970), invented the term '**conscientisation**' to describe the process by which a person becomes conscious of the power structures in society. Freire thought that education should liberate people by raising their consciousness, teaching them how to read not only words but also the power structures in society. He was opposed to the idea that education was simply about moving information from one generation to the next; he wanted it to transform society.

> 66 When I give food to the poor they call me a saint. When I ask why the poor have no food, they call me communist. 99
>
> Dom Hélder Câmara, Brazilian Archbishop, cited in Zildo Rocha, *Helder, The Gift: A Life that Marked the Course of the Church in Brazil*, 2000, p. 53

Traditionally, theology is something that is explained to people by theologians: theological facts move from the heads of theology teachers to the heads of their pupils. Theological explanation comes first and action comes second. Liberation theology turns this around. It argues that action should come first and then explanation. Orthopraxy (right practice) should come before orthodoxy (right belief). Liberation theology is, therefore, a theology of doing, and everyone can do it. It requires Christians to reflect critically on their experience of life.

Orthopraxy (right practice) comes before orthodoxy (right belief)

Think question

If theology begins with action, who decides what action is right?

The concept of the Kingdom of God is central to liberation theology. It is the world made anew, not somewhere to go after death. The coming of the Kingdom of God is something that must be hoped for, and worked for, in this world: '[t]he growth of the Kingdom is a process which occurs historically in liberation, insofar as liberation means a greater fulfilment of man' (Gutiérrez, *A Theology of Liberation*, 1973, p. 177). Christians must destroy the roots of exploitation and oppression by living a Christian life and working for peace and justice in the hope of creating the Kingdom of God on earth. In this way, liberation theology offers hope to the poor and the oppressed that things may change for them. This implies a real revolution, not just a revolution in word and thought.

For Gutiérrez, liberation happens in two distinct ways. First, there must be social and economic liberation. Poverty and oppression are caused by humans and can be remedied by them. Therefore, people must take responsibility for liberation and act to bring it about. Secondly, people must be liberated from sin, reconciled with God and all of God's brothers and sisters in Christ. Both methods of liberation are essential. It is not enough to focus on liberation from sin without liberation from socio-economic injustices, and vice versa. This means that the political liberation of people is the work of salvation. Sin is not just personal, it is historical and collective because it is found in the social structures and institutions that harm people.

Liberation theologians disagree about whether earthly liberation or spiritual liberation should come first. Juan Segundo argues that, 'Liberation is first and foremost liberation from the radical slavery of sin' (Segundo, *Theology and the Church: A Response to Cardinal Ratzinger and a Warning to the Whole Church*, 1985, p.160), but others, such as Gutiérrez, seem to emphasise earthly liberation.

Liberation theology draws on a number of key biblical texts:

- The Exodus story and the liberation of the people of Israel from oppression:

66 Then the Lord said to Moses, 'Go to Pharaoh and say to him, "This is what the Lord, the God of the Hebrews, says: 'Let my people go, so that they may worship me.'" 99

Exodus 9:1, New International Version

- The Magnificat, with the announcement of a coming change:

66 He has performed mighty deeds with his arm;
he has scattered those who are proud in their inmost thoughts.
He has brought down rulers from their thrones

but has lifted up the humble.
He has filled the hungry with good things
    but has sent the rich away empty. 🙶

> Luke 1:51–53, New International Version

- Jesus' denouncement of the wealthy, including lawyers, Pharisees and the rich:

🙶 Again I tell you, it is easier for a camel to go through the eye of a needle than for someone who is rich to enter the kingdom of God. 🙶

> Matthew 19:24, New International Version

- The requirement to treat all those in need as if they were God:

🙶 The King will reply, 'Truly I tell you, whatever you did for one of the least of these brothers and sisters of mine, you did for me.' 🙶

> Matthew 25:40, New International Version

- The Resurrection, which is the ultimate form of liberation:

🙶 For my Father's will is that everyone who looks to the Son and believes in him shall have eternal life, and I will raise them up at the last day. 🙶

> John 6:40, New International Version

- The Beatitudes, a kind of road map to liberation:

🙶 Blessed are the poor in spirit, for theirs is the kingdom of heaven. 🙶

> Matthew 5:3, New International Version

Liberation theology is a theology of hope. These Bible passages are not just metaphors for what will happen. They are parables of the struggle for liberation of the poor, the oppressed and the unjustly treated today, in this world, in this time. Liberation theology emerged in Latin America in the 1960s, a part of the world where many governments were corrupt and many people were very poor. Christians formed discussion groups, called **basic Christian communities**, where they talked about their experiences and the challenges they faced, searching for practical solutions, supported by the Gospel.

Liberation theology is a theology of hope

Apply your knowledge

1. What should education be about?

   a. Moving facts from the minds of teachers to the minds of students.

   b. Equipping students to recognise the power structures at play in the world around them, in the knowledge they are learning and in the language they are using.

2. Explore what is meant by a structure being sinful. What sorts of structures in the world today might be sinful?

3. If the Kingdom of God is a social reality and not just a private reality, does that imply a need for radical revolution? If so, does radical revolution lead to the taking of life, something Jesus seemed to be opposed to? Discuss the implications of these questions.

4. If Christianity is really about a social and political revolution, how can we explain Jesus' reluctance to overthrow the Romans or the fact that Christ was crucified and did not lead a revolution to replace the government of the time? Discuss.

5. If the Kingdom of God and salvation require liberation, what happens to those people who are imprisoned. Are they not fully saved?

Liberation is part of God's continuing work of creating and sustaining the world. The people of God (in the Hebrew Scriptures they are described as the people of Israel) were liberated and God made a new covenant with them so that they may become a new people. God's love, therefore, involves both liberation and creation.

Marx, alienation and exploitation

Karl Marx (1818–83)

The world is filled with incredible technology: space travel, genetic engineering, robots, the Internet, etc. Many of these technological developments, which were unimaginable even a short while ago, have revolutionised our lives. Yet, at the same time, human beings seem to feel helpless in the face of the extraordinary forces, such as the threat of nuclear destruction and climate change, that technology and industrialisation have unleashed. Paradoxically, the more human beings have the power to control the world, the more they feel they are not in control. Karl Marx's writing reflects this feeling.

Marx was a nineteenth-century German economic theorist and philosopher who is best known for laying the foundations of socialism and communism. His most famous works are *The Communist Manifesto* (1848) and *Das Kapital* (Capital) (1867). He wrote:

> **"** On the one hand, there have started into life industrial and scientific forces, which no epoch of the former human history had ever suspected. On the other hand, there exist symptoms of decay, far surpassing the horrors of the Roman Empire. In our days everything seems pregnant with its contrary. Machinery, gifted with the wonderful power of shortening and fructifying human labour, we behold starving and overworking it. The new-fangled sources of wealth, by some strange weird spell, are turned into sources of want. The victories of art seem bought by loss of character. **"**
>
> Karl Marx, 'Speech at the Anniversary of the Peoples' Paper', quoted in Eugene Lunn, *Marxism and Modernism*, 1984, p. 31

Marx's theory of alienation reveals that there is human activity behind this experience of powerlessness. The social institutions that foster it seem to have developed naturally, but they are not natural. They have been shaped by human action. Specifically, they have been shaped by the appropriation of the means of production by the powerful.

Marx did not think that humans have a fixed nature, but he believed they have to work to survive and, unlike other animals, they are conscious of their work and can develop new ways of doing things. He also believed that humans are social beings: 'Society does not consist of individuals; it expresses the sum of connections and relationships in which individuals find themselves' (Marx, *Grundrisse*, 1858, p. 77).

When human society reached a point that it could create a surplus (e.g. grow more wheat than was needed to make bread to feed everyone in the community) it began to fracture. Class divisions emerged between those who had control over the means of producing this surplus and those who did not. This was first evident through the ownership of land:

> In feudal landownership we already find the domination of the earth as of an alien power over men. The serf is an appurtenance of the land. Similarly the heir through primogeniture, the first-born son, belongs to the land. It inherits him. The rule of private property begins with property in land which is its basis.
>
> Karl Marx, *Early Writings*, [1833–4] 1975, p. 318

The feudal lords own the land and, therefore, the means of producing food. The serfs, who work the land but do not own it, are reliant on the lords for access to the means of producing food and must give their surplus to the lords in return for working the land. The serfs are alienated from the land they work and subservient to their feudal lords.

The advent of capitalism (an economic system in which the means of production are privately owned and operated for profit) changed the relationship between people and the means of production. Workers no longer had the right to dispose of what they produced. Wage labour replaced other forms of labour; labour, just like any other commodity, could be bought and sold for money. This resulted in social division, with the wealthy who owned the means of production divided from the workers. The worker:

> is depressed, therefore, both intellectually and physically, to the level of a machine, and from being a man becomes an abstract activity and a stomach, so he also becomes more and dependent on every fluctuation in the market price, in the investment of capital and on the whims of the wealthy.
>
> Karl Marx, *Early Writings,* [1833–4] 1975, p. 285

Charlie Chaplin in the film *Modern Times (1936)*. Are workers cogs in the machine?

According to Marx, workers cannot work independently of capitalism. To work means to be part of the capitalist machine. And work is a living death; labour becomes forced labour because without work, without money to buy food, people die. This is most visible in the factory system, where the stages of production are separated, people only relate to the part of the process they are working on, and have no sense of the whole; they only understand the part of the machine that they serve. They are dehumanised and unable to live fulfilling lives because they are being exploited by the factory owners as a means to an end. Marx predicted the emergence of a class struggle between the different groups in society. He said that in order to create a fairer society, those who were oppressed would begin to violently resist the structures that alienated them.

Human beings are forced into relationships defined by the part of the capitalist machine they work in, but they are also connected to others through the buying and selling of commodities. Today we can use a debit card online to buy a new pair of jeans from a retailer that manufactures them in factories on the other side of the world and ships them to your front door. The pair of jeans that reaches us has passed through many hands, yet we may meet or even think about only the postal worker who brings the package to the door. We do not see the people in the supply chain as fellow individuals with equal rights. They become dehumanised and, as part of the supply chain, we are dehumanised as well. Capitalism means everyone appropriates the produce of others, alienating them from their own labour. As some factories make technological improvements that reduce costs and make it cheaper for them to produce a pair of jeans, other factories drive down wages in order to compete. We celebrate because our jeans are cheaper today than they were yesterday, but our happiness comes at a price: the exploitation of others.

Apply your knowledge

6. Describe five purchases you regularly make that involve people you do not know as individual human beings.

7. 'Education is part of the machine of capitalism and pupils are the cogs in that machine.' To what extent do you agree or disagree with this statement? Give reasons for your answer.

8. Look at some recent newspapers and find examples from the political and business pages of stories that seem to validate Marx's thinking on alienation and exploitation.

Liberation theology's use of Marx to analyse social sin

Liberation theology grew in popularity at a time when Latin America was a key battleground in the cold war conflict between the USA and the USSR, and between the competing ideologies of capitalism and communism. Latin America was an under-developed part of the world where many people lived in poverty, and it was at a crossroads: would it stick with capitalism or would it choose socialism (the first stage in the journey towards communism)? This ideological battle impacted on general elections and caused violence and revolution: socialist governments were overthrown with the support of the USA, and communists led rebel movements. The violent uprising that Marx had predicted seemed to be happening in Latin America.

Liberation theology drew on the idea that the purpose of development is not to increase wealth but to increase human well-being.

While industrialisation might lead to greater wealth, it might do so in a way that sacrifices human well-being for some or all people, especially if the benefits of development are not shared. If workers are alienated and exploited there is injustice. The structures of sin that support industrialisation become part of the organisational structure of society, part of schools, systems of government and other institutions, and injustice becomes institutionalised.

Gutiérrez mentions Marx's theories of alienation and exploitation in his theology, and also Marx's belief that human beings have the power to change the world they live in. He cautioned against endorsing every aspect of Marxism, but believed that the people of Latin America had a deep-rooted desire for liberation from the burdens of capitalism. Gutiérrez identified political movements in Latin America as responding to this need and called for the Church to stand with those movements:

> 66 In Latin America to be Church today means to take a clear position regarding both the present state of social injustice and the revolutionary process which is attempting to abolish that injustice and build a more human order. 99
>
> Gustavo Gutiérrez, *A Theology of Liberation*, 1974, p. 265

For Gutiérrez, to not get involved in politics is helping to keep things as they are. This is impossible for a Christian. Being Christian requires a person to be political. He argues that it is the responsibility of the Latin American Church to denounce every dehumanising situation that is contrary to brotherhood, justice and liberty. The Church must be a voice against alienation and exploitation, and right action (orthopraxis) should come before right belief (orthodoxy). Working to change people's lives for the better should come before concerns about the official doctrines and teachings of the Church.

Gutiérrez draws on Marx's language of class struggle in his theology:

> 66 Unity is one of the notes of the church and yet the class struggle divides men; is the unity of the Church compatible with class struggle? […] the class struggle is a fact and neutrality in this matter is impossible. The class struggle is a part of our economic, social, political, cultural and religious reality […] moving towards a classless society […] It is a will to build a socialist society, more just, free, and human, and not a society of superficial and false reconciliation and equality. 99
>
> Gustavo Gutiérrez, *A Theology of Liberation*, 1974, pp. 273–4

To reject the class struggle is to legitimise the existing system and work as part of it. The current system embraces structural inequality and this creates **structural sin**, which is seen most clearly in the injustices suffered by the poor and oppressed masses. The acceptance of the class struggle against the structures of sin is, arguably, Marx's most important impact on liberation theology.

Liberation theologians are clear that liberation theology is not Marxist but uses Marx's analysis of society:

> 66 In liberation theology, Marxism is never treated as a subject on its own but always from and in relation to the poor. Placing themselves firmly on the side of the poor, liberation theologians ask Marx: 'What can you tell us about the situation of poverty and ways of overcoming it?' Here Marxists are submitted to the judgement of the poor and their cause, and not the other way around. Therefore, liberation theology used Marxism purely as an instrument. It does not venerate it as it venerates the gospel. And it feels no obligation to account to social scientists for any use it may make – correct or otherwise – of Marxist terminology and ideas […] To put it in more specific terms, liberation theology freely borrows from Marxism certain 'methodological pointers' that have proved fruitful in understanding the world of the oppressed. 99
>
> Leonardo Boff and Clodovis Boff, *Introducing Liberation Theology,* 1987, p. 28

The Marxist analysis of structural inequality informs the liberation theology concept of structural sin. Marx's understanding of the development of capitalism and the concentration of the means of production in the hands of the wealthy and powerful, as well as his belief that humans could change the world they live in, also informs liberation theology. Liberation theology concludes that capitalism has failed to satisfy the basic needs of the poor and, although socialism may not be a perfect solution, the socialist ideal is better than the capitalist ideal. Fitzgerald sums up the appeal of Marxist ideas to liberation theologians thus:

> 66 According to liberation theology, capitalism has clearly been incapable of satisfying basic needs in Latin America, despite the fact that government and business leaders are professed Christians. Socialism in practice has not provided a satisfactory solution either: although advances have been made in basic needs provision […] None the less, the socialist ideal is more suitable than capitalism. 99
>
> Valpy Fitzgerald, 'The Economics of Liberation Theology'. In *The Cambridge Companion to Liberation Theology,* 1999, p. 222

Think question

Is neutrality on the issue of poverty impossible for Christians?

Liberation theology concludes that capitalism has failed to satisfy the basic needs of the poor

Apply your knowledge

9. Discuss the following points of view:

    a. Christianity should stay out of politics. It should not get involved in political movements.

    b. Christianity is a religion of the poor and so it should seek to bring about actual change for the poor.

    c. Christianity is about spiritual salvation, not violent revolution.

Liberation theology's teaching on the 'preferential option for the poor'

The phrase **'preferential option for the poor'** was first used in 1968 by Father Pedro Arrupe, Superior General of the Jesuits, and was picked up by the Catholic bishops of Latin America. It refers to a trend in the Bible that shows a preference for individuals who are on the margins of society and who are powerless, and also refers to the way in which Jesus associated himself more closely with the poor and the dispossessed ('Whatever you did for one of the least of these brothers and sisters of mine, you did for me.' See Matthew 25:40, New International Version.) The preferential option for the poor became a central feature of liberation theology and is encapsulated in the writing of the Jesuit theologian Juan Segundo (1925–96).

Juan Segundo argues that whatever criticisms can be levelled at liberation theology for its use of Marxist theories, there is an authentic Christian response in the preferential option for the poor. Christians should not maintain an attitude of neutrality in the face of tragic and pressing problems of human misery and injustice. He writes:

> 66 [N]umerous Christians […] are committed to live the Christian life in its fullness, [and] become involved in the struggle for justice freedom and human dignity because of their love for their disinherited oppressed and persecuted brothers and sisters. More than ever, the Church intends to condemn abuses, injustices and attacks against freedom wherever they occur and whoever commits them. She intends to struggle, by her own means, for the defence and advancement of the rights of mankind, especially of the poor. 99

> Juan Segundo, *Theology and the Church: A Response to Cardinal Ratzinger and a Warning to the Whole Church*, 1985, pp. 169–70

The biblical claim that human beings were made in the image and likeness of God (Genesis 1:26–27) placed the importance of human dignity at the centre of Segundo's thinking. The Gospel advocates living a peaceful and just life, and being oppressed by the crushing effects of poverty or allowing the inequalities between rich and poor to continue is not compatible with peace and justice. Just as God is the defender and liberator of the poor and the oppressed, so liberation theology has a special concern for the poor and the oppressed, and it urges people to act to defend and liberate them.

Segundo differed from Gutiérre, for while Gutiérrez held that social and economic liberation must precede liberation from sin, Segundo believed that liberation from sin should come first because it might not be possible to change the world's social and political structures. For example, Paul's letter to Philemon acknowledges the possibility that unjust social structures, in the form of slavery, will continue. Nevertheless, Christians must give priority to helping the poor and stand in solidarity with them.

Although the preferential option for the poor became central in liberation theology, in time it gained wider acceptance. In 1991, Pope John Paul II used the term in his encyclical *Centesimus Annus*, which celebrated the 100-year anniversary of Pope Leo XIII's encyclical *Rerum Novarum On Capital and Labor*. John Paul II argued that it reminded the Church to have:

> 66 constant concern for and dedication to categories of people who are especially beloved to the Lord Jesus. The content of the text is an excellent testimony to the continuity within the Church of the so-called 'preferential option for the poor', an option which I defined as a 'special form of primacy in the exercise of Christian charity'. Pope Leo's Encyclical on the 'condition of the workers' is thus an Encyclical on the poor and on the terrible conditions to which the new and often violent process of industrialization had reduced great multitudes of people. Today, in many parts of the world, similar processes of economic, social and political transformation are creating the same evils. 99
>
> Pope John Paul II, *Centesimus Annus*, 1991, para 11

John Paul II went on to argue that the advancement of the poor constitutes a great opportunity for the moral, cultural and even economic growth of all humanity. However, he made it clear that the preferential option for the poor includes a concern for spiritual poverty, and does not focus exclusively on material or economic poverty:

> 66 This option is not limited to material poverty, since it is well known that there are many other forms of poverty, especially in modern society – not only economic but cultural and spiritual poverty as well. 99
>
> Pope John Paul II, *Centesimus Annus*, 1991, para 57

And spiritual poverty is something that can be caused by an over-emphasis on material goods and consumerism. He wrote:

> 66 A striking example of artificial consumption contrary to the health and dignity of the human person, and certainly not easy to control, is the use of drugs. Widespread drug use is a sign of a serious malfunction in the social system; it also implies a materialistic and, in a certain sense, destructive 'reading' of human needs. In this way the innovative capacity of a free economy is brought to a one-sided and inadequate conclusion. Drugs, as well as pornography and other forms of consumerism which exploit the frailty of the weak, tend to fill the resulting spiritual void. 99
>
> Pope John Paul II, *Centesimus Annus*, 1991, para 36

Following his election in 2013, Pope Francis has developed this thinking even further, by rejecting many of the trappings of papal luxury and challenging the Catholic Church to be a poor Church for the poor.

Pope Francis continues to drive his old second-hand car in Rome

Apply your knowledge

10. What does spiritual poverty mean, according to Pope John Paul II?

11. 'Pope Francis seems to emphasise the preferential option for the poor in a more direct way than previous recent popes.' Discuss.

The Catholic Church's response to liberation theology

The Catholic Church became concerned with liberation theology's use of Marx's theories. In the *Instruction on Certain Aspects of the 'Theology of Liberation'* (Congregation of the Doctrine of the Faith, 1984), Cardinal Ratzinger articulated the Catholic Church's disquiet. The liberation theologians may have felt that adopting Marx's theories was the only immediate and effective response to the desperate situation in Latin America, but:

- it is dangerous to take parts of Marx's theories and use them in theology because Marxism contains intolerant aspects, including the denial of the individual and the emphasis on class and communal action

- it is a perversion of the Christian message for the Eucharist to become a celebration of power struggle

- there is a danger that violent revolution will take precedence over evangelism

- Christian liberation should be primarily understood as spiritual liberation from sin

- ultimately, only God can remove the suffering that human beings experience.

Ratzinger argued that the Catholic Church will continue to struggle for the poor, but using its own means and in its own way. Christian theology cannot adopt a Marxist analysis without changing from a Christian world view to a Marxist world view because Marxism is inherently unchristian:

Christian theology cannot adopt a Marxist analysis without changing from a Christian world view to a Marxist world view

....

66 Thus no separation of the parts of this epistemologically unique complex is possible. If one tries to take only one part, say, the analysis, one ends up having to accept the entire ideology [...] Let us recall the fact that atheism and the denial of the human person, his liberty and rights, are at the core of the Marxist theory. 99

Congregation of the Doctrine of the Faith, *Instruction on Certain Aspects of the 'Theology of Liberation'*, 1984, para 7.6

....

In *Temptations for the Theology of Liberation* (1974), Bonaventure Kloppenburg, a Brazilian theologian, summarises the criticisms of liberation theology. He argues that liberation theology emphasises practical opposition to oppression above the message of the Gospel, thereby equating theology with political action and sidelining the spiritual messages of Christianity. It emphasises structural sin over personal sin, despite the fact that Jesus reached into people's personal lives and spoke of the individual coming back to God through forgiveness and reconciliation. It places too much emphasis on people being able to deliver liberation and salvation, whereas ultimately the Kingdom of God is brought by God's intervention and salvation is a gift from God. If, Kloppenburg asks, theology is linked to a political movement, what happens if that movement fails? Has theology also failed?

This leads to the general criticism that liberation theology is so concerned about action that it has not paid sufficient attention to Christian theology and, specifically in the case of Catholic theologians, the teachings of the Catholic Church. In starting from action it cannot determine which actions might be right and which might be wrong.

In an article written in 1984 for www.liberationtheology.org, Richard McBrien adds that liberation theology seems to focus almost exclusively on some biblical themes (poverty, Exodus, concern for the poor and the Kingdom of God) at the expense of others, and it is much more interested in Luke's Gospel than John's Gospel. It defines oppression in economic terms, ignoring other kinds of oppression that derive from cultural forces, such as sexism and racism.

Nevertheless, even taking these critical observations into account, there are still questions that point to the need for a new theology like liberation theology:

- For the starving oppressed poor, is liberation from personal sin the most important liberation?

- Is change happening for the people in our world who live in poverty?

- Salvation and liberation may first be about inner spiritual change, but is there not a point when someone has to do something: see Matthew 25 New International Version, which focuses on human actions for the most needy.

Although liberation theology was formally viewed with suspicion by the Catholic Church, the election of the first Latin American pope may indicate a change of heart. In 2015, Pope Francis asked Gustavo Gutiérrez to be a keynote speaker at an event at the Vatican. While Pope Francis is said to have been critical of Marxist liberation theology in the past, he has certainly criticised capitalism and named Óscar Romero, the Salvadoran archbishop who was assassinated by right-wing death squads in 1980, as a martyr. Perhaps the impact of liberation theology on Christianity has only just begun? The Catholic Church's official position has not changed, but some in the media write of a thaw between the Vatican and the Latin American Christian thought of the 1960s and 1970s.

Discussing liberation theology and Marx

Should Christian theology engage with atheist secular ideologies?

The Vatican's key concern about liberation theology is its adoption of a Marxist account of human development. Marxism offers a comprehensive analysis of the world and clearly articulates how the workers can liberate

---

Apply your knowledge

12. Explore the strengths and weaknesses behind these points of view:

   a. Theology should be prepared to hear new ideas that respond to crises in the world. This might help it focus on parts of Christian thought and the Bible that have been forgotten.

   b. Liberation theology should focus more on established teaching and less on thinking linked to non-Christian philosophies, which are in danger of distracting it from right belief.

themselves from oppression by developing a socialist society. This world view contradicts Christianity. Christianity offers an account of the world centred on the creation of human beings by a loving God. The account focuses on the ways in which humans sin and turn away from God and God's response, as he seeks to bring people back to him by sending his son Jesus Christ to save the world. In Marxism, the analysis is economic; in Christianity, the analysis is spiritual. Therefore, if Christian thought adopts elements of Marxism (a theory that is not expressed in Christian sources of faith, including the Bible, and makes no space for God) then it is abandoning the Christian world view and adopting an alternative world view. Consequently, it can be argued that Christianity should avoid such atheist secular ideologies.

However, others argue that Christian theology has a strong record of engaging with and adapting in response to new insights, and will not be corrupted if it borrows from Marxist thinking. For example, scientific developments that have brought about a better understanding of how our universe and human life first came about have led to a re-evaluation of the creation story in Genesis, and developments in psychology and medicine have helped to shed new light on some of the healing stories in the New Testament. From Genesis 2:19 onwards, God even gives human beings a duty to learn about and look after the world around them when he asks man to name the livestock, birds and wild animals. Furthermore, some Christians believe that God can be encountered in all things, including human thought, making 'Christian Marxism' (which both draws from Marxism and seeks to inform Marxism) possible.

Many liberation theologians are aware of Marxism's limitations and they counsel against adopting it wholesale and without critical analysis. For example, José Míguez Bonino argues that:

> 66 The rigid Marxist orthodoxy or dogmatism is immediately rejected [...] The Marxist scheme cannot be taken as a dogma but rather as a method which has to be applied to our own reality in terms of this reality 99
>
> Bonino, *Doing Theology in a Revolutionary Situation*, 1979, p. 35

Meanwhile, Leonardo Boff argues that, ultimately, liberation for Christians must draw inspiration from the Gospel, and that Marxism can never be allowed to become a central principle of Christian thinking. Christians must, he suggests, be vigilant in their criticism of Marxism and must reject Marxism's closed, monolithic socialist system that denies God and the dignity of the human person. Marxism, as a system, is in opposition to Christianity (see Boff and Boff, *Introducing Liberation Theology*, 1987, p. 66).

If Christian theology applies to all aspects of human life then, arguably, it must engage with secular thought. However, there remains a question about the extent to which it adopts political ideologies and interprets its own core messages through the lens of those political ideologies.

Apply your knowledge

13. Discuss the following points of view:

   a. I think that Christian thought should only pay attention to recognised sources of Christian faith, such as the Bible.

   b. I think God can be encountered in all things, even atheist theories. I think God wants us to challenge and develop those theories and make them Christian.

Does Christianity tackle social issues more effectively than Marxism?

Social issues are widespread and wide ranging. They affect people in less economically developed countries and people in more economically developed countries, people in the global north and people in the global south. They include poverty, low rates of literacy and numeracy, poor physical and mental health and well-being, hunger, child abuse, child labour, human trafficking, modern-day slavery, alcoholism and drug abuse. As Marx identified, many people around the world are oppressed and marginalised by those in power who control the means of production. It can be argued that there is, as Marx believes, a struggle at the centre of life.

Marx claimed that, through revolution, many social problems would ultimately lead to a socialist, classless society. Yet many today would argue that communism was unable to respond effectively to suffering and poverty in society. For example, it was unable to hold back the tide of globalisation. China and Cuba, both communist countries, have begun to open up their close economies to capitalism in recent years. This is despite the fact that, while globalisation has made a tiny minority much richer, it has also increased social fragmentation and made the lives of the vast majority much more precarious.

In contrast, Christianity, with its emphasis on the spiritual and on the individual as part of a community, may be of more practical help for people struggling with unhappiness and oppression. Suffering cannot be removed from life, even in a truly classless society, and people therefore need something to help them respond to this suffering. Marx does not provide any comfort for those who die in the struggle to achieve a classless society, but Christianity can provide hope and solace by teaching that God loves you and is there for you during difficult times. Christianity offers insights into the human experience and provides spiritual strength to help people live with suffering and through uncertain times. For some Christians, the belief in eventual salvation in heaven is a comfort.

The concept of the coming Kingdom of God is a concept in Christian thought. The Kingdom of God is both here now, in righteous actions, and in the future, in the realisation of a fully just and fair and loving world. Performing charitable acts, out of love and concern for the alienated and the oppressed, is a manifestation of the Kingdom of God. Marx once said that religion was 'the opiate of the people', acknowledging that religion helps people to live with life as it really is, supporting them through difficult times (*Critique of Hegel's 'Philosophy of Right'*, 1843, p. 1). For Marx, this means it helps to maintain the status quo and limits people's desire for revolutionary change. But, looking at it from the opposite perspective, religion also helps people to live in the present and not spend their lives wishing for a future that might never happen.

Apply your knowledge

14. Two young, single women go to confession at a city church. The first woman is a single mum, who can only find temporary low-paid work with zero-hours contracts. Her poor qualifications mean she cannot get a better job. She is finding it difficult to pay her rent, is drinking heavily and using drugs. The second woman belongs to a wealthy family so does not need to work. She lives independently in an affluent part of the city and spends her time going to an endless round of parties, where she takes drugs and has casual sex. She finds her life utterly empty but cannot bear to leave it and all her friends behind. What might Christianity have to offer each of these people? Would Marx be able to offer them more, or less?

Has liberation theology engaged with Marxism fully enough?

It can be argued that liberation theology fails to fully appreciate the significance of Marx's fundamental belief in the need for revolution. Of course some liberation theologians do call for revolution, and there were cases of priests taking off their dog collars and taking up arms in South American struggles in the 1960s and 1970s. But many liberation theologians adopt a Marxist analysis of society to promote social change without engaging with the wider aspects of Marxism.

66 Placing themselves firmly on the side of the poor, Liberation Theologians ask Marx: 'What can you tell us about the situations of poverty and ways of overcoming it?' Here Marxists are submitted to the judgement of the poor and their cause, not the other way round. Therefore, liberation theology used Marxism purely as an instrument. It does not venerate it as it venerates the Gospel. 99

Leonardo Boff and Clodovis Boff, *Introducing Liberation Theology*, 1987, p. 28

Therefore, some argue for a deeper dialogue between Marxism and Christianity:

66 At one time Marx's contributions to both disciplines were disdainfully considered as less than irrelevant; now there is an overwhelming need to study his theses with great dedication. But institutions have always demonstrated a conspicuous inability to repent, to recognize errors and injustices and remedy them. Thus we must realize that it is not enough merely to take seriously today the Marx whom we scorned yesterday; [...] If we are to abandon yesterday's position, we must also revise the whole system of ideas and values which made such a position necessary. Real conversion is needed, not lukewarm concealment of changes which are made underhandedly. 99

José Miranda, *Marx and the Bible: A Critique of the Philosophy of Oppression*, 1974, pp. xiii–xvii

Here, Miranda is talking not just about theology's rejection of Marxism, but also its rejection by the disciplines of economics and history in the West during the height of the cold war. With the decline of communism, Marxist thinking is seen by many as less relevant now than ever before. However, there is an indication of a revival of Marxist socialism. In recent years, a number of South American countries have been led by socialist leaders including Hugo Chávez of Venezuela, Rafael Correa of Ecuador, Evo Morales of Bolivia, and Luiz Inácio Lula da Silva of Brazil. Miranda's argument from the 1970s might, therefore, have some relevance today. He believed a compelling dialogue between Marxism and Christianity was possible. There are similarities between the two: both Marxism and the Bible emphasise history, for example, and both have a sense that an approaching event will bring about a change (revolution in the case of Marxism, the coming of the Kingdom of God in the case of Christianity). But how can Christianity deal with the atheism that is at the heart of Marxism?

In 'Marxism, Liberation Theology and the Way of Negation' (*The Cambridge Companion to Liberation Theology,* 2nd edition, 2007), Denys Turner argues that liberation theology should go further and embrace the apophatic way to more effectively engage with Marx. The apophatic way is a way of speaking about God and theological ideas using only negative terms. Drawing on the works of Pseudo-Dionysius, Meister Eckhardt and John of the Cross, Turner shows how an apophatic theology need not affirm or deny the essence of God, and if Christian thought asserts that God does not exist, then Marxism has no God to deny. If theology disposes of its language of affirmation, then Marxism can dispose of its atheist language of denial. Turner is not arguing that Christian theology abandons belief in God, but rather that it abandons any attempt to try to describe God because only a theology based around a God that is beyond language and experience can have any meaningful interaction with Marxism.

Is it right for Christians to prioritise one group over another?

One of the more controversial aspects of liberation theology is the extent to which it prioritises one group, the poor and oppressed, over other groups.

A case can be made that Christianity is, and should be, centrally focused on the poor. This begins with the biblical observations of the actions and teachings of Jesus, which emphasised that God is close to the poor and the poor are close to God, and that trappings of power, wealth and social status do not raise a person's standing in the eyes of God. Boff and Boff argue that God does not sit back, dispassionate and disengaged with the world, but gets involved and takes sides with the poor:

> 66 God is especially close to those who are oppressed; God hears their cry and resolves to set them free. God is father of all, but most particularly father and defender of those who are oppressed and treated unjustly. Out of love for them, God takes sides, takes their side against the repressive measures of all pharaohs. 99

Leonardo Boff and Clodovis Boff, *Introducing Liberation Theology,* 1987, pp. 50–1

However, while many Christians are deeply concerned about the poor and the oppressed, and many religious orders focus their vocation on working with those in greatest need, liberation theology takes things one step further. Liberation theology suggests that God takes the side of the poor against the rich and actively works for the poor:

66 He is a God who takes sides with the poor and liberates them from slavery and oppression [...] the reciprocal relationship between God and the poor person is the very heart of biblical faith. 99

Gustavo Gutiérrez, *The Power of the Poor in History*, 1983, pp. 7–8

For Gutiérrez, 'to know God as liberator is to liberate, is to do justice' (Gutiérrez, *The Power of the Poor in History*, 1983, p. 8).

Some liberation theologians have been criticised by the Vatican for focusing on the poor in opposition to the wealthy. Writing about the works of Jon Sobrino, the Vatican says he manifests a dangerous preoccupation with the poor and oppressed in Latin America and, whilst that preoccupation is shared by the Catholic Church, it believes it is wrong to prioritise one group over the needs of others, for all are to be saved.

John Paul II argued that wealth does not shelter people from spiritual poverty, that rich people can be just as profoundly unhappy as poor people, and this spiritual poverty was as much of a concern for the Gospel writers as material poverty: 'Blessed are the poor in spirit' (Matthew 5:3). More fundamentally, the message of salvation that Jesus brings is a message for all of humanity, not just the poor. Emphasising one group as mattering more than another puts us in danger of forgetting the universal nature of salvation. However, it is difficult to make a case that churches should not be deeply concerned with the poor and the oppressed. Equally, the Catholic Church invests poverty with special status through, for example, the vows of poverty taken by many in religious orders.

One solution might be to define 'poverty' widely, to encompass both material and spiritual poverty. If Christians work to reduce poverty of all kinds, then they will make the world a better place. If work to reduce spiritual poverty encourages the wealthy to live more socially responsible lives and to share their wealth with their poorer neighbours, then it will operate alongside efforts to reduce material poverty to improve the lives of the poor and the dispossessed.

66 Liberation theologians are quite clear that the Kingdom belongs to the poor (Luke 6.20) and the rich as such have no part in it (Luke 6.24 et seq.; Luke 16.19–31; Mark 10.23–25) because

> **Think question**
>
> Does God take sides with the poor, *against* the rich?

money is an idol which becomes an absolute value: we cannot serve God and Mammon (Matt. 6.24) – private property is by definition exclusive. However, Jesus does not idealise the poor, because poverty is the consequence of the sin of exclusive possession. Rather, his aim is for abundance for everyone – expressed symbolically by the banquet of the Kingdom – so that this can be possible. He teaches us to abandon the goods of this earth (Matt. 6.25–33) and invites us to share what we have with the poor (Luke 12.14 et seq.). **"**

Valpy Fitzgerald, 'The Economics of Liberation'. In *The Cambridge Companion to Liberation Theology*, 2008, p. 249

Apply your knowledge

16. Discuss the following points of view. Which do you find most compelling and why?

   a. Jesus spent most of his time with the poor and so Christianity is a religion for the poor in their struggle against the rich. It should encourage people to rise up against the status quo, against the establishment and the wealthy.

   b. Jesus spent time with those who were wealthy and who had been corrupted by wealth and power, including tax collectors and the Pharisees. The poor will be always with us, but it is vital to reach out to those in positions of wealth and power to try to make things better for everyone.

   c. If Jesus is the redeemer of all then he is interested in everyone, irrespective of their economic background.

Learning support

Points to remember

» For Marx, the concentration of the means of production in the hands of the wealthy few leads to the alienation and oppression of the masses. He believed that capitalism was inherently unstable and would eventually lead to revolution and the establishment a new (socialist) order.

» Liberation theology is more than Marxism. While some of its critics reduce it to Marxism, it draws more deeply on biblical texts than on Marxist literature.

» Liberation theology takes the situation people find themselves in, their suffering, as its starting point. This is distinctive and empowering for those in poverty.

» Liberation theology is often discussed as a failed theology because it was rejected by the Catholic Church, but the preferential option for the poor has become central to Catholic thought, and since the appointment of Pope Francis there has been a change in the relationship between the Vatican and the once condemned liberation theologians.

Enhance your learning

» *Introducing Liberation Theology* (1987) by Leonardo Boff and Clodovis Boff is an excellent introduction to liberation theology.

» Gustavo Gutiérrez is, arguably, the father of liberation theology and his book *A Theology of Liberation* (1974) is highly readable and quite revolutionary, and direct in tone. Chapters 1–3 in particular, set out both the method of practising liberation theology and its relationship with Marx. Chapter 13 explores the Catholic Church as a movement for protest and solidarity with the poor.

» *Instruction on Certain Aspects of the 'Theology of Liberation'* by the Congregation of the Doctrine of the Faith (1984) is readable and readily available on the Internet. It summarises the Catholic Church's official response to liberation theology.

» 'Liberation Theology's Temptations', an article by Richard McBrien, summarises Bonaventure Kloppenburg's criticisms of liberation theology. It is available at http://liberationtheology.org/library/liberation_theology_temptations---article_by_richard_mcbrien.htm.

» Valpy Fitzgerald's article, 'The Economics of Liberation Theology' in *The Cambridge Companion to Liberation Theology*, 2008, contains a detailed discussion of the economics of liberation theology.

» An article in *The Guardian* on 11 May 2015 discusses possible signs of change in the relationship between the Papacy and liberation theology: 'Catholic Church Warms to Liberation Theology as Founder Heads to Vatican'. It can be found at: www.theguardian.com/world/2015/may/11/vatican-new-chapter-liberation-theology-founder-gustavo-Gutiérrez.

Practice for exams

At A level, essay questions invite you to demonstrate your knowledge and understanding of factual material (AO1) and also your critical ability in putting forward a coherent, balanced argument (AO2). You should aim to write essays that are persuasive responses to the question throughout, rather than writing a lot of description and then tacking an opinion on at the end of each paragraph.

'Christianity is better than Marxism at tackling social issues.' Discuss.

This question invites a comparison between Christianity and Marxism in relation to social issues such as poverty, low literacy rates and substance abuse.

In order to gain high marks for AO1, you should show knowledge and understanding of the ways in which both Christianity and Marxism understand and tackle these issues. For example, you might refer to the Christian understanding of social issues as symptomatic of a world that has been corrupted by human sin since the Fall, and the Marxist understanding of social issues as symptomatic of alienation due to private ownership of the means of production.

For AO2, you need to make a comparison between ways in which Christianity and Marxism tackle these issues, and say which you think is better. You could explain what you mean by 'better', for example whether you mean that it has longer-lasting results or reaches a greater number of people. You might want to argue that some kind of combination of Christianity and Marxism is most effective.

When an essay question asks you to make a comparison, try to look at the two ideas side by side throughout the essay rather than writing about Christianity on its own and then Marxism on its own.

Discuss the claim that Christianity should not show preference to the poor and oppressed, but should treat everyone equally.

This question invites a critical evaluation of the concept of Christianity showing a 'preferential option for the poor'.

For AO1, you should be able to demonstrate knowledge and understanding of the idea that Christians should be actively involved with the world in fighting injustice and seeking to help the poor. You should be able to refer to the ideas of liberation theologians to support your answer. You might also want to make use of biblical passages that can be used to support different points of view.

For AO2, you should evaluate the reasons why some people think that Christianity should show preference to the poor. You could consider biblical teachings about poverty and wealth alongside teachings that everyone is made in the image of God.

In formulating your argument, make sure that you consider counter-arguments and try to give persuasive reasons to support your own point of view.

Glossary

Absolutism: the view that morals are fixed, unchanging truths that everyone should always follow

Agnosticism: the view that there is insufficient evidence for God, or the view that God cannot be known

Alienation: the process of becoming detached or isolated

Analogy: a comparison made between one thing and another in an effort to aid understanding

Apophatic way (*via negativa*): a way of speaking about God and theological ideas using only terms that say what God is not

Basic Christian communities: Christian groups that gather together to try to directly resolve difficulties in their lives

Betrothal: traditionally the exchange of promises, which in earlier times marked the point at which sex was permitted

Capitalism: an economic system in which the means of production are privately owned and operated for profit, in contrast with communism where trade and industry is controlled by the state

Cataphatic way (*via positiva*): a range of ways of speaking about God and theological ideas using only terms that say what God is

Cognitive: having a factual quality that is available to knowledge, where words are labels for things in the world

Cohabitation: an unmarried couple living together in a sexually active relationship. Sometimes known pejoratively as 'living in sin'

***Conscientia*:** this is the name Aquinas gives to the process whereby a person's reason makes moral judgements

Conscientisation: the process by which a person becomes conscious of the power structures in society

Consent: freely agreeing to engage in sexual activity with another person

Consummation: an act of sexual intercourse that indicates, in some traditions, the finalisation of the marriage

Davidic Messiah: a Messiah figure based on the kingly military images of the Hebrew scriptures (the Old Testament)

Demythologising: removing the mythical elements from a narrative to expose the central message

Ego: Freud uses this word to describe the mediation between the id and the super-ego

Emotivism: ethical theories that hold that moral statements are not statements of fact but are either beliefs or emotions

Empirical: available to be experienced by the five senses

Encyclical: an open letter sent to more than one recipient

Equivocal language: words that mean different things when used in different contexts

Eternal: timeless, atemporal, being outside the constraints of time

Everlasting: sempiternal, lasting forever on the same timeline as humanity

Exclusive: a commitment to be in a sexual relationship with a person to the exclusion of all others. This is the opposite of an 'open marriage' or a 'casual relationship'

Exclusivism: the view that only one religion offers the complete means of salvation

Existentialism: a way of thinking that emphasises personal freedom of choice

Exploitation: treating someone unfairly in order to benefit from their work or resources

Extramarital sex: sex beyond the confines of marriage, usually used to describe adulterous sex

Falsification: providing evidence to determine that something is false

Feminism: the name given to a wide range of views arguing for, and working for, equality for women

Free will: the ability to make independent choices between real options

Gender biology: the physical characteristics that enable someone to be identified as male or female

Gender expression: the ways in which people behave as a result of their gender identification

Gender identification: the way people perceive themselves in terms of masculine, feminine, both or neither

Homosexuality: sexual attraction between people of the same sex

Hume's Law: you cannot go from an 'is' (a statement of fact) to an 'ought' (a moral)

Id: for Freud, this is the part of the mind that has instinctive impulses that seek satisfaction in pleasure

Immutable: incapable of changing or being affected

Inclusivism: the view that although one's own religion is the normative (setting the standard of normality) means of salvation, those who accept its central principles may also receive salvation

Inter-faith dialogue: sharing and discussing religious beliefs between members of different religious traditions, with an aim of reaching better understanding

Intuitionism: ethical theories that hold that moral knowledge is received in a different way from science and logic

Invincible ignorance: this is how Aquinas describes a lack of knowledge for which a person is not responsible, and cannot be blamed

Logical positivism: a movement that claimed that assertions have to be capable of being tested empirically if they are to be meaningful

Missionary work: activity that aims to convert people to a particular faith or set of beliefs, or works for social justice in areas of poverty or deprivation

Multi-faith societies: societies where there are significant populations of people with different religious beliefs

Naturalism: ethical theories that hold that morals are part of the natural world and can be recognised or observed in some way

Naturalistic fallacy: G.E. Moore's argument that it is a mistake to define moral terms with reference to other properties (a mistake to break Hume's law)

Non-cognitive: not having a factual quality that is available to knowledge; words are tools used to achieve something rather than labels for things

Noumena: a Kantian term to describe reality as it really is, unfiltered by the human mind

Omnibenevolent: all-good and all-loving

Omnipotent: all-powerful

Omniscient: all-knowing

Particularism: an alternative name for exclusivism, meaning that salvation can only be found in one particular way

Patriarchal society: a society that is dominated by men and men's interests

Phenomena: a Kantian term to describe reality as it appears to us, filtered by the human mind

Pluralism: the view that there are many ways to salvation through different religious traditions

Post-Christian theology: religious thinking that abandons traditional Christian thought

Preferential option for the poor: the idea that Jesus Christ stood with the poor and oppressed, and that the Church should focus on the poor and oppressed and stand in solidarity with them

Premarital sex: sex before marriage

Ratio: the word used by Aquinas to describe reason, something which is placed in every person as a result of their being created in the image of God

Reform feminist theology: religious thinking that seeks to change traditional Christian thought

Relativism: the view that moral truths are not fixed and are not absolute. What is right changes according to the individual, the situation, the culture, the time and the place

Secular: not connected or associated with religious or spiritual matters. Used colloquially in widely differing ways by atheists, pluralists and those who are anti-religion. Historically, the term was used to distinguish priests who worked in the world (secular priests) from those who belonged to religious communities, such as monasteries

Secularisation: a theory developed in the 1950s and 1960s, developed from Enlightenment thinking, that religious belief would progressively decline as democracy and technology advanced. Sociologists now doubt such a linear decline

Secularism: a term that is used in different ways. It may mean a belief that religion should not be involved in government or public life. It may be a principle that no one religion should have a superior position in the state. It often entails a belief in a public space and a private space, and that religion should be restrained from public power

Servant king: an understanding of the Messiah that focuses on service rather than overlordship

Social cohesion: when a group is united by bonds that help them to live together peacefully

Socialisation: the process by which people learn cultural norms

Sophia: Greek for 'wisdom', personified in female form in the ancient world

Structural sin: the idea that sin is not just a personal action, but something that can be brought about through unjust organisations and social structures

Super-ego: Freud uses this word to describe the part of the mind that contradicts the id and uses internalised ideals from parents and society to make the ego behave morally

Symbol: a word or other kind of representation used to stand for something else and to shed light on its meaning

Symposium: a group of people who meet to discuss a particular question or theme

Synderesis: for Aquinas, this means to follow the good and avoid the evil, the rule that all precepts follow

Synod: the legislative body of the Church of England

Thealogy: studying God based around the goddess ('thea' is Greek for 'goddess')

Theology of religion(s): the branch of Christian theology that looks at the relationship between Christianity and other world religions from a Christian perspective

Truth-claim: a statement that asserts that something is factually true

Univocal language: words that mean the same thing when used in different contexts

Vatican II: the Second Vatican Ecumenical Council, held from 1962 to 1965 to discuss the place of the Catholic Church in the modern world

Verification: providing evidence to determine that something is true

Vienna Circle: a group of philosophers known as logical positivists who rejected claims that moral truth can be verified as objectively true

Vincible ignorance: this is how Aquinas describes a lack of knowledge for which a person is responsible, and can be blamed

Wish fulfilment: according to Freud, wish fulfilment is the satisfaction of a desire through a dream or other exercise of the imagination

Index

Acknowledgements

The authors and publisher are grateful to the parties indicated for permission to reprint extracts from copyright material:

Scripture quotations from the *Holy Bible, New International Version,* Anglicised copyright © 1979, 1984, 2011 Biblica, used by permission of Hodder & Stoughton Ltd, an Hachette UK company. All rights reserved. 'NIV' is a registered trademark of Biblica, UK trademark number 1448790.

Scripture quotations from the *Revised Standard Version of the Bible,* copyright © 1946, 1952, and 1971 the Division of Christian Education of the National Council of Churches of Christ in the United States of America, used by permission. All rights reserved.

Extracts from the following works published by the Libreria Editrice Vaticana, www.vatican.va, Pope Paul VI: *Lumen Gentium* (1964) and *Humanae Vitae* (1968); John Paul II: *Mulieris Dignitatem* (1988), *Redemptoris Missio* 'In Dialogue with our brothers and sisters of other religions' (1990), and *Centesimus Annus* (1991); Pope Benedict XVI 'Good Friday Reflection on the Gospel' (2005); Pope Francis: *On Love in the Family* (2016); *Catechism of the Catholic Church,* and *Instruction on certain aspects of the 'Theology of Liberation'* (Congregation of the Doctrine of the Faith, 1984); all copyright © Libreria Editrice Vaticana, used by permission of the publishers.

Extracts from *The Book of Common Prayer* (1979), the rights in which are vested in the Crown, used by permission of the Crown's Patentee, Cambridge University Press.

Extracts from *Anglican Alternative Service Book* (1980), copyright © The Central Board of Finance of the Church of England 1980, copyright © The Archbishop's Council 1999; General Synod's report 'Sharing the Gospel of Salvation' (2009), copyright © The Archbishop's Council 2009; and *Some Issues in Human Sexuality: a guide to the debate* (2003), copyright © House of Bishops 2003, copyright © The Archbishop's Council 2003; all used by permission of the Archbishop's Council of the Church of England, c/o Hymns Ancient & Modern.

Kwame Anthony Appiah: from 'Mistaken Identities: Creed, Country, Colour, Culture', BBC Radio 4 Reith Lecture 2016, used by permission of Professor Appiah c/o Janklow & Nesbit Associates and of the BBC.

A J Ayer: from *Language Truth & Logic* (Palgrave 2004), first published in 1936, used by permission of Dover Publications, Inc.

Tina Beattie: from *The New Atheists: the twilight of reason and the war on religion* (Darton Longman and Todd, 2007), copyright © Tina Beattie 2007, used by permission of the publishers.

Peter L Berger: from *Desecularization of the World: Resurgent Religion and World Politics* (W B Eerdmans, 1999), copyright © Peter L Berger 1999, used by permission of Wm B Eerdmans Publishing Co.

Anicius Manlius Severinus Boethius: from *The Consolation of Philosophy* translated by Victor E Watts (Penguin Classics, 1969), copyright © Victor Watts 1969, 1999, used by permission of Penguin Books Ltd.

Luke Bretherton: from 'Post secular politics? Interfaith relations and civic practice', *The Lambeth Interfaith Lecture,* Lambeth Palace, 4 June 2009, used by permission of the author.

The British Humanist Association: on faith schools from website www.humanism.org.uk, used by permission of the British Humanist Association.

Bernado Carducci: from *The Psychology of Personality: Viewpoints* (2e, Blackwell, 2009), used by permission of John Wiley & Sons via Copyright Clearance Center.

José Casanova: from 'Rethinking secularization: A global comparative perspective', *The Hedgehog Review,* 8:1, 2 (2006), used by permission of The Hedgehog Review, Institute for Advanced Cultural Studies, University of Virginia.

Simon Chan: from 'Why we call God "Father": Christians have good reasons to resist gender-neutral alternatives', *Christianity Today,* 13 August 2013, used by permission of the author.

Carol Christ: from 'Feminist theology and post-traditional theology', in *Cambridge Companion to Feminist Theology* (Cambridge, 2002), copyright © Carol Christ 2002, used by permission of Cambridge University Press.

Brian Davies: from *An Introduction to the Philosophy of Religion* (3e, OUP, 2004), used by permission of Oxford University Press.

Richard Dawkins: from *The God Delusion* (Bantam Press, 2006), used by permission of The Random House Group Ltd.

Valpy Fitzgerald: from 'The economics of liberation theology' in *Cambridge Companion to Liberation Theology* (Cambridge, 1999), used by permission of Cambridge University Press.

Philippa Foot: from *Natural Goodness* (OUP, 2001), copyright © Philippa Foot 2001, used by permission of Oxford University Press.

Sigmund Freud: from *The Ego and the Id* (Vol 19); from *Civilization and its Discontents* (Vol 21); and from *The Future of an Illusion* (Vol 21) in *Standard Edition of the Complete Psychological Works of Sigmund Freud* translated and edited by James Strachey (Hogarth Press, 1953/Vintage, 2001); from *New Introductory Lectures on Psychoanalysis* (Hogarth Press, 1933), used by permission of The Random House Group Ltd, and The Marsh Agency Ltd on behalf of Sigmund Freud Copyrights.

Erich Fromm: from *Beyond the Chains of Illusion: My Encounter with Marx & Freud* (Continuum, 2007), copyright © Erich Fromm 1962, used by permission of Bloomsbury Continuum, an imprint of Bloomsbury Publishing Plc.

General Medical Council: from *Personal beliefs and medical practice* (2013), copyright © GMC, used by permission of the General Medical Council.

The Guardian: Graphic showing religious affiliation from 'People of no religion outnumber Christians in England and Wales - study', *The Guardian*, 23 May 2016, copyright Guardian News & Media Ltd 2016, based on figure in *Contemporary Catholicism in England and Wales: A Statistical Report Based on Recent British Social Attitudes Survey Data* by Stephen Bullivant (Benedict XVI Centre for Religion and Society, St Mary's University, Twickenham, 2016), used by permission of Stephen Bullivant and Guardian News & Media Ltd.

Gustavo Gutierrez: from *A Theology of Liberation: History, Politics Salvation* translated by Sister Caridad Inda and John Eagleson (SCM, 2001), used by permission of the publishers, SCM Press, Hymns Ancient & Modern.

R M Hare and **Antony Flew:** 'Theology & Falsification the university discussion' in Antony Flew & Alasdair MacIntyre (eds): from *New Essays in Philosophical Theology* (Macmillan, 2012), copyright © SCM Press 1955, 1983, used by permission of the publishers, SCM Press, Hymns Ancient & Modern.

Jack W Hayford: lines from 'Majesty' (1997), copyright © 1981 Rocksmith Music/Omagem/Small Stone Media BV Holland, administered by and used by permission of Song Solutions, www.songsoultions.org. All rights reserved.

John Hick: from *God and the Universe of Faiths: Essays in the Philosophy of Religion* (Oneworld, 1993), copyright © John Hick 1973, used by permission of Oneworld Publications; from *Philosophy of Religion* (2e, Prentice-Hall, 1983), copyright © John Hick 1973, used by permission of Pearson Education, Inc, New York.

Nicholas Humphrey: from 'What shall we tell the children?', Oxford Amnesty Lecture, 21 February 1997, first published in *Social Research* 65 (1998), used by permission of the author.

Lisa Isherwood: from *Introducing Feminist Christologies* (Sheffield Academic Press, 2001), copyright © Lisa Isherwood 2001, used by permission of Sheffield Academic Press, an imprint of Bloomsbury Publishing Plc.

Peter Kropotkin: from *Memoirs of a Revolutionist* (1989), translated and quoted in Philippa Foot: *Natural Goodness* (OUP, 2001), used by permission of Oxford University Press.

J L Mackie: from *Ethics: Inventing Right and Wrong* (Penguin, 1990), copyright © J L Mackie 1977, used by permission of Penguin Books Ltd.

Jo Marchant: from *Cure: a Journey into the Science of Mind Over Body* (Canongate, 2016), copyright © Jo Marchant 2016, used by permission of Canongate Books Ltd.

Paul Victor Marshall: *Prayer Book Parallels,* Volume 1 (2000), copyright © Church Publishing 2000, used by permission of Church Publishing, New York, NY 10016.

David Martin: from 'The Evangelical Upsurge and its Political Implications', copyright © David Martin 1999, in Peter L Berger: *Desecularization of the World: Resurgent Religion and World Politics* (W B Eerdmans, 1999), used by permission of Wm B Eerdmans Publishing Co.

Karl Marx: from *Early Writings* translated by Rodney Livingstone and Gregor Benton (Penguin Books in association with New Left Review, 1992), used by permission of *New Left Review*.

Jose Miranda: translated by John Eagleson: from *Marx and the Bible: A Critique of the Philosophy of Oppression* (SCM, 1974), used by permission of the publishers, SCM Press, Hymns Ancient & Modern.

G E Moore: from *Principia Ethica* (Cambridge, 1994), copyright © G E Moore 1903, used by permission of Cambridge University Press.

Samuel Pepys: from entry for 14 October 1663 in *The Diary of Samuel Pepys,* Vol 1, edited and translated by Robert Lathem and William Matthews (Collins, 2010), used by permission of Peters Fraser & Dunlop (www.petersfraserdunlop.com) on behalf of the Estate of Robert Lathem.

H A Pritchard: from 'Does Moral Philosophy Rest on Mistake?', *Mind*, Vol XXI (81), 1912, used by permission of Oxford University Press via Copyright Clearance Center.

W D Ross: from *The Right and the Good* (OUP, 2001), copyright © W D Ross 201, used by permission of Oxford University Press.

Rosemary Radford Ruether: from *Sexism and God-Talk: Toward a Feminist Theology* (SCM, 2002), used by permission of the publishers, SCM Press, Hymns Ancient & Modern.

Juan Segundo: from *Theology and the Church: a response to Cardinal Ratzinger and a Warning to the whole Church* translated by John W Diercksmeier (T & T Clark, 1987), translation copyright © 1984, used by permission of Bloomsbury T & T Clark, an imprint of Bloomsbury Publishing Plc.

Brendan Sweetman: from *Religion: Key Concepts in Philosophy* (Continuum, 2007) copyright © Breandan Sweetman 2007, used by permission of Continuum, an imprint of Bloomsbury Publishing Plc.

Richard Swinburne: from *Coherence of Theism* (2e, OUP, 2016), used by permission of Oxford University Press.

The United Methodist Church: from *The Book of Discipline* (2016), used by permission of The United Methodist Publishing House.

The United Reformed Church: statement from the website at www.urc.org.uk, copyright © 2016, used by permission of The United Reformed Church.

Peter Vardy: from *The Puzzle of Evil* (Routledge, 2015), copyright © Peter Vardy 1992, used by permission of Routledge via Copyright Clearance Center.

The publishers would like to thank the following for permission to use their photographs:

Cover: Alexandr Pakhnyushchyy/123RF

p22: BUGNUT23/Shutterstock; **p30:** JohnnyGreig/iStock; **p37:** Ruslan Guzov/Shutterstock; **p54:** Martin Anderson/Shutterstock; **p55:** ullstein bild/Getty; **p56:** Christian Delbert/Shutterstock; p61: Ashley Cooper pics/Alamy; **p67:** radub85/123RF; **p69:** Geoff A Howard/Alamy; **p70:** ullstein bild/Getty; **p72:** Lovattpics/iStock; **p76:** Andriy Lipkan/Shutterstock; **p95:** The Warden and Fellows of Merton College Oxford; **p96:** PAINTING/Alamy; **p98:** Steve Pyke/Getty; **p99:** RHIMAGE/Shutterstock; **p100:** University of Sydney Archives; **p102:** Pictorial Press Ltd/Alamy; **p103:** The President and Fellows of Trinity College, Oxford; **p105:** Kurt Hutton/Getty; **p108:** Popperfoto/Getty; **p118:** AFP/Getty; **p119:** DEA/VENERANDA BIBLIOTECA AMBROSIANA/Getty; **p121(T):** jorisvo/Shutterstock; **p121(B):** A-R-T/Shutterstock; **p125:** IanDagnall Computing/Alamy; **p128:** Jim Noetzel/Shutterstock; **p150:** John Robertson/Alamy; **p153:** dpa picture alliance/Alamy; **p154:** London Stereoscopic Company/Getty; **p175:** Pitu Cau/